Alone in the World?

Alone in the World?

HUMAN UNIQUENESS

IN SCIENCE AND THEOLOGY

The Gifford Lectures
The University of Edinburgh
Spring 2004

J. Wentzel van Huyssteen

William B. Eerdmans Publishing Company

Grand Rapids, Michigan / Cambridge, U.K.

Published 2006 in the United States of America by
Wm. B. Eerdmans Publishing Co.
255 Jefferson Ave. S.E., Grand Rapids, Michigan 49503 /
P.O. Box 163, Cambridge CB3 9PU U.K.
www.eerdmans.com
and in Germany by
Vandenhoeck & Ruprecht GmbH & Co., KG, Göttingen
www.v-r.de

Printed in the United States of America

11 10 09 08 07 06   7 6 5 4 3 2 1

Library of Congress Cataloging-in-Publication Data

Van Huyssteen, J. Wentzel.
    Alone in the world: human uniqueness in science and theology / J. Wentzel van Huyssteen.
        p.   cm.   (The Gifford lectures)
    Includes bibliographical references and index.
    ISBN-10 0-8028-3246-6 / ISBN-13 978-0-8028-3246-7 (cloth : alk. paper)
    1. Theological anthropology — Christianity.   2. Human evolution — Religious aspects —
Christianity.   3. Human evolution.   4. Religion and science.   I. Title.   II. Series.

        BT701.3.V36   2006
        233′.5 — dc22

                                                2006000783

Bibliografische Information Der Deutschen Bibliothek

Die Deutsche Bibliothek verzeichnet diese Publikation in der Deutschen Nationalbibliografie;
detaillierte bibliografische Daten sind im Internet über <http://dnb.ddb.de> abrufbar.

ISBN 13: 978-3-525-56977-1 / ISBN 10: 3-525-56977-7

Images from the caves of Gargas, Niaux, and Cougnac are from the personal collection of Dr. Jean
Clottes, and are reprinted with his permission.

The image of the "Dotted Horses" (front cover) from the cave of Pech-Merle is reprinted with the
permission of the Centre de Préhistoire du Pech-Merle, 46330 Cabrerets (France):
Chevaux ponctués © Centre de Préhistoire du Pech-Merle, Cabrerets (Lot, France).

The images from the cave of Lascaux are reprinted with the permission of the
Centre National de Préhistoire, Département d'Art Pariétal, Perigueux, France.
Crédit photographique: CNP — Ministère de la Culture.

For Hester,

   our children,

      and our grandchildren

Contents

Acknowledgments

The invitation to deliver the Gifford Lectures at the University of Edinburgh in the spring of 2004 presented me with a unique and challenging opportunity to develop further my own thoughts on the complex relationship between religion and science. Preparing for and delivering the Gifford Lectures has been a remarkable personal journey and has opened up new and exciting ways of thinking about the problem of interdisciplinary reflection. In this specific instance, the rather concrete focus of my research would be the topic of *Alone in the World? Human Uniqueness in Science and Theology,* a topic that would not only directly stimulate my reflection on the more philosophical problem of interdisciplinarity, but would also afford me the challenge of rethinking, and ultimately revisioning, Lord Gifford's requirement for doing "natural theology in the widest sense of the term." Most importantly, however, it finally gave me the opportunity to explore the uncharted but fascinating relationship between theology and paleoanthropology.

I am very grateful to the University of Edinburgh for honoring me with this invitation. I would like to express my very special gratitude to Professor T. M. M. O'Shea, Principal and Vice-Chancellor, and to the Gifford Committee for the warm hospitality my wife Hester and I were privileged to receive during our stay in Edinburgh. Our host, Professor David Fergusson, did everything to make us feel welcome and to enhance the experience of being part of a very distinguished community of scholars at the University of Edinburgh. A word of thanks must also go to Ms. Isabel Roberts, Secretary of the Gifford Committee, for the highly professional and skillful way she took care of every possible detail during our stay in Edinburgh.

I am deeply indebted to my colleagues and students at Princeton Theological Seminary, and to the president and administration, for their remarkable support during this particular time in my professional life. I remember with much gratitude all my colleagues who were willing to read my lectures in their various incarnations, and especially for their constructive feedback and responses at a much appreciated "pre-Gifford" evening, organized by our friends Chip and Leslie Dobbs-Allsopp in Princeton. The support of Princeton Theological Seminary followed me all the way to Edinburgh, not only thanks to colleagues and students who traveled to Scotland to attend my lectures, but also in the form of a wonderful and festive Princeton reception in Edinburgh, planned and organized by our colleague Steven Hamilton.

I am immensely grateful to students and other colleagues at Princeton Theological Seminary who were directly involved with this project: Rachel Baard, who did an extremely professional job as my research assistant prior to my lectures in Edinburgh; Jennifer Thweatt-Bates, who was an excellent editorial assistant for both the lectures and various drafts of the manuscript; and my research assistant, Erik Wiebe, who did all final editing, prepared the bibliography and index, and without whose expertise and outstanding work this book would not have been possible. I am also very grateful to Denise Schwalb, Faculty Secretary at Princeton Theological Seminary, for her unfailing support and assistance during the preparation for my lectures, and during the time this book was written. A very special word of thanks must also go to Julie Dawson, Associate Librarian at Princeton Theological Seminary, and Jon Wood, Ph.D. student, for their invaluable assistance and linguistic competence that finally helped me obtain permission from various institutions in France to publish the remarkable photographs of prehistoric cave paintings that appear in this book.

I want to thank a special group of friends and scholars who read, and re-read, various versions of my lectures and gave me important critical feedback. Others directly contributed to the content of this work through in-depth conversations and invaluable suggestions for interdisciplinary reading material that enriched immeasurably my own research and writing. These colleagues are: Patrick Miller, Richard Osmer, Chip Dobbs-Allsopp, Dennis Olson, James Kay, and Steven Hamilton (Princeton Theological Seminary); Angela Creager (Princeton University); George Newlands (University of Glasgow); LeRon Shults (Bethel Theological Seminary); Rudie Botha, Julian Müller, Robert Vosloo, Deon Bruwer (South Africa), and Ockert Meyer (Australia). A dear friend of many years, Jerome (Jerry) A. Stone, not only read the entire manuscript several times, but enriched it with his thorough comments and important critical questions.

Directly after delivering the Gifford Lectures in May 2004, I had the great privilege of being part of a group of scientists who met in Les Eyzies, France, under the joint leadership of Colin Renfrew and Mary Ann Meyer, sponsored by the John Templeton Foundation. At this seminar, "Innovation in Material and Spiritual Cultures," I had the privilege of finally meeting those leading scholars in paleoanthropology and archeology whose research work and publications have so definitively shaped my own interdisciplinary work on the elusive relationship between theological anthropology and paleoanthropology. I am deeply indebted to the following scientists for their inspiring work, for their sustained and genuine interest in the kinds of questions a philosophical theologian would ask, and for their critical feedback and contributions to my own thinking about the shared problem of human uniqueness: Jean Clottes, Margaret Conkey, Francesco d'Errico, Christopher Henshilwood, David Lewis-Williams, Paul A. Mellars, Steven Mithen, Paul Taçon, and my colleague Keith Ward.

In the months following my lectures in Edinburgh, I was invited to speak on this topic at various institutions, an opportunity that greatly contributed to the fine-tuning and structuring of the final manuscript of this book. I would like to express my sincere gratitude to the following institutions: the Metanexus Institute (Philadelphia); the Institute of Theology (Princeton); the North Central Program for Science and Theology (St. Paul, Minnesota); the Divinity School at Yale University; St. John's University (Collegeville, Minnesota); the Evangelische Akademie Arnoldshain (Germany); and in South Africa, the Faculty of Theology, University of Pretoria, and the Presbyterian Church of St. Columba's, Johannesburg. An invitation by the University of Uppsala, Sweden, to deliver the Olaus Petri Lectures in December 2004 enabled me once again to return to, and work through, this manuscript. I am especially grateful to my colleagues in Uppsala, Mikael Stenmark, Carl Reinhold Bråkenhielm, and Eberhard Herrmann, for their extremely constructive conversations and contributions on the topics of interdisciplinarity and "human uniqueness."

I also want to specially thank Ian Tattersall, Curator at the Department of Anthropology at the American Museum of Natural History, New York City, for his ongoing support of my work, and for assisting me with the detailed planning of my very first visit to the prehistoric caves in southwestern France and the Basque Country in northern Spain. I am also enormously indebted to Rick Potts, Director of Human Origins at the National Museum of Natural History, Smithsonian Institution in Washington, D.C., and to Paul Wason, Director of Science and Religion at the John Templeton Foundation, for their encouragement, for their critical reading of my work, and for really believing in this project.

I am very thankful to Jean Clottes for meeting with me, first in Foix, and later in Les Eyzies, France, and for guiding me through the wealth of information available on Upper Paleolithic cave art today. He has not only been an inspiration for this book but has also very graciously supplied me with spectacular photos of paintings from the caves of Gargas (Hautes-Pyrénées), Cougnac (Lot), and Niaux (Ariège). I am also very grateful to Norbert Aujoulat, Director of the Département d'Art Pariétal in Périgueux, France, for making available, and giving copyright permission for, the stunning images from the cave of Lascaux that are printed in this text. Bertrand Defois from the Centre de Préhistoire du Pech-Merle provided me with the most beautiful image of the famous "Dotted Horses" from the cave of Pech-Merle that I have ever come across. I thank him for that, and for the permission to reproduce it here.

These acknowledgments cannot end without thanking a group of dear friends who traveled from different parts of the world to attend my lectures in Edinburgh. This encouraged me in ways I will never forget.

The ongoing support and enthusiasm for this project from our family, our children, their spouses, our grandchildren, and my mother, Annie van Huyssteen, has been a true inspiration. The fact that some of them managed to join us for the lectures in Edinburgh meant the world to us. Their presence was indicative of the continuous support of the rest of our family who were unable to be with us at that time. I would like to dedicate this book to my wife Hester, to our four children Henk, Ilse, Daniël, and Nina, to their spouses Charmaine, Jac, Gretchen, Dale, and to our beautiful grandchildren Benjamin, Wentzel, Ava, and Jada.

List of Plates

Introduction

The long and rich tradition of the Gifford Lectures has always, in one sense or another, challenged the way religious faith relates to culture, or more specifically, how religion and theology critically respond to the remarkable success of contemporary science. It is this specific challenge that finally gave me the opportunity to contextualize, as it were, my own recent work in philosophical theology. In my work *The Shaping of Rationality: Toward Interdisciplinarity in Theology and Science* (1999), I focused on how the fragile but uniquely human ability to be rational infuses our everyday lives as well as our deep involvement with religious faith, theology, and the spectacular achievements of the sciences of our time. The development of a postfoundationalist notion of rationality helped me move beyond any position that would want to regard either science or theology as a superior form of rational thinking. Moreover, I argued that if human rationality is alive and well in all the various facets of our lives, then this uniquely human ability should also be able to help us successfully bridge the many domains of our intellectual lives.

This lecture series gave me the special opportunity to develop further this interdisciplinary approach. More importantly, though, it challenged me for the first time to apply this methodology to a highly concrete interdisciplinary case study by focusing specifically on the notion of "human uniqueness" in science and theology. Quite concretely it afforded me the exciting opportunity to explore the uncharted waters of the interdisciplinary relationship between theological anthropology and paleoanthropology, if such exists. This very specific interdisciplinary problem would not only resonate well with some of Lord Gifford's original intentions for this lecture series, but would give me the opportunity to argue that theological anthropology has much to learn from human origins, from the dimension of meaning in which *Homo sapiens* have always existed, and from our close relationship to other animals. Moreover, theology might suggest to science the interdisciplinary relevance of those elusive but distinctly human characteristics that do not fossilize but are crucial for defining the human condition. Most importantly, though, this interdisciplinary case study has revealed some of the most challenging opportunities, but also important limitations, of interdisciplinary work.

In chapter 1, I reject the idea that the domain of religious faith and the domain of scientific thought are exemplified by rival and opposing notions of rationality. I argue instead that these different and seemingly incompatible reasoning strategies actually share in the resources of human rationality and are therefore able to be linked in interdisciplinary dialogue. This will set the stage for developing both themes that are strongly implicit in Lord Gifford's original charge: that of an integrative and interdisciplinary praxis for theology and the sciences, and the basic conviction that there is something about being human, something perhaps uniquely human, that is constituted by the way we relate to ourselves, to the world, and even to God. I argue that it is precisely in interdisciplinary dialogue that we find an adequate vehicle for a concrete case study like science and theology on human uniqueness. I also argue for the idea of transversality as a heuristic device that opens up new ways for crossing boundaries between disciplines, and for identifying those interdisciplinary spaces where the relevance of scientific knowledge can be translated into the domain of Christian theology, and vice versa.

In chapter 2 a multidimensional interdisciplinary discourse, where perspectives from theology, epistemology, and the sciences can unfold along diversely intersecting lines, is authenticated by linking the question of human uniqueness to evolutionary epistemology, with a special focus on the prehistory of the human mind. I argue that Charles Darwin's understanding of human identity and of human nature still functions as the canonical core of the ongoing discourse on human evolution, and that the powerful galaxy of meaning of these Darwinian views, now maybe more than ever, shapes our views on the evolution of human cognition. The epistemic implications of these views on reason, imagination, consciousness, linguistic ability, and moral awareness are represented in a most challenging way in contemporary evolutionary epistemology. Evolutionary epistemology, with its focus on the embodied human mind, not only embraces the core of Darwin's ideas on human cognition, but also reveals the evolution of human cognition as a bridge between biology and culture. Moreover, arguments from evolutionary epistemology demonstrate the plausibility of distinctions between biological and cultural evolution and, importantly, that the problem of human uniqueness is directly related to the problem of human origins. Evolutionary epistemology also clearly shows that a human propensity for metaphysical and religious beliefs should be seen as the result of specific interactions between early humans and their lifeworlds. The question for any theology would be whether this tells us anything about the integrity of religion, and about the rationality or meaningfulness of religious belief.

In chapter 3, against the backdrop of arguments for human distinctiveness in evolutionary epistemology, the focus shifts to one of the core traditions of the Christian faith, the doctrine of the *imago Dei,* and the deep-seated religious belief that humans are different and distinct because they were created in the image of God. To argue for the elusive point where theology and the various sciences may intersect transversally on the issue of human uniqueness, a theory of traditions will be applied as a methodological link to this increasingly interdisciplinary discourse. This will facilitate important questions like: Is there an intrinsic biblical meaning that can be ascribed to the idea that humans were created in the image of God, or has the meaning of this crucial term shifted dramatically through history? Is the theological notion of the *imago Dei* helped or hindered by the diverse interpretations of human uniqueness revealed by various sciences, and what does that tell us about our relations to earlier hominids, and to the uniqueness of our sister species in the animal world? It will be argued that the porousness of the boundaries between theology and the sciences allows for a creative rethinking of the notion of the *imago Dei* in Christian theology. The relative convergence of theological and scientific arguments on the issue of human uniqueness may give us an argument for the plausibility and comprehensive nature of religious and theological explanations for a phenomenon as complex as *Homo sapiens.* At the same time, scientific notions of human uniqueness may help us ground theological notions of human distinctiveness in the reality of flesh-and-blood, real-life, embodied experiences, and thus protect theological reflection from overly complex abstractions when trying to revision the notion of the *imago Dei.*

In chapter 4 I complement the very distinct and diverse lines of reasoning for human uniqueness in both evolutionary epistemology and theology by weaving, transversally, a third argument into the pattern of this emerging discourse. The history of the evolution of human cognition is deeply embedded in the question of human origins, and quite naturally leads to the question of human distinctiveness or uniqueness. The most obvious and plausible scientific voice on this crucial issue, but much neglected in the broader theology and science dialogue, is found in contemporary paleoanthropology. The argument from paleoanthropology will show that the prehistory of the human mind, including the evolution of consciousness and self-awareness, reveals the remarkable cognitive fluidity of our mental abilities. The most spectacular evidence of symbolic behavior in humans — and some of the earliest — can be found in the Paleolithic cave art in southwestern France and the Basque Country in northern Spain. The materiality of these prehistoric images might not tell us much about our remote human or hominid origins, but the images certainly reveal much of what it means to be human, and as such, dramatically reveal the complexity of the cognitively fluid human mind. This cognitive fluidity generates imagination, the capacity for symbolic thought, and the creative ability to generate complex mental symbols and to manipulate them into new combinations. This kind of cognitive ability holds the key to our species' exceptional creative abilities, and is therefore closely tied to the emergence of art, science, and religion. As such, the Upper Paleolithic holds an all-important and intriguing key to the naturalness of the evolution of religion, to the credibility of the earliest forms of religious faith, and to what it means for *Homo sapiens* to be spiritually embodied beings.

In chapter 5 I evaluate the fact that three distinct disciplinary lines of argument on human uniqueness have now transversally intersected: the *epistemological* argument from evolutionary biology, the *historically* diverse and rather fragmented argument from theology, and complex, multileveled *scientific* arguments from contemporary paleoanthropology. In this chapter, also, new interdisciplinary proposals on the origins of the human mind will be introduced by additional arguments for a theory of human cognitive evolution, drawing on linguistics, neuroscience, and neuropsychology. The primary focus will be on how symbolic representation, as the principal cognitive signature of humans, is grounded in our remarkable mimetic and linguistic abilities. In language, in fact, we find our most unique capacity for symbolic communication. What it means to be uniquely human, then, clearly includes biologically unprecedented ways of experiencing and understanding the world, from aesthetic experience to spiritual contemplation. In fact, both the special adaptations for language and language itself have played important roles in the origins of human moral and spiritual capacities. In this sense it will be argued that the capacity for spirituality can be understood as an emergent consequence of the symbolic transformation of cognition and emotions. This symbolic nature of *Homo sapiens* will also explain why the propensity for religion and religious experience can be regarded as an essentially universal human attribute. At the same time, a postfoundationalist approach to human uniqueness as an interdisciplinary problem should alert us to the fact that religious imagination cannot be discussed abstractly or treated as a generic given, but can be discussed and evaluated only within the concrete context of specific religions and concrete theologies.

Finally, in chapter 6 the question can be asked: What can theologians learn from the insights the sciences have provided about the evolution of human uniqueness? At the very least a serious interdisciplinary conversation with the sciences should inspire theologians to revisit the way notions of the *imago Dei* are constructed. Interpretations of the *imago Dei* have indeed varied dramatically throughout the long history of Christianity. Theologians are thus challenged to rethink what human uniqueness might mean for the human person, an embodied being that has emerged biologically and sexually as a center of self-awareness, identity, and moral responsibility. Personhood, when richly reconceived in terms of imagination, symbolic propensities, and cognitive fluidity, may enable theologians also to revision the notion of the *imago Dei* in a way that acknowledges our close ties to the animal world, challenging us to rethink our own species specificity, while focusing on what our symbolic minds might tell us about the emergence of the uniquely human propensity for religious awareness and religious experience. The emergence of this kind of mental complexity does resonate with theology's deepest convictions about human uniqueness, and does argue for the plausibility of a distinctly theological explanation of a phenomenon like the emergence of the human mind. After all, our ability to respond religiously to ultimate questions in worship and prayer is deeply embedded in our species' symbolic, imaginative nature. However, if the sciences are taken seriously on what is unique about humans, the theological notion of the *imago Dei* will have to be revisioned as emerging from nature itself. Thus, in this interdisciplinary case study our vital connection with nature is honored precisely by focusing on our species specificity, and by rethinking, theologically, the "image of God" as having emerged from nature by natural evolutionary processes.

one *Human Uniqueness as an Interdisciplinary Problem?*

"The *I* is the producer of inwardness."

Jean-Paul Sartre, *The Transcendence of the Ego*
(New York: Hill and Wang, 1960), 38

On August 21, 1885, Lord Gifford signed into existence his last will and testament, creating the Gifford Lectures and along with that the now famous charge to all future lecturers:

"I having been for many years deeply and firmly convinced that the true knowledge of God, . . . and the true and felt knowledge . . . of the relations of man and of the universe to Him, and of the true foundations of all ethics and morals — being, I say, convinced that this knowledge, when really felt and acted on, is the means of man's highest well-being, and the security of his upward progress, I have resolved . . . to institute and found . . . lectureships or classes for the study and promotion of said subjects." The purpose and goal of these lectureships at the four Scottish universities would be "promoting, advancing, teaching and diffusing the study of Natural Theology in the widest sense of the term," and the lecturers should "treat their subject as a strictly natural science, the greatest of all possible sciences, indeed, in one sense the only science, . . . without reference to or reliance upon any supposed special exceptional or so-called miraculous revelation. I wish it to be considered just as astronomy and chemistry is."[1]

1. Cf. *Lord Gifford's Will*, in Jaki 1986: 71f., 74.

Lord Gifford's very specific demand for a generally conceived natural theology that would treat its object of study as "a strictly natural science," and indeed in one sense as "the only science," has of course become a completely impossible task today. The emerging interdisciplinary, and increasingly international, research field of "theology and science" clearly exemplifies a diversity of approaches, and a pluralism of opinions and methodologies that starkly reveals a rather complex intellectual journey from modernity to postmodernity and beyond. Against the background of this intellectual history, the mere idea that "true knowledge of God" might be "the means of man's highest well-being, and the security of his upward progress," and that all this could be achieved by a natural theology "in the widest sense of the term," seems remote, even quaint, were it not for the obvious passion and sincerity that shine through the carefully worded paragraphs of Lord Gifford's will. Every Gifford lecturer, of course, is confronted with the serious and daunting challenge of successfully embedding his or her lecture series in the long and rich tradition of the Gifford Lectures and thereby establishing a meaningful connection with the intellectual climate of the Edinburgh of 1885. Clearly, any Gifford lecturer should feel at least some moral and intellectual obligation to live up to the charges of Lord Gifford's will. But, as Alasdair MacIntyre argued in his Gifford Lectures at the University of Edinburgh (1988), Adam Gifford's will is a document from a cultural milieu so significantly different from and alien to our own that it might be difficult, and really hard work, to determine what fidelity and loyalty to Lord Gifford's intentions might mean today. This is all the more true since we are not all participants in a common culture, and therefore no longer share the philosophical and theological presuppositions of Lord Gifford and his peers.

In the introduction to his lectures, MacIntyre correctly argued that any public lecture or lecture series should demand of us an astute awareness of the radical contextuality of who the lecturer is, who the audience is, and how the problems at hand are to be defined (cf. 1990: 1). In the Gifford Lectures, I believe, this radical contextuality, embodied by a specific lecturer, a very specific audience, and a specifically defined problem, should be deepened and broadened even further to include past audiences and past lecturers, and also very specifically the dominant voice of the influential conditions of Lord Gifford's will. This should be true in spite of the philosophical and cultural differences we face as we try to relate to Gifford's intentions. For anyone engaged in interdisciplinary work, possibly the biggest challenge comes from the now dated and problematical modernist worldview expressed in a sentence like the following: "I wish the lecturers to treat their subject as a strictly natural science. . . . I wish it to be considered just as astronomy and chemistry is" (cf. *Lord Gifford's Will,* in Jaki 1986: 74).

This now famous statement clearly exudes a very specific, if not typical, modernist yearning for a lofty and universal notion of human rationality.[2] Clearly the intention here is that natural theology, however conceived, be done in such a way that it would qualify for natural scientific status, so that also the discipline of theology can partake in one of the most important and defining characteristics of the natural sciences, namely, its successful history as one of clear and distinct rational progress in intellectual inquiry. Lord Gifford is thus revealed as a strong and representative figure of his own cultural time and place (cf. MacIntyre 1990: 9, 14). However, even if in a sense the history of the natural sciences could be interpreted to witness a progressive evolution of new breakthroughs and spectacular discoveries, surely theology — and even "natural theology," conceived in whatever form — has no such history of rational problem-solving and progress to fall back on. Not only has the notion of "progress" become seriously problematical today, even in the natural sciences (cf. van Huyssteen 1989: 24-71), but the contemporary intellectual context of theological reflection has become so radically pluralist that there is little chance of any agreement on what rational progress might be conceived to be, or whether it is even something that theology should strive for.

MacIntyre was right, of course, in identifying this kind of radical intellectual pluralism not only as exemplifying the academic context of the culture(s) we live in (cf. MacIntyre 1990: 11), but also as typical of the history of the Gifford Lectures. For MacIntyre this raised the troubling question whether the history of the Gifford Lectures, instead of accomplishing some form of universal rational progress in natural theology, might represent only dissensus, or in his striking words, a kind of "museum of intellectual conflict" (10), so that delivering these lectures might in the end make one a prisoner in a world of incommensurable rationalities. In my recent work I have challenged precisely this kind of polarization, especially when trying to relate Christian theology to the sciences. We are obliged neither to commit to some form of universal rationality nor to plunge into a sea of relativism where many rationalities proliferate. A multidimensional or interdisciplinary understanding of rationality, rightly conceived, should enable us to move away from ab-

2. In MacIntyre's words: "For Adam Gifford and almost all his educated Edinburgh contemporaries it was a guiding presupposition of thought that substantive rationality is unitary, that there is a single, if perhaps complex, conception of what the standards and the achievements of rationality are, one which every educated person can without too much difficulty be brought to agree in acknowledging" (MacIntyre 1990: 14).

stract, overgeneralized models or blueprints for "doing" interdisciplinary work,[3] and specifically for doing theology and science. This should instead help us focus on developing, first contextually, and then transversally, the merits of each concrete interdisciplinary problem in terms of the very specific science and the very specific theology involved.

Against this background, it seems clear why it has become impossible and unrealistic even to contemplate developing a universal natural theology that would rival the empirical excellence of the natural sciences. But what does all this mean for the interdisciplinary dialogue between theology and the sciences? Pluralism in both theology and the sciences, along with a rising awareness that science and religion are vastly different cognitive domains, has of course intensified this problem. We can summarize some of the most important factors determining the complexity of the theology and science dialogue as follows:

- clear and profound differences as to the nature and identity of these very different reasoning strategies
- important differences in how we form and hold on to beliefs in these two very different cognitive domains
- obvious differences in how we justify holding our beliefs in disciplines as radically different as theology and the sciences

Moreover, contemporary forms of postfoundationalist epistemology have convincingly shown that it has become impossible, and certainly implausible, even to talk about "theology and science" in any generic, abstract, or a-contextual sense. This increasing awareness of the radical social and historical contextuality of all our rational reflection should make it abundantly clear that in interdisciplinary dialogue the rather vague terms "theology and science" should be replaced by a focus on specific theologians who are trying to do very specific kinds of theologies and are attempting to enter into interdisci-

3. Richard Osmer has helpfully distinguished between four levels of cross-disciplinary thinking: *interdisciplinary* reflection focuses on the dialogue between different disciplines or fields, and on the enhancing role different disciplines may play in the construction of theories within disciplines; *intradisciplinary* reflection focuses on the various methodological or theoretical options within a specific discipline; *metadisciplinary* reflection focuses on the nature and specific epistemological integrity of individual disciplines; *multidisciplinary* reflection is based on the assumption that various disciplines are needed to comprehend complex phenomena (cf. Osmer 2000: 186f.). In what follows I will presuppose these conceptual distinctions and in addition argue that a multidisciplinary approach to complex phenomena invariably leads to interdisciplinary results.

plinary dialogue with very specific scientists, working within specified sciences on clearly defined, shared problems.

In the light of the rather complex recent history of the theology and science dialogue, these questions ultimately focus on the very last issue: Would it be possible to identify, between radically diverse disciplines, something like a common issue, a shared problem, a kind of mutual concern, or even a shared, overlapping research trajectory that might benefit precisely from interdisciplinary dialogue? Is it too ambitious to hope that a multidisciplinary approach may yield interdisciplinary results, or do we, at the end of the day, remain prisoners of our incommensurable belief systems and isolated disciplines? In *The Shaping of Rationality: Toward Interdisciplinarity in Theology and Science* (1999), I rejected the idea that the domain of religious faith and the domain of scientific thought are in any sense exemplified by rival or opposing notions of rationality. I also argued that different, and seemingly incompatible, reasoning strategies actually share in the resources of human rationality. The question is, of course, whether this approach might help us circle back to some of Lord Gifford's original intentions.

I hasten to add that an argument that celebrates diversity, pluralism, and contextuality, while at the same time pursuing shared resources of human rationality and interdisciplinary conversation, does not in the least imply a retrieval of modernist notions of rationality. The rationality of modernity resided in a centered human subject, functioning as an epistemological foundation from which all claims for the justification of knowledge proceeded (cf. van Huyssteen 1999: 22f.). In this sense modernity not only characteristically represented a comprehensive metanarrative strategy that described the historical construction of the modern world, but it even more fundamentally represented a widespread cultural understanding. This modernist notion of universal rationality can also be described as taking for granted not only that all rational persons conceptualize data in one and the same way, but also that — because honest observers are allegedly able to put aside or rise above the prejudices of prior commitment to belief — they would report the same data, the same facts, in the same way (cf. MacIntyre 1990: 16). Closely related to this is the typically modernist development of distinct domains of knowledge and practices the disciplinary autonomies of which were ultimately institutionally recognized and protected but which, at the same time, were unified by a formal and universal notion of human rationality (cf. Rouse 1996: 49). On an epistemological level this modernist mode of inquiry was definitively dealt with first by Michael Polanyi, then by Thomas Kuhn, and post-Kuhn by various strands of postmodern science. What this move has made increasingly clear is that all our inquiry, whether scientific or theological, is highly contextual and already presupposes a particular theoretical, doctrinal, or personal stance and commitment (cf. van Huyssteen 1989: 47-71; 1999: 1-60).[4]

In a modernist world that confessed utmost faith in universal rationality, and that saw the history of genuine science as a history of continuous progress, it was therefore impossible to see that commitment to some particular theoretical or doctrinal standpoint may be a prerequisite for, rather than a barrier to, an ability to characterize data in a way that will enable inquiry to proceed rationally. In this world all sciences, also the human sciences, exhibited progress, and progress of all kinds — moral, scientific, technological, theological — was the central and defining subject matter. These kinds of conceptions of progress and of its inevitability were among the most unifying conceptions of this modernist worldview (cf. MacIntyre 1990: 17, 21). This gets even more interesting if we ask what scientific knowledge in theology might truly have meant to Adam Gifford and his contemporaries. In natural theology, as a "science still in the making," specific data would function as starting points for inquiry: both the data of nature that supplies the starting point for natural theology, and the data provided by the Bible that supplies the starting point for a theology of revelation. For Gifford, furthermore, natural theology took over from philosophy the role of an organizing principle, the overarching view that provided the encyclopedic context for all the different sciences. This is why in his will he called natural theology "the greatest of all possible sciences, indeed, in one sense the only science" (Jaki 1986: 74). What we have here, then, is a conception of universal science that comprehends both God and nature (cf. MacIntyre 1990: 22f.).

Against this background I now have to answer the question that has haunted so many recent Gifford lecturers: *Are Gifford Lectures really possible today?* And I too answer it with a qualified yes and no (cf. MacIntyre 1990: 24). We may not be able to go back in time to Lord Gifford's context in Edinburgh, and we may no longer be able to accomplish natural theology, or natural theology in exactly that universalizing way. But we can go back to the central idea of Gifford's charge and from that glean two crucially important themes. Gifford phrased it as follows:

> I having been for many years deeply and firmly convinced that the true knowledge of God, . . . and the true and felt knowledge . . . of the relations

4. MacIntyre is therefore right: "What is true of physical enquiry holds also for theological and moral enquiry. What are taken to be the relevant data and how they are identified, characterized and classified will depend upon who is performing these tasks and what his or her theological and moral standpoint and perspective is" (1990: 17).

of man and of the universe to Him, and of the true foundations of all ethics and morals — being, I say, convinced that *this knowledge, when really felt and acted on, is the means of man's highest well-being, and the security of his upward progress,* I have resolved . . . to institute and found . . . lectureships or classes for the study and promotion of said subjects. (Jaki 1986: 72, 74, my italics)

The very explicit and well-known statement here is that, *in knowing God, and in knowing the world, and our relationship to the world in relation to God, we may actually find and achieve something unique, i.e., humankind's "highest well-being."* As I will now argue, implicit in this statement are two important themes that can be revisioned to reach out to us transversally across time: there is a direct challenge to a form of multidisciplinary reflection that may lead to interdisciplinary insights, and there is a clear and unambiguous relational statement on what is unique about our human species, which can be optimally understood only in terms of our broader connection to the universe and to God. Lord Gifford seems to be making a theological statement about human uniqueness, and might just as well have said that what is unique about us as humans can be found in exactly this remarkable ability we have to know God through our relationships to this God, and through the way we know the relationship of the universe to this God.

MacIntyre argued in his Gifford Lectures that even if we are obliged to reject some of the central beliefs of Gifford and his Edinburgh contemporaries so steeped in a modernist, nineteenth-century mode of rationality, we are still able to continue the tradition of his charge, and to identify with his project because of the way he held that inquiry into God and inquiry into the good are not separable (MacIntyre 1990: 25f.). I want to take this one step further and argue that the call for a comprehensive, universalizing natural theology in Gifford's will can be transformed into an integrative and contemporary interdisciplinary challenge for theology and the sciences. This is so precisely because Gifford's basic conviction — that there is something about being human, even uniquely human, that is constituted by the relationship of ourselves and of our world to this God — transcends the rigid modernist contours of the time. For me as a Christian theologian, this today means that we have not understood our world, or ourselves, until we have understood them in relationship to God. This profoundly links us to Gifford's original intentions, even as we move beyond the philosophical worldview of these intentions and radically revise our knowing of God, and of ourselves, in the light of our own natural origins.

The call for a comprehensive, universalizing natural theology in Lord Gifford's will can therefore be revisioned to reveal an integrative and interdisciplinary contemporary praxis for "theology and the sciences." Also, precisely because of Gifford's basic theological conviction that there is something about being human, even uniquely human, that is constituted by the *relationality* of ourselves and our world to God, his charge transcends the rigid modernist contours of the time. The two themes of interdisciplinarity and relationality thus merge in a powerful theological appeal: we have not understood our world, and ourselves, until we have understood ourselves and our world in relationship to God.

In this lecture series I will directly pursue these two crucial themes that reach out to us transversally from Lord Gifford's original charge: revisioning a contemporary notion of interdisciplinary reflection, and pursuing as an interdisciplinary problem the issue of human uniqueness. I will argue that theology and the sciences find a shared research trajectory precisely in the topic of human uniqueness. The question, of course, is how reasonable it is to expect a theologian to enter into the formidable dangers of interdisciplinary discourse on a topic that, at first blush, seems to present itself as a common or shared concern but is certainly going to be fraught with all kinds of methodological and epistemological dangers. How reasonable is it for a theologian, after examining, for instance, the results and accomplishments of some of the sciences dealing with anthropological issues, to expect these sciences to provide a basis, or important links, or even a stage for discussion of issues on human origins, human nature, human uniqueness, and human destiny? How realistic is it for a theologian to expect scientists to take theological contributions to this central topic seriously? And when the dialogue is finally narrowed down to theology and paleoanthropology, how may paleoanthropology enrich theology, and what — if anything — may theological anthropology contribute to paleoanthropology?

In dealing with these questions, we are immediately confronted with two more difficult issues, issues that Jean-Pierre Changeux and Paul Ricoeur have identified as serious obstacles for any interdisciplinary conversation. First, we face the prejudices of a public that easily places all its trust in science and, I would add, unabashed scientism. Second, there exists an equally serious problem with theology and philosophy, two disciplines that seem so concerned to assure their own survival and, preoccupied by immense textual heritages, also seem uninterested in recent developments in the sciences (Changeux and Ricoeur 2000: 1). For theology the challenge is even more daunting: Even if it wanted to, can a theology that has willingly abandoned all grand claims to be an inclusive, comprehensive natural theology ever be a legitimate part of a multivoiced interdisciplinary conversation? Why would the theologian try to speak publicly? And who would care to hear this voice?

In the kind of multileveled, integrative interdisciplinary conversation that I will argue for, terms like "transversality" and "contextuality" will take center stage, and will have the value of identifying shared concerns and points of agreement, and maybe more importantly, of exposing areas of disagreement and putting into perspective specific divisive issues that need to be discussed. We also need to keep in mind that in any interdisciplinary conversation, different discourses often represent radically diverse perspectives, and also different and distinct methods of investigation, which means they cannot be reduced to each other or derived from each other (cf. van Huyssteen 1999: 235ff.; Changeux and Ricoeur 2000: 4). The challenge, however, is to show that it is often at the boundaries between disciplines that new and exciting discoveries take place. But a timely warning should be issued here: an interdisciplinary approach is likely to be fruitful only as long as one is scrupulously attentive to the meaning of words and the proper use of concepts (cf. Changeux and Ricoeur 2000: 25). When a concept like human uniqueness is used in theology, it may mean something entirely different than when it is used in the sciences. But these diverse uses of the same phrases may, at the same time, alert us to promising liminalities between the disciplines. Indeed, interdisciplinary discourse may begin at this very point of transversal intersection and tension. Thanks to the multiplicity, abundance, and completeness of human experience, our different discourses do continually intersect with one another at many points.

Interdisciplinary discourse, then, is an attempt to bring together disciplines or reasoning strategies that may have widely different points of reference, different epistemological foci, and different experiential resources. This "fitting together," however, is a complex, multileveled transversal process that takes place not within the confines of any given discipline (cf. Changeux and Ricoeur 2000: 87), but within the transversal spaces between disciplines. For the theologian the achievement of this kind of shared rational space might at the same time signify the arrival of an authentic public realm in which all participants, whatever their particular differences, can meet to discuss any claim that might be rationally redeemable (cf. Tracy and Reynolds 1992: 19).

Interdisciplinarity in Theology and Science

In a context where the public trust in science, and often unabashed scientism, is still so dominant, it does seem warranted to ask whether science as such has finally claimed rationality, that allegedly most unique of our human abilities, at the expense of religious faith and theological reflection. And if it has, would that mean that theology is now left without any interdisciplinary criteria to "qualify" for epistemic credibility at all? In *The Shaping of Rationality* I explored the complex relationship between the cultural forces of theology and science, and answered these questions with a resounding no. A more nuanced approach would be to ask whether theology exhibits a rationality that is comparable to, overlaps with, or is informed by the rationality of science (cf. van Huyssteen 1999: 119). Against this background I have argued that the identities of both science and theology have been challenged by postmodern culture. This challenge has revealed the typically modernist notions of objective truth, universal rationality, and autonomous individuality as untenable. In developing my notion of a postfoundationalist rationality, I argue for the abandonment of modernist notions of rationality, typically rooted in foundationalism and in the quest for secure foundations for our various domains of knowledge. With postmodernism I have rejected all forms of foundationalism, but I have also argued against extreme forms of deconstructive postmodernism and the adoption of relativist forms of nonfoundationalism or contextualism (cf. also Stenmark 1995: 301ff.) as reactions against universalist notions of rationality. Over against the objectivism of foundationalism and the extreme relativism of most forms of nonfoundationalism, a postfoundationalist notion of rationality helps us to acknowledge contextuality, the shaping role of tradition and of interpreted experience, while at the same time enabling us to reach out beyond our own groups, communities, and cultures, in plausible forms of inter-subjective, cross-contextual, and cross-disciplinary conversations.

On this postfoundationalist view embodied persons, and not abstract beliefs, should be seen as the locus of rationality. We, as rational agents, are thus always socially and contextually embedded. Moreover, it is as embodied rational agents that we perform rationally by making informed and responsible judgments in very specific personal, communal, but also disciplinary and interdisciplinary contexts. In fact, in all domains of rational behavior we make these judgments for what we perceive to be good reasons. And it is precisely in our very human ability and responsibility for informed judgments in all areas of life that we find what I have called the shared resources of human rationality (cf. van Huyssteen 1999: 145ff.). On this view rationality is alive and well in *all* the domains of our human lives. Rationality turns out to have many faces, and human rationality, rightly interpreted in its complex, embodied form, may even ultimately define who we are as a species. This notion of human rationality presupposes the evolutionary epistemological insight that all forms of human cognition are grounded in biological evolution even as it reaches out beyond the limitations of strictly evolutionary explanations. Moreover, a postfoundationalist approach to rational reflection teaches us that rationality can never be adequately housed within only one specific reasoning strategy, and as will become clear, the very human ability for reasoning actually holds the important and only key to bridging the different domains of our lives responsibly (4ff.).

In fact, rationality is all about epistemic responsibility: the responsibility to pursue clarity, intelligibility, and optimal understanding, as ways to cope with ourselves and our world. In this dialogue the pursuit of intelligibility and optimal understanding emerges as possibly the most important epistemic goal that shapes the way we interact with others, ourselves, and our worlds on a daily basis. In my recent work I have argued that all the many faces of human rationality relate directly to this pretheoretical reasonableness, a "common-sense rationality" that informs and is present in all our everyday goal-directed actions. The origins of a rationality of interdisciplinarity, therefore, lie not in abstract theories of reason but in the everyday and ordinary means by which we make rational judgments and decisions, i.e., the performance of rationality in everyday life. From these everyday activities in ordinary time we can identify epistemic values like intelligibility, discernment, responsible judgment, and deliberation, which guide us when on an intellectual level we come to responsible theory choice and commitment (cf. 171). It is in the pursuit of these goals and ideals that we become rational persons as we learn the skills of responsible judgment and discernment, and where we articulate the best available reasons we have for making what we believe to be the right choices, those reasons we have for holding on to certain beliefs, and the strong convictions we have for acting in certain ways. For this reason we cannot talk abstractly and theoretically about the phenomenon of rationality anymore; it is only as individual human beings, living with other human beings in concrete situations, contexts, and traditions, that we can claim some form of rationality. In this sense human rationality is revealed as always person- and domain-specific, as we discover it as present and operative in and through the dynamics of our words and deeds.

Against this background I have argued for a *postfoundationalist notion of rationality* with significant challenges for the interdisciplinary dialogue between theology and the sciences (cf. van Huyssteen 1999). Leaving behind modernist notions of absolutist, universal reasoning, and accepting the postmodern challenge of fragmentation and pluralism in both theology and the various sciences, I have argued for important and distinct differences between reasoning strategies used by theologians and scientists. At the same time, however, I have argued that shared rational resources may actually be identified for the very different cognitive domains of our lives precisely in the pragmatic performance of rationality in different reasoning strategies. In dialogue with philosophers like Nicholas Rescher, Calvin Schrag, and Larry Laudan, I have tried to plot a course between, on the one hand, modernist, metanarrativist overstatements of universality and objectivity and, on the other hand, the extremes of postmodernist overemphases on contextuality and personal judgment. In exactly this sense, then, the move beyond modernist forms of foundationalism does not mean that we should retreat to nonfoundationalist communities of discourse that have only their own epistemologies, and their own isolated rationalities. On a postfoundationalist view, however, "splitting the difference between modernity and postmodernity" (Schrag 1989: 89ff.) is taken with utmost epistemological seriousness, and does not imply that either modern themes or postmodern concerns are cast aside, but that they are creatively revisioned in a move beyond these extremes, precisely by constructing plausible forms of intersubjective, rational accountability.

This postfoundationalist view is certainly meant to remind those who "dance on the grave of the Enlightenment that funeral arrangements for reason are premature" (cf. Keating 2002). With Schrag I have argued against a notion of universal rationality that assumes a common mode of rationality for all domains of our cognitive lives, but I have also argued against the reduction of rationality to mere communal consensus and local contextuality. This certainly means that theology cannot formulate its own idea of reason independent of philosophy or the rationality of other reasoning strategies. A postfoundationalist approach to rationality does however allow theology to remain tied to specific communities of faith without being trapped by these communities. For this reason I have argued for a form of transversal reasoning that honors precisely the universal intent of human reason and, consequently, yields a "cognitive parity" between various and diverse fields of inquiry (cf. van Huyssteen 1999: 172). This clears the way for a more "catholic" or holistic notion of rationality that enables the sciences and theology, as well as the arts and humanities, to enter into meaningful cross-disciplinary conversation. This emerging, broader view of postfoundationalist rationality is interdisciplinary (cf. also Schneider 2001: 30f.), but by definition it also yields interpersonal, and all forms of cross-cultural, dialogue, and ultimately enables us to interpret multiple aspects of our embodied experience by attuning our beliefs, convictions, and judgments to our own self-awareness, and because of that, to the overall patterns of our interpreted experience. On a postfoundationalist view of rationality, the narrative quality of one's experience, therefore, is always going to be rationally compelling. And in this sense a postfoundationalist notion of rationality is never going to function as a superimposed, modernist metanarrative, but will always develop as an emerging pattern that unifies our experience without in any way totalizing it (cf. van Huyssteen 1999: 176f.).

Crucial to a postfoundationalist theory of rationality, then, is a theory of experience that will enable us to reason adequately about the various facets of our human experience. In dialogue with Jerome Stone, Susan Haack, and others, I have understood experiential adequacy as crucial for the understanding of a postfoundationalist notion of rationality (cf. van Huyssteen 1999: 202ff., 222f.). On this view human experience is always interpreted experience, our observations and perceptions are always theory-laden, and they interact with our world(s) in terms of life views to which we are already committed. A postfoundationalist notion of rationality thus yields a form of compelling knowledge (cf. Solberg 1997) that must seek to strike a balance between the way our beliefs are anchored in interpreted experience and the broader networks of beliefs in which our rationally compelling experiences are already embedded (cf. van Huyssteen 1999: 232). Against this background I have agreed with Haack that our epistemologies, as well as our standards of rationality, are always contextually shaped yet not hopelessly culture-bound (cf. Haack 1995: 222). This made possible the jettisoning of universal rules of reason that would dictate the proper rational forms for all our reasoning strategies. But this also prevents us from seeing the celebration of diverse forms of rationality as a capitulation to epistemological tribalism: we do not have to eschew the free deployment of our diverse modes of rationality as we transversally cross cultural and disciplinary boundaries.

Thus an interdisciplinary rationality is revealed that supports the claims, by at least some in our epistemic community, for a public voice for theology in our complex, contemporary culture. On this view theologians, and also scientists of various stripes, should be empowered to protect the rational integrity of their own disciplines, while at the same time identifying overlapping issues, shared problems, and even parallel research trajectories as we cross disciplinary lines in multidisciplinary research. This should be a challenging answer to one of modernity's most powerful demands, namely, that theological reflection, as well as the many forms of contemporary scientific reflection, ultimately requires universal epistemological guarantees to qualify as "real science." In fact, postfoundationalist theology, like science, relies on a community, a community that converses with itself but also seeks to engage in dialogue across the disciplines because of the rational resources we share. And as Larry Laudan has argued, one of the most important shared resources between diverse disciplines is surely problem solving as the central activity of research traditions (cf. Laudan 1977: 190ff.; van Huyssteen 1989: 172-89; 1999: 164ff.). Also, the very diverse reasoning strategies of theology and the sciences overlap in their respective quests for intelligible problem solving, whether empirical, experiential, or conceptual.

Philosophically Lord Gifford's charge can now be liberated from its modernist intentions and revisioned to express its implicit and powerful interdisciplinary challenge precisely in terms of what I have called a postfoundationalist notion of rationality. Within the context of this model of thought, we do not have to succumb to the modernist view that somehow there exists a necessary, universal rule of reason that dictates the proper rational forms for all humans and all disciplines, nor do we have to capitulate to the relativism of epistemological tribalism. A postfoundationalist notion of rationality reveals the way we live and reflect on our lives as deeply embedded in historical, cultural, and conceptual contexts, but also shows, at the same time, that we are free to employ our rather unique modes of rationality across contextual, cultural, and disciplinary barriers. For this reason it would be in interdisciplinary dialogue, correctly conceived, that we rediscover the public voice of religion and theology. Here theology is neither transformed, modernistically, into natural science nor rejected as nonscience. It emerges as a reasoning strategy on par with the intellectual integrity and legitimacy of the natural, human, and social sciences, even as it defines its own powerful domain of thought that in so many ways is also distinct from that of the sciences. On this view the theologian may join forces with the critical scientist in drawing clear boundaries vis-à-vis all forms of scientism, but also has a moral obligation to resist all forms of theological imperialism: two ideologies that have the power to destroy interdisciplinary dialogue.

As an important step beyond any universalist and generic notions of rationality, I have argued for developing a postfoundationalist notion of rationality where as rational agents situated in the rich, narrative texture of our social practices and traditions, our self-awareness and our self-conceptions are not only intrinsically embedded in our own rationality, but are indispensable starting points for any account of the values that shape human rationality. But if rationality and personal convictions go together so closely, and the experiential bases of our rational decisions and actions are acknowledged, then, from an epistemological point of view at least, conscious self-awareness indeed lies at the heart of human rationality, and at the heart of what it might mean to be uniquely human. What follows from this is that the patterns of our ongoing interpreted experiences naturally emerge as integral to the way we rationally cope with our world. And precisely because rationality is so person-relative and thus requires that we attune our beliefs, decisions, and actions to our self-awareness, rationality will also require that we attune our beliefs, decisions, and actions to the overall pattern of our experience. It is in this sense that a postfoundationalist notion of rationality acknowledges the fact that one's embodied experience is always going to be rationally compelling, even as we reach out beyond personal awareness and conviction to interpersonal (and interdisciplinary) dialogue. The need for this kind of experiential accountability seems to lie at the heart of our human self-awareness, and deeply influences our actions.

The need for accountability to our experience also reveals another important epistemological overlap between theological and scientific modes of inquiry. Because we relate to our world epistemically only through the mediation of interpreted experience, it may be said that our diverse theologies, and also the sciences, offer alternative interpretations of our experience (cf. Rolston 1987: 1-8). Alternative, however, not in the sense of competing or conflicting interpretations, but of complementary interpretations of the manifold dimensions of our experience. I have therefore argued that all religious language, and certainly all theological language, invariably reflects the structure of our interpreted experience (cf. van Huyssteen 1997: 40f.). In science, too, our concepts and theories can be seen as products of an interaction in which both nature and we ourselves play a formative role. In exactly this sense scientific knowledge of our world is also always epistemically mediated through interpreted experience. Empirical scientific observation is theoretically selected and interpreted, and functions only within the network of presupposed theories that constitute a specific reasoning strategy.

In a modernist world, the "objective" natural sciences were carefully demarcated from those disciplines that study human beings, their artifacts, and their institutions, i.e., the human and social sciences. In a world challenged by postmodernism and pluralism, stereotypical distinctions between the natural and human sciences fall away, especially when hermeneutics surfaces in the heart of the sciences and we discover that even in the natural sciences we study nature as theoretically interpreted. Thus we discover that, because of the shared resources of rationality, we use similar kinds of interpretive and evaluative procedures to understand nature and other humans, as well as the social, historical, and religious aspects of our lives. Consequently, the world as we encounter it is already interpreted, and our theories play an important role in our received interpretations (cf. Rouse 1987: 9). If in this way we relate to the manifold dimensions of our world(s) epistemically only through the filter of interpreted experience, then our attempts to locate theology in the ongoing and evolving interdisciplinary discussion acquire new depth and meaning. It also brings us a few steps closer to reconstituting theology as a rational form of inquiry in its own right.

Moreover, if it is possible to identify important epistemological overlaps and *similarities* between diverse reasoning strategies (like a shared quest for intelligibility, the shaping role of personal judgment, an ongoing process of problem solving, and experiential accountability), then it is also important to highlight *differences* between these strategies. These differences are revealed as differences in the very specific *epistemological focus,* the *experiential resources,* and the *heuristic structures of* different disciplines (cf. Stoeger 1988: 232ff.). What this means for theology and the sciences is that the differences between these reasoning strategies are far more complex and refined than just differences in objects of study, language, or methodology. These differences in foci, experiential resources, and heuristic structures obviously give rise to different disciplinary languages, contexts, and the methodologies of diverse reasoning strategies, and as such make meaningful interdisciplinary communication and understanding very difficult. But this difficult and demanding process of entering interdisciplinary dialogue in a complex, pluralist situation, with our strong personal convictions intact, is just what a postfoundationalist model of rationality hopes to facilitate. As members of specific epistemic communities who would like to plausibly claim some form of expertise in our various fields of inquiry, we hope to discover in disciplines other than our own — and often in the hazy interfaces between disciplines — clues, indications, or some form of persuasive evidence that will help us push the limits of our own disciplines (cf. 232). At the heart of interdisciplinary reflection lies precisely this kind of challenge: standing within specific research traditions, we often realize that a particular tradition may generate questions that cannot be resolved by its own resources alone. Exactly this kind of interdisciplinary awareness may lead us to reach out for rational support to other disciplines.

For theology a postfoundationalist model of rationality should include an interpretation of religious experience that not only facilitates an evaluation of the problem-solving effectiveness of religious and theological traditions, but also transcends pitfalls like the kind of dualist approach that sets up a false dilemma between the "natural" and the "supernatural" and then demands a reductionist choice between the two (something that was clearly evident also in the text of Lord Gifford's will). Surely in theological reflection our choices can no longer be restricted to either seeing the divine as interrupting or intruding on the natural, or the reductionist option of only a naturalist interpretation of religious experience (cf. Gill 1981: 117ff.). This postfoundationalist choice for an interactionist, interpretive dimension in religious experience should have important consequences for any Gifford lecturer who feels challenged to revision Gifford's idea of natural theology. This approach opens up the possibility of interpreting religiously the way in which some of us believe God comes to us, in and through our manifold experiences of nature, persons, ideas, emotions, places, things, and events. And because of what appears to be a typical human quest for ultimate meaning, various dimensions of our experience may reveal an element of mystery, a religious disposition that, when responded to, may be plausibly said to contain, within specific interpretative contexts, the potential for divine disclosure. With this we have also arrived at possibly the most crucial and telling difference between theology and the sciences. The focus on this kind of ultimacy or mystery is unique to the experiential resources and epistemic focus of theology, and definitively sets it apart from the very focused empirical scope of the natural sciences. It is also the response to the element of mystery in all religious reflection that has often led to modernist claims that theology and the sciences, even if not conflictual, should at least be seen as incommensurably different paradigms from one another.

Would this element of mystery, when followed by the typical faith of a religious commitment, again force theology out of the shared domain of interdisciplinary discussion? This confronts us with the serious question whether deep and personal religious convictions are radically opposed to and different from other forms of knowledge, and whether this again implies a radical difference between scientific and theological rationality. The postfoundationalist notion of rationality for which I have been arguing above claims the exact opposite: because of the multidimensional nature of human rationality, we should be able to enter the pluralist, interdisciplinary conversation with our full personal convictions intact, and at the same time be theoretically empowered to step beyond the limitations and boundaries of our contexts or traditions in critical self-reflection.

In *The Shaping of Rationality* (1999) I argued *against* theology's epistemic isolation in a pluralist, postmodern world, and *for* a postfoundationalist notion of rationality that reveals the interdisciplinary, public nature of all theological reflection. In an earlier work, *Duet or Duel? Theology and Science in a Postmodern World* (1998), I also argued that some forms of contemporary evolutionary epistemology may hold the key to understanding not only the propensity for but also the naturalness of religious awareness. I will return to this argument in chapter 2, and show why evolutionary epistemology, by revealing the biological origins and roots of human rationality, may facilitate a more comprehensive and integrative approach to human knowledge. In *Duet or Duel?* I also argued that evolutionary epistemology may facilitate the kind of postfoundationalist notion of rationality that could take us beyond the confines of traditional disciplinary boundaries and modernist cultural domains. This interdisciplinary notion of rationality allows us to revision human rationality along the following lines.

Firstly, it acknowledges contextuality and the embeddedness of all our reflection in human culture, and therefore in specific scientific and confessional traditions, and thus acknowledges that also our theological presuppositions are already influenced by the scientific culture of our times.

Secondly, it takes seriously the epistemically crucial role of interpreted experience or experiential understanding, and the way that tradition shapes both the epistemic and nonepistemic values that inform our reflection, our thoughts about God and (what some of us believe to be) God's presence in the world.

Thirdly, it allows us to explore freely and critically the experiential and interpretive roots of our beliefs from within our deep commitments, and to discover patterns in our lives and thought that might be consonant with what we regard as the canon(s) of our respective religious/theological traditions (cf. Brown 1994: 55ff.). The persuasiveness of these patterns should be taken up in critical theological reflection, where their problem-solving ability should then be evaluated and judged in an interpersonal and cross-contextual conversation.

Fourthly, rationality itself can now be seen as a skill that enables us to gather and bind together the patterns of our interpreted experience through rhetoric, articulation, and discernment. It is on this point that the important postfoundationalist notion of *transversality* replaces modernist, static notions of universality in a distinct move to see human reason as dynamic and practical in the way we use it to converse with one another through interpretative critique, narration, and rhetoric. In *The Shaping of Rationality* I argued for the "transversal performance" of rationality precisely when referring to this dynamic and multileveled interaction of our discourses with one another (cf. van

Huyssteen 1999: 135-39, 247-50). The notion of transversality is hugely helpful for highlighting the human dynamics of consciousness that enables us to move between domains of intelligence with a high degree of cognitive fluidity, and as such it is at the heart of my notion of interdisciplinary reflection (cf. also Mithen 1996: 70ff., 136ff.).

In the dialogue between theology and other disciplines, transversal reasoning facilitates different but equally legitimate ways of viewing, or interpreting, issues, problems, traditions, or disciplines. On this view interdisciplinary dialogue can therefore be seen as multidimensional and thus on convergent paths moving toward an imagined vanishing point: a transversal space where different voices are not in contradiction, nor in danger of assimilating one another, but are dynamically interactive with one another (cf. Capps 1999: 332ff.). In this multidisciplinary use of the concept of transversality there emerge distinct characteristics or features: the dynamics of consciousness, the interweaving of many voices, the interplay of social practices are all expressed in a *metaphor* that points to a sense of transition, a lying across, extending over, intersecting, meeting, and conveying without becoming identical. Transversality thus provides a philosophical window to the wider world of communication through thought and action. It also represents a strong reaction against rationalist/modernist impulses to *unify* all faculties of knowledge into a seamless unity, or the positivistic impulse to claim science as a superior form of knowing. It clearly also represents a protest against the imperialism of all kinds of ideological thought. In this sense it is a vibrant and constructive postmodernist move to integrate all our ways of knowing without again totalizing them in any modernist sense.

Philosophically, transversality implies the distinct move away from the unity and domination of reason, to the pluralization of human rationality (cf. Welsch 1996: 432ff.). In his important contribution to the notion of tranversality, Wolfgang Welsch sees transversal reasoning as a move away from static notions of rationality: the axis of reason is rotated from verticality to horizontality, and human reason itself now becomes a dynamic faculty of performative transitions that interconnects the various forms of human rationality (Welsch n.d.: 31f., 46f.). But on this view the plural nature of human reason does not imply that different rationalities now exist independent of one another as incommensurable intellectual domains. In fact, different domains of human rationality, and therefore also different disciplines, while having their own integrity and specific identities, are in many ways connected and intertwined with one another precisely by the dynamic performative faculty of reason (cf. Novakovic 2004: 159ff.). This plurality is nonhierarchical and irreducible (cf. Welsch 1996: 555ff., 603f.), and highlights important differences between various domains of rationality, and between disciplines, even as it opens up the exploration of transversal spaces that allow for the connection of different domains of rationality. This also allows for the emergence of paradigmatic interdisciplinary networks and opens up the possibility that different disciplines in dialogue, although never fully integrated, can learn from one another and actually benefit by taking over insights presented in interdisciplinary dialogue.

On this view transversal rationality facilitates a multiperspectival approach to dialogue, where rationality exists in the intersecting connections and transitions between disciplines. In interdisciplinary dialogue, it is precisely these shared domains of rationality, these intersecting, overlapping concerns, that have to be carefully identified. This interwovenness of many different disciplinary voices opens up spaces for the performance of human cognitive fluidity at work, reveals the interdisciplinary conversation as transitional and interrelational, and the performance of human rationality as transversal. Welsch puts this quite succinctly: transversal rationality is rationality in movement, it is an ability, a skill, and as such is dynamically realized in these interactive processes (cf. Welsch 1996: 764).

In his use of the metaphor of transversality, Calvin Schrag takes his cue from mathematicians, who take up the vocabulary of transversality when speaking of a line as it intersects a system of other lines or surfaces, but also from physicists and physiologists. In the interdisciplinary and varied use of this concept a shared meaning emerges indicating a sense of extending over, lying across, and intersecting with one another (cf. Schrag 1994: 64). All these images enrich and enlighten what happens in concrete, contextual situations where we start down the risky and precarious road of interpersonal and interdisciplinary conversation. The use of the concept of transversality has important roots in Jean-Paul Sartre's existentialist theory of consciousness. In a critical move away from Husserl's transcendental ego, Sartre found the unity of human consciousness in the performative act of human consciousness. In Sartre's own striking words: "The *I* is the producer of inwardness. . . . Consciousness is defined by intentionality. By intentionality consciousness transcends itself. It unifies itself by escaping from itself. . . . It is consciousness which unifies itself, concretely, by a play of 'transversal' intentionalities which are concrete and real retentions of past consciousnesses" (Sartre 1960: 38, 39).

This was Sartre's way of anchoring subjectivity in performative intentionality, by weaving different strands of past experiences into a concrete pattern of subjective intentionality. On this view consciousness is from the bottom up intentional and emerges in the transversal continuity of the self-referential subject (cf. Shirin 2005: 195). Schrag has connected deeply with Sartre's notion of a unifying play of transversal intentionalities, but relocates it within a rich and multidimensional notion of transversal rationality, or what I have called a postfoundationalist notion of rationality. Transversal rationality is now fused with consciousness and self-awareness, and this consciousness is then unified by an experience of self-presence, emerging over time from a re-membering self-awareness/consciousness in which diverse past experiences are transversally integrated as we reach out to others. In appropriating the notion of transversal rationality in this truly rich and creative way, Schrag eventually wants to justify and urge an acknowledgment of multiple patterns of interpretation as one reaches out in interpersonal dialogue, and as one moves across the borders and boundaries of the different disciplinary matrices (cf. Schrag 1994: 65). Influenced by Guattari, Deleuze, and Foucault, Schrag ultimately aggressively moves beyond the restrictions of Sartre's subject-centered consciousness to transversality as an achievement of communicative praxis (cf. Schrag 1992: 153ff.). Talk about the human subject is now revisioned by resituating the human subject in the space of communicative praxis. Thus the notion of transversal rationality opens up the possibility of focusing on patterns of discourse and action as they happen in our communicative practices, rather than focusing on only the structure of the self, ego, or subject. On this view it is clear that transversal rationality is not just a "passage of consciousness" across a wide spectrum of experiences held together by our memory. It is, rather, a lying across, extending over, and intersecting of various forms of discourse, modes of thought, and action. Transversal rationality thus emerges as a performative praxis where our multiple beliefs and practices, our habits of thought and attitudes, our prejudices and assessments, converge.

In interdisciplinary conversation the degree of transversality achieved depends on the effectiveness of our dialogue across different domains of meaning. But the important thing in this notion of a transversal rationality is discovering the shared resources of reason precisely in our very pluralist beliefs or practices, and then locating the claims of reason in the transversal connection of rationality between groups, discourses, or reasoning strategies. The implications of the notion of transversal rationality, however, go even further than this. Schrag also distinguishes between *discursive* (the performance of articulation in language and conversation) and *nondiscursive* practices, the latter comprising, specifically, the performance of embodied rationality beyond the realm of language and the spoken word. Thus, "as there is a time and space for discourse, so there is a time and space of action, mood, desire, bodily and institutional inscriptions — a vast arena of *nondiscursive* dispositions and practices that also exhibit an articulatory function" (83). Transversal rationality thus emerges as a deeply embodied rationality, and our actions, desires, emotions are all ways of also understanding and articulating ourselves and our world(s). And in this sense, what Schrag calls the "event or articulation" lies transversally across both our discursive and our nondiscursive actions in time and space. Thus our experiences as "events of interpretation" are always situated temporally and spatially (cf. 83).

Exactly at this point Schrag helpfully appropriates Russian philosopher and historian Mikhail Bakhtin's notion of the *chronotope,* or value-imbued space-time, as the marker of the intrinsic connectedness of time and space as concrete dwellings for our varied discourses. The notion of the chronotope expresses for Bakhtin the inseparability of space and time, the place where time thickens, takes on flesh, becomes visible (cf. Bakhtin 1981: 84). For Schrag transversal rationality concretely exists in what Bakhtin has called the chronotopical moment, in our embodied existence in valued space and time, the performative here and now where time and space are intrinsically connected (cf. also Shirin 2005: 187). Epistemically this way of thinking is always concrete, local, and contextual, but at the same time it points beyond local context to transcontextual and cross-disciplinary conversation. Its initial perspectives are highly contextual, but its performances transcend the local and the concrete and ultimately facilitate interdisciplinarity. In this transversal, performative sense, then, rationality *happens*. And in this concrete sense time and space become vitalized and vibrant as existential dwellings rather than dead frames of reference. Most importantly, when we take seriously the radical situatedness of our existence, a multiplicity of language games and cultural domains comes into play as we attempt to articulate our situatedness in historical time and historical space. In this sense one could say that the texts of our discourses always remain embedded in the contexts — scientific, moral, legal, economic, aesthetic, and religious — from which they emerge (cf. Schrag 1992: 84).

In this way, finally, a postfoundationalist notion of rationality enables us to retain the language of epistemology by fusing it with hermeneutics. Our different genres of discourse can now certainly be identified by our making of scientific claims, moral statements, aesthetic evaluations, religious judgments, theological assessments, or by our participation in the praxis of prayer. This determination of whether a certain discourse should be recognized as scientific, ethical, political, aesthetical, or religious unfolds against the background of a wide spectrum of social practices and linguistic usages (cf. 86).

This discussion has given new depth to the important notion of *transversal rationality.* The modern epistemological paradigm was typified by claims for universality. The postmodern challenge typically calls into question any search for such universals; instead of a "God's-eye view," a perspective from the other side of history, we are offered only a fragmented vision from this side of history that typically leaves us with a complete relativization of all forms of thought and all contents of culture. Schrag's response to this has been the pursuit of a third option, i.e., the "splitting of the difference" between modernity and postmodernity. In this move the postmodern problematization of modern claims for universality is embraced, but then postmodernism is used against itself by showing how transversal reason can more productively address the issues at hand. On this view, therefore, transversality ultimately replaces universality (cf. Schrag 1994: 75). By rediscovering the resources of reason in transversal rationality, modernist epistemology finally has to make room for a fusion of a refigured epistemology and hermeneutics in postfoundationalist rationality.

A postfoundationalist notion of rationality thus creates a safe space where our different discourses and actions are seen at times to link up with one another and at other times to contrast or conflict with one another. It is precisely in the hard struggle for interpersonal and interdisciplinary communication that the many faces of human rationality are revealed. On this view interdisciplinary assessments are still possible, and indeed required, thanks to the transversal play of our social practices, our webs of belief, and our societal engagements that demand from us an ongoing response to that which is said and done. It is this "performance of the fitting response" (76), the practice of responsible judgment, that is at the heart of a postfoundationalist notion of rationality, and that enables us to reach fragile and provisional forms of coherence in our interpersonal and interdisciplinary conversations.

In revisioning interdisciplinary dialogue as a form of transversal reasoning, human rationality is not seen anymore as a universal and austere form of reasoning, but as a practical skill that enables us to gather and bind together the patterns of all our daily experiences and make sense of them through communal, interactive dialogue. The notion of transversality also enables us to honor the nonhierarchical asymmetry between various disciplines, and specifically between the sciences and theology, and to see human reason as dynamic and practical as we use it to converse with one another through critical interpretation, through dialogue and rhetoric. The notion of transversality opens up interdisciplinary dialogue in a new and challenging way, and identifies the voices of science, theology, religions, and art as different but equally legitimate ways of looking at the world. Most importantly, though, a postfoundationalist notion of rationality claims to point beyond the boundaries of any local community, group, tradition, or culture, toward a plausible form of interdisciplinary conversation. Also in theology, as we will see, true interdisciplinary reflection will be achieved when the conversation proceeds not in terms of imposed "universal" rules, nor purely ad hoc rules, but in terms of the intersubjective agreements we reach through persuasive rhetoric and responsible judgments, and where both the strong personal convictions so typical of Christian commitment and the public voice of theology are acknowledged in cross-disciplinary conversation.

Tradition and Communicative Understanding

Postfoundationalism in interdisciplinary reflection thus claims to be a viable third epistemological option beyond the extremes of absolutism and the relativism of extreme forms of pluralism. In these lectures I want to show concretely that, in developing this notion, the "fabric" of my postfoundationalist notion of rationality can be woven together by demonstrating what this kind of interdisciplinary conversation would look like if one literally goes into a multilayered conversation with a whole array of important voices in philosophy, theology, and the sciences. As we just saw, as rational agents situated in the rich, narrative texture of our social practices and traditions, our self-awareness and our self-conceptions are indispensable starting points for any account of the values that shape human rationality. But if rationality and personal convictions go together so closely, then, from an epistemological point of view at least, the patterns of our ongoing experience naturally emerge as integral to the way we rationally cope with our world. And precisely because we are embedded in the rich narrative texture of our social practices and traditions, the overall patterns of our experience also transversally reach back to experiential patterns, contexts, and traditions of the past. In this sense a theory of traditions not only is necessarily implied in a postfoundationalist notion of rationality, but should in fact shape the way we approach interdisciplinary dialogue.

It is precisely in theoretical issues like our embeddedness as rational agents in our social practices and traditions, the fact that human rationality and personal convictions go together so closely, that we reach out to our world(s) as interpretive agents, that as situated agents we function within the complexity of multiple traditions, which have been made intelligible by the postfoundationalist turn in philosophy. In an enlightening recent article that deals directly with the impact of postfoundationalist thought on politics, democracy, and theories of governance, Mark Bevir also analyzed the epistemic importance of thinking of social context in terms of traditions (Bevir 2004).[5] On this view the concept of tradition evokes a social context into which individuals are born and which then acts as the necessary background to their beliefs and actions even while, in the course of time, they might modify, develop, or even reject much of this inheritance. What this means in real life is that our embeddedness in cultural and other traditions is in a sense unavoidable. But a specific tradition is unavoidable only as a starting point, not as a final destination, i.e., not as something that determines or defines later performances. In this sense the traditions (and I would add, disciplinary research traditions) we live by have a distinct initial influence on our thoughts and actions, but are in no sense an inevitable presence within all our beliefs and actions. Although traditions are unavoidable only as starting points and not as final destinations, and most traditions do not possess fixed contents, they certainly may have identifiable core ideas that may persist over time (cf. Bevir 2004: 618).

In this sense tradition is a helpful explanatory concept in that it allows properly for situated agency and thus even provides a means for analyzing social change. Bevir's description of the malleability and plurivocity of tradition as it passes through different individuals and groups clearly echoes the sentiments of theologian Delwin Brown (1994), pointing not only to the inevitable role of culture in tradition, but also to the unavoidable role of tradition(s) in other cultural and intellectual processes (cf. Gideon 2005: 24). This unambiguously points to the fact that whether in the sciences, theology, or politics, traditions change to accommodate dilemmas that challenge previously held beliefs.

This helps us to understand even better how a postfoundationalist approach illuminates what happens when actual interdisciplinary dialogue takes place. Because of our irrevocable contextuality and the embeddedness of all belief and action in networks of social and cultural traditions, beliefs, meaning, and action arise out of our embedded lifeworlds. A postfoundationalist approach helps us realize, however, that we are not the intellectual prisoners of our contexts or traditions, but that we are epistemically empowered to cross contextual, cultural, and disciplinary borders to explore critically the theories, meanings, and beliefs through which we and others construct our worlds. This

Human Uniqueness as an Interdisciplinary Problem?

25

5. I am much indebted to my former student Bethany Gideon for alerting me to this work with its quite remarkable philosophical parallels to my own postfoundationalist approach to interdisciplinary dialogue.

leads directly to what Bevir has called a postfoundationalist sympathy for bottom-up forms of inquiry (cf. Bevir 2004: 709). I want to expand this to mean a direct rejection of all foundationalist approaches to reason or experience, and the acknowledgment that people in the same social-historical situation could in fact hold very different beliefs, and for a variety of reasons. This is true because experiences within even the very same context or situation could be laden with very different prior theories, and therefore often interpreted in radically different ways. This focus on bottom-up inquiry acknowledges the complex interaction between traditions and culture, and the ways in which our beliefs and practices are created and sustained but also transformed through the (contextual and intercontextual) interplay and contest of beliefs and meanings embedded in human activity (cf. 709).

Given the embeddedness of all our knowledge in tradition(s), it seems clear that if we want to reflect critically on the nature of a specific interdisciplinary problem like human uniqueness in science and theology, we will have to be ready and willing to reflect critically on exactly those traditions that underlie our knowledge claims. And if we want to avoid what Schrag calls the "twilight zone of abstraction" (cf. Schrag 1989: 90), we need to realize that a crucial notion like *human uniqueness,* which may be at the heart of some of our most important traditions in science and theology, can no longer be discussed within the generalized terminology of a metanarrative that ignores the sociohistorical context of the scientist(s) or theologian(s) who are entering this very specific interdisciplinary space (cf. van Huyssteen 1998: 26). For theology this will imply that its embeddedness in specific traditions will first of all mean theology should be done locally and contextually. But the awareness of this contextuality and locality does not imply the choice for some notion of tribal rationality, or for a kind of rampant relativism or easy pluralism. Precisely the open acknowledgment of this kind of contextuality, and of epistemic and hermeneutical preferences, can facilitate, rather than obstruct, transcontextual and interdisciplinary dialogue.

Therefore, in theology we are not only called to acknowledge and articulate the way our belief in God is embedded and shaped by our personal and ecclesial commitments. We are also obliged to return critically to exactly these beliefs and traditions, acknowledge their flexible and fluid nature as they are shaped by the ongoing process of history, and then rethink and reconstruct them in interdisciplinary conversation. An important suggestion for such a theory of traditions, which also significantly dovetails with my proposal for a postfoundationalist notion of rationality, has been made by Delwin Brown (1994). Brown argues persuasively that traditions exhibit both change and continuity, and that at its heart the behavior of a tradition — whether in changing or in staying the same — is fundamentally pragmatic, and as such is indeed concerned with survival, power, and legitimation (cf. 26ff.). The identity and integrity of a tradition are preserved by what we may call its heart, or *canon*, which functions as an authoritative narrative and conceptual framework that shapes and molds continuity and change in traditions as lived realities. The relationship between a tradition and its canon(s) is always dialectical; the creation of identity and continuity, but also of discontinuity and novelty, occurs both as a rearrangement within its canon and as a rearrangement of the place of canon in tradition.

In theology as well as in the sciences, our traditions, paradigms, and worldviews, like all other traditions, are historical creatures. As such they are created and articulated within a particular intellectual milieu, and like all other historical institutions, they wax and wane. If in all theological reflection, as in other modes of knowledge, we relate to our worlds epistemically through the medium of interpreted experience, then this interpretation of experience always takes place within the comprehensive context of living and evolving traditions. These traditions are epistemically constituted by broader paradigms or research traditions. Because of their historical nature, research traditions in all modes of human knowledge can change and evolve, and they do this either through the internal modification of some specific theories or through a change of some of their most basic core elements. Larry Laudan has correctly pointed out that Kuhn's famous notion of a "conversion" or paradigmatic revolution from one paradigm to another can most probably be better described as a natural, creative evolution within and between research traditions. Traditions, however, not only imply ongoing change and evolution, but also exhibit continuity. In this sense it would be right to claim that in any adequate theory of traditions, continuity and change would be primary categories (cf. Laudan 1977: 77ff.).

To understand what continuity and change might mean in the dynamic of evolving traditions, Laudan, like Imre Lakatos (1970), suggests that certain elements of a research tradition are sacrosanct and can therefore not be rejected without repudiation of the tradition itself. Unlike Lakatos, however, Laudan insists that what is normally seen as sacrosanct in traditions can actually change with time. He thinks Lakatos and Kuhn were right in thinking that a research tradition or paradigm always has certain nonrejectable, canonical elements associated with it, but were mistaken in failing to see that the elements constituting this core can shift through time. From this he concluded that by relativizing the "essence" of research tradition with respect to place and time we come closer to capturing the way scientists and historians of science utilize the concept of tradition (cf. Laudan 1977: 99f.).

This reveals again not only the radical historical nature of all traditions, but also that intellectual revolutions do not necessarily take place through complete shifts but often occur through the ongoing integration and grafting on of (research) traditions. From this we can now glean the following characteristics of research traditions, which will all apply to our imminent analysis of human uniqueness in science and theology (cf. van Huyssteen 1999: 257f.; Brown 1994: 26f.).

First, because we are deeply embedded in history, traditions are constitutive of the present and finally explain why we relate to our world epistemically only through the mediation of interpreted experience. In this sense we may argue that the world we live in is always a conceptualized reality (cf. Herrmann 1998: 109).

Second, research traditions — like all traditions — cannot be reduced to the activities of individuals and groups within them, but they also have no reality outside of specific (epistemic) communities.

Third, (research) traditions are dynamic, evolving phenomena that live precisely in the dialectic of continuity and change.

Fourth, (research) traditions are never isolated from one another, because the borders separating traditions from their milieus and from other traditions are usually, if not always, exceedingly porous (cf. Brown 1994: 26f.).

Fifth, all traditions have sacrosanct elements that, even if they shift or change over time, form the canons of traditions and define their identity. These canons serve as the source of creativity as well as the principle of identity of traditions.

These characteristics of research traditions have important consequences for theological reflection, and clearly show why any uncritical retreat, or fideist commitment to a specific tradition or its canon(s), would seriously jeopardize the epistemic status of theological reflection as a credible partner in a pluralist, interdisciplinary conversation. Within a fideist context all commitment and religious faith seem to be irrevocably arbitrary. But the most serious limitation to any fideist epistemology would be its complete inability to explain why we choose certain viewpoints, certain networks of belief, certain traditions over others. Surely there is more to using religious language than understanding and adopting the internal workings of some specialized linguistic system that is not answerable to anything or anybody outside itself. There also should be more to the making of commitments than just being embedded in traditions that can never be questioned. Theology's critical relation to tradition thus shows us that all religious and theological language is indeed human convention, the result of creative intellectual construction, which — along with the commitments to the canon or canons it serves to express — should be examined and critiqued as well.

Canons, or the sacrosanct elements of traditions, not only define the integrity of traditions but also form the boundaries that often function to protect traditions, and as such are often strongly resistant to change. At the same time, the boundaries that separate tradition from its milieu are always exceedingly porous (cf. Brown 1994: 26f.), although as theologians we often notoriously invent protective strategies that mask the necessary fluidity of traditions. Important changes in a tradition, though often provoked from outside, are ultimately accomplished by the recovery and re-formation of internal elements crucial to a specific tradition. In this sense continuity and change continually exemplify the dynamics of traditions. Furthermore, novelty or change in theological traditions can emerge *unintentionally*, when a tradition is swept along in political-social changes, but also *intentionally*, when change or novelty becomes the result of a conscious human choice.

What this really means is that we cannot be separated from our past, whether in our religious practices, our ecclesial, theological, cultural, scientific, or art traditions. However much freedom we have, we still are constrained by the traditions and rituals of our recent and distant ancestors, and we use this past to negotiate our way through contemporary culture. But in a postfoundationalist approach to theology, there would be no recourse to foundationalist certitude by bestowing on our canon(s) objective truth or indubitable knowledge. For a theology that is open to interdisciplinary standards of rationality and public debate, the canonical structures of its core traditions will be less structured and fixed than in foundationalist conceptions of tradition(s).

Against this background Brown has helpfully suggested that the complexity of a canon and its function in a tradition are analogous to a kind of galaxy, *a galaxy of meaning* (cf. Brown 1994: 76f.). Just as a galaxy is composed of a vast and varying multiplicity of elements, a canon too, as the sacrosanct core of a tradition, is dynamic and pluriform. But a galaxy has enough unity and structure to be one thing rather than another; in the same sense a canon has a rough and practical unity that can be differently construed from different perspectives. A canon, as a complex but identifiable core identity of a tradition, as a galaxy of meanings, thus has gravitational force, or a gravitational pull that is the result of the way its own internal structure relates to, and is construed in the history of, its interpretative relations. Through the dynamic interaction of construction and constraint in the historical evolution of our traditions, these galaxies of meanings creatively give way to interpretive constellations of meaning that we construct in direct interaction with the different challenges presented to theology by contemporary culture (cf. 77). It is exactly this point that will prove to be of primary importance as we find our way into the origins and history of the notion of human uniqueness in science and theology. In this sense both our theological and scientific traditions on human uniqueness will emerge as cultural negotiations, shaped by what we see as the continuing gravitational pull of the specific canon(s) of specific traditions in science and theology.

For the Christian theologian it would be impossible to think or act except through an experiential understanding of, and engagement with, very specific traditions. Our task, however, is also to stand in a *critical* relation to our respective traditions. In this imaginative and critical task of reconstructing tradition(s), the theologian in fact becomes, in Brown's striking phrase, the *caregiver of* his or her tradition(s) (cf. 82, 119ff., 138). This also implies a conscious critical step beyond the confines of particular traditions, and is warranted by a revisioned postfoundationalist notion of rationality, where the task and identity of theology are revealed as definitively shaped by its location in the living context of not only tradition but also interdisciplinary reflection. The fact that we lack a clear and "objective" criterion for judging the adequacy or problem-solving ability of one tradition over another should not however leave us with a radical relativism, or even with an easy pluralism. Because we can make rational judgments and share them with various and different epistemic communities means we should also be able to communicate with one another meaningfully through conversation, deliberation, and evaluation in an ongoing process of collective assessment. Sharing our views and judgments with those inside and outside our epistemic communities can therefore lead to conversation, which we should enter not just to persuade but also to learn from. Such a style of inquiry can provide ways of thinking about rationality that respect authentic pluralism — it does not force us all to agree or to even share the same assumptions, but it finds ways we can talk with one another and criticize our own traditions while continuing to stand in them.

On this view, in an open, postfoundationalist conversation, Christian theology should be able to claim a "democratic presence" in interdisciplinary conversation. Theology would share in interdisciplinary standards of rationality that, although always contextually and socially shaped, would not be hopelessly culture- and context-bound. And theology could become an equal partner in a democratic, interdisciplinary conversation with the sciences, where an authentic Christian voice might actually be heard in a postmodern, pluralist situation. This kind of theology will share in interdisciplinary standards of rationality, even as we respect our widely divergent personal, religious, or disciplinary viewpoints, and the integrity of our widely diverse disciplines.

In my most recent work I have argued for a revisioning of theology's public voice — for the clearing of an interdisciplinary space where not only very diverse and pluralist forms of theological reflection but also science and other disciplines might explore shared concerns and discover possible overlapping epistemological patterns in an ongoing interdisciplinary conversation. A postfoundationalist notion of rationality thus enables us to communicate across boundaries, and to move transversally from context to context, from one tradition to another, from one discipline to another. The tentative and shared mutual understanding that we achieve through this I have named, following various other scholars, a *wide reflective equilibrium*.[6] This wide reflective equilibrium points to the optimal but fragile communal understanding we are capable of in any given moment. It never implies complete consensus, but it does exemplify the fragile accomplishments of our interpersonal and interdisciplinary communication, a sense of mutual agreement and of "not being puzzled anymore" (Herrmann 1998: 104). As such it also establishes the necessity of a multiplicity of voices and perspectives in our ongoing processes of mutual assessment.

In this wide reflective equilibrium we finally find the safe but fragile public space we have been searching for, a space for shuttling back and forth between deep personal convictions and the principles that finally result from responsible interpersonal judgments. Francis Schüssler Fiorenza has eloquently captured this postfoundationalist strategy by stating that, through a back-and-forth movement, the communicative strategy of reflective equilibrium seeks to bring into balance or equilibrium the principles reconstructed from practice with the ongoing practice itself (cf. 1984: 301f.). On this view our already agreed-upon principles and background theories provide a critical, independent constraint that prevents these principles from being mere generalizations of our contextual judgments and practices, while at the same time allowing them to be critically questioned too. Aiming for a wide reflective equilibrium

6. Cf. van Huyssteen 1999: 277ff.; cf. also Nielsen 1987; Schrag 1989: 176ff.; Schüssler Fiorenza 1984: 301ff.; and Herrmann 1998: 103-14.

as an epistemic goal of interdisciplinary dialogue is, finally, truly post-foundationalist and nonhierarchical because no one disciplinary voice, and no one set of judgments, practices, or principles, will be able to claim absolute priority over, or be foundational for, any other. On the contrary, on this view interdisciplinarity is achieved when different disciplinary voices successfully manage to identify mutual concerns in shared transversal spaces, and use these moments of intersection between theology and other disciplines as the key to interdisciplinary conversation.

The dynamics of a postfoundationalist rationality is thus finally revealed in this fragile process where, through responsible judgment, we strive to attain the most coherent and most consistent sets of beliefs in the interdisciplinary conversation between theology and the sciences. In a postfoundationalist notion of rationality this kind of evaluative judgment plays a crucial role, and is resituated within the dynamics of our sociohistorical contexts. And as we strive for optimal understanding, and in interdisciplinary dialogue for a wide reflective equilibrium, critical evaluation becomes a truly communicative project (cf. Schrag 1989: 88). The judgments we make of the possibilities or impossibilities of interdisciplinary dialogue are therefore inseparable from the social practices of our various communities of investigators, as we attempt to understand and explain that the various domains of our personal and public lives are inexplicably connected to the contextuality and social practices of the species — ourselves — that we are trying to understand. As I will show later, it is exactly this point that has proven to be true for disciplines as diverse as theology and paleoanthropology.

In a modernist context the demands for a universal mode of rationality and judgment were construed as a quest for certainty, and finally fused into the impossible epistemological requirement of unimpeachable foundations for certain knowledge. Within a postfoundationalist notion of rationality, however, critical and responsible judgment pursues neither the modernist desire for true foundations nor its hope for certainty (cf. Schrag 1989: 89). In a postfoundationalist sense, interpersonal and interdisciplinary judgment is content to discern and evaluate our beliefs, our convictions, and our practices against the background of ever-changing and historically conditioned patterns of meaning, and to discover significant connections between them. The wide scope of a postfoundationalist notion of rationality also encompasses the separated cultural domains of modernity (science, morality, art, religion), but it is the dynamics of this process of intercontextual and cross-disciplinary reflection that enables one to move across discourses, effecting an integration of sorts that ultimately could yield the wide reflective equilibrium of interdisciplinary understanding in reasoning strategies as diverse as theology and the sciences. Whether this can be true for the elusive issue of human uniqueness in disciplines as vastly different as theology and paleoanthropology is exactly the challenge of this lecture series.

What should already be clear, however, is that on this view genuine religious, theological, and scientific pluralism emerges as normal and natural, and ought to allow for conversations between people from different traditions or cultural domains who may enter the conversation for very different reasons, and who may in fact disagree about many issues. This pluralism also allows for a legitimate diversity; the fact that different people represent divergent experiential situations because they come from different traditions, and in addition commit themselves to different research traditions, makes it normal, natural, and rational that they should proceed differently in cognitive, evaluative, and practical matters. Consequently, we must accept that also, and maybe especially, in theology, complete cognitive agreement or consensus is unattainable. What Nicholas Rescher (1993: 3f.) called *dissensus tolerance* will prove to be a positive and constructive part of pluralism in the theology and science dialogue. It is at this point that we reach beyond our specific traditions in cross-contextual conversation to a shared wide reflective equilibrium where the diversity of our traditions will yield the diversity of our experiences, the diversity of our epistemic situations, the diversities of our values and methodologies. In the theology and science dialogue, the most sensible posture is therefore to accept the reality of cognitive pluralism within a shared public realm of discourse, to accept the unavailability of complete consensus, and to work at creating an optimally coherent, communal framework or wide reflective equilibrium of thought and action. This is what true coherence is about — a coherence where dissensus and a variety of opinion provide for creative enhancement rather than impoverishment of our intellectual culture.

This also means that even if we lack the universal rules for rationality that were so much a part of the intellectual culture of Lord Gifford and nineteenth-century Edinburgh, and even if we can never again judge the reasonableness of statements and beliefs in isolation from their cultural or disciplinary contexts, we are not the prisoners of our contexts or disciplines. We can retain the "universalizing intent" (cf. Rescher 1992: 11) of Gifford's charge while, at the same time, letting go of the universalism of modernist rationality. For this reason we can still meaningfully engage in cross-contextual evaluation and conversation and give the best available cognitive, evaluative, or pragmatic reasons for the responsible choices we hope to make in interdisciplinary conversation. True interdisciplinarity in theology and science, therefore, will be achieved only when our conversations proceed not in terms of imposed "universal" rules nor in terms of purely ad hoc rules, but when we identify this interdisciplinary space where both strong religious convictions and the public voice of theology are fused in public conversation. A postfoundationalist acknowledgment of the pluralist character of such an ongoing process of collective assessment should open our eyes to how our various traditions, our various discourses, our communities, our sciences and practices make up our social and intellectual domains and shape our behavior and our different modes of understanding. Each of our domains of understanding may have its own logic of behavior, as well as an understanding unique to the particular domain, but in each the rich resources of interdisciplinary rationality remain.

Against this background I have argued for a theology that would be acutely aware of its deeply interdisciplinary nature, and of the epistemological obligations implied with this status. The overall thesis of this project is that a constructive appropriation of some of the epistemological issues raised by the postfoundationalist challenge to theology and the sciences will make it possible (1) to collapse rigid, modernist disciplinary distinctions and create more comprehensive interdisciplinary spaces where (2) traditional epistemic boundaries and disciplinary distinctions are blurred precisely because the same kinds of interpretative procedures are at work in all our various reasoning strategies and (3) through a creative fusion of hermeneutics and epistemology, reasoning strategies as distinctive and different as theology and the sciences may be revealed to share the rich resources of human rationality.

Interdisciplinarity and Human Uniqueness

The final question before us today is the following: Could this kind of transversal, interdisciplinary dialogue be an adequate vehicle for a concrete case study like the one before us — human uniqueness in science and theology? I believe that only in a carefully developed interdisciplinary discourse would we be able to discern whether a theological perspective on *human origins* and *uniqueness* even remotely relates to what scientists of various stripes may mean when they talk about *human origins* and *human uniqueness*. Developing a postfoundationalist approach to interdisciplinary dialogue in this first chapter is therefore my response to the first of the two themes so strongly implicit in Lord Gifford's original charge, namely, the possibility of an integrative and interdisciplinary praxis for "theology and the sciences." Developing this model for interdisciplinarity has now cleared the way, so to speak, for approaching his important second theme: the basic theological conviction that there is something about being human, even uniquely human, that is constituted by the relationship of ourselves, and of our world, to God. It will now be my task to take up and evaluate various scientific, philosophical, and theological claims for human distinctiveness, and to see whether a multidisciplinary research program can yield interdisciplinary results.

As has now become abundantly clear, to develop a very specific multidisciplinary discourse on a very specific problem we need to identify the various disciplinary voices that are going to be part of this conversation. And maybe more importantly, we need also to identify the very specific problem and historical/contextual environment of the discipline(s) in which it is embedded. For true multidisciplinary research to achieve any interdisciplinary insights, we have to move out of the kind of "twilight zone of abstraction" where the issue at hand is decontextualized from the space of beliefs and social practices that provided its original habitat (cf. Schrag 1989: 90). A postfoundationalist notion of rationality should alert us to the kind of flawed methodology by which many of us often overgeneralize broadly when discussing specific issues in specific fields of research. This kind of a-contextual thinking, from which stems the belief that broad conclusions can be drawn regardless of agent and context, almost always reveals a preference for underspecifying an event or an issue, and invariably, therefore, for overgeneralizing. This will turn out to be the biggest challenge in pursuing a theme like *human uniqueness in theology and science,* since the central concept of "human uniqueness" can be used so abstractly that it is rendered almost useless (cf. Kagan 1998: 2f.).

Ambitious overgeneralizing quickly transforms itself into an epistemological problem when we ignore subtle shifts in meaning as we cross disciplinary boundaries. In a multidisciplinary approach to a problem like human uniqueness, recognition of the significance of specific local contexts in specific different disciplines will eventually help us bridge the gap between disciplines. In pursuing the problem of human uniqueness in theology and the sciences, then, we will have to be very specific, aware of the ramifications of the question of human uniqueness within the very different contexts of different disciplines and also aware of the historical background and the history of ideas behind such contexts.

Scientists who treat the issue of human uniqueness as if it were only a biological or anthropological event, and theologians who treat it as only a spiritual or religious issue, want the book of human nature to be written in only one language. No one disciplinary language, however, can ever completely capture every aspect of the complex issue we are trying to understand here, and this will become an important argument against those disciplinary purists who are made uneasy by the messiness of multiple vocabularies in interdisciplinary research (cf. 45f.). I will argue that the problem of human uniqueness, correctly defined, not only benefits from but also needs many disciplinary voices, and also benefits from and needs the presence of the theological voice. In fact, this kind of multidisciplinary holism is not only epistemologically sound and plausible, it will also finally enable us to align this postfoundationalist argument with Lord Gifford's original comprehensive, interdisciplinary charge.

The phenomenon of "species uniqueness," as well as the more specific issue of human uniqueness, is certainly alive and well in our commonsense understanding of ourselves and our world. Various animals, and certainly *Homo sapiens,* do seem to possess at least a small number of unique qualities that are not present in others: snakes shed their skin, dogs do not; bears hibernate, cats do not; monkeys form dominance hierarchies, mice do not. Humans experience guilt, shame, and pride; anticipate events far in the future; invent metaphors, speak a language with a grammar, and reason about hypothetical circumstances. No other species, including the great apes, apparently possesses this set of talents (cf. 9). Certainly, because a great deal of important, informative research is performed on animals, scientists may feel considerable social pressure to generalize and transfer conclusions based on evidence from animals to the human condition. Jerome Kagan has warned, however, that equally confident generalizations are not possible for all human qualities: only humans seem to engage in symbolic rituals when they bury kin, draw on cave walls, hold beliefs about the self and the origin of the world, and worry about their loyalty to family members (cf. 9). Here again is an argument for contextual reasoning, and in this case for replacing overgeneralizations with species specificity.

What is already clear, and will become increasingly so, is that our species' remarkable intellectual capacity for the kind of fluid, cross-disciplinary reflection that I have been arguing for will be properly understood only if we listen to what science is telling us today about how the human mind works. And when, as theologians, philosophers, or scientists, we try to understand how the human mind works, we must inevitably inquire about its origins and evolution. So in a sense we are back at the problem of human uniqueness, and the unavoidable question seems to be: How special are we as a species? Are we created in the *image of God,* as Christian theology has traditionally maintained, or should we rather follow the classic philosophical route and think of ourselves as *rational animals?* My argument will be that framing this important question in this way already presents us with a false dilemma, a choice we do not have to make. A careful look at the origins and prehistory of the human mind will show that we can transcend the limitations of both these polarizing perspectives and embrace a third option that will include a scientifically informed, complementary view of the nature of human uniqueness. In these lectures I want to look at some of the evidence gleaned from the transversal dialogue between Christian theology, evolutionary biology, evolutionary epistemology, paleoanthropology, and archeology, and at what these disciplines tell us today about the evolution of a creature called *Homo sapiens,* who is, of course, none other than *us.* As we will see, sometime in our past our ancestors were part of a remarkable emergence: an emergence into self-awareness, with an increasing capacity for consciousness, the possibility for moral responsibility, and the yearning and capacity for aesthetic and religious fulfillment. This fact alone offers fascinating challenges to traditional Christian theology, since it is no longer possible to claim some past paradise in which humans possessed moral perfection, a state from which our species has somehow "fallen" into perpetual decline.

The unavoidable question seems to be: *How special are we really?* Normally, when we refer to ourselves as rational animals, what we mean is that humans have evolved within nature in such a way that much of what we think and do proceeds under the formative guide of *intelligence.* Human intelligence should indeed be seen as the product of a long and complex process of biological evolution. Our possession and use of intelligence should, therefore, first be understood in evolutionary terms, or in Nicholas Rescher's apt words, as our very "useful inheritance," our survival mechanism par excellence (cf. Rescher 1990: 1). Our possession of intelligence and our capacity for rationality are easily understood within evolutionary principles: these peculiar human resources are clearly a means to adaptive efficiency, enabling us to adjust our environment to our needs, rather than the reverse. The ability of our brains to make intelligent judgments and appropriate decisions is the survival instrument of our species, in much the same way that other creatures ensure their survival by being prolific, tough, or well sheltered. In Rescher's words, intelligence is our functional substitute for the numerousness of termites, the ferocity of lions, or the toughness of microorganisms (2f.). And because of this basic fact, our need for information and proper cognitive orientation in our environment is as important as the need for food and sex, and in a sense even more insatiable. The imperative to *understand,* therefore, is something altogether basic for us as humans, and we cannot thrive without reliable information regarding what goes on around us. Our inherited, basic intelligence thus demands of us a cognitive commitment to intelligibility, an abiding need for a comprehensive and coherent account of things. Rescher has pointed out that the rationale for our cognitive resources, therefore, is indeed fundamentally Darwinian, and that the conception of knowledge as a tool for survival, as I will argue in the second lecture, is as old as biological Darwinism itself (cf. 5; also Darwin 1985: 443f.; and especially Darwin 1981: 137, 404f.).

Intelligence can therefore be seen to constitute our particular competitive advantage, but while biological evolution accounts for the *possession* of intelligence, explaining the way we actually *use* this intelligence requires a different and broader approach. What this means is that the process of selection does not function only on a biological level, but seems also to operate — albeit in a limited way — on an aphysical or cultural level, and serves to favor survival of those cultural forms that prove to be the most advantageous. On the one hand, then, we deal with the biological transmission of physical traits by biological inheritance across generations, and on the other with the social propagation of cultural traits by way of generation-transcending influence. But the fundamental structure of the process is the same on either side. Both involve the conservation of structures over time (cf. Rescher 1990: 6).

With this it becomes clear that, for cognitive matters, the biological evolution of our capacity for rational thought is not the only issue we have to consider seriously. Not only do our various capacities for intelligent reflection and action have an evolutionary basis, so does the way we go about using them, even if on a cultural level it is more about *rational* selection than *natural* selection (cf. 6). Most importantly, cognitive evolution will challenge us by raising the question of how rational selection is superimposed on natural selection. Against the background of all the millions of species that have come and gone over the millennia, it still is a fact that a complex transmissible culture has developed in only one of them. In this one it developed explosively with radical innovations. There is indeed only one line that leads to persons, to self-awareness and consciousness, and in that line the steady growth of cranial capacity makes it difficult to think that intelligence was not being selected for. And at exactly this point, evolution by natural selection passed into something else as nature transcended itself into culture (cf. Rolston 1996: 69). The historical emergence of our thought mechanisms, therefore, is doubtless biological (Darwinian), but the development of our thought methods is governed by the complicated social process of cultural evolution. In Rescher's words, thinking people are by and large just as interested in the fate of their ideas as in the fate of their descendants: the survival of their *values* is no less significant for them than the survival of their *genes* (cf. 1990: 12).

As will become increasingly clear in these lectures, with human consciousness and culture, radically new elements like conscious experiences have emerged, and along with thoughts have also come values and purposes and ultimately a propensity for rational knowledge (cf. van Huyssteen 1998: 38). It is precisely in an attempt to understand our ability to cope intelligently with an increasingly intelligible world through *knowledge* that the impact of the theory of evolution is felt far beyond the boundaries of biology. So we can now say that an individual's heritage comes from two main sources: a *biological heritage* derived from parents and a *cultural heritage* derived from society. Given this perspective, then, evolution does lead to emergent qualities that can actually radically transcend their biological origins. Rescher's views on this topic resonate well with Arthur Peacocke's well-known description of the emergence of complexity (cf. Peacocke 1993: 61-83), and with important work now being done by complexity theorists like Stuart Kauffman, in addition to other scientists like Ian Stewart and Simon Conway Morris. These scientists, however diverse in their fields and research, all share the view that the emergence of new modes and levels of operation, function, self-organization, and behavior that transcend the narrow capabilities of their causal origin should in fact be seen as characteristic of evolutionary processes as well.

Conclusion

In this first chapter I have argued that in an intellectual culture shaped by postmodernity and increasing pluralism, it has become virtually impossible to follow Lord Gifford's demands for a universalizing natural theology that would treat its object of study as a "strictly natural science." I do believe it is possible, however, to revision the central idea of Gifford's charge and glean from it two crucially important contemporary themes. As famously stated in his will, Gifford argued that in the "true knowledge of God," and in our knowing the world, and our relationship to the world in relation to God, and in acting on this knowledge, we may actually find and achieve something unique, i.e., humankind's "highest well-being" and the security of our "upward progress" (cf. Jaki 1986: 71f.). I have now argued that implicit in this rather modernist statement are two themes that can be reconstructed to reach out to us transversally across time: a direct challenge to a contemporary form of multidisciplinary reflection that may actually yield interdisciplinary results, and a clear and unambiguous statement that as a species we humans can be optimally understood only in terms of our broader connection to the universe and to God. Against this background it was possible to argue that the call for a universalizing natural theology in Gifford's will can be revisioned more specifically to reveal, first, the challenge for an integrative and interdisciplinary contemporary praxis for theology and the sciences, and second, the challenge to pursue as an interdisciplinary problem the issue of "human uniqueness." I will argue, furthermore, that precisely in the topic of human uniqueness do theology and the sciences today find a shared research trajectory.

More specifically I have argued that:

1. Contemporary forms of postfoundationalist epistemology have convincingly shown that it has become implausible today even to talk about "theology and science" in any generic, abstract sense. In fact, the radical social and historical contextuality of all our rational reflection reveals that in interdisciplinary dialogue the rather a-contextual terms "theology" and "science" should be replaced by a focus on specific theologians, engaging in specific kinds of theologies, who are attempting to enter the interdisciplinary dialogue with very specific scientists, working within specific sciences on clearly defined, shared problems.

2. The idea that the domain of religious faith and the domain of scientific thought in any sense exemplify rival or opposing notions of rationality should be rejected outright. In fact, different and seemingly incompatible reasoning strategies share what I have called "the resources of human rationality." For this reason a postfoundationalist notion of rationality, rightly conceived, should enable us to leave behind abstract, overgeneralized "blueprints" for engaging in interdisciplinary research and help us to focus on developing, first contextually and then transversally, the merits of specific interdisciplinary problems. It is in this sense that a multidisciplinary approach to specific problems may yield interdisciplinary results.

3. A postfoundationalist notion of rationality thus reveals not only a more holistic, embodied way to think about human rationality, but also arguments for the public voice of theology in our rather complex contemporary culture. On this view theologians, but also scientists of all stripes, should be empowered to argue for the rational integrity of their specific disciplines, while at the same time being free to pursue overlapping concerns and identify shared problems, and even parallel research trajectories, as they cross disciplinary lines in multidisciplinary research. Here theology is neither transformed modernistically into natural science nor rejected as nonscience. On this interdisciplinary mode theological reflection emerges as a reasoning strategy on par with the intellectual integrity and legitimacy of the natural, social, and human sciences, even as it delineates its own domain of thought that in so

many ways is also distinct from that of the sciences. At the heart of this kind of interdisciplinary reflection, therefore, we find a new opportunity: as we find ourselves deeply embedded in specific research traditions, we may now realize that a particular disciplinary tradition may generate questions that cannot be resolved by its own resources alone. It is exactly this kind of interdisciplinary awareness that may lead us to cross disciplinary boundaries and reach out to other disciplines for intellectual support.

4. Because of the multidimensional, transversal nature of human rationality, we are enabled to enter the pluralist, interdisciplinary conversation with our full personal convictions intact; at the same time, we are theoretically empowered to step beyond the limitations and boundaries of our contexts, traditions, and disciplines. It is in this sense that in the dialogue between theology and other disciplines transversal reasoning facilitates different but equally legitimate ways of evaluating issues, problems, traditions, or even disciplines themselves. Transversal rationality thus emerges as a performative praxis where our multiple beliefs and practices, our habits of thought and attitudes, our prejudices and judgments, converge. In this way a postfoundationalist notion of rationality enables us to retain the language of epistemology by fusing it with hermeneutical concerns. Our different genres of discourse can now be performatively integrated by our making of scientific claims, moral statements, aesthetic evaluations, religious judgments, and theological assessments. Precisely in revisioning interdisciplinary dialogue as a form of transversal reasoning, human rationality does not have to be identified with isolated and austere forms of reasoning anymore; it is a practical skill that enables us to gather and bind together the patterns of our daily experiences, and then make sense of them through communal, interactive dialogue.

5. On this view Christian theology should be able to claim a public or "democratic" presence in interdisciplinary dialogue. Here theology will share in interdisciplinary standards of rationality, which, although always contextually and socially shaped, will not be hopelessly culture- and context-bound. This will enable our theological reflection to aim for the reasoned coherence of a wide reflective equilibrium as the optimal epistemic goal of interdisciplinary dialogue. This postfoundationalist approach to interdisciplinarity also revealed interdisciplinary reflection as nonhierarchical because no one disciplinary voice, and no one set of judgments, practices, or principles, will be able to claim absolute priority over, or be foundational for, any other.

In this specific research project I will now combine the two themes gleaned from Lord Gifford's original charge and pursue an interdisciplinary conversation quite specifically between theology and paleoanthropology on the shared problem of "human uniqueness." However, does my focus on a transversal approach to interdisciplinarity mean that we are already focusing on the evolution of human cognitive capacities as an answer to the question, *how special are we really?* Moreover, will theology be able to learn from the insights science is providing about the evolution of human uniqueness and the emergence of complexity, and how will these insights affect the already complex dialogue between these very diverse reasoning strategies? I have argued that there is indeed no clear philosophical blueprint or timeless recipe for relating the bewildering complexity of contemporary theologies to the increasingly complex spectrum of contemporary sciences (cf. van Huyssteen 1999: 235-86). This does not mean, however, that we cannot develop focused dialogues between theology and the sciences on issues that are quite specific and that resonate with both partners in this dialogue. I do believe that the evolution of "human uniqueness," brought to the fore by especially paleoanthropology and evolutionary biology, presents us with an outstanding and exciting case study for precisely this kind of interdisciplinary dialogue.

Christian theology has traditionally assumed a radical split between human beings (as created "in the image of God") and the rest of creation. This split has mostly been justified by reference to cognitive traits like human rationality or intelligence, which in the dominant part of the history of Christian thought served to define what exactly was meant by "human uniqueness." However, current research in animal cognition, and on protolanguage, protomorality, ritual, and levels of consciousness, has shown that we may not be as unique as we think we are (cf. Peterson 1999: 283ff.). But even if we were to agree that various levels of consciousness extend over, and deeply connect, the animal and human world (as is argued by Damasio 1999: 195-233), it will become unambiguously clear that our emerging conception of "human uniqueness" should be broadened to account for crucial cultural issues like the emergence of art, of technology, of religion, and eventually of science.

As will become clear during this series of lectures, science, art, and religion, as direct products of cultural evolution in *Homo sapiens,* are all deeply embedded in the advanced consciousness and cognitive fluidity (cf. Mithen 1996: 70f., 136f.) of the human mind. As such, these cultural accomplishments rely on psychological processes that originally evolved in specialized cognitive domains and emerged only when these processes could actually work together. Cognitive fluidity, and the symbolic mind that goes hand in hand with this unique human mental ability, also enabled the development of a technology that could catalogue problems and store information. Of perhaps even greater significance, it allowed for the possibility of powerful metaphors and analogy, without which science, religion, and art could not exist. What is eminently clear, as we will see in the work of various scientists, is that *the potential arose in the human mind* to undertake science, create art, and discover the need and ability for religious belief, even if there were no specific selection pressures for such abstract abilities during our past.

A positive theological appropriation of the results of these sciences should at the very least inspire the theologian to carefully trace and rethink the complex evolution of the doctrine of the *imago Dei*. Interpretations of the *imago Dei* have varied dramatically throughout the long history of Christianity. In much of contemporary theology, the notion is seen as grounding personhood, and theologians are now challenged to rethink what human uniqueness might mean for the human person, a being that has emerged biologically as a center of self-awareness, identity, and moral responsibility. What does human distinctiveness mean in terms of the evolution of imagination, of symbolic propensities, of cognitive and linguistic abilities, and of moral awareness, and should we review our theological notions of the *imago Dei* so that it does not imply a value superiority over animals? I will eventually argue for a revisioning of the notion of the *imago Dei* that acknowledges our close ties to the animal world and *its* uniqueness, while at the same time focusing on what our symbolic and cognitively fluid minds might tell us about the emergence of embodied human uniqueness, consciousness, personhood, and the propensity for religious awareness and experience.

Finally, it is precisely in the transversal spaces between the porous boundaries between theology and the science of paleoanthropology that we will find the key for a creative rethinking of the notion of the *imago Dei* in Christian theology. However, we should take care not to mistake any convergence or resonance we might identify between scientific facts and Christian theology's deepest convictions as being some kind of "proof" for God's purpose or design in the universe. The emergence of this kind of complexity may however resonate with theology's deepest convictions about human uniqueness, and may give us an argument for the plausibility and comprehensive nature of a *theological* explanation of a phenomenon — the emergence of the human mind — that has now become so fascinating for the sciences. Human nature does seem to be imperfectly understood if we do not take into account the emergence of religion, and the plausibility of religious and theological explanations. After all, our ability to respond religiously to ultimate questions in worship and prayer may be deeply embedded in the history of our species' symbolic and imaginative behavior, as well as the cognitively fluid minds that make such behavior possible.

two *Human Uniqueness and Cognitive Evolution*

"And it is true that while we are embodied, and firmly rooted in the natural world we are also reflective. We can, and should, in various ways transcend and refine the given."

> Anthony O'Hear, *Beyond Evolution*
> (Oxford: Clarendon, 2002), 100

"The *Imagination* is one of the highest prerogatives of man. By this faculty he unites, independently of the will, former images and ideas, and thus creates brilliant and novel results."

> Charles Darwin, *The Descent of Man, and Selection in Relation to Sex* (Princeton: Princeton University Press, 1981), 45

In the first chapter I argued for a *postfoundationalist* approach to interdisciplinary dialogue, which implied two important moves for theology. First, as theologians we should acknowledge the contextuality and the epistemically crucial role of interpreted experience, and the way tradition shapes the values that inform our reflection about God and what some of us believe to be God's presence in the world. Secondly, however, a postfoundationalist notion of rationality in theological reflection should open our eyes to an epistemic obligation that points beyond the boundaries of the local community, group, or culture, toward a plausible form of interdisciplinary dialogue. The overriding concern here is as follows: while we always come to our interpersonal and cross-disciplinary conversations with strong personal beliefs, commitments, and even prejudices, a postfoundationalist approach should enable us to realize that there is also much that we share, and help us identify these shared resources of human rationality in different modes of knowledge so as to reach beyond the boundaries of our traditional communities in cross-contextual, cross-disciplinary conversation.

Taking seriously context and interpreted experience also makes it virtually impossible to talk about interdisciplinary theology — or any kind of public theology, for that matter — without first talking about the role of tradition in the task of theological reflection. The philosophical and epistemological challenges that undergird this kind of claim, and the very basic fact that epistemic and moral traditions shape our patterns of research in both science and theology, will be of central importance for the very specific case study in interdisciplinary dialogue that I am arguing for here. I have argued that for both theology and the sciences the following would be true.

First, we always relate to our world through interpreted experience only. As such we have no standing ground, no place for evaluating, judging, and inquiring, apart from that which is provided by some specific tradition or traditions. In this sense interpretation is at work as much in the process of scientific discovery as in different forms of knowledge; it goes all the way down and all the way back, whether we are moving in the domain of science, morality, art, or religion.

Second, because we cannot think and act apart from our embeddedness in tradition(s) and worldviews, our epistemic task is to stand in a *critical* relation to our tradition(s) and worldviews. This requires a conscious and deliberate step beyond the confines of particular traditions and disciplines, and implies that the task and identity of a discipline is definitively shaped, not only by its location in the living context of specific tradition(s), but also by the more comprehensive, transversal space of interdisciplinary reflection.

In chapter 1, I argued that the problem of interdisciplinarity is the first clear theme that could be reconstructed from Lord Gifford's charge to his lecturers. A second theme emerges in the issue of human distinctiveness, or human uniqueness, and along with this the challenge of finding a possible shared interdisciplinary research trajectory on this very specific topic for theology and the sciences. The problem of human uniqueness, of course, must have existed for as long as humans have found it necessary to distinguish themselves from the rest of the living world. As human beings, it seems, we are doomed forever to agonize over what it means to be human (cf. Tattersall 2003: 232). Some, like historian of science Robert Proctor, see the idea of "humanness" as a notion we invented to elevate ourselves over other creatures, and it usually has as much to do with the myths we create as with the empirical realities that science focuses on. As such we humans seem to be animals with an odd capacity for self-*aggrandizement,* and one common, shared way in which we are all human is that we constantly involve ourselves in exercises of both self-definition and self-deception (cf. Proctor 2003: 228). On one level our remarkable capacity (some would call it mania) for self-definition could no doubt also be seen as one of the crowning achievements of our species. No one single trait or accomplishment, however, should ever be taken to signal definitively what it means to be human. Moreover, we will soon see that whatever we define as our true "humanness," or even our human uniqueness, ultimately reveals a deeply ambivalent moral choice, for we are not just biological creatures, but as cultural creatures we have the ability to determine whom we are going to include, or not, as part of "us" (cf. 228f.). Therefore, talking about human uniqueness when defining ourselves implies a crucially important moral dimension precisely because the inclusion or exclusion of others as "fully human," or not, gives shape to the social and cultural contexts we create and experience.

Ian Tattersall has argued recently that from a scientific point of view, the problem of human uniqueness may have seemed a relatively simple one, at least as long as our closest known relatives were the living apes, for what makes us human is simply whatever makes us different from the great apes (cf. Tattersall 2003: 232). In recent years, of course, it has become increasingly difficult to pinpoint what exactly this difference is, especially in light of the quite stunning 99 percent genetic similarities between humans and chimpanzees. All this is complicated even further because we now know that humans had an evolutionary past of more than 5 million years, containing a great diversity of now-extinct hominids that were much more closely related to us than the living apes are, but that still seem to be somehow different from us. In this work I will follow Tattersall and other paleoanthropologists in using the term "human evolution" in the quite specific sense of covering the history of the hominid family, excluding the great apes. Furthermore, what is highly significant, and will most certainly have ramifications for an interdisciplinary study such as this, is that a paleoanthropologist like Tattersall regards only living and historic *Homo sapiens* (and those fossils that were anatomically and behaviorally like them) as "fully human" (cf. 233). In addition, definitions of what it means to be "human" or even "fully human" have not only shifted and changed with time but have also been deeply influenced by reigning cultural ideologies and worldviews, thus exposing science itself as deeply influenced by worldviews and moral perspectives. Center stage here will be the timing of human evolution, that is, the antiquity or recency of the emergence of creatures called *Homo sapiens,* who are, of course, none other than *us.*

With this it already becomes clear that, as far as cognitive matters go, the biological evolution of our capacity for rational thought may not be the only issue we have to consider seriously when trying to define "human uniqueness." Certainly our various capacities for intelligent reflection and action have an evolutionary basis, but the way we use these capacities on a cultural level seems to be more about complex *rational* selection than *natural* selection (cf. Rescher 1990: 6). Most importantly, the problem of cognitive evolution will challenge us by raising the question of how rational selection is superimposed on natural selection. Against the background of all the millions of species that have come and gone over the millennia, it still is a fact that a complex transmissible culture developed in only one of them. In this one it developed explosively with radical innovations. As I briefly mentioned in chapter 1, there seems to be only one line that leads to persons, to self-awareness and consciousness, and in that line the steady growth of cranial capacity makes it difficult to think that intelligence was not being selected for. And at exactly this point, evolution by natural selection passed into a higher level of complexity as nature transcended itself into culture (cf. Rolston 1996: 69).[1]

With human consciousness, conscious self-awareness, and culture, radically new elements like conscious experiences have emerged, and along with thoughts have also come values and purposes and ultimately a propensity for rational knowledge (cf. van Huyssteen 1998: 38). It is precisely in an attempt to understand our ability to cope intelligently with an increasingly intelligible world through *knowledge* that the impact of the theory of evolution is felt far beyond the boundaries of biology. The emergence of new phenomena at different levels of scale and organizational complexity in nature necessarily entails the emergence of new processes and laws at these levels. Evolution in na-

1. The historical emergence of our thought mechanisms, therefore, is doubtless biological (Darwinian), but as will become clearer later, the development of our thought methods is also governed by the complicated social processes of cultural evolution. In Nicholas Rescher's words, thinking people are by and large just as interested in the future fate of their ideas as in the future fate of their descendants: the survival of their *values* is no less significant for them than that of their *genes* (cf. Rescher 1990: 12).

ture thus reflects a succession of new strata of operational complexity. New products and processes constantly develop from earlier modes of organization, bringing new orders of structure into being. Consequently, the emergence of intellectual and psychological processes (and the accompanying realms of meaning and purpose) is simply another step in the established developmental process of increasing functional complexity. This "purposive intelligence" could be seen as a novel phenomenon that emerges at a new level of operational complexity. On this view, then, having a causally productive account of the biological origins of our mental processes differs markedly from actually having reflective and experiential access *to what we are thinking about.* Coming to grips with cognitive issues like meaning, intention, and purpose means understanding them. And understanding them means also performing them, and performing them requires having the kind of mind that has access to those particular and unique mental experiences (cf. Rescher 1990: 122).

In this chapter I will quite specifically ask how diverse disciplines like contemporary paleontology and evolutionary epistemology may support or conflict with our commonsense notions of human uniqueness. First, we will look at how notions of humanness in paleontology have shifted and changed with time, and how cultural ideologies and moral worldviews have deeply affected notions of human distinctiveness. This will confirm not only that ideologies and worldviews deeply influence science, but also that, ironically, well-intentioned moral perspectives can at times actually constrain scientific development. Secondly, I will argue that Charles Darwin's views on human identity and human nature still function as the canonical core of the ongoing discussion on human uniqueness. It is Darwin's views on human distinctiveness, moreover, that very specifically are still shaping our views on the evolution of human cognition. Thirdly, I will argue that the epistemic implications of these views on the evolution of human cognition are today most clearly represented in contemporary evolutionary epistemology. Evolutionary epistemology's focus on the evolution of human cognition will not only reveal embodied human cognition as a mediator between biology and culture, but will link the question of human uniqueness directly to embodied consciousness, aesthetic imagination, moral awareness, and the propensity for religious belief.

Human Distinctiveness in Paleontology

The intriguing fact that in paleoanthropology definitions of human uniqueness have changed with time and are deeply influenced by worldviews and
ideologies is discussed by historian of science Robert Proctor in an important
recent article in *Current Anthropology* (Proctor 2003). Proctor succeeds admi-
rably in contextualizing and historicizing research on human antiquity and
recency, and convincingly shows how much this subject matter is inextricably
interwoven with seemingly "extrascientific" factors (cf. also Hochadel 2003:
231). Like all our disciplinary ventures and reasoning strategies, the development of paleoanthropological ideas should always be understood in the context of their times, i.e., within the historical-cultural network of ideas in
which they are, or were, embedded (cf. Tattersall 2003: 233). One such seminal
idea that has often been greatly influenced by the moods and ideologies of the
times is the origin and timing of human evolution. There is, of course, still
radical disagreement over the timing of human evolution, understood as the
coming-into-being of the language-using symbolic cultural creatures we are
today (cf. Proctor 2003: 212). Conceptions of human antiquity have changed
rather radically over time, with the most recent evidence and opinion pointing to the relatively recent emergence of consciousness, language, kindled fire,
compound-tool use, and other aesthetic, creative signs of human symbolic
intelligence.

One of the most fascinating historical examples of the influence of
"extrascientific," political or moral views on the definition of human uniqueness is found in the influence of post-Holocaust definitions of humanness in
paleoanthropology. For many years after the horrific events of World War II it
was fashionable, and politically correct, to project "humanness" onto every
early hominid discovered by paleontologists — even Lucy, an australo-
pithecine female, one of our "oldest ancestors," and other earlier hominids
were granted humanity. Today, however, it is more common to see the australopithecines as more chimplike, while distinctions between anatomically modern *Homo sapiens* and behaviorally modern *Homo sapiens* have become com-
monplace. At the same time, paleoanthropologists are also arguing against
seeing our closest human relatives, the Neanderthals, as "fully human" (cf.
Proctor 2003: 212; also Tattersall 1998). Proctor has provocatively called this recent trend the "dehumanizing" of early hominids, a transformation clearly visible in the separate sciences of archeology, paleontology, and molecular anthropology (cf. 2003: 213). But how important is this so-called dehumanizing
of early hominids for understanding humanness in our own species?

A. Human Uniqueness as a Moral Issue

The idea that humanness is a relatively recent phenomenon certainly includes both anatomically modern *Homo sapiens,* in a biological sense, and even more recently, behaviorally modern *Homo sapiens,* in a cultural sense, taking into account the best-established dates for the first forms of human ornamentation, abstract or representational art, compound-tool use, deliberate grinding and polishing, and similar signs of human symbolic intelligence (cf. Proctor 2003: 312). What is fascinating to observe, however, is that the so-called dehumanizing of early hominids, by focusing on the recency of the humanness of *Homo sapiens,* has made earlier hominid diversity acceptable and even politically correct. This important change in perspective can certainly be seen as a response to new discoveries in these fields. It is also, however, a distinct move away from the immediate political and moral influence of post–World War II and post-Holocaust understandings of race and brutality. On this view conceptions of hominid and racial diversity were deeply intertwined, and one impact of racial liberalism after World War II seems to have been a delay in the recognition of the richness of fossil hominid diversity as a result of fears of excluding and "dehumanizing" one or another now-extinct hominid from the so-called family of man. For this reason there seems to be an inherent arbitrariness in deciding when "they" became "us," and precisely because of this the question, When did humans really become human? must also be seen as, among other things, a very specific moral question (cf. Proctor 2003: 213).

Against this background Proctor has shown clearly why, following the 1950 UNESCO Statement on Race, which rightly rejected race as an unscientific, social myth, the idea of "humanness" was pushed back so far in time that some scholars even suggested that *Ramapithecus,* a creature that lived around 14 million years ago, should be seen as a hominid and a tool user, implying that this creature was "human" in some deep and inclusive sense (cf. 214). By the mid-1970s this approach was widely accepted, but this kind of reigning consensus that equated "hominid" with "humanity" has significantly broken down in the past two decades. Very important also, and highly publicized, is the discovery of *biological* recency, i.e., the idea that humans share with chimpanzees a common ancestor who lived as recently as 5 million or 6 million years ago. This close temporal kinship was not discovered until the 1960s, and not widely accepted until the 1980s, by which time it was also shown independently by Richard Lewontin that genetic differences between races are minor and racial differentiation cannot be very old (cf. Proctor 2003: 214; Lewontin 1974: 152-57). In this way contemporary scientists have successfully argued for both the animality of our humanity and the triviality of racial distinctions (cf. Proctor 2003: 214). The fascinating result of this research was that both the break between humans and the great apes and the separation of races from one another were thus diminished, while at the same time human uniqueness was ever more carefully defined. This is illustrated well when we take a closer look at the origins of the idea that human evolution is a truly recent phenomenon, and the clear trend in the past few decades to push forward the dates for many of the qualities we often regard as central to being human, qualities like language ability, control of fire, consciousness, and ritual behavior. Early hominids are now actually seen as "less human" because some of the earliest dates for some of the traits seen as typically "modern" have not held up to scientific scrutiny, especially data from archeology, paleontology, and molecular anthropology (cf. 214).[2]

The paleontological argument focuses specifically on the crisis caused by fossil hominid diversity. In the 1960s and 1970s spectacular South African and East African hominid fossil finds showed clearly that more than one species of hominids must have coexisted at many points in the course of hominid evolution.[3] Many paleoanthropologists today place the total number of hominid species at about twenty, divided into four or five distinct genera, two of which are *Homo* and *Australopithecus*. Hominid diversity seems to have peaked about 2 million years ago when three, four, five, or possibly even more separate hominid species coexisted on our planet, all in East Africa (cf. 215). All this makes the present state of affairs, where there is only one surviving species, namely, us, a very unusual situation in the 5-million-year span of hominid evolution. In fact, from this particular scientific point of view we humans are indeed "alone in the world."

Of course, in nature the persistence of only one species, and of one suc-

2. The archeological argument focuses on the crisis or turning point in interpreting some of the oldest tools, specifically the Oldowan and Acheulean assemblages of the Lower Paleolithic. A popular view, for instance, was that the Acheulean hand axes that were found widely in the terrain of the Lower Paleolithic from more than a million years ago were evidence of complex foresight and planning, and a primitive appreciation of symmetry and proportion. The more common view today is that such tools were produced according to a sequence of operations that does not necessarily have the "hand ax" as an end-in-view, and that the makers of these tools did not have the capacity of speech (cf. Proctor 2003: 214; also Noble and Davidson 1996: 196ff.). On this view the users of these tools were not transmitting knowledge by means of abstract symbols, and therefore no language could have been involved (cf. Proctor 2003: 215).

3. Mary Leakey's *Zinjanthropus*, Louis Leakey's *Homo habilis*, and Donald Johanson's *Australopithecus* Lucy, etc. (cf. Proctor 2003: 315).

cessful lineage, is rare, and is a distinction that *Homo sapiens* share with the aardvark (Lewin 1993: 5). Modern humans are the sole surviving representatives of the hominid lineage, and as a result we now seem to lack the imagination to think of ourselves otherwise. The trappings of culture and the world we humans create through language, consciousness, and the force of mythology are so powerful and all-enveloping that by definition they seem to exclude the possibility of sharing such an adaptive niche with another species like us. We have to realize, therefore, that whatever we mean by "human uniqueness" today, that which separates humans from other animals, is something that might not have been conceived of in this way earlier in human prehistory. Any contemporary notion of human uniqueness thus reflects an acknowledgment that this "uniqueness" is a product of the evolutionary process, or as Roger Lewin forcefully puts it, it reflects "the accretion over time of powerful adaptations by a bipedal ape" (cf. 5-11).

Against this background the importance of the moral dimension of our decisions for defining human uniqueness becomes even more apparent. Proctor's argument, that the earlier hominid fossil diversity was initially not accepted without a struggle, thus points directly to the resistance of the liberal antiracialist climate of the post-Auschwitz era, when it was dogmatically assumed that only one hominid species could exist at any given time. As we just saw, this was tied to the reevaluation of race in the early post–World War II era, when a broad cultural consensus began to emerge that all humans living today are equal in cultural worth, part of the "family of man," culminating then in the 1950 UNESCO Statement on Race, which correctly branded race as an "unscientific" category and humankind's "most dangerous myth" (cf. Proctor 2003: 215). In the 1950s and 1960s the hypothesis that there was only a single species of humans present on earth at any time envisioned a linear nonbranching evolutionary sequence according to which, as Proctor puts it, *Australopithecus* begat *erectus, erectus* begat Neanderthal, and Neanderthal begat *sapiens*. In this climate it was very difficult, and politically incorrect, to accept the rich diversity of the fossil hominid history. What happened, however, was that not just racism but also *racial diversity* became unfashionable after the revelation of the crimes of the Nazis, with the resultant worldwide and important campaigns to end racial discrimination in all its many forms. As a result, *fossil hominid diversity* was deliberately underplayed as attitudes toward the ancestral (or extinct) hominid "other" got caught up in race relations (cf. 221).

The single-species hypothesis was dealt its first solid blow in 1959, when Mary Leakey discovered the 1.8-million-year-old *Zinjanthropus* at Olduvai

Gorge in Tanzania, a fossil with hyper-robust features, now known as *Australopithecus boisei* (cf. 221f.). *Homo habilis,* found at Olduvai in the early 1960s, further undercut the assumption of a single-stalk, nonbranching evolutionary tree. *Homo habilis* was clearly more humanlike than *Australopithecus* but quite older than had previously been imagined for our genus, and was the first real evidence that *Homo* must have lived at the same time as australopithecines. The idea that apelike hominids were not just replaced by more humanlike hominids, but that multiple hominid genera coexisted, took some time to assimilate. The final "nail in the coffin," to quote Proctor directly, came when Richard Leakey announced the discovery of a *Homo erectus* skull old enough to have coexisted with *Australopithecus boisei,* followed by the discovery that there were at least two kinds of *Australopithecus* (cf. 222).

Since the 1970s the trend has been to argue that hominids prior to *Homo sapiens* were not, after all, as "human" as once thought. This argument was accompanied by an increasing appreciation for the fact that it might not be such a bad thing *not* to be fully human, and also a growing sense that it is not really racist at all to believe that non*sapiens* hominids were radically different from us. This overview of shifting perspectives of how scientists have viewed hominid history not only confirms how ideologies and worldviews influence science, but is also a fascinating example of how a well-intentioned, highly moral viewpoint can curb and restrain scientific development. Hominid diversity became more acceptable when purged of its earlier racist overtones, and because of this difference finally became something that could be celebrated (cf. 222f.).[4]

The question of hominid evolution and the likelihood of the emergence of some form of "human uniqueness" in *Homo sapiens* also leads to another important set of questions. For most paleoanthropologists the emergence of a gulf between humans and other animals was in no sense inevitable. Evolution is generally seen as a contingent process of the moment, responsive to prevailing circumstances, especially those of climate and environment, and different conditions would have led to a different, subsequent evolutionary history. On this dominant view human beings, like all species, also seem to be the product of historical contingence. Retrospect lends the evolutionary process the appearance of inevitability, but the final pattern we are trying to reconstruct and understand is the result of environmental circumstances as they happened to

---

4. Cf. Proctor 2003: 225f. Proctor also discusses the highly problematical "Out of Africa: Thank God!" hypothesis, which subtly implied that Africa is a good place *to be from*, and that hominids therefore became human in the process of leaving Africa.

have occurred (cf. Lewin 1993: 12). There are, however, also important and challenging exceptions to this view, most notably proposed in the recent work of scientists like Ian Stewart and Simon Conway Morris.

In his *Life's Other Secret: The New Mathematics of the Living World* (1998), Stewart probes the relationship between intelligibility, evolution, and the mathematical order of the world of nature. Pointing to the way in which mathematics may describe the structure and evolution of life, Stewart in this book invites us to enter a world "deeper than DNA." He argues forcibly against biological or genetic reductionism, but not along the well-known lines that many scientists, philosophers, and theologians have followed in challenging the genetic determinism presented by much of neo-Darwinism and sociobiology. He argues that a world where everything blindly obeys instructions coded in its DNA is precisely what science does *not* find. DNA was indeed the *first* secret of life discovered by science, but Stewart wants to turn our attention to life's *other* secret — the universal mathematical principles of growth and form that even DNA exploits (cf. 1998: 93).

Stewart places his argument within the broader context of the important notion of *emergence*. We know that our universe obeys simple rules, the laws of nature. We also know, however, that life behaves in ways that do not seem to be built explicitly into those rules. Life is flexible, life is free, life seems to transcend the rigidity of its physical origins. And it is this kind of transcendence that is called "emergence." Emergence is not, however, the absence of causality; rather, it is a web of causality so intricate that the human mind cannot grasp it (cf. 7). Any attempt to understand life, then, is ultimately incomplete without an effective theory of emergent features.[5] In the end Stewart reminds us that the organic world is just as mathematical as the inorganic world, but that the mathematical basis of *living* things is just more subtle, more flexible, and more deeply hidden (cf. 14). We should not, however, be naive about the expression of mathematics in the living world, we should not expect life to display *only* mathematical patterns, and we most definitely should not expect to see pure mathematical patterns, undecorated by genetic and evolutionary thinking (cf. 23). Genes fit into this picture by adding significant flexibility to growth and form because they control and select the physical patterns that an organism

5. In Stewart's own words: "We need to understand how complicated rule-based systems manage to produce robust high-level features that themselves obey their own kind of emergent rules. We also need to develop an understanding of the high-level commonalities among different systems — the underlying unities, the common features that do not depend on particular interpretations and realizations, the features that life exploits to make itself possible, the universals, God's book of patterns" (8).

needs. In this sense physics imposes constraints on what biology can do, and in this sense genes are not the laws of life but are the means through which these laws operate.

It is here that Stewart identifies the reason genes should *not* be called the "key to life": they are *a* key, and an enormously important one, but behind them lie something much deeper — the true laws of biology, the mathematical rules into which the genetic code is plugged (cf. 25ff.). This thesis forms the basis for much of the argument in his book: there is mathematics at every level of life, and it concerns not just the growth and forms of organisms, but also their molecular bases, their microstructures, their control systems, their movements, their patterns, their behaviors, their means of communication, their relationship with each other and with their environment, and the historical paths by which they have evolved. The role of genetics in the development of organisms can therefore be understood only if we also bear in mind the effect of physical constraints. These constraints are not so much limiting as liberating; what we do *not* see is a world where everything blindly obeys instructions coded in only its DNA. Genes, therefore, are not a blueprint, but should rather be seen as something like a recipe: a cell carries out its genetic instructions; the laws of physics and chemistry produce certain consequences; and only when you put the two together do you get an organism (cf. 88).

Stewart also introduces the concept of *phase space* as the heart of this argument. Phase space is an image for the fact that every event that does happen is surrounded by a ghostly halo of nearby events that did not happen but could have. Phase spaces are large, since they comprehend a wide range of all possibilities. So if a rule system is sufficiently rich, then all sorts of possibilities lurk within its phase space. For Stewart this idea reveals the true significance of mutations in evolution — they do not just make evolution possible, they also enable the system to explore its phase space (cf. 118f.). The role of selection also now becomes clearer, since it makes the exploration of this space very efficient. If all that happened were just random mutations, "the system would wander around in its phase space like a drunkard, tottering one step forward, two steps back" (118). With selection, however, bits of phase space that do not work (i.e., that fail to promote fitness) are eliminated. Selection thus helps the system to home in on the most interesting regions of phase space, the places where useful things happen, and which are the central features of the evolutionary landscape.

Stewart's research here interestingly dovetails with that of paleontologist Simon Conway Morris, whose work on the Burgess Shale in British Columbia has placed the history of life in a new set of contexts and so by implication has shed new light on our place in the history of evolution. The Burgess Shale, with its remarkable richness of fossil remains, has become an icon for every student of the history of life, and Conway Morris guides us through this landscape and its significance, ultimately arguing for a radical reconsideration of the whole concept of evolution in the Darwinian framework.

In his *Crucible of Creation: The Burgess Shale and the Rise of Animals* (1998), and more recently, *Life's Solution: Inevitable Humans in a Lonely Universe* (2003a), he argues that although the Darwinian framework provides the logical underpinning to explain organic evolution, the actual *pattern of life* we observe may require a more complex set of explanations. Conway Morris also famously engages the work of Stephen Jay Gould, as well as "hard" or ultra-Darwinists like Daniel Dennett and Richard Dawkins.[6] Conway Morris starts his argument against Gould by developing his own interpretation of evolution and evolutionary continuity. Although there certainly is an evolutionary continuity in the history of life, he argues, nearly all the species that have ever lived are currently extinct and entire ecosystems have also vanished. In these past worlds there was much that was novel and has no counterpart today. But much is familiar too. This has not so much to do with evolutionary continuity as with the phenomenon known as *convergence* (cf. 1998: 13). Conway Morris

6. Conway Morris has an interesting view of Dawkins's position, which he considers too focused on the primacy of the gene, and therefore highly reductionist. Conway Morris sees Dawkins's worldview not so much as wrong, but as seriously incomplete: while few doubt that the development of form is underwritten by the genes, at the moment we have almost no idea how form actually emerges from the genetic code (cf. 1998: 7-14). The central problem that arises here is finding mechanisms that connect genes and developmental processes to morphological evolution, and what has quite unexpectedly emerged is *how seemingly very different organisms share the same fundamental genetic information*. This leads to a huge paradox: vast contrasts in morphology and behavior need have no corresponding differences in the genetic code. It is precisely these complex issues that cannot be satisfactorily explained by Dawkins's severely reductionist approach (cf. Conway Morris 1998: 91). Dawkins's view is exposed as incomplete in failing to explain how information (the genetic code) gives rise to the phenotype, and by what mechanisms.

The real focus of Conway Morris's critique, however, is the work of Stephen Jay Gould, who at first blush seems to have a much richer view. Dawkins's world is narrow and one-dimensional, but Gould's is much more difficult to encompass, but also much more deeply flawed. Gould's work has perhaps been overshadowed by his hypothesis of punctuated equilibria. Lately, though, Gould has promulgated a different set of notions that emphasize the role of the *contingent* in evolution. His argument basically is that the range of variation in the Cambrian was so huge and the end results in terms of diversity in today's world so restricted that this history could be regarded as one colossal lottery. On this view chance and contingency reign supreme, and what to us constitutes the utterly familiar was in principle no more inevitable than a million other possible outcomes (cf. Conway Morris 1998: 12, 199ff.).

claims that there has been no systematic, focused study of convergence, and of the constraints of form and pattern in evolution. One reason for this is that it is often just taken for granted. It does hide, however, a circular argument in which scientists can easily become trapped: *Are organisms similar because they have converged or because they are the descendants of a common ancestor?* Conway Morris's point is that whichever way one looks at it, some form of order, as well as distinct convergent features, has almost invariably emerged in the evolutionary process. This becomes a central feature of his argument, and he goes on to claim that this effectively undermines Gould's argument on the role of contingent processes in shaping the tree of life. In his words: "Contingency is inevitable, but unremarkable. It need not provoke discussion, because it matters not. There are not an unlimited number of ways of doing something. For all its exuberance, the forms of life are restricted and channeled" (13).

This discussion on construction and constraint is especially important for the very specific problem of the emergence or rise of human intelligence. For Gould, if the history of evolution were to be repeated, the likelihood of humans again evolving is virtually nil, and humankind is just a quirky, evolutionary accident. Conway Morris makes the point that what is important here is not so much the origin, destiny, or fate of a particular lineage, but the likelihood of the emergence of a particular property, like human *consciousness* (cf. 14). Here the reality of convergence suggests that human intelligence would almost certainly always emerge,[7] and we are in fact, as the subtitle of his latest book suggests, "inevitable humans in a lonely universe." Thus, Conway Morris makes an important argument against Gould's overstatement of the role of contingencies in evolution, and argues that the constraints we see imposed on evolution suggest that underlying the huge diversity of forms there is in fact an interesting predictability.

As for *Homo sapiens,* we may be the product of evolution, but we certainly seem to have the ability to transcend our biological origins. Whether we

7. Conway Morris also makes the important — and much neglected — point that our views of the processes of evolution always have metaphysical implications for us. Gould's view of humankind as an evolutionary accident includes an impoverished metaphysic and a libertarian attitude whereby, by virtue of cosmic accident, we have no choice but to take sole responsibility for our destiny and mold it to our desire. We do, however, seem to have a choice, and we can exercise free will. This is not only because of the gift of intelligence, but because there seems to be uniquely inherent in our human situation the possibility of transcendence. The fact that we arrived here via an immensely long string of species is a wonderful and crucially important scientific story, but it cannot be the last word in explaining who and how we are (cf. Conway Morris 1998: 14).

like it or not, we are a unique species, with unique responsibilities (cf. 218). What this finally implies, as we saw with Stewart, is that in evolutionary development DNA is not the sole determining factor of human distinctiveness. It exists in interaction with the spectrum of (restrained) possibilities provided by the laws of nature. Ultimately, the arguments of both Conway Morris and Stewart imply that when we go beyond biological evolution — beyond mathematics and biology, beyond even the natural sciences — to richer notions of culture, the notions of phase space and convergence should include not only human self-awareness, creative intelligence, and consciousness, but also the fact that we actually use our conscious, self-aware minds in creative new ways to do uniquely human things in art, science, and religion. As we will soon see, precisely this argument has recently been developed by Anthony O'Hear.

The burning question that now demands our attention is, what does the emergence of this kind of complexity tell us about the actual process of cognitive evolution in the human species? The evolution of the human brain can certainly be seen as nature's struggle to provide the machinery of information management and control needed by creatures of increasing versatility (cf. Rescher 1990: 108). The interesting question, certainly for those of us who are theologians, now becomes the following: If ultra-Darwinists are correct, why would this amazing brain, so intricately developed and emerged through a stunning, interactive evolutionary process, so massively deceive us only as far as the propensity for religion is concerned? This is especially pressing if we keep in mind that once intelligence is let in the door, it gets, in Rescher's words, the "run of the house," and becomes a catalyst for further development simply because intelligence is, as it were, developmentally self-energizing (111). To this important point I will return after an analysis of contemporary evolutionary epistemology.

Biological accounts of the origins of human intelligence and rationality can therefore effectively explain the origins and development of mental operations, but they cannot make their experiential character intelligible. What Rescher argued earlier in another context can now tentatively be suggested for the emergence of religion and religious faith: the *existence* of mental functions that lead to the creation of epistemic values like meaning and purpose can certainly be explained in terms of evolutionary principles (as can the propensities for religion and religious faith), but their *qualitative nature* is nevertheless something that can be adequately comprehended only "from within," from a performer's rather than an observer's perspective (cf. 122f.). What this implies is that we cannot in any way reduce the "inner dimension" of intentionality, purpose, faith, and meaning — always embedded in broader cultural contexts

— to an evolutionary account of physical processes. Biological evolution tells us how human minds arise and come to acquire their talents and capacities, but what we do with them is explained only by cultural evolution. Similarly, biology can explain the emergence of the human mind and of that unique ability we call rationality, but the ways in which we use this ability for rational thought lie beyond the scope of biology and of evolutionary explanations. A Darwinian account of the development of human rationality does leave open the possibility of a more complex understanding of notions like purpose and meaning, and therefore what we call religion or religious faith. If in fact there are limitations to evolutionary explanations, then a Darwinian account of the origin of mind cannot exhaust the understanding of human consciousness, and of traits like intentionality and purpose, because intrinsically different issues are at stake here. An acceptance of the biological origins of human rationality should leave ample scope for the development of meaning, values, and purpose in the broader cultural domain of our thought and action (cf. 126).

B. *Human Uniqueness and Hominid Evolution*

As for actual human origins, scientists are now arguing that molecular evidence indicates that the hominid group was established about 5 million to 6 million years ago, although the earliest putative hominid fossil (a small fragment of a cranium) is just 5 million years old. Indeed, the evidence is extremely fragmentary until we reach a little in excess of 3.5 million years ago: the jaw fragments and famous footprint trail at Laetoli, Tanzania. The record begins to improve substantially with material from the Hadar region in Ethiopia, the Lake Turkana sites in northern Kenya, Olduvai Gorge in Tanzania, and various famous South African sites like the Swartkrans and Sterkfontein caves. It is significant that virtually all hominid fossil remains that date earlier than about 1 million years ago have been found in Africa (cf. Lewin 1993: 15ff.).

The primary hominid adaptation, in the sense of a true evolutionary innovation that established the group, and that today is of supreme importance in discussions about human uniqueness, was *bipedalism.* Bipedality was most probably an adaptation for efficient locomotion. The first hominid species might well have been hominid only in the way it stood and moved. However, in the first known hominid species, *Australopithecus afarensis,* dated to 3.75 million years ago, the dentition already differs from that of the ape. It is humanlike to the extent of displaying relatively small canines, a thick enamel layer, and cheek teeth better designed for grinding tough material than for dealing with fleshy fruit (24). The overall appearance of the head is apelike, but the fossilized leg and pelvic bones indicate a strong adaptation to upright walking, although this creature was very much a bipedal ape, though not completely so.[8] After this a pronounced second shift occurred. This novel adaptation can be described as a large-brained, small cheek-toothed, bipedal ape, the true beginning of the genus *Homo*. The earliest known species to follow this adaptation was *Homo habilis*, the oldest fossils of which are close to 2 million years old. *Homo erectus* followed, beginning about 1.7 million years ago. The new anatomy probably involved a dietary shift that included meat. With the emergence of *Homo*, the hominid group was at its most densely branched, and at this time at least three species coexisted (cf. 28).

From the limited amount of skeletal evidence available, there is no question that by 2 million years ago all hominids were fully capable bipeds: the overall shape of the pelvis, the angle of the thigh bone, and the platform structure of the feet attest to that. One of the most spectacular discoveries of the century was a 1.6-million-year-old *Homo erectus* youth from west of Lake Turkana, the so-called *Turkana Boy*. Although powerfully muscled, this creature was tall and slender, having shed all apelike proportions, and the newly evolved, slender build was clearly an adaptation to greater activity, including the ability to be an effective runner (cf. 28). After about 1.5 million years ago, the two types of hominid adaptation coexisted, and after that a new trend was developing: australopithecines were becoming extinct, with the extreme version *(Australopithecus boisei)* persisting the longest. Most anthropologists would argue that by about 1 million years ago, only one species of hominid existed in Africa: *Homo erectus,* the species that eventually expanded into the lower latitudes of the Old World.

About half a million years ago there began to appear hominids that bore *Homo erectus* features together with certain modern ones, including expanded brain size. This new form of hominid, specimens of which have been found in Africa, Europe, and Asia, is generally known as "archaic *sapiens*."

---

8. Until about 2 million years ago, all hominid species followed this basic pattern: they were small-brained, large cheek-toothed, bipedal apes, but the curvature of the hand and foot bones was not pronounced, as far as can be determined. Lewin puts it well: "By this time adaptive radiation had clearly moved the bipedal ape away from an apelike diet, exploiting a much wider range of plant foods. In some species the adaptation to processing tough plant foods was extreme, the molars becoming enormous and the anterior teeth tiny. *Australopithecus robustus* and *Australopithecus boisei* are two examples of this pattern, and both display the bony keel along the top of the head. A less extreme variant was *Australopithecus africanus*" (Lewin 1993: 25).

The use of this term indicates an uncertainty by anthropologists as to the status of these individuals: they were neither *Homo erectus* nor *Homo sapiens,* but may have been a transitional form between the two (cf. 29). The term "archaic *sapiens*" is more a descriptive shorthand than a formal classification. The crucial problem for paleoanthropologists, however, was the following: *What exactly was the evolutionary trajectory along which our ancestors eventually became modern?* And was it a steady, gradual, accumulative process, or a relatively sudden, late transformation? The fossil record — as always, rather patchy — shows that *Homo habilis* may have appeared first around 2.5 million years ago, but the first good fossil evidence is a little less than 2 million years old. The transition from *habilis* to *erectus* involved a slight enlargement of the brain and a change in facial features, including the development of prominent ridges about the eyes, the browridges. Once this configuration evolved, it persisted throughout the history of the *Homo* lineage and can clearly be seen as a stable adaptation (cf. 30).

With the origin of modern humans, however, there was a change in skeletal build, not so much in shape as in strength. *Homo erectus* bones are very much the same shape and size as those of *Homo sapiens,* but are more thickly buttressed. In other words, modern humans were physically active, like *Homo erectus,* but not quite as strong. At the same time, increase in brain size was quite prominent. To evolutionary biologists the trajectory of evolutionary change, *gradual* versus *punctual,* or *continuist* versus *discontinuist,* has been the subject of lively debate, and still dominates the discussion on human uniqueness. Those who favor gradual change see evolution as a continuous response to selection pressure. Those who emphasize sudden, punctuational change interspersed between periods of stasis argue that factors relating to evolutionary development may constrain evolutionary responses to selection pressure, so that change, when it comes, comes rapidly. The latter pattern, proposed in 1972 by Niles Eldredge and Stephen Jay Gould, is known as *punctuated equilibrium.* Lewin has argued persuasively that two decades of debate and empirical study clearly indicate that both punctuational and gradual modes of evolutionary change occur, though there are still differences of opinion as to their relative importance (cf. 31f.).

Importantly though, as *Homo erectus* expanded from Africa into the Old World, tool technology naturally went with it. It would be the evolution of language, however, and not just the development of technology, that would provide the evolutionary foundation upon which natural selection would build the bigger brain. In fact, some scholars believe that spoken language reaches back to the beginning of the *Homo* lineage and was the prime cause of brain expansion (cf. 32). This position obviously supports the gradualist evolution of language capacities, and contrasts with the punctualist view that language capacity was the defining element in the biological shift to modern humans, and happened late in this evolutionary process. This strikingly reveals how different scholars may place different interpretations on the same evidence because of their differing theoretical preconceptions. But what are the dominant interpretations of human evolution today? Two of the strongest contenders are the so-called *Out of Africa hypothesis* and the *Multiregional Evolution hypothesis.*

We can come to terms with these very different theories more easily if we first look briefly at the arrival of the Upper Paleolithic in western Europe. About 40,000 years ago the long-established and relatively limited flake technology of the Middle Paleolithic was suddenly replaced by an exquisitely refined and rapidly evolving blade technology of the Upper Paleolithic, which also included extensive use of bone and antler as raw material. In addition, evidence of body ornamentation began to emerge, as did spectacular artistic expression on cave walls. In Lewin's striking words, the Upper Paleolithic people, modern humans, had apparently burst on the scene with dramatic effect, leaving the less refined Middle Paleolithic people behind (cf. 66). If, however, the origin of modern humans is the real issue, one may have to go back much further in history. The archeological signal in Europe 40,000 years ago is strong and clear, although it almost certainly indicates an event in the history of modern humans that relates not so much to human origins as to what it means to be *human* in the modern sense of the word. But when talking about the *origins* of modern humans, we do have to be careful not to express a too Eurocentric archeological point of view.

Radiocarbon dating strongly suggests that the Upper Paleolithic period lasted from about 45,000 to 10,000 years ago. The Upper Paleolithic in western Europe was the period of fully anatomically human people, the period of *Homo sapiens,* or the so-called Cro-Magnons, no different from ourselves, people who had the same bodies and brains that we do. The period that preceded the Upper Paleolithic in western Europe, the Middle Paleolithic, was characterized by the presence of *Homo neanderthalensis.* The Neanderthals, much debated today for their alleged capacities or noncapacities, did not seem to make art, and clearly had a simpler "tool kit" of intellectual capacities. Various dating techniques show that the Middle Paleolithic period lasted from approximately 220,000 years ago to about 45,000 years ago. It was preceded by the Lower Paleolithic, which lasted from nearly 3 million years ago to about 220,000 years ago. The Lower Paleolithic was characterized by the presence of a number of hominids, including *Homo erectus* and *Homo habilis* (who made the first stone tools), whose fossils have been found in Africa (cf. Lewis-Williams 2002: 39f.).

During the Upper Paleolithic transition, which in western Europe lies between 45,000 and 35,000 years ago, the Neanderthals gave way to *Homo sapiens*, with the two forms living side by side, at least in some areas, for some thousands of years. This transition clearly was an immensely important period in the human story: it is during this time that human consciousness and intelligence emerged, and with it creative, artistic, and religious imagination. For this reason this important period is also called the Upper Paleolithic Revolution or the "Creative Explosion" (cf. Lewis-Williams 2002: 40). What clearly emerged in the Upper Paleolithic was a distinct morphological gulf between the Neanderthals and the Upper Paleolithic people. The most recent version of the Out of Africa hypothesis will pick up on this important issue and not require that Neanderthals evolved into Upper Paleolithic or Cro-Magnon people.

The difficult task of archeologists and paleoanthropologists has been made a little easier by the emergence of new specimens and better dates, and also the emergence of new techniques for comparing anatomy. What is important is that there seems to have been no genetic continuity between the archaic populations (including the Neanderthals) in Europe and the Near East, and the modern humans that eventually became established there. In other words, the early populations in that region of the world were not the ancestors of the people who lived there later (cf. Lewin 1993: 69). Outside of Europe the fossil evidence is scarce, but in Africa it was becoming apparent that certain specimens with modern human characteristics (such as fragments from the Klasies River Mount in South Africa, and Border Cave) were among the oldest anywhere in the world, in fact, most probably the oldest (cf. 69).

Uncertainties in dating these specimens have plagued their interpretation for years. New techniques such as thermoluminescence and electron spin resonance have been applied recently with some considerable success, however (cf. 70). Both techniques depend on natural radioactivity in the soil, which boosts electrons to higher energy levels in "target" materials such as flint or tooth enamel. The longer such material is buried, the greater will be the accumulation of boosted electrons, thus providing a measure of the passage of time since burial. The thermoluminescence technique measures the higher-energy electrons by the release of light that occurs when the target material is heated. Electron spin resonance detects the high-energy electrons more directly. As a result of new dates from these techniques, confidence is building that some of the early anatomically human species in southern Africa are close to 100,000 years old, making them contemporaries of Neanderthals in Europe and Asia. In this way the Out of Africa model (the notion that anatomically modern humans arose somewhere in sub-Saharan Africa) was firmly established, although only later would geneticists argue that modern humans from Africa spread out into the rest of the world, completely replacing all existing populations of premodern people (cf. 71ff.). On this view *two* migrations are in fact discerned: that of *Homo erectus*, about a million years ago, often referred to as Out of Africa 1, the original and still influential Darwinian view;[9] and a second, Out of Africa 2, beginning around 100,000 years ago, of modern human populations. Thus there seems to have been an early appearance of anatomically modern humans in Africa at least 100,000 years ago, followed over the next 70,000 years by a disappearance of archaic forms and the establishment of these modern forms in the rest of the world. Whether this change was the result of newly evolved language, superior technology, environmental factors, new forms of social organization, or sharper cognitive skills that gave *Homo sapiens* an edge over archaic *sapiens* people, is still being hotly debated.

In direct opposition to the Out of Africa hypothesis stands the Multiregional Evolution hypothesis. According to this model, *Homo sapiens* emerged throughout the Old World through gradual evolutionary change, the direct product of existing archaic populations. This view requires no population movements, nor is there any replacement of populations by evolutionarily advanced people. This model, however, is not as extreme as earlier versions of the unilinear hypothesis that envisioned complete isolation of geographically separate groups (races) stretching back as far as a million years, and that also implied a deep genetic division between living races. This model does argue for a degree of contact among different populations, promoting gene flow between them and effectively maintaining a network of evolutionary interconnections. Multiregional evolution does however argue that some of the features that distinguish major human groups such as Asians, Australian Aborigines, and Europeans evolved over a long period in the regions where they are still found today (cf. 73ff.). There remains an ultimate African source for all these groups, but this refers to the population expansion out of Africa of *Homo erectus*, at least a million years ago (Out of Africa 1). Regional differ-

9. Cf. Proctor 2003: 224 n. 26: Darwin's original Out of Africa 1 insight, according to which humans evolved in Africa and spread from there to other parts of the world, is still widely accepted by the scientific community.

ences began to develop at the far reaches of the population expansion throughout Africa, Asia, and Europe, laying down the typical racial characteristics that we all know today. The move from *Homo erectus* to archaic *sapiens* to *Homo sapiens* is then seen as occurring throughout the Old World with sufficient interaction among populations to maintain a rough contemporaneity. Regional characteristics were then maintained through a degree of isolation, while genetic cohesion was favored by a degree of gene flow. In this model there is clearly no significant mutation that produces a key innovation, such as implied by the Out of Africa 2 hypothesis.

A third and novel source of evidence would ultimately make an important difference in current paleoanthropological discussions, namely, the so-called *Mitochondrial Eve* and other genetic evidence (cf. 87ff.). Mitochondrial DNA analysis unequivocally supports the Out of Africa 2 hypothesis. In fact, molecular data pushed the hypothesis even further than its anthropological authors initially envisaged, by indicating a complete replacement of established archaic *sapiens* populations by incoming modern humans. The Out of Africa 2 hypothesis, all things considered, now outranks the Multiregional Evolution model (cf. 108ff.). Of special importance is the surprising lack of genetic variation among modern human populations. Most genetic variation among modern humans as a whole is accounted for by variation among individuals, not between populations. Such a pattern is clearly consistent with the Out of Africa 2 hypothesis, in which all modern humans derive from a single genetic pool, and which recognizes that all living humans have descended from a small group of Africans who lived around 100,000 to 200,000 years ago. These behaviorally modern humans are therefore relatively recent in a biological sense. The Out of Africa 2 scenario has risen to great prominence, not only because of its central idea of an "African Eve," but also through the clarity and simplicity of its opposition to the so-called multiregional hypothesis, based on the strength of its molecular methods, which cast doubts on a multiregional model that might presume deep and invidious racial distinctions (cf. Proctor 2003: 215).

Interestingly, in addition, both gradualists and scholars who have followed Gould and Eldredge's punctuated equilibrium model are now arguing for the recency hypothesis. Recency may not be the same as suddenness, but it has become as popular among Gouldians as among anti-Gouldians (cf. 215). And here the focus is on the dramatic so-called cultural big bang, the Upper Paleolithic revolution and the explosive growth of human creativity around 45,000 years ago. As will become clear in the fourth chapter, this cultural breakthrough gave us not only spectacular prehistoric imagery and representational "art," but also the first evidence of ornamentation, new and changing tool styles, and the first evidence of religion and possibly religious ritual (cf. Klein 1999: 512-17). If moral choices can play such an important shaping role within science, then it will come as no surprise that in our interdisciplinary attempts to understand human origins, the narratives of paleoanthropologists and other scientists may interweave with the specific moral choices of theologians working in their own disciplines. Whether this happens or not will clearly hinge on ideological and worldview choices. No wonder, then, that on the problem of human uniqueness, science and theology may at times conclude with stunningly conflicting perspectives: on the one hand, *Homo sapiens* can be seen, and has been seen for about 2,000 years in Christian theology, as created in "the image of God," both rationally and morally superior to all other creatures; on the other hand, in the wake of post–World War II horrors, *Homo sapiens* has also been described as a "mentally unbalanced predator" endowed with vigorous and destructive aggressive instincts (cf. Cartmill in de Waal 2003: 230).

I believe there is an important interdisciplinary way out of this very real dilemma, and that is by following the lead of the theory of traditions as developed in chapter 1, and asking about the origin of the problem of the evolution of human uniqueness within the context of the biological sciences. Here it becomes important to go back to the way Charles Darwin viewed this issue, then to ask what the canonical heart of this tradition was, and how it has since shaped views on human identity.

Charles Darwin on Human Uniqueness

Is our pursuit of some description or definition of human uniqueness a valid interdisciplinary research project, or are we victims of a rather arrogant form of species narcissism? There clearly seems to be something at least to our "commonsense" perception of human uniqueness; it is human beings, after all, who are reaching out to understand the immensity and complexity of our universe, the complexity of ourselves, of one another, and even of God. Also, there does seem to be a distinctly higher level of complexity and organization, and a richness of experience, that occurs in humans more than anywhere else, or in anything else, in our universe, at least as far as we can tell.

In fact, this is true not only of our everyday conceptions of ourselves. In an unparalleled focus on what it means to be human, a large number of the sciences now are not only building on commonsense perceptions of human uniqueness, but also seem to be invading some of the most traditional theological territories. Christian theologians, like Christians everywhere, tradition-ally believe that there is something absolutely unique about being human, pre-cisely because humans are believed to be created in the image of God, as Genesis 1:26-28 so clearly states. However, sciences like evolutionary biology and genetics, studies in artificial intelligence and robotics, neuroscience, cog-nitive science, cognitive psychology, and evolutionary epistemology (to name just a few) are all now directly challenging any unnuanced notion(s) of human uniqueness, and by implication, therefore, this traditional Christian doctrine of the *imago Dei.*

The troublesome question is, how should theology respond to the way the sciences are challenging, and even deconstructing, the notion of human uniqueness? Would any Christian theology that ventures forth bravely into in-terdisciplinary dialogue still be able to maintain, for instance, that there is some deeper, divine purpose to being human, and by implication then also to human evolution? Would Christian theology be able to argue that a cosmic process producing intelligent persons is what one would expect if God is intel-ligent and personal (cf. Barbour 2002: 56f.)? My answer to these and related questions will unfold against the background of the brief theory of traditions developed in chapter 1. I believe the history of ideas of theological reflection shows that theological traditions have always been extremely sensitive to the culture(s) in which they are embedded. I will suggest that we get at this prob-lem by looking at how theological traditions, specifically the doctrine of the *imago Dei,* evolve and respond to cultural pressure. In this specific case study on human uniqueness, we will attempt to facilitate a transversal intersection of various voices as theology goes into conversation with the sciences of paleo-anthropology and archeology. What kind of dialogue will result, and what kind of challenges will be revealed, if we happen to uncover some common concerns, some overlapping interests between these very diverse reasoning strategies? For Christian theology the question will undoubtedly be: How much of a heart, a canon or unchanging identity, does the notion of the *imago Dei* have? And how much of the distinctiveness of this canon, as embedded in the rich galaxy of meaning of this historical doctrine, is protected by its own gravitational pull, its core Christian identity? How much of this core identity might be open and receptive to cultural pressure? And if this core notion of human uniqueness in theology does turn out to be somewhat fluid and chang-ing, what would be the limits and boundaries that this galaxy of meaning would allow? Finally, and maybe most importantly, is this process of pursuing the intelligibility and integrity of the doctrine of the *imago Dei* helped, or hin-dered, by the ever increasing volume of voices from the sciences?

In my first chapter the argument was made that a postfoundationalist approach to interdisciplinary conversation will always emphasize how the contextual and pragmatic nature of different forms of rational inquiry will reveal important epistemological overlaps between the natural sciences and other modes of intellectual reflection such as theology. In this way I argued against promoting an already existing universal rationality that assumes a common, shared rationality for all, but I also argued against the reduction of human rationality to mere local contexts. Instead, I argued for a transversal rationality that honors the universal intent of all human rationality, thereby enabling a cognitive parity between various and diverse fields of inquiry (cf. van Huyssteen 1999: 172, 176). This move toward a richer notion of embodied rationality enabled us to interpret multiple aspects of our experience, thus opening up a place for the theological voice in interdisciplinary discourse. The fact that our beliefs are always anchored in interpreted experience, and our rationally compelling experiences are always already embedded in even broader networks of disciplinary beliefs, also necessitated a theory of traditions that revealed how dependent our research is on reliable traditions, even as we critically reevaluate them in an ongoing process of interdisciplinary reflection.

At this point, then, we turn to science and ask: How is our perception of the origins and heart of a *scientific* tradition hindered or helped by this theory of traditions? My argument now will be, first, that Charles Darwin's conception of human identity and human nature still functions as the canonical core of the ongoing discourse on human evolution, and that, second, the powerful galaxy of meaning of this canonical core of Darwin's views on human distinctiveness, maybe more than ever before, is shaping our views on the evolution of human cognition. The epistemic implications of these views are most clearly represented today in contemporary evolutionary epistemology. Finally, teasing out the interesting evolutionary route from Darwin to evolutionary epistemology will set the interdisciplinary stage, so to speak, and create the necessary transversal space, for a dialogue between theology and the sciences on human uniqueness.

The canonical core of Darwin's views on human identity is most clearly spelled out in his major work, *The Descent of Man, and Selection in Relation to Sex* (1981). The dominant theme of this groundbreaking work, as the title clearly states, is that humans descended from other animals and were not specially created. In it, however, Darwin does more than just marshal evidence for the continuity between humans and other animals. The book also represents his attempt to study intelligence as a central figure of adaptive change, and to study it in that organism in which he saw it as most prominent, the human being (cf. Bonner and May 1981: viii). The idea that evolution by natural selection could account for the origin of humans was taken up quickly by others as a direct result of Darwin's new ideas, notably by T. H. Huxley in his *Evidence as to Man's Place in Nature* (1863), and by the German biologist Haeckel, who even invented an imaginary missing link between ape and human, which he called *Pithecanthropus alalus,* the speechless ape-man. It is especially interesting to look back on the dissenting voice of Alfred R. Wallace, who published an essay in 1864 saying that the bodily structure of humans could be entirely accounted for by natural selection, but that the "mind of man" was created by some "higher intelligence" (cf. Bonner and May 1981: xi). In this sense one could say that the real controversy surrounding the relation between humans and other animals in Darwin's time was essentially already a problem of science versus religion (cf. xxi).

In their introduction to the *Descent of Man,* John Tyler Bonner and Robert M. May make the interesting observation that in today's ongoing and lively debate about human evolution, the idea that the unique place of humans in evolutionary history was guaranteed by divine intervention (as Wallace believed) has now been replaced by an argument that is interestingly similar in structure to that of Wallace and other nineteenth-century religionists: the human body is indeed a biological structure, clearly descended from the apes, but human culture, which stems from the extraordinary and unique minds of humans, is on a new, higher hierarchical level of its own, and biology cannot tell us much about this level (cf. xxii). We will focus on this issue again later, but we seem to have here the conviction that human culture and civilization is so special, and so different from anything in the animal world, that it can be analyzed only on its own terms. Thus the quest for human uniqueness, in spite of sociobiology and recent studies in animal behavior that challenge such a notion, lives on, and human attributes like consciousness, moral awareness, language, and other mental qualities, as in Darwin's time, are still seen to separate "man from the beasts" (cf. xxii). Darwin himself, of course, argued for an unbroken continuum between animals and humans and saw the difference between them as one of degree only.

How does Darwin argue for this continuity and for the peculiar identity of humans? Insofar as "it has often and confidently been asserted, that man's origins can never be known," Darwin warns us that "ignorance more frequently begets confidence than does knowledge: it is those who know little, and not those who know too much, who so positively assert that this or that problem will never be solved by science" (Darwin 1981: 3). From this Darwin famously argued that humans are the codescendants with other species of some ancient, lower, and extinct form — a conclusion he did not see as spectacularly new, especially in light of the earlier work of Lamarck, and the German naturalist Haeckel, and others (cf. 4f.). Darwin's acceptance of the shared descent between humans and animals is strikingly illustrated in the following statement: "But the time will before long come when it will be thought wonderful, that naturalists, who were well acquainted with the comparative structure of man and other mammals, should have believed that each was the work of a separate act of creation" (33).

For Darwin "there is no fundamental difference between man and the higher mammals in their mental facilities" (35). In the second chapter of *The Descent of Man,* Darwin discusses how animals and humans share emotions, attention, and even memories (cf. 34ff.). He saw *imagination,* however, as one of the "highest prerogatives of man," although animals admittedly possess some power of imagination (for instance, they clearly have vivid dreams). By this faculty the human being unites, independently of the will, former images and ideas, and thus creates brilliant and novel results (45).

Darwin was very clear, however, about what really seemed to be unique about humans: "Of all the faculties of the human mind, it will, I presume, be admitted that *Reason* stands at the summit" (46). Darwin does carefully show that even here there is continuity, and it must be admitted that animals do possess some power of reason: animals are often seen to pause, deliberate, and resolve, although it is often difficult to distinguish between the power of reason and that of instinct (46). Therefore, instead of being separated from the higher animals by their mental faculties as an inseparable barrier, it was clear for Darwin that animals possessed the same faculties of imitation, attention, memory, imagination, and reason, though in very different degrees (cf. 49).

Darwin does agree that the language faculty has justly been considered one of the chief distinctions between humans and the lower animals (cf. 53ff.). Animals of various kinds, however, do communicate by expressing cries of many kinds. Articulate language certainly is peculiar to humans, although even humans, in common with the lower animals, use inarticulate cries to express meaning, aided by gestures and the movement of the muscles of the face (54). For Darwin language undoubtedly has as its origin the imitation and modification, aided by signs and gestures, of various natural sounds, the voices of other animals, and the instinctive cries of humans themselves. And as the human voice was used more and more, also in interaction with the superior development of the human brain, the vocal organs would have been strengthened and perfected through the principle of the inherited effects of use, and this would have reacted on the power of speech (cf. 57). Furthermore, Darwin concluded, the "extremely complex and regular construction of many barbarous languages, is no proof that they owe their origin to a special act of creation" (62).

As for discussing and possibly pinpointing the issue of human uniqueness, Darwin was rather skeptical: "It would be useless to attempt discussing these high faculties, which, according to several recent writers, make the sole and complete distinction between man and the brutes, for hardly two authors agree in their definitions" (62).

These special faculties could certainly not have developed fully in humans until their mental powers had advanced to a high standard, and this implies the use of a perfect language. Darwin goes on to show that even the sense of beauty is not exclusive to humankind, as the way female birds respond to the often spectacular beauty of the males of the species clearly shows (cf. 63-65). But how about humankind's sense of *religion*?

For Darwin there certainly was no clear evidence that humankind was "aboriginally endowed with the ennobling belief in the existence of an Omnipotent God" (65). In fact, Darwin saw ample evidence that many humans had no idea of one or more gods. Should a person choose to include under the term "religion" the belief in unseen or spiritual agencies, however, everything is different, for this kind of belief seems to be almost universal, especially for what Darwin referred to as "the less civilized races" (cf. 65). This belief clearly arose in the following way: as soon as the important faculties of the imagination, wonder, curiosity, together with some power of reasoning had begun to develop, the human being would have naturally craved to understand what was happening around him or her, and would have "vaguely speculated on his own existence" (65). Furthermore, the belief in spiritual agencies would easily pass into the belief in the existence of one or more gods. "The feeling of religious devotion is a highly complex one, consisting of live, complete submission to an exalted and mysterious superior, a strong sense of dependence, fear, reverence, gratitude, hope for the future, and perhaps other elements. No being could experience so complex an emotion until advanced in his intellectual and moral facilities to at least a moderately high level" (68).

Darwin was clear that these facilities tracked the biology of earlier stages of life, for instance in the state of mind of the dog that deeply loves its master. Finally, only as our reasoning powers develop and we move beyond religious superstitions do we realize what an infinite debt of gratitude we owe to the improvement of our reason, to science, and to (what Darwin called) our accumulated knowledge (cf. 69).

In his discussion of allegedly unique human traits, Darwin finally focuses on moral sense or conscience, which he clearly regarded as the most important characteristic to be discussed regarding differences between humans and lower animals. This moral sense "is summed up in that short but imperious word *ought*, so full of high significance. It is the most noble of all the attributes of man, leading him without a moment's hesitation to risk his life for that of a fellow-creature" (70). Moreover, Darwin wanted to do something that he felt other scholars at the time had not done: discuss the issue of moral awareness exclusively from the perspective of natural history (cf. 71). In opting for this approach Darwin was convinced that the study of the lower animals could throw light "on one of the highest psychical faculties of man" (71).

What Darwin basically proposed is that any animal, well endowed with social instincts, could in principle acquire a moral sense or conscience, "at least as soon as its intellectual powers had become as well developed, as in man" (72). This could happen for various reasons: social instincts would lead animals to take pleasure in the society of their fellows; or the evolution of the power of language would lead to a situation where the wishes of the members of the same community could be distinctly expressed, and the common opinion of how each member ought to act for the public good would naturally become the guide for all action, and thus be reinforced and strengthened by habit, and obedience to the wishes and judgment of the community (cf. 72f.). This does not mean that social animals would become exactly like humans. It means that just as various animals have developed a sense of beauty, so they might have a sense of right and wrong. A certain class of animal actions certainly points to this, such as what looks like a manifestation of conscience in dogs, and obedience in baboons (cf. 73ff.), but for Darwin a moral being clearly is one who is capable of comparing past and future actions or motives, and approving or disapproving of them (cf. 88).

These views now get Darwin very close to identifying human uniqueness: "We have no reason to suppose that any of the lower animals have this capacity; therefore when a monkey faces danger to rescue its comrade, or takes charge of an orphan monkey, we do not call its conduct moral. But in the case of man, who alone can with certainty be ranked as a moral being, actions of a certain class are called moral, whether performed deliberately after a struggle with opposing motives, or from the effects of slowly-gained habit, or impulsively through instinct" (89).

A clear pattern of Darwin's views on human nature and identity has now emerged, and I believe that the canonical core of his views on human identity can be summarized as follows.

1. For Darwin there can be no doubt that the difference between the mind of the "lowest man" and that of the highest animal is immense (cf. 104).

2. Nevertheless, the difference in mind between humankind and the higher animals, great as it is, is certainly one of degree and not of kind (cf. 104).

3. If we do want to maintain that certain abilities, such as self-consciousness, intelligence and abstraction, moral awareness, etc., are peculiar to humans, it might very well be that these are the incidental results of other highly advanced intellectual faculties. And these faculties again are mainly the result of the continued use of a highly developed language. Darwin also intriguingly speaks of "the half-art and half-instinct of language" that still bears the stamp of its own gradual evolution (cf. 105).

4. As for a religious sensibility, Darwin clearly argued that "the ennobling belief in God is not universal with man; and the belief in active spiritual agencies naturally follows from his other mental powers" (105). Darwin thus denied that the idea of God is innate or instinctive in humans, although he did concede that a belief in spiritual agencies seemed to be universal in all humans, and is directly connected to human imagination (cf. 394f.).

5. It is, however, specifically our moral sense that perhaps best defines "the highest distinction between man and the lower animals" (106). Also, a natural explanation for the foundation of morality suffices; thanks to humankind's social instincts, with the aid of its intellectual powers and the effect of habit, both the mental and moral faculties of humankind gradually evolved (cf. 105f.).

6. We humans, then, are "unique" as a result of, as Darwin himself would put it, the evolution of our superior intellectual facilities and our social habits. Our "wonderful advancement," however, is ultimately dependent on the unique evolution of language (cf. 137). In the final sentence of the final page of *The Descent of Man*, Darwin speaks of our "God-like intellect," but also of the fact that in our bodies we still bear the indelible stamp of our lowly (animal) origins (cf. 404f.).

For Darwin the many superior attributes we have (including the fact and advantages of bipedalism; cf. 140ff.), and the wonderful inventions this has led to, are all the direct result of the evolutionary development of human cognition, our powers of observation, memory, curiosity, imagination, reason, and moral sense (cf. 138). For this reason Alfred R. Wallace's position on human uniqueness continued to perplex him: "I cannot, therefore, understand how it is that Mr. Wallace maintains that 'natural selection could only have endowed the savage with a brain a little superior to that of an ape'" (137). Darwin had no doubt that the case for that distinct place of humans in the process of evolution had been clearly argued: "I have now endeavoured to shew that some of the most distinctive characters of man have in all probability been acquired, either directly, or more commonly indirectly, through natural selection" (151).

In this way Darwin not only wanted to aid in overthrowing the dogma of what he called "separate creations," and with that the idea that each species had been purposely created (cf. 151). He also established the core Darwinian view, in different shapes and forms, that to this day defines the canon of the ongoing tradition of the theory of human evolution.

My developing argument in this chapter is that Darwin's conception of human identity and human nature, with its very specific focus on the evolution of human cognition, still functions as the canonical core of the ongoing discourse on human evolution, and that the powerful galaxy of meaning of this canonical core of Darwin's views on human identity, maybe more than ever before, is shaping our current views on the evolution of human cognition. The epistemic implications of these views on cognition are most clearly represented today in contemporary evolutionary epistemology. Finally, teasing out the interesting evolutionary route from Darwin to contemporary evolutionary epistemology will set the interdisciplinary stage, so to speak; create the necessary transversal space for a dialogue between theology and the sciences on human uniqueness; and in doing so will provide us with specific transversal links to paleoanthropology. In fact, it is precisely evolutionary epistemology's focus on the evolution of human cognition that will reveal cognition as the mediator between biology and culture, and in so doing provide paleoanthropology with a crucial role in the wider debate about human origins (cf. Lake 1992: 268).

Evolutionary Epistemology and Human Uniqueness

In *Duet or Duel? Theology and Science in a Postmodern World* (1998), I argued that when we take the evolution of human cognition seriously, we quickly realize that even theological reflection is radically shaped by the ongoing influence of its traditions, and therefore by its social, historical, and cultural embeddedness, and is also definitively shaped by the deeper biological roots of human rationality. And yet it is precisely the voice of evolutionary epistemology that has been almost totally neglected by contemporary theology. The very basic assumption of evolutionary epistemology is that we humans, like all other living beings, result from evolutionary processes and that, consequently, our mental capacities are constrained and shaped by the mechanisms of biological evolution. Clearly, if all human knowledge is in some sense or another shaped by its biological roots, then the study of evolution should be of extreme importance, not only for an understanding of the phenomenon of human knowledge (cf. van Huyssteen 1999: 4f.), but also for what we might want to define as the uniquely human aspect of this process. It may turn out that Darwin was right: the evolution of human cognition ties us directly to the animal world, even as it also sets us radically apart from our animal ancestors.

Various philosophers have argued that it should not surprise us that as human beings we could have acquired intelligence, enabling us to secure information and survive in the world. Nicholas Rescher has correctly argued that human intelligence naturally arises through evolutionary processes precisely because it provides one very effective means of survival. Human rationality, seen in the broadest sense of the word as our particular human ability to cope intelligently with an intelligible world, can therefore be seen as conducive to human survival, which makes the explanation of our cognitive resources fundamentally Darwinian (cf. Rescher 1992: 3f.). The implication for a sense of human uniqueness seems to be clear; the imperative to understand is something altogether basic for *Homo sapiens*. In fact, we cannot function, let alone thrive, without reliable information of the world around us.

The phrase "evolutionary epistemology" was introduced into academic discourse mainly by Donald T. Campbell (cf. 1974: 47-89).[10] All evolutionary epistemologists would agree that the theory of evolution in essence is a theory of knowledge precisely because the process of evolution is the principal provider of the organization of living things and their adaptations. Therefore, if adaptations of all sorts are forms of knowledge, then evolution itself is the process by which knowledge is achieved. Evolution thus turns out to be more than just the "origin of species"; it is a much richer process that leads to, among other things, the thoughts and ideas that we have in our heads, and thus to knowledge as commonly understood (cf. Plotkin 1993: 21). Evolutionary epistemologists would take the evolutionary explanation for human intelligence much further, however, and would also locate the discipline of evolutionary

10. "An evolutionary epistemology would be at minimum an epistemology taking cognizance of . . . man's status as a product of biological and social evolution. In the present essay it is also argued that evolution — even in its biological aspects — is a knowledge process, and that the natural-selection paradigm for such knowledge increments can be generalized to other epistemic activities, such as learning, thought, and science. Such an epistemology has been neglected in the dominant philosophical traditions" (Campbell 1974: 47).

epistemology within the broader context of the history of contemporary epistemology and philosophy in general.[11]

Already in *Duet or Duel?* I argued that evolutionary epistemology might offer us a postfoundationalist way out of the problem of having to choose between foundationalist and nonfoundationalist approaches to human rationality. The shift away from positivism, and from all varieties of foundationalism, remains significant, especially in our attempts to critically define human uniqueness. Evolutionary epistemology highlights the fallibilist nature of our rational judgments and explains that there is progress in the growth of knowledge, but does not assess such progress as an increase in the accuracy of depiction or as an increase in the certainty of what we know. Evolutionary epistemology also reveals extreme nonfoundationalist and antirealist positions as forms of epistemic narcissism, because it makes us think that knowledge is not a relation between the knower and what is known, but a narcissistic reflection of our own image in our society, or of our society in us (cf. Munz 1985: 7). Biology suggests that our power of abstraction and our ability or faculty for having distinct expectations are the result of natural selection, that our cognitive apparatus is adaptive, and that the whole of our knowledge consists of theories that are embodied proposals (i.e., organisms) or disembodied proposals (i.e., conscious theories) made to the environment. On this evolutionary epistemological point of view it is possible to see knowledge as an interactive relationship between an embodied knower and something that is known, and one can now actually cease to identify the knower with a subjective, mental, inner consciousness and the known with the rest of the outside, "real" world (cf.

11. Peter Munz, in a fascinating account of the failure of positivism to account for the growth of human knowledge, has argued persuasively that positivism was unable to account for major paradigm shifts, like the shift from Newtonian mechanics to general relativity. More importantly, however, positivism could not explain how in philosophy of science itself there were occurring two different and competing moves away from positivistic forms of philosophy of science. One move was toward Wittgenstein's philosophy of language games and Thomas Kuhn's theory of paradigms. The other was toward Karl Popper's evolutionary epistemology and the important injection of Darwinism into philosophy (cf. Munz 1985: 4). Thus we found earlier in the twentieth century not only the kind of growth of knowledge for which positivism had no explanation, but also the emergence of metascientific theories that positivism could never anticipate (cf. 5). Wittgenstein, and later Polanyi and Kuhn, as is well known, led the way to the acknowledgment of the theory ladenness and paradigm dependency of all knowledge, and showed that we have the knowledge we have because it is based on the prevailing norms of speech habits of a given community of speakers. At the same time, however, we also find the beginnings of what soon would become known as *evolutionary epistemology*, which sought to explain the knowledge we have precisely as an extension of the adaptive evolutionary process that began millions of years ago (cf. 6).

12). For the rich and complex development of evolutionary epistemology, the works of Karl Popper, Konrad Lorenz, and Donald Campbell have been seminal. In this discussion I will briefly focus on Popper, and then specifically evaluate the contributions of Henry Plotkin and Franz Wuketits to our understanding of the evolution of human cognition.

The general thrust of Popper's thought links up directly with Darwinism, and with Darwin's momentous insight that evolution proceeds by natural selection. In Darwinism there is no teleology, no goal, no instruction, and the relentless elimination of nonfitting organisms produces better results than any design or plan could have produced. Popper's immense contribution to our knowledge of human knowledge lies in his extension of Darwinian evolution to knowledge in general. As is well known, Darwin's theory of natural selection as the motor of evolution finds its complement in Popper's theory that we do not gain knowledge by induction, but propose theories to the environment, which subsequently falsifies most of these theories and thus provides the criteria for the retention of those it fails to falsify. We are able to know, and we are here, because of the relentless elimination of all those pieces of knowledge or organisms that are not a fit to the environment; Popper's views of the acquisition of knowledge, then, like Darwinian evolution, very specifically focused on a negative process of elimination and falsification (cf. Munz 1985: 15).

Although Popper began by examining the growth of knowledge in science, ultimately his inquiry developed into an evolutionary epistemology in which the growth of knowledge is seen as continuous with biological and cultural evolution. Popper famously did not accept Darwinism as a testable scientific theory because of its near tautological nature (the best fitted to survive will survive) and its lack of testability (cf. Stanesby 1988: 54f.). However, it did provide a "metaphysical research program," also for evolutionary epistemology, and for understanding the emergence of human consciousness as something irreducible to any lower level of existence, a comparatively rapid evolution that has enabled the human mind to become to a large extent emancipated from dependence on its immediate environment. It is exactly this phase of cultural evolution, where language plays a crucial and defining role, that provides the link between the human being's biological and cultural evolution. Through language, then, humans have created a body of objective knowledge. And this knowledge is an evolutionary artifact that enables us humans to profit from the trials and errors of our ancestors (cf. Popper 1998: 126ff.). Derek Stanesby puts it well: from this point on, human evolution is the evolution of knowledge (cf. Stanesby 1988: 59, 65). It is especially through Popper's views, then, that evolutionary epistemology became a metatheory of science (cf. Wuketits 1990: 45ff.).

The link of Darwinism to Popperian philosophy of science clearly signaled the arrival of a new conception of rationality. For Darwin human rationality consisted in the making of mistakes, in comparing mistakes, and in retention of those forms of replication that are the most adaptive fits to the environment. Thus, already Darwin introduced us to the idea that rationality does not consist in the avoidance of error, but in the occurrence of error and the elimination of error by natural selection. We can therefore say that on this view rationality consists in making bold guesses and conjectures and then subjecting them to ruthless criticism. "In this view of rationality, the path of reason is not a secure path which leads from certainty to certainty; rather, it is a wild display of the imagination, the products of which are scrutinised by criticism" (Munz 1985: 16).

The rational person, on this view, is not the person who controls his or her imagination, but the person who subjects the products of his or her imagination to criticism. In this novel view of rationality the rational person learns through his or her mistakes, without necessarily implying any teleology in this process of falsification.

A. Evolutionary Epistemology as Embodied Epistemology

An even richer development in contemporary evolutionary epistemology is found in the interdisciplinary work of Henry Plotkin and Franz Wuketits. Plotkin links together evolutionary biology, psychology, and philosophy, and thus presents a new science of knowledge that picks up exactly on the canonical core of Darwin's notion of human distinctiveness by tracing an unbreakable link between instinct and our human ability to know. Since our ability to know our world depends primarily on what we call intelligence, Plotkin wants to understand intelligence as an extension of instinct. Thus emerges what is at the heart of the argument of evolutionary epistemology: the idea that the capacity for knowledge is deeply rooted in our biology and, in a special sense, is shared by all living things. Ultimately he develops an interactionist epistemology that refines the notion of knowledge as a kind of "incorporation of the world" by the knower (cf. Plotkin 1993: ix). In doing so he carefully explores the question why we, both as a species and as individuals, ever came to know anything about our world and ourselves.

Plotkin develops his argument by pointing to the central role of the apparent "fit," or matching, of all living things to the features and conditions of their world. This "matching" can be seen as a result of the way living creatures somehow incorporate into themselves those aspects of the world that they actually interact with. It is these amazing and often beautiful forms of harmonious interaction between living things and the world that we call *adaptations* (cf. xiii). Adaptations have formed the most powerful foci of the study of biology and are formed by a very long process of interaction between the environment and successions of organisms that make up lineages of organisms extending over thousands, hundreds of thousands, and millions of years. They are the crucial determinants of whether organisms survive and reproduce or not. The study of adaptations is not only central to biology, distinguishing it from other sciences, but is also rather central to the human sciences because we human beings are, in Plotkin's words, a finely woven cloth of adaptations, as are all other animals (cf. xiv). But what is the exact connection between these adaptations and knowledge? Plotkin gives two closely related answers to this, which reveal his stance as a contemporary evolutionary epistemologist. First, the human capacity to gain and impart knowledge is itself an adaptation, or a set of adaptations. In developing this point Plotkin correctly argues that we would simply not understand human rationality and intelligence, or human communication and culture, until we understood how these seemingly "unnatural" attributes are deeply rooted in biology. In his words, they are the special adaptations that make us special (xiv). Our amazing ability to know our world with sophisticated intelligence is an unarguable product of human evolution, and there are no substantive alternative ways of understanding our extraordinary capacity for knowledge. Second, adaptations, in an evolutionary sense, are themselves knowledge, forms of "incorporations" of the world into the structure and organization of living things. In a sense, then, all adaptations are forms of biological knowledge, and knowledge as we usually understand it would then be a special case of biological knowledge (cf. xv). The structure of all organisms is therefore directly informed by their environment, and that is why adaptations, by definition, almost always work. Rescher's well-known argument for a direct correlation between intelligence and intelligibility clearly resonates with Plotkin's argument that human knowledge in much the same way conforms to the relational quality or fit that all adaptations have (cf. Rescher 1988: 176ff.).

Plotkin's most valuable contribution to the question of the evolution of human cognition, however, is found in the way he develops the relationship between instinct and rationality. Plotkin considers instinct as unlearned and unthinking adaptive behavior, a kind of behavior that is knowledge in the same way that any form of camouflaging coloration of an insect constitutes knowledge of its surroundings. In this sense adaptations are instances of knowledge, and human knowledge is a special kind of adaptation (cf. Plotkin 1993: 117ff.). Plotkin goes further and importantly links human knowledge and its adaptive development to the concept of *epigenesis*, the notion that development is not a simple and inevitable unfolding or growing process, but instead is highly variable within certain constrained limits. This variability results from a cascade of immensely complex interactions between genes, developing features of the organism, and the environment in which development occurs (cf. 247). Epigenesis tells us something very important: although adaptive structures and even behavior in part have genetic causes, they are not necessarily invariant in form and may sometimes vary quite widely as a result of the environment in which the development occurs (cf. 124). Plotkin goes even further and talks about this kind of "developmental plasticity" as in itself an adaptive device and as such a knowledge-gaining device.

What emerges here is that knowledge and its development clearly have two components, one *internal* and the other *external*. These developmental processes and the genes that initiate and participate in them should therefore be seen as the integrated way in which all knowledge is gained. Human knowledge, then, is a product of this complicated, interactive, and dynamic developmental process. This has direct consequences for the way we should view the distinction between behavior that occurs without thought, which is not affected by the processes of learning and memory, and behavior that is affected by such processes. The first we may call *instinct,* the second *rationality,* which as such is the product of reason, intelligence, learning, and memory (cf. 125ff.). Darwin had a lot to say about instinct in *Origin of Species,* but little about rationality. All that changed with *The Descent of Man,* which was very much concerned with the "mental powers of man." Darwin, however, made little attempt to consider the function of rationality or what the relationship might be between rational powers and instinct. For Darwin much of human rational powers begin in the rational abilities of "lower" animals, and Darwin's main message, according to Plotkin, was that, extraordinary as human rational powers may seem, they do not set human beings apart from their fellow creatures (cf. 127). On this view rationality is an attribute we share with other species, from whom we have inherited it. So, for Darwin, also for instincts or rational abilities, in the end it was the *continuity* between species that had to be stressed.

For Plotkin it would obviously be tremendously important to refute the false assumption that instinctive behaviors should conceptually be kept apart from behaviors that arise through processes of learning and intelligence. It does seem important initially, however, to keep apart instinctive and learned behaviors if we really want to understand why rationality evolved in the first place. Knowledge, as commonly understood, is a product of the processes of rationality, and if we are to understand what knowledge is, we must understand the origins and nature of rationality (cf. 130). What this means is that we must be able to answer the question why *all* behavior isn't instinctive. This is the same as asking why rationality evolved at all. This question — why all behavior is not instinctive and why therefore rational powers evolved in the first place — concerns the ultimate causes of rationality. Remarkably, this issue attracted little attention until quite recently. Darwin never put the question in this form, and for a hundred years almost none of his followers did either. Today, however, we realize that rationality, intelligence, thought, and the ability to learn and remember are never just open-ended activities but are, rather, constrained, limited, and directed by genetically determined instinctive behavior. Learning, for instance, is primed by our genes, and in this sense instincts are more basic and reliable than our rational abilities. And yet, in spite of this, rationality did evolve. This must mean that the balance has shifted from favoring instincts to favoring intelligence and rationality. To understand this we have to ask what the *limitations* of instinct are, and how rationality makes up for these limitations (cf. 133).

On this view human knowledge is just one kind of a more widely defined biological knowledge, and science itself is then a very special case of this human knowledge. Along these lines Plotkin wants to develop a *universal Darwinism* where evolution not only produces all transformations in time, but even our brains are to be seen as "Darwin machines," and the way we gather knowledge as another form of universal Darwinism (cf. xvii). For human knowledge this will have huge ramifications: *all animals, including our species, that can learn and think are born knowing implicitly what they must learn and think about.* In humans this touches directly the way we come to master language, recognize significant people in our lives, reason, react emotionally, and share knowledge through culture. Plotkin thus correctly presupposes that our extraordinary capacity for gaining and communicating knowledge must always be understood, first, as a part of our nature, and only then as an issue in nurture (cf. xviii).

This prompts Plotkin, in a very interesting argument, to warn against a too simple solution to the old "nature-nurture problem." We often hear that the regular dichotomies that characterize the nature-nurture distinction, like the instinct-intelligence and the genes-experience dichotomies, are false dichotomies. Behind this argument lies the strong conviction that all genes require an environment to develop. Since development requires both genes and experience, however, every trait acquired by the process of evolution requires both nature and nurture. For Plotkin this argument is fundamentally wrong because the solution it provides is "horizontal" in that it still maintains the separation of genes, on the one side, and the role of the environment, on the other side, with some kind of developmental integration in the middle (cf. 164). This kind of "interactionism" does not match up to the "verticalism" that Plotkin wants to propose: intelligence, as a "secondary heuristic," is subsumed under, embedded in, and enclosed by instinct as the "primary heuristic." The horizontal components of interactionism, the internal and external causes, still remain present at both levels. The really important issue, however, is the comprehensive concept that includes all the levels of the hierarchy, and that concept, Plotkin argues, is *adaptation,* and therefore *knowledge* (164). On this view intelligence, nested under development and under the genetic process, does not allow any claims that something is caused by either nature only or nurture only. This kind of language and imagery is wrong because intelligence *is* an adaptation, and the required integration can only be achieved vertically, not horizontally (164). What Plotkin, therefore, wants to refute is the doctrine of "separate determination," i.e., that behavior controlled by *rationality and intelligence* should be viewed as quite separate from the kind of behavior controlled by *biology and instinct.* But these two can never be separated in this way, and rationality and intelligence should rather be seen as extensions of instinct that cannot be separated from it. On this more embodied, holistic view of human knowledge, instinct can indeed be called the mother of intelligence (cf. 165). Importantly, because of its nesting under the primary heuristic, namely, its embeddedness in instinct, intelligence cannot easily and automatically be equated across species. The intelligence of each and every species is directly tied to its genes, and human intelligence too can be understood only in context of human genes. This, then, is Plotkin's argument for *species-typical intelligence,* or *domain-specific intelligence* (cf. 165, 237).

On this view the causes of intelligent behavior are still clearly divided between genes and development, on the one hand, and the capacity to gain knowledge and act on it through creative intelligence, on the other. The causes of intelligent behavior, however, can never be reduced exclusively to genetics, because intelligence then would only passively reflect the nature of those instructional processes and the circumstances of the world that are imposed on it. On this view intelligence would become merely a rather extended but entirely deterministic device understandable entirely in terms of genetic determinism, on the one hand, and the history of the organism-environment interaction on the other. What saves intelligent behavior from such a reductionist account is the presence of selectional processes in the mechanism of intelligence itself (cf. 176). Genetic reductionism can never be invoked, then, as an explanation of the behavior and evolution of beings that are intelligent. And this is of course especially true for *Homo sapiens:* once intelligence has evolved in a species, self-conscious brains have a causal force equal to that of genes. For evolutionary theory to be complete regarding humans, intelligent behavior has to be included, and so does a very peculiar feature of intelligent behavior, namely, *culture* (cf. 177). Plotkin's view on cultural evolution here clearly emerges in opposition to the faulty Lamarckian view that wanted to include behavior as one of the causes of evolution. Plotkin plausibly argues that behavior becomes causally significant in the process of evolution only if the behavior itself is driven by intelligence, itself an evolutionary process involving unpredictable variant generation.

Finally Plotkin wants to make the point that culture should be seen as a third-level heuristic, another form of "Darwinian machine," and hence another means of gaining knowledge of the world based on evolutionary processes (cf. 225). On this view human cognition is revealed as the mediator between biology and culture, and human knowledge emerges as a web of relationships that matches different levels of the hierarchy with different features of the world. The leitmotiv of Plotkin's argument thus is clear: knowledge as commonly understood is a special kind of adaptation, and all adaptations should be seen as forms of knowledge. This clearly means that knowledge is a complex set of relationships between genes and past selection pressures, between genetically guided developmental pathways and the conditions under which development occurs, and between a part of the consequent phenotypic organization and specific features of environmental order (cf. 228). This is also what Plotkin means when he argues that it would be human conceit to think that knowledge is something both unique to our species and located only in our heads. He clearly maintains the canonical core of Darwin's notion of human evolution and sees knowledge as a pervasive characteristic of all life, exemplified by all adaptations in all living creatures (cf. 229).

This now implies that the natural-selection paradigm can be generalized (or rather, metaphorized) to include some of our most crucial and broadly conceived epistemic activities such as learning, thinking, imagination, science, and even religion (cf. van Huyssteen 1998: 140ff.). Franz Wuketits explains this move very well by saying that any living system is an information-processing system. Echoing Plotkin, he argues that information processing should be seen as a general and typical characteristic of all organic nature. We as humans do indeed exhibit the most sophisticated type of gathering and preserving of information about certain important aspects of reality, and this information processing too can certainly be explained as an evolutionary phenomenon (cf. Wuketits 1990: 4). Also, therefore, especially for theologians the following should be true: if we take the theory of evolution seriously, we should take evolutionary epistemology seriously. This will of course mean that, precisely as far as our cognitive abilities go, we will ultimately be challenged to discern whether the theory of evolution by natural selection can be seen as adequate for explaining the moral, aesthetic, and religious dimensions of human knowledge and rationality.

Wuketits, while arguing positively that evolutionary epistemology is not destined to "destroy" religion, unfortunately does not grasp how religion and religious knowledge can and should be integrated into this broader, comprehensive epistemology. He ultimately avoids this difficult issue, but at the same time correctly states that the main purpose of this kind of (evolutionary) epistemology is still to meet the need for a comprehensive approach to the problem of knowledge that will take us beyond the limitations of traditional disciplinary boundaries. He thus importantly argues that evolutionary epistemology, rightly understood, has to lead to an *interdisciplinary* account of our epistemic activities (cf. 4ff.). As I see it, not only philosophy but also theology will benefit greatly by incorporating scientific research regarding ourselves as conscious "knowing subjects" and our genetic makeup, anatomy, and physiological abilities into this comprehensive paradigm. In this broader sense evolutionary epistemology becomes not just an interesting option for theology, but a necessary one, as it opens up a way for re-visioning our study of human knowledge by giving us a fresh epistemological look at interdisciplinary issues.

Wuketits has correctly called the emergence of evolutionary epistemology a truly Copernican turn in philosophical epistemology (cf. 6). He calls his own version of evolutionary epistemology *a systems theory of evolution*, which argues for an approach based on, but also going beyond, Darwin's theory of evolution by natural selection. For this reason he turns to conceptions that specifically go beyond Darwin. He wants to argue, first, that evolution is determined not only by external selection but also by *intraorganismic constraints* on evolutionary change, and second, that the flow of biological information is not unidirectional but bidirectional (cf. 22). Wuketits now unfolds his systems-theoretical approach to evolution that first of all implies that environmental change by itself does not suffice as an "evolutionary pressure." In fact, organic evolution exhibits patterns of its own dynamics that effectively go beyond environmental constraints. It indeed seems plausible that evolution is influenced by structures and functions of the organism itself. Wuketits thus proposes a flow of cause and effect in two directions and concludes that in the process of evolution by natural selection, organism and environment are codetermined (cf. 23).

As with Henry Plotkin's interpretation of the evolution of cognition, Wuketits argues that the evolution of life results from internal (intraorganismic) as well as external (environmental) selection. These internal and external forms of selection work together to build the systems conditions of evolutionary change. And in this sense the systems theory of evolution is a revised and extended version of the classical theory of natural selection. The point is that for Wuketits evolution is an "open process" and in fact creates its own laws a posteriori (cf. 24). At the biological level the principles of organic evolution apply fully to the human species; humans, like other organisms, result from organic evolution caused by genetic recombination, mutations, environmental selection, and intraorganismic (internal) constraints. But the story of our species is virtually the story of the growth of the human brain; the ascendance of humankind is due to the preeminence of the brain and not only to bodily prowess (cf. 27ff.). And as we have seen, one thing that makes our species unique in the animal kingdom is our capacity for culture. The crucial question then becomes: Can evolution be extended to culture? Can culture be explained in terms of organic evolution?

Wuketits deals with this extremely important issue by arguing in the following way. First he stresses the thesis that human culture relies on specific brain structures and functions: it is a result of the peculiar development of the human brain and can be regarded as the most sophisticated expression of the brain's power. The main problem that now arises, of course, is whether biological explanations of the brain will be enough to explain the particular paths of our cultural evolution. Wuketits wants to show that it is unwarranted to reduce the complex patterns of human culture to the principle of organic evolution alone (cf. 30f.). Cultural evolution exhibits its own characteristics and systems conditions. Certainly the emergence of culture has been propelled by organic forces, but, however crucial, the biological approach will not be sufficient to explain the complex and peculiar paths of cultural evolution. Clearly, the principles of biological evolution can therefore not be translated directly into explanations for culture, religion, or society.

On the one hand, then, organic evolution — particularly the evolution of the human brain — can be seen as the basis of cultural evolution. On the other hand, the latter can never be reduced to the former. Cultural evolution requires explanations beyond the biological theory of evolution in its strictest sense. Therefore the term "evolution" applies to both the development of the organic world, from unicellular organisms to humans, and the development of culture. Or in Wuketits's words, biology offers the necessary conditions of culture, but it does not offer the sufficient conditions (cf. 31). Cultural evolution (including the evolution of ideas, scientific theories, and religious worldviews) cannot be reduced to biological evolution. Echoing Plotkin, Wuketits argues that the study of human evolution can therefore clarify the preconditions of cultural evolution, but it cannot explain the particular paths a culture will take (cf. 33).

Closely following Plotkin's views on the relationship between instinct and intelligence, one of the central claims of evolutionary epistemology can now be restated as follows: not only has evolution produced cognitive phenomena, but evolution itself can be described as a cognition process or, more precisely, a cognition-gaining process. The thesis that evolution is a cognition process obviously implies that knowledge, and the ability for gaining knowledge, is an information-processing procedure that would increase an organism's fitness. And already at the prerational level information processing is characterized as a cycle of experience and expectation. So, when we come to the uniqueness of human knowledge, this process of knowledge gaining as information processing turns out to be a universal characteristic of all living beings, which again confirms that human rationality has a biological basis, and as such can be seen only as embodied rationality. And precisely because human rationality everywhere shares deeply in this biological basis, human rationality as such reveals a universal intent that links together all our diverse and complex epistemic activities.

It is thus that evolutionary epistemology opens our eyes to the kind of comprehensive, integrative epistemology that does not have to emerge as a modernist metanarrative for human knowledge. And if our various and diverse cognitive activities are linked together by the evolutionary resources of an embodied human rationality, then evolutionary epistemology succeeds, on an intellectual level, in revealing a space for true interdisciplinary reflection, the kind of epistemic context that would be a safe and friendly space for the ongoing conversation between reasoning strategies as diverse as theology and science (cf. van Huyssteen 1998: 149).

The biological resources of human rationality are enhanced, furthermore, by Wuketits's very helpful distinction between three levels of information processing that we all share as human beings:

1. The *genetic level,* which refers to the development (ontogenesis) of living systems. Genetic information can be transmitted from one generation to the next only by inheritance. Wuketits importantly stresses, however, that this kind of information processing is not to be confused with any kind of cognitive structure (cf. 1990: 55).
2. The *preconscious level,* where all animals require an information-processing system like the nervous system.
3. The *conscious level:* which is the level of rational knowledge that comes with consciousness. At the conscious level we encounter a level of intellectual information processing and self-awareness that represents the particular state of human consciousness (55).

What we see, then, in the work of both Plotkin and Wuketits is a hierarchy of information processing and also a hierarchy of cognition processing in the living world, with human rational knowledge emerging as the most sophisticated type of information processing to which we have access (cf. 55). Wuketits correctly stresses that information processing, and therefore the gaining of knowledge, is an important biofunction and indeed can be regarded as a characteristic that increases the organism's fitness in a Darwinian sense. It is hard to imagine Darwin *not* agreeing with the formula "without cognition no survival" (cf. 58). And in the process of the evolution of knowledge, our interpreted experiences and expectations have a central role to play. I argued earlier that we as humans relate to our worlds through interpreted experience only, that our expectations are therefore always based on our interpreted experiences, and that these experiences in turn lead to new expectations (cf. van Huyssteen 1999). Evolutionary epistemology helps us to understand this connection as a result of long-term evolutionary processes. Changing experiences will obviously lead to changed expectations, and the cycle of experience and expectation in the individual is thus clearly the result of evolution.

In a broader sense the members of a population or a species have often managed to have the same experiences again and again. In the long run these experiences will be genetically stabilized so that any member of the species will be equipped with what we might call "innate expectations," i.e., a "program" of expectations based on the accumulation of the experiences of a species. In this sense, again, evolution can be described as a universal learning process or cognition process (cf. Wuketits 1990: 68). The evolution of living systems thus implies an overall increase in cognitive abilities. In Wuketits's words: "Thus we may argue, their evolutionary history has prepared animals to grasp at least some important aspects of the world — those aspects of the world that have been experienced by thousands of individuals during a long line of evolutionary processes" (68).

This process, also called *phylogenetical memorizing*, explains why kittens snarl at dogs, why many of us almost irrationally fear snakes, and so on. And although genetic information itself does not have the character of cognitive structures, such structures certainly can be transmitted genetically. An organism gathers experience through its sense organs and processes this experience through the nervous system. The development of these sense organs and the nervous system in an individual animal depends on specific genetic coding, and in this sense the peculiarity of experiencing aspects of the world is indeed genetically programmed (cf. 68f.).

Evolutionary epistemology thus reveals the process of evolution as a holistic, embodied belief-gaining process, a process that in humans, too, is shaped preconsciously. All our beliefs, and also, I would argue, our religious beliefs, thus have distant evolutionary origins and were established by mechanisms working reliably in the world of our ancestors, even if on a broader cultural level our beliefs and convictions are not explained by biological origins. This is the reason that the theory of evolution by natural selection cannot offer an adequate explanation for beliefs that far transcend their biological origins. It does, however, again underline the fact that cognition is a general characteristic of all living beings, and that human rationality can be fully understood only if its biological roots are understood. This is true even if human rationality at some important point transcends these biological roots. Precisely this important point has also been argued by Plotkin, who has shown that there is a clear evolutionary link between evolution on a genetic level and the evolution of our intellectual and rational capacities — a relationship, however, that can never be seen to be deterministic in any reductionist sense of the word (cf. Plotkin 1993: 176ff.). Our rational capacities are thus part of the process of evolution by natural selection, but cannot be understood deterministically. In Plotkin's work, as became clear earlier, this has led to the bold suggestion that the evolution of human rationality becomes comprehensible only if on this level we reject the deterministic influence of genes (cf. also Hančil 1999: 17).

Peter Munz also gives an excellent interpretation of how not only so-called "a priori knowledge" but also "expectations of regularities in nature" are deeply embedded in the embodied, biological origins of human rationality. Someone like Immanuel Kant could not explain this, but the biological explanation shows that precisely the emergence of a priori expectations is shaped by the process of evolution. Taking seriously the biological origins of rationality should therefore finally convince us that there are regularities in nature, and that the a priori expectations we have of them are justified, and that their presence in our minds or nervous systems can be explained by the theory of evolution by natural selection (cf. Munz 1985: 29f.). The biology of evolution and regularities in nature thus go together very closely; without such regularities there could be no adaptation by natural selection because every organism that is adapted is actually adapted to the *regularities* of its environment. In this sense one could state that evolution by natural selection and adaptation would not be possible, let alone conceivable, without the assumption that there really are regularities in nature. It is precisely the organisms that have the right expectations that are selected, are "adapted," and ultimately survive. In this sense one could also argue that we would not be here if there were no regularities in nature (cf. 30).

The more important question, however, is how it has happened that we know about these regularities and have expectations about them. The answer cannot be found in observation only, because without specific expectations we would not even be able to recognize these regularities. For Munz this is a strong argument for the plausibility of evolutionary epistemology, with its focus on the origin and evolution of our cognitive abilities, our powers of abstraction, and the ability to have expectations; evolutionary epistemology is a successful program precisely because of its wider scope and problem-solving ability (cf. 34). As for our powers of abstraction (i.e., our ability to recognize differences and similarities, and the capacity to abstract from individual observations and experience), this specific critical intellectual ability would not have been there if we did not have expectations of similarities and differences. Precisely this power to abstract is the result of evolution and the most basic form of adaptation to the environment (cf. 37).

Evolutionary epistemologists are therefore clearly making the strong point that there is a congruence between "external" and "internal" reality, i.e., between nature and embodied cognition. Any organism's perception of certain aspects of reality is conducted by genetically programmed dispositions that are the results of evolutionary learning processes/experiences. Every species thus lives in its own cognitive niche. The human cognitive niche is constrained by the experiences of our phylogenetic ancestors, so that we have developed organs for the perception of only those aspects of reality of which it was imperative for our species to take account (cf. Wuketits 1990: 101). On this view it is very clear why an exclusively adaptationist view, according to which cognition (like all other biofunctions) has been just an adaptation to given, external structures, does not suffice as an explanation of the relations between cognition and reality. In the place of this, evolutionary epistemologists like

Wuketits, Plotkin, and Munz are clearly suggesting a more holistic, systems-theoretical approach that makes clear that organisms are active systems and problem solvers, and that their cognitive capacities are constrained by their own architecture and not just formed by external requirements. From this follows the important conclusion, then, that there are indeed regularities in nature, and that those life-forms that are adapted (in the sense that they behave as if they expected the regularities in their environment) have a better chance of survival than those that are not. In this sense, through the process of natural selection and through heredity, the ability to have expectations of regularities is phylogenetically a posteriori: organisms "learn" from the environment, not as individuals but as a species, precisely because only those that are adapted to expecting the regularities survive and reproduce (cf. Munz 1985: 34f.). Ontogenetically the expectation of regularities is, however, a priori, and each individual and organism, as Karl Popper already argued (cf. Popper 1998: 47ff.), is born with "expectations" in place, which is why Wuketits could refer to our "phylogenetic memories." Munz phrases it well: in this way the regularities that exist in nature are eventually transferred by the organisms that survive by natural selection, and in this way the "order of nature becomes the nature of order" (cf. Munz 1985: 35).

At this point it is important to realize that two distinct programs seem to be emerging in contemporary forms of evolutionary epistemology. One is the attempt to account for the cognitive mechanisms in animals and humans by extension of the biological theory of evolution to those structures of living systems that are the biological substrates of cognition, like brains, nervous systems, and sense organs (cf. Wuketits 1990: 5). The other is the attempt to explain human culture, including science and religion, in terms of evolution, but not in a sociobiological sense. Both programs are interrelated, but they help us make an important distinction between two levels of evolutionary epistemology: that of a natural history or *biology of knowledge,* and that of evolutionary epistemology as a *metatheory* for explaining the development of ideas, scientific theories, religious views, and theological models in terms of evolutionary models. Whether we approach this kind of metatheory from a religious, a specifically theistic, or a resolutely naturalistic viewpoint will of course determine whether there will be a legitimate place for religion and theological convictions in it. So, again we see that the choice is never just *for* science and *against* religion (or vice versa), but for or against certain comprehensive worldviews from which religion and science will emerge with either a significant level of compatibility or locked in serious conflict.

Implicit in the evolutionary explanation for the origins of human rationality is also evolutionary epistemology's crucial contribution to what, in the first chapter, I called a *postfoundationalist epistemology*. Evolutionary epistemology breaks through the traditional modernist subject-object polarization and reveals the basis for a postfoundationalist epistemology by showing:

> first, that all cognition is a function of active embodied systems that relationally interact with their environments;
>
> second, that cognitive capacities are the result of these interactions between organisms and their environments, and these interactions have a long evolutionary history; and
>
> third, that cognition is a process to be described not as an endless, accumulative chain of adaptations building on one certain foundation, but rather as a complex interactive process in which we move beyond our biological roots without ever losing touch with them (cf. also Wuketits 1990: 96). It is therefore clear that human knowledge is indeed constrained by biological factors, but that it also very much depends on cultural determinants. Precisely in an interactionist epistemology the cultural and biological determinants of knowledge would therefore be directly interrelated, and precisely for this reason our rational knowledge also goes beyond what is genetically fixed.

Our ongoing focus on human evolution helps us to realize that the acquisition of rational knowledge is the latest achievement in the long chain of the evolution of information processing, and in this sense it can be seen as an amazing evolutionary novelty. Wuketits sees the emergence of human rationality as such an epoch-making event that it has given evolution a new direction (cf. 108). This leads him to the perception that, because of their rationality, humans are unique among all living organisms. However, many who would otherwise agree with evolution sometimes hold that humans are unique because human rationality can be seen "supernaturally" (almost like Darwin's contemporary, Alfred R. Wallace) as "God's work" (cf. 108). In direct opposition to this so-called supernaturalist view, Wuketits argues that from the point of view of evolutionary theory there really is nothing suprarational about our species, although our unique status in nature certainly is uncontestable. But Wuketits wants to explain the emergence of life on earth, and of human consciousness and rationality, without resorting to any supernatural or "mystical factor" (108). But God, supranaturalism, and mysticism are all indiscriminatingly lumped together.

Wuketits's basic argument, however, that human rationality and its emergence might be ascribed to a principle of integration and self-organization, i.e., a self-organizing brain providing for ever more and increasingly complex properties, does not have to be in conflict with religion, and with faith in God, at all (cf. van Huyssteen 1998: 153f.). He is certainly right in that if self-organization can be regarded as one of the most important characteristics of our universe, then human rationality may also be traced back to the formation or self-organization of brain mechanisms (cf. Wuketits 1990: 109). His main point, therefore, is that the brain alone is responsible even for the most sophisticated mental phenomena and that these phenomena are to be explained as particular expressions or properties of the brain. From an evolutionary point of view, then, the human brain is an information-processing system that has increased fitness in the human race, since information processing generally has a certain survival value for any organism.

The simple message of evolutionary epistemology thus is that the information that living organisms get from the world is sufficiently accurate to allow for survival and reproduction. The world in which we live seems to be intelligible, at least to some extent, and the structures of this world do not seem to exist only in our imaginations. As epistemological fallibilists, we also know that even in science it is never possible to arrive at a complete and definitive understanding of reality. But precisely the epistemological ramifications of the process of evolution allow us to hypothesize about the reality of our world. In this sense most evolutionary epistemologists would claim that the ability to arrive at a relatively accurate understanding of our world is in a sense the ultimate survival value (cf. Hančil 1999: 21). Human rationality, when defined as our ongoing quest for the deepest and most accurate level of understanding of reality, thus emerges from the heart of the process of evolution by natural selection.

B. Evolutionary Epistemology and Religion

A theological redescription of the ramifications of evolutionary epistemology for human rationality and culture at this point will clearly reveal the possibility of exciting links between theology and the sciences. If our genes do not completely determine our culture and our rational abilities, then it might be as reasonable to expect that our genes, our cultures, and our rational abilities may also *not* completely determine the enduring and pervasive need of humans for symbolic thought, metaphysics, and ultimately life-transforming religious faith. This certainly is no argument for the existence of God, but it is an argument for the rationality of religious belief in terms of a nondeterministic theory of evolution by natural selection.

Even Wuketits would argue that the need for metaphysics, and metaphysical explanations, seems to be a general characteristic of all humans (cf. Wuketits 1990: 117). In all human societies we find metaphysical systems that include notions of life after death, the "other" world, etc. As to how this is to be explained, Wuketits gives a surprisingly clear answer: metaphysical belief is a result of particular interactions between early humans and their external world and thus results from specific life conditions in prehistoric times (cf. 118). My question, however, would be: Why should we, so suddenly and only at this point — the development of this metaphysical aspect of our cultural evolution — so completely distrust the phylogenetic memory of our ancestors? In the end, this version of evolutionary epistemology reveals a naturalist and reductionist prejudice against the very human propensity for religion, as well as a very reductionist view of religious faith itself.

This prejudice is clearly revealed when not only a reductionist view of religion, but also an inadequate and scientistic view of human rationality, suddenly surfaces. Wuketits now defines metaphysics as the human need for metaphysical beliefs, including religion and all other *irrational* worldviews (cf. 118). He skims over this superficial treatment of religion by remarking that human beings, as rational beings, are obviously also capable of irrationality, for ever since the emergence of rationality humans have invented irrational belief systems whenever they lacked "rational" explanations and then projected them onto their worlds. Here Wuketits follows rather blindly the popular idea of anthropomorphistic projection, in which humans cannot imagine that there might be processes in the universe without any purpose, so they invented the purposeful universe according to their own teleological actions. He seems to want to explain away all religion by seeing all metaphysics as constrained by emotions and illusions reaching back to the living conditions of prehistoric humankind (cf. 118).

But if metaphysical beliefs, on this naturalistic view at least, do not really tell us anything about "first causes" or "last purposes" (i.e., God), but rather about our own *propensity* for such beliefs (cf. 118), why did they evolve on such a massive scale in the history of our species? And why should we distrust our phylogenetic memories *only* on this point? Obviously, my arguments here should not be seen as an attempt to reconstruct an argument for the existence of God, but only as making a case for the naturalness of religion, the meaningfulness, necessity, and rationality of religious belief, which cannot just be explained away rather naively by seeing it as "invented" earlier by our sometimes wildly irrational species. I would much rather argue that Darwin (cf. 1981: 68f.) was right in his thesis that metaphysical and religious beliefs in humans were related to evolutionary processes, and therefore could be explained like any other mental capacity in the light of human evolution. But this would make invalid, or help to explain away, only exotically abstract and excessively constructivist notions of the divine, or God, not necessarily theistic belief as such, and certainly not the phenomenon of religion. Wuketits is right on one important point, and that is that our "marvelous brain" has indeed given rise to creative imagination (cf. 1990: 119), but why would not his earlier relational, or interactionist, epistemological viewpoint (his "systems approach" that even included a weak form of hypothetical realism; cf. 73ff.) now again be plausible in at least explaining the existence of religion(s) too? Wuketits finally has no "rational" reason for explaining away religion as "irrational." A resolute naturalism, thinly disguising a rather positivistic view of natural scientific rationality, not only seems to be inconsistent with his argument that biology can never fully explain culture, but also blinds him to what may lie beyond a strictly scientific rationality and may be only tentatively caught through imagination and religious faith.

Anthony O'Hear (2002) has argued along similar lines that while the theory of evolution is successful in explaining the development of the natural world in general, it is of more limited value when applied to humans, human nature, and culture. It is rather puzzling that O'Hear, in his evaluative critique of evolutionary epistemology, never mentions or discusses the seminal contributions of Plotkin and Wuketits to this debate (cf. 50-83), and therefore fails to see how closely these evolutionary epistemologists relate to his own views on these matters. O'Hear has argued that because of distinctive traits like consciousness, self-awareness, reflectiveness, and rationality, we humans indeed have the ability to take on cognitive goals and ideals that cannot be justified in terms of survival-promotion or reproductive advantage only. Therefore our very typical quest for rational knowledge, but also our moral sensibilities, and our aesthetic appreciation of beauty, while all deriving in important ways from our biological nature, once they emerge cannot be analyzed only in biological or evolutionary terms. In this sense, then, we clearly transcend our biological origins, and in doing so have the ability to transcend what is given us in both biology and culture. O'Hear, however, wants to push even further: we are prisoners neither of our genes nor of the ideas we encounter as we each make our personal and individual way through life (vii).

Closely resembling the evolutionary epistemologists we have encountered in this chapter, O'Hear sees as the first and most distinctive trait for humanness the fact that we human beings are *material* beings. We are, first of all, embodied beings, and as such what we do and think and feel is conditioned by our embodiment. In this sense, in our very typical ways of obtaining knowledge, in our capacity for moral awareness, and in our perceptions of beauty (and, I would add, in our ancient religious disposition), our materiality is presupposed and exploited in a host of ways. Our senses condition and filter our knowledge in interaction with the material world, and our moral, aesthetic (and religious) sensibilities are intimately linked to the perception of visible, tactile, and aural things, and to embodied suffering and pain due to the limitations of our very embodied physicality (1f.). It is this materiality of our existence that has come about through the process of biological evolution.

It is also obvious, however, that in various respects we do not behave like most material objects. We are self-aware and critically conscious, and although degrees of consciousness are something we share with a fairly large proportion of the animal world, we have developed the ability, over and above mere consciousness, to think critically and discursively, to be aware that we are so thinking, and to express these thoughts in language and other symbolic forms. In fact, the presence of thought, reflection, and self-conscious belief is what makes human activity different from the conscious but unreflective behavior of nonlinguistic animals (cf. 49). It is precisely in the expression and development of this propensity for self-conscious thought that we have produced a large diversity of cultural artifacts and systems by which our lives are surrounded, conditioned, and made meaningful. Our comparatively large and complex brains clearly play a crucial role in the production of thought and culture. Nevertheless, human thought and culture do exhibit certain important characteristics that are rare if not unique in the rest of nature (2f.). It is against this background that we have to look at the very human abilities for reflective knowledge, moral awareness, aesthetics, and, I would add, a propensity for religious awareness and religious belief. And it is these propensities of the human mind that cannot be explained by naturalistic evolutionary accounts of human nature and behavior only.

O'Hear does present us with an interesting and important perspective on religion. The inbuilt ambivalence of human reason, with its very specific limitations and at the same time its transcendence as a process, has the further ability of finding concrete expression (some would say fulfillment) in religion and religious belief (26f.). What this means for O'Hear is that there is in our very nature as self-conscious but finite beings an ontological tension that naturally expresses itself religiously, and comes close to what I have called the "naturalness of religion." Therefore religious awareness, with its intimations of human limitations and our natural disposition to try to overcome these limitations, mirrors very precisely our nature as reflective thinkers. In this sense religious belief does not simply understand and express the ambivalence of the limitations and transcendence of our rational abilities. It also sees our drive toward something transcending human powers as reflected in the fabric of the universe, a reality that is greater than, and transcends, empirical reality. Religious belief, therefore, implies that there is this transcendent aspect to reality, and that we humans are part of, and related to, this dimension of transcendence. For religious believers it will be natural to interpret the emergence of consciousness and self-consciousness as revelatory of something deep in the universe, something inexplicable by physics, something behind the material face of the world (cf. 27).

Like all evolutionary epistemologists, O'Hear takes seriously the fact that important epistemological conclusions can be drawn from the fact that we human beings are products of evolutionary development. While our activities, including all forms of our knowledge, are certainly rooted in our biological inheritance, as human beings operating in a human-cultural world we have taken on goals and activities whose aims and rationales cannot be explained in biological terms only (50). It is exactly on this point that O'Hear is very close to Plotkin and Wuketits. While evolutionary epistemology tells us that it clearly is biologically advantageous to have survival-promoting beliefs, human knowledge is also about more than survival-promoting beliefs. It is in this sense, when considering the nonadaptive aspects of our cognitive drives, that we can say that in human knowledge, in moral awareness, in aesthetic appreciation, and in religious awareness we transcend our biological origins. This perspective enables us to see human cognition as the mediator between biology and culture, and cultural evolution as requiring explanations beyond the biological theory of evolution. It is in this sense of the word that Wuketits could argue that biology offers the necessary conditions for culture, but not the sufficient conditions (cf. Wuketits 1990: 31). Also for O'Hear, the study of human evolution can clarify the preconditions of cultural evolution, but it cannot explain the particular paths that human culture will take through rational knowledge, moral awareness, aesthetic appreciation, and religious propensity. Evolutionary epistemology, therefore, clearly functions on two levels: that of a natural history or biology of knowledge, and that of a metatheory for explaining the development of ideas, scientific theories, religious views, and even theological models in terms of evolutionary models.

And as eventually we turn to notions of human uniqueness in paleoanthropology and in theology, maybe the most important lesson learned from evolutionary epistemology is that we are embodied in and interactive with the world, and taking this fact as a premise in our epistemology will pull us away from pure forms of idealism and antirealism, as well as from naive realism, which downplays our embodiment, and treat all our knowledge as the result of perceiving an already divided up and categorized world. O'Hear, when discussing this kind of embodied, interactive knowledge, concludes by making a truly strong postfoundationalist claim: "[T]here is no theory of the world, no knowledge which is not the result of interaction between organism and world, and which is not, in its classifications and conclusions, coloured by the interests and perspectives of the organism" (2002: 99).

Precisely because experience, and the experience of embodied living, is the basis of all our knowledge, our species' sensory knowledge and its knowledge by scientific inference cannot suddenly be seen as the only "rational" form of knowledge, with religious knowledge isolated as a type of knowledge gained only by "mere belief," and therefore irrational (cf. Wuketits 1990: 121). Amazingly this point of view is actually supported by Wuketits's next argument. If we should ask whether we are justified in speaking of cultural evolution as we do of biological evolution, the answer, as we saw in our discussion of Plotkin's work, should be yes. We are not only justified to do this, but it is necessary, since there is one common trait here: both organic and cultural evolution can be regarded as complex learning processes, with human cognition as the crucially important mediator between them. Culture can therefore be understood as the most sophisticated learning process requiring particular modes of explanation and a particular type of evolutionary epistemology that goes beyond strict Darwinism. Wuketits, therefore, correctly argues that although there are biological constraints on cultural evolution, culture is not reducible to biological entities. Cultural evolution indeed depends on specific biological processes, and our cultures therefore are part of a grandiose universal natural history, but cultural evolution, once it started, obeyed its own principles and gave human evolution an entirely new direction, even acting back on organic evolution (cf. 130f.). In chapter 4 we will see how this recognition that the evolution of human cognition functioned as a mediator between biological and cultural evolution will open up the exciting possibility of acknowledging the crucial role of paleoanthropology in the wider debate on human origins. Only through paleoanthropology and cognitive archeology will we be able to grasp something of the cognitive abilities of our remote ancestors by studying the cultural expressions of their amazing, symbolic minds.

Wuketits's arguments strongly support the contention that it would be a serious fallacy to use the principles of biological evolution to explain cultural evolution, let alone the evolution of religion. Certainly the necessary condition for the emergence of cultural evolution was biological evolution, and particularly the evolution of the human brain. Cultural evolution has channeled the creative human brain, and Wuketits himself has argued that although the human brain is the producer of all culture, this does not mean that the particular pathways of cultural evolution are prescribed by any single brain mechanism. Hence, cultural evolution has its own dynamics, going beyond the dynamics of biological, organic change. Exactly on this point evolutionary epistemology differs seriously from the genetic determinism of sociobiology. But for evolutionary epistemology to be truly nonreductionistic and nondeterministic, we should take seriously the argument, made even by Wuketits, that we humans are in a sense genetically disposed to religious and metaphysical beliefs (cf. 155, 199).

Holmes Rolston argued a similar point very clearly. In nature information travels intergenerationally through genes, while in culture information travels neurally, as people are educated into transmissible cultures. In nature the coping skills are coded on chromosomes. In culture the skills are coded in craftsmen's traditions, in technology manuals, or in religious rituals, texts, and traditions (cf. Rolston 1996: 69). This information transfer on a cultural level can be several orders of magnitude faster than on a genetic level, and can in fact leap over genetic lines. As human beings we have developed a great diversity of cultures, and each heritage is historically conditioned, perpetuated by language, and conventionally established precisely by using symbols with locally effective meanings. Therefore, while animals adapt to their niches, human beings adapt their ecosystems to their needs. For this reason animal and plant behavior are never determined by anthropological, political, technological, scientific, ethical, or religious factors, and in human evolution natural selection pressures are finally relaxed in the emergence of culture (cf. 69). From this it naturally follows that two of our most enduring, most meaningful, and most dominant cultural achievements, science and religion, are both products of this remarkable historical development; they are intimately entwined with the process of biological evolution, although ultimately not determined by it.

In his Gifford Lectures (1999) Rolston developed further the convincing argument against any easy reduction of religion and ethics to biology. In this specific argument he takes on both ultra-Darwinism and the kind of sociobiological orthodoxy that ultimately would want to "naturalize" not just science, but also ethics and religion. The particular focus of his book is the emergence of complex biodiversity through evolutionary history, with as its focal point the remarkable genesis of human beings with their capacities for science, ethics, and religion. The most crucial conceptual task of the book, however, is to relate cultural evolution to natural/organic evolution, and to account for the way values are created and transmitted in *both* natural and human cultural history. Rolston acknowledges that Darwinian biology is a brilliant achievement, all the more so when coupled with that of genetic and molecular biology. Biology has been less successful, however, in relating itself to culture (cf. Rolston 1999: xi). It is on this point that Rolston argues that there is a genuine novelty that emerges with culture, and that while it is important to see how biological phenomena give rise to culture, it is just as critical to realize how culture exceeds biology.

Rolston finds the "uniqueness" of our species in our remarkable ability to be conscious, self-aware, intelligent, and capable of rational decisions. Unlike other animals, we humans are not just what we are by nature, but we come into this world by nature quite unfinished and then become what we become through culture. As Rolston puts it, the products of culture are myriad — languages, rituals, tools, clothing, houses, computers, and rockets — and are directly tied to ideas, and the home of ideas is the human mind (cf. xii). Other higher animals may also have minds, but the human mind is the only mind that permits the building of complex transmissible cultures. Humans are indeed the only species that think about their ideas, that teach their ideas to the next generation, and that make creative ideological achievements that can be transmitted from generation to generation. Some of these most outstanding achievements of human culture are science, art, ethics, and religion, achievements that rightly could be called emerging phenomena in culture. Historically ethics, art, and religion have been present in every classical culture, oral or literate, but science — in its current form at least — is a relatively late arrival in literate cultures. And among these cultural achievements of our species, science, ethics, and religion are the principal carriers of value (cf. xii).

This argument is enhanced by what evolutionary epistemologists are arguing about objectivity, and about the realist quality of our experiences. Munz even believes that biology can "help" philosophy by providing the missing link in arguments about objectivity. He does this by carefully unpacking the way Popper's philosophy of science was embedded in Darwinian evolution. If we accept that we are here in the world, we must accept that the world is the sort of world that has brought about our existence. Our presence, therefore, is not only a guarantee of an objective reality as the result of which we are; it is also evidence of the fact that objective reality must be of a certain kind, for if it were different we would not be here (cf. Munz 1985: 237). Certainly for Popper, and for Munz, the theory of evolution by natural selection implies simply taking the presence of an objective world for granted. In this sense, as we have seen, evolutionary epistemologists speak of a "hypothetical realism"; the world we want to explore epistemically is the kind of world that has produced the sorts of beings who would want to explore it (cf. 238).

Implied in evolutionary epistemology's notion of hypothetical realism is that, instead of asking what kind of mind is required to know the world, we should rather ask what kind of world the world must have been to produce the sort of mind we have. The "realism" involved here is "hypothetical" because, since we have embodied minds, it is a reasonable hypothesis that there must be a real world that, by a process of evolutionary selection, has produced our minds (cf. 242). This hypothetical realism is a realism without correspondence theories, and without the kind of empiricism that would claim only sense experience as a foundation of all knowledge. Munz argues that Darwin also used the argument that one need not follow a plan to bring about the achievement of design (256). So, Darwin was not in the first place arguing against design; the sheer constraints of the environment on evolving organisms were bound to produce design. He did, however, attack the argument *from* design, i.e., the belief that since there was design in evolution, there must have been a plan, a divine providence. Evolutionary epistemologists have therefore been able to characterize evolution as a process that, though lacking intentionality and foresight, is nevertheless creative and productive of design (cf. 256).

Like our ancestors in the plant and higher animal kingdoms, we humans store the kind of *correct knowledge* that is conducive to our survival. In our prehuman ancestors this knowledge was stored in the gene pools of populations and was species-specific, so that each species had a different knowledge of the reality it lived in because it was a temporarily successful adaptation to a specific environment. In human beings this knowledge is partly stored in the gene pools and partly held collectively in the memories and traditions of each society. This knowledge is not private opinion, or the convictions of individuals, because human beings know what to eat, what foods are poisonous, how to conceive babies, how to deliver them, how to rear them, and how to find food. Without such "correct" knowledge, handed down from generation to generation, human beings could not survive. With the enlargement of the brain and the development of the neocortex, this knowledge became consciously held knowledge, and with consciously held knowledge humans can now learn by trial and error (cf. 295).

We have now seen that the argument from evolutionary epistemology confirms the rather dramatic, mediating role that the evolution of human cognition plays between biology and culture, and that the evolution of human cognition strengthens the argument for the plausibility of the naturalness of religious belief. The final question is whether the nature of this process of complex cognitive evolution, revealed as interactive and epigenetic, and the hypothetical realist claims that flow from this on a philosophical level, tells us anything about the realist claims of some religions.

If we limit our understanding of reality to the more naturalist/reductionist views of an evolutionary epistemologist like Wuketits, then religious faith should be interpreted as an adaptation that has become obsolete and irrational, even if it might have been beneficial for our remote ancestors. Czech scholar Tomáš Hančil has recently made a strong theological argument that this kind of reductionist objection can be raised only on the assumption that God does not influence our world in any way, and that all processes in this world are therefore determined by natural laws only. For Hančil, breaking out of the circularity of this scientistic argument could open our eyes to the fact that God does in fact influence events in our world. And if God does influence events in this world, then God's influence would be part of the data that the adaptive process uses for the selection of available variants. Against the background of this strong view, Hančil wants to argue that it may be logical to claim that such a cognitive adaptation would have given us humans the abilities also to reason about the reality of God (cf. Hančil 1999: 240; cf. also Hančil and Ziemer 2000: 11ff.).

The critical question we have to ask, however, is whether this stronger realist claim still is consistent with evolutionary epistemology's implied hypothetical realism. Evolutionary epistemology has certainly shown that the principles of evolutionary development can and should be extrapolated to the evolution of human cognition, and to its bridging function between biology and culture. Precisely for this reason, as we will see in chapter 4, paleoanthropology will take a central role in the wider discussion of the evolution of human cognition in this project. Not only is there overwhelming evidence of the interaction between physical and cultural evolution in the evolution of the human mind, but we can understand the modern human mind only by understanding the prehistory of the human mind (cf. Mithen 1996: 66ff.). This is the reason why a scientist like Ian Tattersall can claim that we humans are not just *more* intelligent than our ancestors, but are *differently* intelligent (cf. Tattersall 1998: 32), intelligent in ways that allow us to manipulate the environment around us in a qualitatively unique manner. In this sense evolutionary explanations of the development of the human brain during a long period of 5 million or 6 million years point to the uniqueness of our human cognitive capacities (cf. Hančil 1999: 240).

In chapter 4 I will return to this argument, with a special focus on the work of Steven Mithen (1996), Ian Tattersall (1998), Terrence Deacon (1997), and David Lewis-Williams (2002). The issue of human uniqueness has also functioned prominently in the work of Christopher Wills (1998), who has argued provocatively that the evolution of *Homo sapiens* is actually accelerating, and that our power over nature has done nothing to halt evolution's unrelenting march. Our physical evolution is certainly continuing, according to Wills, perhaps at the same rate it always has, but it is cultural change that is exploding and laying the groundwork for a far more rapid evolution of our mental abilities in the future. What is unique about us as humans is precisely the speed and power with which evolutionary processes have acted on our minds, and even the ability to devise religion and powerful mythology is due to the same evolutionary forces (cf. Wills 1998: 6f., 202f.).

Merlin Donald (1991; 2001) has also argued that the bridge from biology to culture is necessarily cognitive, and that a complete evolutionary proposal for human evolution should address the cognitive level and its capacity for cultural change (cf. 1991: 10ff.). Instead of seeing it as hovering free from its biological embeddedness, culture is connected closely to the process of evolution via the cognitive capacities of the brain. In this sense, then, human cognition will prove to be the link or mediator between cultural and biological levels, a claim that supports the redefinition of evolution as a knowledge-gaining process, as suggested by evolutionary epistemologists like Plotkin and Wuketits.

Hančil, in his theological evaluation of these claims of evolutionary epistemology, has correctly argued that the evolution of religion and religious beliefs must be closely dependent on the development of human cognitive abilities (cf. Hančil 1999: 243). This does not mean, of course, that religion can be reduced to what can be ascertained through paleoanthropological or archeological research. Religion and religious belief, on the contrary, are clear examples of how the development of the human mind distinguishes humans from other species, even from our closest relatives, *Homo neanderthalensis* (cf. 244). On this evolutionary epistemological view religion and religious belief become part of what in essence it means to be human. Hančil's conclusion is supported by an argument by Tattersall, who has stated that precisely because every human society possesses religion of some sort, complete with origin myths that purportedly explain the relationship of humans to the world around them, religion cannot be discounted from any discussion of those human behaviors we see as unique (cf. Tattersall 1998: 201). And if human cognition is the link between biology and culture, as Donald and Hančil have argued, and if, as I am arguing, it is only through paleoanthropology that we can come to a fuller understanding of the cognitive capacities of our earliest ancestors, then Philip Hefner's claims about our distant evolutionary past become theologically relevant: in the Upper Paleolithic period, our earliest human ancestors met a challenge and confronted it through the formation of myths and rituals, and these ancient myths and rituals must have organized the kind of information that was necessary for survival through elaborate cultural systems (cf. Hefner 1993: 278; cf. Hančil 1999: 244).

This is where Hančil wants to make the *theological* point that it is not enough to conclude that the human mind has a unique ability for religion and myth. Not just the use of myth, but also the contents and messages of particular myths must have greatly influenced the behavior of our ancestors, as they still do for us today. For Hančil this means applying evolutionary principles to the development of the structure and also the contents of human religious reasoning. In fact, evolutionary principles must be used for discerning the validity and appropriateness of the content of our religious traditions (cf. 1999: 254). At this point Hančil falls back on the promise of evolutionary epistemology and its principle of hypothetical realism. The interactive systems theory approach of evolutionary epistemology implies that every development is "caused" by interacting with the environment. In culture and religion, however, biological explanations would not suffice, and a much broader picture is needed. In Christian theology even more is needed, and Hančil now includes God as one of the explanatory factors of evolutionary reality. He claims that religion and culture can be interpreted as evolutionary adaptations to the external reality of God, and that these religious beliefs, correctly reflecting the nature of God, are beneficial to believers (cf. 259; also Hančil and Ziemer 2000: 16). In this strong if not startling claim, the principles of hypothetical realism are now stretched to comprehend a divine or ultimate reality to which religion, also the Christian faith, has responded responsibly. On this view our bodily structures, as well as our cognitive capacities, culture, and religions, are the products of an evolutionary process that responds to the reality of our environment, now conceived of in the widest possible sense to include God.

I believe Hančil has given us serious arguments for why theologians should engage in an interdisciplinary dialogue with evolutionary epistemology precisely on the issue of human uniqueness. Evolutionary epistemology can become a tool for theological reasoning (cf. Hančil 1999: 271), but clearly in a much more limited sense, and with much more limited but still profound claims. Indeed, in the transversal connection with evolutionary epistemology, theology can most probably find, in the rich notion of cognition, shades of an important historical trend in theology to closely associate human distinctiveness with notions of rationality and cognition, as will become clear in chapter 3. Evolutionary epistemology will challenge theology, however, to take aboard seriously the implications of the biological origins of an embodied human rationality, as well as the embodied history of the evolution of human cognition. This will have serious consequences for reductionist and overly abstract theological notions of the *imago Dei*.

In the interdisciplinary conversation between theology and evolutionary epistemology, theology should take seriously the evolution of human cognition, but the evolutionary epistemologist also should learn to appropriate the critical antireductionist message that the theologian ought to voice. In being open to what it could learn from evolutionary epistemology about human uniqueness, theology could then speak out forcefully and appeal to epistemologists, in terms of the principles of their own evolutionary epistemology, to take seriously the phylogenetic memories of our remote ancestors on the origins of imagination and religious awareness. If the origin of the human mind is indeed closely tied to the kind of cognitive fluidity that includes symbolic and mythical dimensions, as we will see in chapters 4 and 5, then the origins of our cognitive behavior are not fully understood unless we also take seriously the origins of religious behavior. On this view, then, the prehistory of the human mind points to the naturalness of religion, and supports the broader argument for the rationality and plausibility of religious belief. This will not provide theologians a generic argument for the existence of God, but it might give more credibility to the way they express themselves contextually in presupposing the existence of God within the boundaries of the discipline of theology.

The principles of evolutionary epistemology, liberated from scientistic reductionism, can support these claims for the plausibility of religious belief as part of the remarkable cognitive capacity that contributes to our notions of human uniqueness. However, it would be too much for a theologian to go beyond this minimal transversal connection with evolutionary epistemology and use the argument from hypothetical realism to claim maximally the existence of God, and of God as an explanatory factor in the evolution of human cognition. Hančil's otherwise excellent and promising interdisciplinary argument takes this one step too far by first invoking the existence of God in the midst of an epistemological argument, not recognizing that at this point the interdisciplinary, transversal moment has passed. The epistemological lesson learned here is that success in the evolutionary struggle, considered on its own, does not guarantee the truth or adequacy of beliefs or perceptual representations (cf. O'Hear 2002: 60f.). It is a huge overstatement, therefore, to try to make the argument theological by including God as an explanatory factor. It is *epistemologically* problematical because it overstretches the capacities of hypothetical realism, and it is *theologically* problematical because it does not take into account the power of imagination, and the spectacular ability of the human mind to delude itself. Positing God as a reality factor in this generic way also weakens theology and makes it vulnerable to interdisciplinary attack. On the other hand, a theology that is already firmly embedded in the history of its own tradition of beliefs, including what it believes about God, may indeed be liberated to find its public, postfoundationalist voice precisely by discovering that the reality claims we make in theology are resonant with, and reinforced by, the defining role that the emergence of religious awareness played in the evolution of human cognition.

Conclusion

In this chapter it became clear that the very human obsession with self-definition is directly related to the evolution of human cognition, and to our distinctive capacity for self-reflective awareness and self-consciousness. The following also became clear.

1. In our search for an adequate definition of humanness, no single trait or capacity like intelligence or rationality should ever be taken as the definitive word on human uniqueness.

2. Talking about human uniqueness, whether in theology or the sciences, always implies a moral dimension; defining ourselves as "fully human" always both includes and excludes others, and thus contributes directly to the sociopolitical and cultural contexts we create and live by. As a direct result of this very contextual nature of all our definitions of human uniqueness, definitions of what it means to be "human" or "fully human" have not only shifted and changed with time, but have also been influenced deeply by worldviews and moral perspectives. What this implies for this interdisciplinary study on human uniqueness is a postfoundationalist understanding of the fact that all our disciplinary ventures and reasoning strategies, in this case specifically the development of our ideas in paleoanthropology and theology, should be understood in the context of their times, i.e., within the historical-cultural network of ideas in which they are, or were, embedded.

3. In this chapter it was argued that Charles Darwin's conception of human identity and human nature, with its very specific focus on the evolution

of human cognition, still functions as the canonical core of the ongoing discourse on human evolution. I also argued that the powerful galaxy of meaning emerging from Darwin's views on human identity, maybe more than ever before, is shaping our current views on the evolution of human cognition. The epistemic implications of these views on cognition are most clearly represented today in some forms of contemporary evolutionary epistemology. Finally, teasing out the interesting conceptual route from Darwin to evolutionary epistemology has now set the interdisciplinary stage, so to speak, and has created the necessary space for a dialogue between theology and the sciences, quite specifically on human uniqueness, and in doing so has provided us with very specific transversal links to paleoanthropology. In fact, it is precisely evolutionary epistemology's focus on the evolution of human cognition that revealed embodied human cognition as the mediator between biology and culture, and in so doing provided paleoanthropology with a crucial role in the wider debate about human origins.

4. Evolutionary epistemology has proved to be very fruitful in investigating the consequences that the theory of evolution by natural selection may have for philosophical epistemology, for our theories of knowledge in different disciplines, and for the origin and development of our cognitive structures, our cognitive maps and abilities (cf. van Huyssteen 1998: 134). As such, evolutionary epistemology facilitates precisely the kind of postfoundationalist challenge for a more comprehensive and integrative, holistic approach to human knowledge that I argued for in chapter 1. Moreover, the qualified form of hypothetical realism implied by evolutionary epistemology reveals embodied human cognition as not only a form of illusion or mere cultural construction. In chapter 5 we will see how transversal connections with neuroscience and paleoanthropology may help us take this argument further in an attempt to understand the spectacular material legacy of cave art that we inherited from our Paleolithic ancestors, and the possible nature of the first religion(s) they might have practiced in those remote, dark caves in southwestern Europe. This will reveal that it is precisely in this sense that human phylogenetic memory is expressed in our genotype as well as in our predisposition to rely on a religious framework when searching for ultimate meaning in life. In this sense one could indeed say that, even though we may aspire critically to understand the cultural pressures that have been influencing metaphysical views and religious convictions in the course of past millennia, our deepest beliefs and firmest convictions reach back further than any cultural influence currently shaping their expressions (cf. Hančil and Ziemer 2000: 15). It is in exactly this way, also, that evolutionary epistemology facilitates a postfoundationalist argument for

the rationality of religious belief, and for the fact that religion, and religious intelligence, has always been a response to the holistic search for meaning in our experience.

5. A postfoundationalist approach to evolutionary epistemology allows us, then, to understand how religion and religious knowledge should be integrated into a broader, holistic epistemology. Franz Wuketits has correctly argued that evolutionary epistemology necessarily leads to an interdisciplinary account of our epistemic activities (cf. Wuketits 1990: 4ff.). It does so because this very comprehensive, holistic approach to the problem of embodied cognition by definition takes us beyond traditional disciplinary boundaries.

6. Evolutionary epistemology thus facilitates a multidisciplinary approach to the central theme of this study, namely, the unprecedented contemporary focus on what it means to be human. It has already become clear that various sciences, but also evolutionary epistemology itself, are now building on and extending our commonsense perceptions of human uniqueness, and by doing that are also crossing over into some of the most traditional theological territories. Christian theologians, like Christians everywhere, traditionally believe that there is something absolutely unique about being human, precisely because humans are believed to be created in the image of God, as Genesis 1:26-28 so clearly states. However, disciplines like evolutionary biology, paleoanthropology, archeology, genetics, artificial intelligence and robotics, neuroscience, cognitive science, cognitive psychology, and evolutionary epistemology (to name just a few) are now all directly challenging any unnuanced notion(s) of human uniqueness, and by implication, therefore, this traditional Christian doctrine of the *imago Dei*.

The important question now will be, how should theology respond to the way the sciences are challenging, and even deconstructing, the notion of human uniqueness? Would any Christian theology that ventures forth bravely into interdisciplinary dialogue still be able to maintain, for instance, that there is some deeper, divine purpose to being human, and by implication then also to human evolution? As indicated earlier, my answer to these and related questions will unfold against the background of the brief theory of traditions developed in the first chapter. I believe the history of ideas of theological reflection shows that theological traditions have always been extremely sensitive to the culture(s) in which they were embedded. I will suggest, therefore, that we get at this problem by looking at how theological traditions, specifically the doctrine of the *imago Dei*, have evolved and responded to cultural pressure. In this specific case study on human uniqueness, I will ultimately attempt to facilitate a transversal intersection of different disciplinary voices as theology goes into conversation with the sciences of paleoanthropology and archeology. What kind of dialogue will result, and what kinds of challenges will be revealed, if we happen to uncover some common concerns, some overlapping interests between these very diverse reasoning strategies? Finally, and maybe most importantly, is this interdisciplinary process of trying to revision the notion of the *imago Dei* helped, or hindered, by voices from the sciences of paleoanthropology, archeology, and neuroscience?

three Human Uniqueness and the Image of God

"Hence, although the soul is not the man, there is no absurdity in holding that he is called the image of God in respect to the soul; though I retain the principle which I lately laid down, that the image of God extends to everything in which the nature of man surpasses that of all other species of animals."

John Calvin, *Institutes of the Christian Religion,*
vol. 1, 15, par. 3, p. 164

"The real situation is that man who is made in the image of God is unable, precisely because of those qualities in him which are designated as 'image of God,' to be satisfied with a god who is made in man's image. By virtue of his capacity for self-transcendence he can look beyond himself sufficiently to know that a projection of himself is not God."

Reinhold Niebuhr, *The Nature and Destiny of Man* (1942), 1:166

In chapter 1, I argued the philosophical point that, from a multidisciplinary point of view, it is possible for different disciplines to identify various shared concerns, or a variety of overlapping or intersecting problems, about which critical interdisciplinary conversation then can become possible. I also argued for the idea of transversality as a heuristic device that opens up new ways for crossing boundaries between disciplines, and for identifying those interdisciplinary spaces where one might ask how to translate the relevance of scientific knowledge into the domain of Christian theology, and vice versa. Even if the problem of human uniqueness qualifies as such an interdisciplinary space, the question still remains: How much will be lost in translation when we move back and forth between theology and paleoanthropology, and how much of a transversal connection can be made between these very different disciplines? As an entry point into this conversation, and setting the stage, as it were, for this kind of interdisciplinary dialogue, I argued in chapter 2 that some forms of contemporary evolutionary epistemology make it possible to talk about the naturalness of religious belief. Evolutionary epistemology, with its focus on the embodied human mind, not only embraces the canonical core of Charles Darwin's ideas on human cognition, but also reveals the evolution of human cognition as a bridge between biology and culture, and rather sharply focuses on human distinctiveness as embodied intelligence and consciousness. However, this helpful focus on the naturalness of religious belief and on embodied intelligence and consciousness does not yet yield any significant transversal connection to theological reflection on human uniqueness. On the contrary, we have seen that both scientistic reductionist interpretations of these characteristics and ambitious theological attempts to appropriate realist conclusions from evolutionary epistemology's hypothetical realist methodology not only fail as an interdisciplinary exercise but leave us undecided as to what exactly an evolutionary perspective may contribute to theological notions of human uniqueness.

Against the background, then, of evolutionary epistemology's argument for the naturalness of religious belief and for embodied intelligence and consciousness, the focus in this lecture will shift to one of the core traditions of the Christian faith, the doctrine of the *imago Dei,* and the deep-seated religious belief that humans are special because they were created in the image of God. To argue for the elusive point where theology and the various sciences may intersect transversally on the issue of human uniqueness, I will again take up the theory of traditions developed in the first lecture as a methodological link to this increasingly interdisciplinary discourse. This view on the pragmatic function of traditions already helped us determine the scope of Darwin's ongoing influence on contemporary views of cognitive evolution. It will now help us ask important questions about (1) why the idea of human uniqueness, so important to all three Abrahamic faiths, is so pervasive in Christian theology, (2) whether there is a deep, core biblical meaning that can be ascribed to the idea that humans were created in the image of God, and (3) how the meaning of this crucial term, thanks to cultural pressure and other theological influences, has shifted dramatically through history.

Finally, of course, we will have to ask whether the theological notion of the *imago Dei* is helped or hindered by the diverse interpretations of human uniqueness that are alive and well in the various sciences, and what that might tell us about our relations to earlier hominids, and to the uniqueness of our sister species in the animal world. I will argue that in a truly interdisciplinary theology it is precisely the porousness of the boundaries between theology and the sciences that will allow for a creative rethinking of the notion of the *imago Dei* in Christian theology. As we saw in chapter 1, however, we should take care not to confuse any convergence we might identify between these sciences and Christian theology's deepest convictions with some kind of "proof" for God's purpose or design in the universe. Then again, the convergence of theological and scientific arguments on the issue of human uniqueness may actually give us an argument for the plausibility of the more comprehensive nature of religious and theological explanations for a phenomenon as complex as the distinctive nature of *Homo sapiens*. At the same time, scientific notions of human distinctiveness may help us ground theological notions of human uniqueness in the reality of flesh-and-blood, real-life experiences, and in this way help protect theological reflection from esoteric and exotically baroque abstractions when trying to revision the notion of the *imago Dei*. More importantly, while the shared interest of theology and the sciences in the problem of human uniqueness may reveal much about the possibilities of interdisciplinary dialogue, we have to be prepared for the possibility that it may also reveal something important about its limitations.

In the first chapter I argued quite specifically for a postfoundationalist approach to interdisciplinary dialogue. This postfoundationalist argument implied that, whatever the cross-disciplinary links we are able to construct transversally between different reasoning strategies, they should always, epistemologically at least, be deeply embedded in highly specified disciplinary contexts. Given the fact that this kind of disciplinary contextuality always implies the embeddedness of all our knowledge in quite specific traditions, it seemed rather logical to me that we will have to be willing to reflect critically on exactly those traditions that underlie our knowledge claims. This is true for reasoning strategies as different as theology and science. I will argue throughout these lectures that the most threatening epistemic danger for a theologian entering interdisciplinary conversation would be to settle for the twilight zone of decontextualized abstraction, as far as the intradisciplinary and interdisciplinary results of this conversation are concerned. It seems clear, then, that we should realize that a crucial notion like *human uniqueness,* which may be at the heart of some of our most important traditions in science and theology, can no longer be discussed within the generalized terminology of a metanarrative that ignores the sociohistorical context of the scientists or theologians who are entering this very specific interdisciplinary space (cf. van Huyssteen 1998: 26). This implies that theology's embeddedness in specific traditions requires first of all that it be done locally and contextually. But the awareness of this contextuality and locality does not imply the choice for some notion of tribal rationality or epistemic isolation, nor for easy pluralism or, worse, rampant relativism. Precisely the open acknowledgment of epistemic and hermeneutical preferences can facilitate, rather than obstruct, trans-contextual and interdisciplinary dialogue.

In theology we are not only called to acknowledge and articulate the way our belief in God is embedded in, and shaped by, our personal and ecclesial commitments, but are obliged to return critically to exactly those beliefs and traditions, acknowledge their flexible and fluid nature as they are shaped by the ongoing process of history, and then rethink and reconstruct them in interdisciplinary conversation. In this way we can begin to solve problems by cultivating the proper relation between belonging to a tradition and, at the same time, keeping our critical distance from that tradition. In the first chapter, therefore, I argued that a significant pointer for developing a theory of traditions that supports this kind of contextual yet interdisciplinary strategy is found, first, in the persuasive argument that all traditions are always defined by continuity and change, and that, second, at its heart the way a tradition behaves, whether in exhibiting fundamental change or in staying the same, is deeply pragmatic. Our research traditions, whether in theology or in the sciences, are in survival mode, and as such they are concerned with legitimating core beliefs in the face of new challenges. The identity and integrity of any disciplinary tradition are preserved by what we may call the heart, or the *canon,* of the tradition, and this canon functions as an authoritative narrative or conceptual framework that shapes and molds continuity and change in the tradition as a lived reality.

In theology and in the sciences our traditions, paradigms, and worldviews, like all traditions, are historical creatures. As such they are created and articulated within a particular intellectual milieu, and like all other historical institutions, they wax and wane. If in all theological reflection, as in other modes of knowledge, we relate to our worlds epistemically through the medium of interpreted experience, then this interpretation of experience always takes place within the comprehensive context of living and evolving traditions. These traditions are epistemically constituted by broader paradigms or research traditions. Because of their historical nature, however, research traditions in all modes of human knowledge can change and evolve, and they do this through either the internal modification of some of their specific theories or a change of some of their most basic core elements.

What this amounts to is that whether in our religious practices or our ecclesial, theological, cultural, scientific, or aesthetic traditions, we cannot be separated from our past. However much freedom we have, we still are constrained by the traditions and rituals of our ancestors, and we use this past to negotiate our way through contemporary culture. In a postfoundationalist approach to theology, or to the sciences, however, there would be no recourse to foundationalist certitude by bestowing the canon(s) of our traditions with objective truth or indubitable knowledge. For a theology that is open to interdisciplinary standards of rationality and public dialogue, the canonical structures of its core traditions would therefore be less structured and fixed than in foundationalist conceptions of the function of traditions.

As was argued in chapter 1, the complexity of a disciplinary canon and its function within a broader research tradition function as a network of ideas, a galaxy of meaning that shapes our ongoing reflection (cf. Brown 1994: 76f.). Just as a galaxy is composed of a vast and varying multiplicity of elements, a disciplinary canon too, as the sacrosanct core of a tradition, is dynamic and pluriform. But a galaxy has enough unity and structure to be one thing rather than another, and in the same sense a canon has a rough and practical unity that can be differently construed from different historical and disciplinary perspectives. A canon, as a complex but identifiable core identity of a tradition, and as embodying a rich galaxy of meanings, thus has gravitational force, or a gravitational pull that is the result of the way its own internal structure relates to and is construed in the always plural history of its interpretative relations. Through the dynamic interaction of construction and constraint in the historical evolution of our disciplinary traditions, these galaxies of meanings creatively give way to interpretative constellations of meaning that we construct in direct interaction with the different contextual challenges presented by contemporary culture. It is exactly this point that will prove to be of primary importance as we find our way into the origins and history of the notion of *human uniqueness* in science and theology. In this sense both our theological and scientific traditions on human uniqueness will emerge as cultural negotiations, shaped by what we see as the continuing gravitational pull of the very specific canon(s) of specific tradition(s) in the sciences and theology.

Human Uniqueness and the History of the *Imago Dei*

It would be fair to say that biblical concepts like the *imago Dei*, along with sets of other concepts like creation, sin, atonement, sacrifice, righteousness, God, etc., once had a great orienting power, a power that has now been greatly reduced by contemporary secularized thought and challenged by the spectacular achievements of science in our time. In a sense some of these well-known concepts come across as remote, metaphysical abstractions, and for contemporary interdisciplinary theology are often like pieces in a museum for the history of theological ideas. As Michael Welker has argued, these formerly crucial concepts now often function only as codes or symbols for a world that has long since ceased to exist. For religious believers, and for theologians concerned about theology's voice in contemporary culture, this is a rather fatal development, because it robs our cultures, our societies, and our churches of fundamental sources of spiritual orientation and important opportunities for self-criticism (cf. Welker 1999: 4).

The biblical idea that human beings are created in the image of God and that *Homo sapiens* are therefore placed more or less at the center of the created universe seems to be especially challenged in our time. For Christian theology one of the most crucial questions today should be whether there is a way in which we may rediscover the canonical function and orienting power of a concept like the *imago Dei* without retreating to metaphysical abstractions. Welker has also argued recently that rediscovering core theological concepts that specifically express the relation between creator and creatures should never be done in abstraction from the way we humans find ourselves concretely situated in the world. Converging closely with my own arguments for a postfoundationalist approach to interdisciplinary theology, Welker warns against constructing "false abstractions" when we attempt theologically to refigure the meaning of some of these crucial theological concepts. To fulfill this task for revisioning core theological concepts that have fallen prey to metaphysical abstractions, Welker also calls for a consciously pluralistic and interdisciplinary theology that should be able to show convincingly that formerly fundamental core concepts from the history of Christian theology can still provide stimuli and insights that are far from exhausted (cf. 2ff.). The question is, therefore, would it be possible to revision the canonical core of the *imago Dei* in such a way that it might again function as a gravitational force in contemporary theological anthropology, while at the same time facilitating interdisciplinary reflection?

Parallel to the way we analyzed the powerful canonical core of the Darwinian tradition on human distinctiveness in chapter 2, we now want to look at the doctrine of the *imago Dei,* one of the most enduring, core traditions of the Christian faith, from a postfoundationalist viewpoint. In this process some crucial questions will naturally emerge: How much of a distinctly Christian and unchanging identity of meaning does this important theological notion of human uniqueness really have? Is there possibly a richer galaxy of meaning to the history of this central concept, and if there is, is this canonical core protected by the gravitational pull of the original historical and textual roots of its own identity? If, then, we find the meaning of this central Christian concept to be nonstatic, and therefore fluid and changing, would there be limits to this fluidity, and what would determine these limits? And most importantly, can this rich and complex theological tradition be woven successfully into an interdisciplinary research project, and if so, would it be threatened, or enriched, by challenges from the sciences?

As we turn to a brief thematic and selective overview of important moments from the history of the doctrine of the *imago Dei,* we should expect that the crucially important biblical notion of human uniqueness would have been handed down to us in the intellectual history of theology as already complexly interpreted minitheories. These central biblical concepts clearly reveal how crucial biblical texts have been received, experienced, interpreted, and negotiated in the multifaceted history of Christian ideas. The idea behind the rich tradition of the *imago Dei* has always been the strong conviction that we humans are in some important sense special and different, since Christians have always believed, according to the rather famous texts in Genesis 1, that human beings were created in the "image of God." Scriptural references to the creation of humans in the image of God are clearly few and far between, and their meaning has always been controversial. On a first, quick reading, these scriptural passages do seem to imply that the divine image is something that all humans participate in, male and female, through succeeding generations, with some form of dominion over nature, and with a specific focus on the value of human life. But what do we find when we read these texts carefully? The first and most important reference to the *imago Dei* is found in Genesis 1:26-28, set within the so-called Priestly creation narrative of Genesis 1:1–2:4a:

26 God said, "Let us make humanity in our image, according to our likeness; and let them rule over the fish of the sea, and over the birds of the skies, and over the cattle, and over all the earth, and over every creeping thing that creeps upon the earth."

27 So God created humanity in his image:

  in the image of God he created him;

  male and female he created them.

28 God blessed them, and God said to them, "Be fruitful and multiply and fill the earth and subdue it. Rule over the fish of the sea and over the birds of the skies and over every living thing that creeps upon the earth."[1]

In its very specific focus on the story of the creation of the human being in antiquity and the essential nature of this creature, this Genesis text clearly raises deep anthropological issues. The significant statement that we humans are made in the image of God certainly seems to imply a profound theological truth claim about human nature itself. As Sibley Towner puts it, theologically it means that we will never be able to talk about human nature apart from God's nature, and that, from a biblical point of view at least, all anthropology is also theology (cf. Towner 2001: 1).

Before we discuss briefly the very diverse and pluralistic interpretations of the *imago Dei* in the history of theology, it might be prudent to look at some contemporary interpretations of these texts, and with that as a background, to briefly evaluate diverse voices from the history of the notion of the image of God. How should we read these texts about the creation of the biblical Adam, and where does this tradition about the "primal human" fit into its ancient Israelite setting? In his historical-critical analysis of these texts, Dexter Callender has persuasively argued that the tradition of the creation of the first mythical human is set within the larger context of an account of creation and humanity from the beginning of the cosmos through the demise of the Israelite kingdom (cf. Callender 2000: 22). This tradition clearly possesses its own oral and perhaps literary prehistory, most specifically its connections with Mesopotamian traditions such as the *Enuma Elish.*[2] Callender also argues that the repetitive nature of Genesis 1:1–2:4a, when the passage is isolated from its present literary context in the Pentateuch, suggests a liturgy, for which it may actually have been used at some point. Yet, in spite of its present literary context, it is anything but a liturgy, but is presented rather as a movement of *history:* not in any modern or literal sense, of course, but as a history nonetheless: the creation of the human is presented simply as an event in the distant past. As such, it forms

1. W. Sibley Towner, *Genesis,* Westminster Bible Companion (Louisville: Westminster John Knox, 2001), 21.

2. The discovery of the Babylonian myth *Enuma Elish* threw new light on the genre of the Genesis texts that use the terms "image" and "likeness." For striking similarities, and how to account for this cultural embeddedness, cf. Shults 2003: 230.

the beginning of the so-called primeval history, the early history of humanity as presented in Genesis 1–11. Only in Genesis 12 does this early history of humanity become, more specifically, the national history of Israel. The significance of this primeval history within the larger context is that of an etiology, i.e., a rather dramatic theory or story of origins. Within this context the purpose of these texts is to explain where humans "came from" and to say something about their nature (cf. 23).

Callender also argues, however, that the roots of this passage lie far deeper than in simple etiology and prelude. To arrive at insights into the priestly conception of the primal human being, we also have to ask about this passage's embeddedness in the ideas and society that inherited and shaped it. Against this background Callender states that, first, the language of this passage derives from the royal imagery of the ancient Near East, and second, its broad scope is indeed meant to include all of humanity. Ultimately the argument is that the Priestly writings (P) recognize the primal human in simple terms not only as the chronological first human, but more importantly as the link between deity and humanity (cf. 24).[3] The plural style of the statement "Let us make humanity in our image . . ." almost certainly indicates the notion that the divine royal court of other *elohim,* in which God exercises God's sovereignty in the human world, is simply assumed by the text (cf. Mays 2005: 89). Also, Patrick Miller has argued persuasively that the move among some recent interpreters to see the plural in these texts as a plural of self-exhortation or self-summons is now outweighed by arguments contending that the divine first-person plural is in fact an address to the heavenly court of Yahweh (cf. Miller 1978: 11).

One of the most vexing problems to Old Testament scholarship has been what specifically is meant by the creation of humanity in the image *(tselem)* and likeness *(demut)* of God. No wonder this has led to a pluriform history of interpretation of these terms in Christian theology. It is also true, however, that biblical uses of the terms *tselem* and *demut* offer only limited help in determining their use in Genesis 1:26-28. The noun *tselem* is the more easily un-

---

3. Not only was the primal human seen as the link between the deity and humanity, but the Garden of Eden was seen as a locus for divine activity. Callender argues that in the ancient Near East a mountainous, oasis-like garden setting is one of the traditionally understood dwellings of the gods. The Garden of Eden in Genesis (and elsewhere in the Hebrew Bible) should then be similarly understood as a divine dwelling, a place where the divine could be encountered unmediated. Just as sacred trees and groves signified the divine presence, so did the Garden of Eden: in Gen. 3:8 God strolls about almost incidentally, as the original hearers would have expected (cf. Callender 2000: 38-50).

derstood of the two terms, and it refers to an image, a physical representation of a thing. As such it refers to statues of idols (Num. 33:52; Ezek. 7:20) or pictorial representations (Ezek. 23:14). The noun *demut,* translated by "likeness" or "form," and "appearance," "model," or "pattern," occurs twenty-five times in the Hebrew Bible, and most frequently in the book of Ezekiel. Various ancient Near Eastern texts also make it quite clear that the language of image and likeness is borrowed from the realm of royal ideology and that the basis for the likeness, first of all, is physical, not spiritual or mental or ethical.[4] Callender argues that this physical similarity should not be taken superficially; its intent is to express some deeper reality, and physical similarity suggests a similarity in nature, content, or function. Many examples from Mesopotamia and Egypt in fact suggest that the king was seen as the "image" of God, and as such represented God as a viceroy. This supports the view of scholars who argue that the text in Genesis presumes an understanding of image and likeness that was widely held at the time, and was best expressed as a fixed formula (cf. Callender 2000: 28). Therefore, in view of the extrabiblical evidence, the theme of the human domination of creation in Genesis 1:26, 28 and the wider context of Psalm 8:5, 6, where humanity has been installed as royalty who ranks just below God and above all living creatures, it is most natural to accept the idea of ruling or dominion as an important aspect of image and likeness, and not as something incidental (cf. 29; cf. also Mays 2005: 90f.).

The inclusion of all humanity in the royal imagery precisely through the primal human clearly shines through here. Because other ancient Near Eastern literatures use the language of the image and likeness in royal contexts, we must recognize that within its present context in Genesis 1, this "royal" imagery applies not only to the primal human but also to humanity in general (cf. Callender 2000: 29). The best textual evidence, however, that the "image" and "likeness" pertain to all humans, and not simply to the first man or couple, is found in that other famous *imago Dei* text, Genesis 9:1-7, which gives as the rationale for the divine prohibition against the shedding of human blood the fact that *every* human is created in the image of God. From this we should conclude that it is not likely that the royal allusions in these biblical passages reflect either innovation or afterthought. Rather, the imagery may have existed in some form already in the *prehistory* of these passages (cf. 29ff.).

It is clear, then, that in the Genesis texts the primal human being is seen as the significant forerunner of humanity, and as such defines the relationship be-

4. Cf. Callender 2000: 26f., for a discussion of various ancient texts that indicate the king is seen in the physical likeness of the gods.

tween humanity and deity (cf. 205). The primal human is therefore revealed as a mediating or intermediary figure standing between the human and divine realms. In fact, the primal human emerges here as a paradigm for intermediary figures in ancient Israelite society. And the language used to describe the primal human being is unequivocally royal; the "first" human is presented as king (Gen. 1:26-28), and in other texts also as priestly (Ezek. 28:11-19) and prophetic (Job 15:7-8). All these roles are expressions of the role of an intermediary. And in this sense the Genesis 1 texts are clear expressions of the uniqueness of the primal human being who occupies a position between God and humanity and is the only one who can lay claim to this distinction. The primal human is not "born of human," and is the only one whose natural state was face-to-face with God (cf. 206). He is the only one who lived in the "actual" (mythical) divine dwelling; others can do so only by mimetically following him. In this sense, against the background of this mythical imagery, the primal human is the significant ancestor who established the paradigm for contact with the divine (cf. 206f.). Clearly, being created in the image of God highlights the extraordinary importance of human beings: humans are walking representations of God, and as such are of exquisite value and importance (cf. Towner 2001: 26).

A close reading of these texts quickly reveals that the idea of dominion is directly linked to the image of God; we are created in God's image so that we may have dominion over the earth, the animals, and the fish of the sea. This means that God's image in us is expressed or manifested in "dominion" as we represent God in this creation (cf. Towner 2001: 28). Dominion is expressed in stewardship, nurture, and responsibility toward the things God loves. Taken as a whole, Genesis 1:1-31 certainly nuances our relationship with other creatures past and present by placing us all in the same framework of divine creative activity. However, the text also unambiguously proposes an ascending sequence of value and importance, and the culminating effort of God's creative work indeed seems to be found in all humans. In this ancient creation story, we humans are therefore the culminating achievement of God: alone of all the creatures, we are said to be made in God's image. Alone of all the mammals, alone of all the plants, we are invited into a personal relationship with God (cf. 30), and in this theological sense we are indeed "alone in the world." As we will see in chapter 4, this biblical perspective on human uniqueness differs strikingly from paleoanthropological views on humanness, where "alone in the world" unambiguously points to the fact that we humans are in reality the last of the hominids on this planet.

Genesis 1:26-28, however, not only has to be read closely with Genesis 9:1-7, but also has to be read within the wider context of Psalm 8:5, 6. In a recent article James Luther Mays argues that it really seems to be an anomaly that the phrase "image of God" does not recur again in the Old Testament. As crucial as it is in the account of the beginning of the world, the phrase as identification of the human being disappears, leaving its one poetic echo in Psalm 8 (cf. Mays 2005: 93). Mays correctly points out that while the notion of the "image of God" is no longer used for the human being in the biblical story, what it stands for theologically does in fact become the structural theme of the biblical account of God and humankind. This becomes especially clear when one takes into account a deeper, second meaning in the early biblical texts for what it means to be created "in the image of God."

When one reads Psalm 8 as interwoven in a network of other psalms, this second meaning emerges in the prayer themes of Psalm 7 and Psalms 9 and 10. In Psalm 8 humanity has famously been installed as royalty that ranks just below God and above all other living creatures:

What are human beings that you are mindful of them,
    mortals that you care for them?
Yet you have made them a little lower than God,
    and crowned them with glory and honor.
You have given them dominion over the works of your hands.

(vv. 4-6 NRSV)

God is here clearly engaged with mortals in an attentive and sustaining way, and the intimation of involvement with the divine is implanted in the human consciousness. But as seen in the broader textual context of prayers, this humanity that is crowned with glory and honor is also deeply distorted. In the prayers framing Psalm 8, hostility, affliction, and oppression mark the human scene, and human conduct features arrogance, ruthlessness, and cunning. Mays has argued rightly that the dissonance between the hymn's portrayal of created humankind and the hymn's contexting prayers' testimony to historical humankind is deafening. To put it another way, in humankind there is a tragic incongruence between what God has done and what the human being has wrought (cf. Mays 2005: 88). The protological account for this dissonance is of course reflected in the sequence of Genesis 1 and 2–3. The story of a humanity that finally leaves Eden (Gen. 2–4) to live the curse instead of the blessing, to murder the brother and to fashion culture as a temple of self-assertion instead of as a room for God's presence, in this sense forms the necessary canonical preface to the enigmatic and ambiguous nature of humanity as portrayed in Psalm 8 and its broader network of prayers (cf. 88).

This also confirms that, in all discussions of the meaning of the "image of God" texts in the Old Testament literature, Genesis 1:26 and 3:22 should be seen as powerfully interacting with one another. In Genesis 3:22 we read: "Then the LORD God said, 'See, the man has become like one of us, knowing good and evil; and now, he might reach out his hand and take also from the tree of life, and eat, and live forever'" (NRSV).

I believe we have here a rather dramatic new dimension to the image or likeness of God, or what Mays has called "the other likeness" (cf. 91). This likeness is not about representing and resembling God in the matter of God's sovereignty, but is in fact the opposite. It stands in tension with the created likeness, and emerges as a disturbing new way of being like God, i.e., by "knowing good and evil." Miller has argued that at this point a narrative tension and contrast emerge between the Priestly and Yahwist texts. Genesis 1 speaks positively of the similarity of the primal human to the divine, but in Genesis 3 the reaction is stunningly different and in fact quite negative (cf. Miller 1978: 21). This apparent paradox is explicable only in the broader context of the biblical story. The line between closeness to the divine, which is God's intention, and human arrogance and its attempt to claim all the prerogatives of the divine is indeed a very narrow one: one is an exaltation given by God in the creation, one is a self-exaltation assumed or attempted by the created human in the face of previously set limitations (cf. 21). That the primal human being should claim unlimited possession of life now puts the human in direct conflict with the divine. The ultimate focus on this thin line between the divine and human worlds finally culminates in the breaking down of the necessary boundaries between these two worlds, and results in the symbolic first sinful act that leads to divine punishment. Nothing in the telling of this dramatic story reconciles the contradiction between these two likenesses of God and humankind, and the "first" humans, now endowed with a moral awareness and the ability to discern good from evil, are left vulnerable to this tragic new dimension of human distinctiveness.

*   *   *

In the New Testament Psalm 8 is cited again, and the theme of the "image of God" reappears in the telling of one man's story, Jesus of Nazareth, in Hebrews 2:6-8. The reference to the Old Testament connects his person with the promise and predicament of the human recounted there, and claims him as the realization of the identity and destiny for which humankind was created (cf. Mays 2005: 96ff.). The author of Hebrews, in quoting Psalm 8 in chapter 2, states that the realization of humankind's original destiny to represent and resemble the sovereignty of God in the world is not yet visible in the world, but "we see Jesus," and in his suffering and death Jesus has become one with humankind: "But we do see Jesus, who for a little while was made lower than the angels, now crowned with glory and honor because of the suffering of death, so that by the grace of God he might taste death for everyone" (Heb. 2:9 NRSV).

Only through the power of his resurrection does he incorporate humankind in his realization of the identity and destiny for which they were originally created. It is in this sense of the crucified, risen Jesus as a perfected human self, or as the "last Adam" (1 Cor. 15:45), whose person opens up a possibility for other humans, that the Pauline letters also refer to "the image of God" (cf. Mays 2005: 97). There Christ is the "image of the invisible God, the firstborn of all creation" (Col. 1:15; cf. also 2 Cor. 4:4). Moreover, Jesus Christ now so absolutely preempts the role of image of God that the vocation and destiny of human beings can be realized only through a transformation of their existence by his Spirit (2 Cor. 3:1-8). Through faith, then, the love and self-giving of the representative and likeness of God begin to reconfigure the selves of others in his own image (cf. Mays 2005: 96). This structural theme of the "image of God" in the texts of the New Testament also reflects a remarkable continuity with the Old Testament texts, and Jesus is now identified as the one who, like the primal human before him, defines the relationship between humanity and God. Moreover, this notion of the *imago Dei* is as contextual and embodied as that of the first Adam: what we know of God, we know only through the story of the suffering and resurrection of the embodied person of Jesus, the Jew.

Against the background of this textual analysis, it is now time to ask how much of a lasting influence the canonical core of these sparse but central biblical texts has had on the theological development of the notion of the *imago Dei*. LeRon Shults has recently argued rather strongly for the enduring power of this notion. He asserts that throughout the biblical tradition, even if the textual evidence for the notion of the *imago Dei* is rare and the Hebrew texts reveal only three specific references, we do find enduring attempts for explaining the persistence of religious hope and awareness by linking what is distinctive in human beings to the concept of the image of God. The idea represented by the notion of the *imago Dei* becomes not only a broader, structural biblical theme, but also the gravitational force of the biblical account of God's relationship to humankind. The remarkable survival of this phrase is fitting because it holds together what has emerged as the canon of this tradition, the intuitions (1) that the nature of humanity must ultimately be understood in terms of its relation to God, (2) that the goodness of the human creature is tied up with its call to responsible stewarding of its relations of solidarity with other creatures, and (3) that for Christian believers humanity is intrinsically oriented to life with God in the Spirit as disclosed in Jesus Christ, who alone is the true image of God (cf. Shults 2003: 217). For Christians this deep conviction makes real theological sense, since it is precisely the task of a Christian theology of human being to explore the metaphysical conditions that render intelligible our characteristic human hoping for some sense of ultimate, religious belonging. For Shults, to become a true human person is to be open to a future outside the self, and that is why we need a metaphysical matrix in which joy and peace can flourish. At the heart of this is a typical human passion for a transcendent reality that ultimately sets us apart from other creatures, and by which we enter the domain of the religious (cf. 218f.).

But is this kind of theological conviction enough for those of us who are theologians and are wondering whether the notion of the "image of God" still makes any *interdisciplinary* sense? If we take seriously the fact that the Hebrew text explicitly refers to the idea of the image of God in only three instances, then the question becomes, why did this idea prevail in early Christian theology? Shults points to two important reasons. First, the New Testament applies the phrase to Jesus Christ, the focus of the Christian faith. From a New Testament perspective, Jesus *is* the image of God, and the ultimate reality and possibility of being human require sharing in his life. Second, early apologists were engaging the important idea of image *(eikōn)* in Greek thought, aiming to articulate the truth claims of Christianity in a way that illuminated and transformed the philosophical self-understanding of that specific cultural context. Shults is certainly correct here: our theological task today is very much an updated version of this, in that we should try to revision theological anthropology in the light of the philosophical and scientific self-understanding of our own culture.

The question contemporary theologians should be asking is how wise it is to still be talking about "human uniqueness" at all. As we will soon see in a broader and more interdisciplinary context, some scientists quite specifically prefer to talk about human uniqueness today, even as they focus on the close connections between humans and animals (especially primates), and are highlighting our close ties to the animal world. It is exactly at this point, I believe, that a conversation with the rich theological tradition of the *imago Dei* can help us to explain whether or not it might still make theological sense to continue speaking of human uniqueness. What I expressed in chapter 1 by focusing on the complex but significant role of traditions in very diverse disciplines like theology and the sciences is wonderfully illustrated in the evolution of the concept of the *imago Dei*. Interpretations of the *imago Dei* differed not only in the early church, but have varied significantly throughout history. In this chapter, in reviewing this vast and complex history, I will focus only on selected aspects and themes that have been shaped by the work of specific theologians. Various contemporary scholars, most recently Noreen Herzfeld (2002) and LeRon Shults (2003), have argued that the intellectual history of ideas that have shaped the *imago Dei* over centuries can be categorized into various distinct patterns. One of the most important and widely accepted of these categorizations is the focus on a three-phased development that historically leads from *substantive* interpretations, to *functional* interpretations, to *relational* interpretations of this crucial, canonical concept. In addition, this well-known triad has also been modified and amplified to include *existential* and *eschatological* interpretations of the *imago Dei* (cf. Hall 1986: 88-112; Herzfeld 2002: 10ff.; Shults 2003: 230ff.).

On a *substantive interpretation*, historically one of the most influential and classical views for interpreting this tradition, the *imago Dei* is seen as an individually held property or capacity that is part of our human nature, and it is most often directly associated with *reason, rationality,* and *intellect.* This individually held property is called "substantive" because it depicts something of substantial form in human nature, a faculty or a capacity that we humans possess over against animals. Historically, substantive interpretations have been dominant in the history of ideas of the West, and in a general sense all Christian writers up to Aquinas saw the image of God as humankind's power of reason. In fact, most writers up to the Reformation, under the strong influence of Greek philosophy (especially Aristotle, who saw the human being as "rational animal") and the early Fathers and scholastics, saw the human intellect as the *imago Dei.* In her recent analysis of the history of the doctrine, Noreen Herzfeld points to the intriguing fact that interest in, and development of, the concept of the *imago Dei* has often been rooted more in philosophy than in scriptural exegesis, and that such interest has been almost exclusively the focus of doctrinal theologians rather than biblical exegetes. Nevertheless, the creation story as told in Genesis 1 has certainly been the starting point for theologians through the ages to develop theories about the nature of humankind. And it is in this sense that the *imago Dei* stands at the heart of questions like: What does it mean to be human, and what is our relationship, as human beings, to God? Historically the *imago Dei* has clearly served as a symbol for Christian theological thought, a symbol of what it is in human beings that makes us uniquely human (cf. Herzfeld 2002: 14ff.).

Traditionally, the matter of the image of God was complicated by classical theologians typically formulating their presentations of the doctrine in response to questions like, what is the difference between the nature of humanity before the fall *(homo creatus)* and after the fall *(homo peccator)?* Furthermore, to what extent was the power of the typically human intellectual and volitional faculties lost, or distorted, by the rebellion of the first two humans? The earliest tradition believed that the *imago Dei* was connected directly to human reason, and also to human righteousness (cf. Shults 2003: 220). One popular approach to this difficult issue, which can be traced from Irenaeus through the Protestant scholastics, is to distinguish between the "image," which is essential to human nature and could not be lost, and the "likeness" to God, which is merely accidental to human nature, and which some theologians believed was lost through sin (cf. 221).[5]

The consensus of the patristic period was that the image of God in Genesis refers to the "intellect," "rationality," and "spirituality" of the human being, wherein then the essence of God (who is both Mind and Spirit) is reflected. This doctrinal emphasis in early Christian theology emerged out of an engagement with the anthropological, philosophical, and theological views that shaped the cultural context of the time. The emphasis on reason was already evident in the work of the Jewish philosopher Philo of Alexandria, who explicitly argued that by the "image of God" the author of Genesis meant "mind" *(nous)*, and quite distinctly did not include any bodily features. In fact, it is on account of its remarkable intellect alone that the human being resembles God as the "Great Director" of the cosmos.[6]

Various scholars have also pointed out that, unfortunately, many of these early theologians also adopted the misogynistic tendencies of their culture, which had an enduring and problematic influence on the developing history of the notion of the *imago Dei*. The image of God was very closely and most directly connected with males, who were allegedly better ruled by reason, while females were tied to their embodiedness.[7] The emphasis on the mind as the im-

5. For more detail, and a discussion of Irenaeus, who introduced a distinction between the terms "image" and "likeness," cf. Shults 2003: 221. For the important role of Irenaeus in shaping Eastern Orthodox thought, where human life is shaped by the goal of *theōsis*, a sharing in the life of God, on the role of the term *eikōn* in Eastern Orthodoxy, and the embeddedness of the doctrine of the *imago Dei* in the mystical relation to God, cf. 222; cf. also Lossky 1974.

6. Cf. Philo, *On the Creation of the Cosmos according to Moses* 12, par. 69, pp. 222-35.

7. For an assessment of misogyny in the Antiochene school, see Frederick G. McLeod, S.J., *The Image of God in the Antiochene Tradition* (Washington, D.C.: Catholic University of

age of God was solidified through the influence of Augustine's modified Neo-platonic anthropology. Augustine's understanding of the image of God was tied to the claim that the individual human mind exists (like God) as a triunity, since it is constituted by memory, understanding, and will, revealing the definitive importance of rationality as reflecting the image of God (cf. Shults 2003: 225ff.). Even Augustine, though, following Paul's infamous statement in 1 Corinthians 11:7,[8] argued that woman was made for man, and from man, and as man's helper could therefore not share directly in the image of God. The man, then, is the image of God, but the woman is the glory of the man (cf. Augustine 1968: 221). Augustine did nuance this argument somewhat: since the image of God is found in the nature of the human mind, the woman together with her husband is the image of God. In his words: "but when assigned as a helpmate, then she is not the image of God: man alone by himself is the image of God" (223). Moreover, this image of God is never found in the human body, but only in the rational mind. It is this rational mind that reflects God's trinitarian being, and it is in the rational mind that the knowledge of God resides (cf. 224).

Augustine's theological ideas on the *imago Dei* would complexly shape the works of Thomas Aquinas, Martin Luther, and John Calvin. In Aquinas we find very clear echoes of Augustine: the intellectual nature of the human being imitates God insofar as, like God, it understands and loves itself. Although Aquinas does not reject outright the idea of women being created in the image of God, his focus is still on the power of rational discernment, which "by nature" is stronger in man. Thomas, therefore, argued that the man is the image of God by reason of his intellectual powers, and in this sense he is the most perfectly "like God." The man thus images God in three ways: in the natural aptitude for understanding and loving God, which as such consists in the very nature of the human mind; inasmuch as man actually knows and loves God, although imperfectly, this image then exists in the conformity of grace; inasmuch as man knows and loves God perfectly, this image consists in the likeness of glory (cf. Thomas Aquinas 1911: I.93.4.471). In its principal signification, namely, as intellectual nature, the *imago Dei* is found in both men and women.

America Press, 1999), especially chap. 6. For the fact that the concept of reason does not exhaust the meaning of the image of God for early theologians, see a brief discussion of Cyril of Alexandria and his additional focus on the human's "capacity for all manners of virtue" as well as humankind's divinely ordained dominion over all creatures. Here an extension of the meaning of the *imago Dei* by now includes the ideas of *virtue* and *dominion* (cf. Shults 2003: 224).

8. "For a man ought not to have his head veiled, since he is the image and reflection of God; but woman is the reflection of man" (NRSV).

In a secondary sense, though, it is found in man and not in woman. On this view the man is the beginning and end of the woman, much as God is the beginning and end of every creature (cf. 472); the *imago Dei* is thus found in men in a way that it is not found in women (cf. Hilkert 1995: 193).[9]

As for the two influential theologians of the Reformation, Luther and Calvin, scholars in the field have pointed out that they never singled out the doctrine of the *imago Dei* as in need of major reformulation, unlike the doctrines of justification and the sacraments. In fact, both Reformers took up the traditional question of the nature of the image of God with heavy dependence on the fathers of the ancient church, especially Augustine, and went to great lengths to show their continuity with that tradition. Luther's most explicit discussion of the topic is in his commentary on Genesis, where he follows Augustine closely in interpreting the image of God as the "powers of the soul," namely, memory, mind or intellect, and will (cf. Luther 1958: 30; also Douglass 1995: 236, 239). Luther also clearly indicated that he found the scholastic distinction between image and likeness not very useful. For Luther both the image and the likeness had to do with original righteousness: the "image and likeness" was in fact holiness, which the primal parents lost with their first sin (cf. Shults 2003: 226). However, for Luther both the intellect and the will remained after the fall, but both were seriously impaired. The restoration of the image and likeness is made possible only through the gospel of Christ. It is interesting to note that, although Luther here strongly appealed to Augustine, he was also very critical of Augustine's equation of the *imago Dei* with the triunity of memory, understanding, and will in the human mind, because this would imply that Satan too was created in the image of God (cf. Shults 2003: 227).

For Luther an important function of the image of God was to show that human beings, though sharing many similarities with animals in their physical lives, were created "by a special plan and providence of God" for a better spiritual life in the future. Moreover, the image of God in paradise was far more excellent than modern people could ever imagine. Adam's "inner and outer senses were all exceedingly pure. His memory was the best, and his will was the most sincere — all in the most beautiful composure, without any fear of death,

9. For a direct link between human reason and the image of God in the *Summa,* cf. *Summa Theologica* I.93.4. On the fact that Aquinas sharpened the Irenaean distinction between the image and likeness, cf. Shults 2003: 226f.: the image of God is our essential nature (rationality), but the likeness was a supernatural gift (righteousness). After the fall, what survived was reason, but the likeness was lost, to be restored only in Christ. Aquinas's hardening of the dichotomy between *imago* and *similitudo* would thus help him explain the difference between human beings before and after the fall.

and without any anxiety."[10] Added to this was a superb body, strong, with acute senses.[11] Importantly, Luther did not appear to make sharp distinctions between male and female with regard to the image of God, and in fact stressed that Eve had abilities that equaled those of Adam. In doing so, he seems to refute very consciously the chauvinist patristic tradition of identifying dominion with the male (cf. Luther 1958: 34). He did, however, introduce gender distinctions that again caused serious ambivalence in his position on the *imago Dei*: on the one hand, men and women were created equal and shared the image of God and ruled over all things; on the other hand, as Luther phrased it, "still, she was only a woman" (34). Women are therefore somewhat different from men, and may be a most beautiful work of God, but still do not equal the glory and worthiness of the male (cf. Douglass 1995: 242).

Jane Dempsey Douglass has argued persuasively that this ambivalence in Luther's notion of the *imago Dei* can most probably be explained by realizing that Luther was a theologian in transition between two worlds. Although Luther was educated as a scholastic and thus deeply imbibed the older tradition of understanding the image of God, he also intended to substitute a biblically derived picture of humankind as created in God's image for the traditional one he regarded as too much derived from Greek philosophy (cf. Douglass 1995: 250). Douglass makes another interesting point: insofar as Luther places the beginning of women's subordination after the fall, as the result of sin, he contributes to genuine reform in theology, stressing a full equality between men and women as intended by God at creation. This teaching has come to dominate modern theology, although Luther himself, by seeing women's inferior place in society as ordained by God's will, effectively eliminated any practical consequences flowing from the creational equality of women with men for the earthly lives of real women (cf. 251).

Calvin mostly followed Augustine by describing the image of God in relation to the human mind. For Calvin the image was spiritual, and its primary seat was in the mind and the soul.[12] In an interesting passage Calvin does re-

---

10. Martin Luther, *Vorlesungen über 1. Mose von 1535-45*, as cited by Douglass 1995: 240.

11. It is interesting, and intriguing, to read Reinhold Niebuhr's negative response in his Gifford Lectures to Luther on this very point: "Luther's extravagant descriptions of the state of perfection before the Fall are so obviously prompted by the desire to accentuate man's present state of sin, misery and death, and they are, compared with both Augustine and Calvin, so inexact that his thought is not very helpful in interpreting the real import of the Christian conception of the image of God" (Niebuhr 1942: 161).

12. On exegetical grounds Calvin rejected the hard distinction between *imago* and *similitudo*, implying that it was simply a Hebrew parallelism (cf. Shults 2003: 227).

veal a remarkably positive, and thus holistic, attitude toward the human body: the divine glory is in fact also displayed in humankind's outward appearance, although the proper seat of the image of God is still the mind or soul (*Institutes* 1.15.3, p. 162). In this sense the *imago Dei* is deeply spiritual and extends to everything in which human nature surpasses the nature of all other species of animals. Although Calvin did find the primary seat of the divine image in the mind or soul, "there was no part even of the body in which some rays of glory did not shine" (164). Moreover, only in the light of our relationship to God can we understand the mystery of humanity, and like Irenaeus before him, Calvin wanted to interpret the image of God primarily in the light of Jesus Christ. In this sense, then, Calvin could describe the image of God as righteousness, knowledge, and holiness, a triad that clearly emphasizes conformity to God, a conformity that restores what the first parents had lost (cf. Shults 2003: 227).[13]

It is interesting to note that in the *Institutes* there is a "new silence" on differences between men and women as far as the image of God goes (cf. Douglass 1995: 253). What Calvin did stress was the corporateness of humanity, and the relationship of all human beings to one another. Moreover, there is a strong implicit suggestion in Calvin's work that the image of God has weighty ethical implications, requiring human justice and mercy. However, although Calvin rarely alluded to women's subordination in the *Institutes*, and certainly did not teach about it there, it remains a fact that his writing and rare allusions do reveal that his work presupposes a social order in which men ruled over women. Although he always insisted that men and women were created in God's image, he also accepted traditional qualifications, i.e., that the woman was derived from the man and therefore possessed the image of God in a derivative sense (cf. 253ff., 259). Douglass has argued, however, that he struggled with the question of women's equality in the image of God more consciously than did Luther, a fact that can most probably be ascribed to his embeddedness in French Renaissance culture. In fact, when Calvin prepared the final edition of the *Institutes* near the end of his life, he included no teach-

---

13. Reformed scholastics later spoke of a "relic" of the image of God that remained after the fall. This implied that most of the image of God was lost, but the remaining relic still differentiates humans from animals. LeRon Shults has argued that here too an appeal could be made to Calvin, who had noted that the image was not totally annihilated, but was almost blotted out: what is left is "fearful deformity" (cf. *Institutes* 1.15.4). The Canons of Dort also used the language of remnants but protected the doctrine of total depravity by emphasizing that there is no part of the human — not even the "remnants" — that is untouched by sin (cf. Shults 2003: 229).

ing of woman's possession of the image of God in any secondary degree, and no teaching of women's inherently subordinate character (cf. 259f.).

Thanks to an ever increasing awareness of the powerful influence of misogynist tendencies in the history of theology, it is possible today to critique why the thrust that the *imago Dei* symbol should have toward justice and human rights, and especially on issues of sexism and heterosexism, has been missed. Not surprisingly, this line of argument has been followed by feminist interpretations of the *imago Dei*. In her critical review of the history of this conceptual tradition, Mary Catherine Hilkert states that in the long and rich tradition of the *imago Dei*, it clearly never was a question whether *man* was created in the image of God. What was never certain was the extent to which *women* were included in the evolution of this theological concept (Hilkert 1995: 193f.). As we just saw, in the early church and the Middle Ages, only males were seen to be created in the image of God, not females. Even Augustine argued that woman was made for man, from man, and as man's helper could therefore not share in the image of God. In Aquinas, although there is no strict rejection, the focus was still on the power of rational discernment, which "by nature" is stronger in man. In this sense a powerful tradition developed around the idea of the image of God and perpetuated the negative idea that the *imago Dei* is found in men in a way that it is not found in women. It is especially interesting to note, as Hilkert has pointed out, that not only feminists but also a consultation of the World Council of Churches have concluded (already in 1981) that the doctrine has traditionally been a source of oppression and discrimination against women (cf. 193). A rethinking of the powerful conceptual resources of the *imago Dei*, however, should reveal that this theological symbol does indeed give rise to justice, and thus exemplifies a root metaphor for a Christian understanding of the human person — an understanding that grounds further claims to human rights, because men *and* women are persons before God (cf. 198).

Contemporary Interpretations of the *Imago Dei*

In her recent analysis of the doctrine of the *imago Dei*, Noreen Herzfeld has argued that among contemporary theologians it has been especially Reinhold Niebuhr who has followed Augustine most closely, and by finding the image of God in human reason or rationality, has significantly prolonged a more substantive interpretation of the *imago Dei* (cf. Herzfeld 2002: 17). At the same time, however, Niebuhr's reading of the image of God in his Gifford Lectures can also be seen as distinctly existentialist (cf. Shults 2003: 235). Rationality by itself is not enough to capture the dignity of humanity, and humans are in fact driven to something beyond reason, a self-transcendence, and it is this existential longing for a God who transcends the world that really sets human beings apart from other creatures. In Niebuhr's words:

> [I]t will suffice to assert by way of summary that the Biblical conception of "image of God" has influenced Christian thought, particularly since Augustine . . . , to interpret human nature in terms which include his rational faculties but which suggest something beyond them. The ablest non-theological analysis of human nature in modern times, by Heidegger, defines this Christian emphasis succinctly as "the idea of transcendence," namely that man is something which reaches beyond itself — that he is more than a rational creature. (cf. Niebuhr 1942: 161f.)

It is important to realize, however, that although Niebuhr sees this remarkable capacity for self-transcendence as going beyond reason or rationality, he does not consider it a quality separate from reason, but rather a quality that is the consequence of reason and self-consciousness (cf. 171f.). Thus self-transcendence is not only a capacity for self-reflection, but is also a defining condition for human freedom, which Niebuhr identifies as a major distinguishing feature of the human race (cf. Herzfeld 2002: 17). Importantly, while Niebuhr points out the significance of the human body as determining the finitude of our human being, his focus is far more on the paradox of human nature as balancing between this creaturely finitude and humankind's self-transcendence (cf. Niebuhr 1942: 166-77). In this sense one could certainly argue that he did not consider the creaturely side of our human nature as being part of the image of God. In fact, our finite embodied nature stands in paradoxical tension over against the *imago Dei*. Moreover, the divine image gives us the ability to see beyond our finite bodies, to think in terms of infinity, although we always remain finite creatures. Thus, while the human body is one defining part of our human nature, it is separate from the image of God, which, although emerging from human rationality, remains for Niebuhr a more spiritual, disembodied quality (cf. Herzfeld 2002: 17).

Substantive interpretations of the *imago Dei*, dominating the history of ideas of Western theology for centuries with an overwhelming focus on reason, intellect, or mind, have now largely fallen out of favor with contemporary theologians. Even in the work of Niebuhr, the focus on reason or self-transcendence, however broadly defined, inevitably led to a mind/body dualism and a rather disembodied, abstract notion of the *imago Dei*. Herzfeld, therefore, rightly concludes that an anthropology that finds the imaging of God only in the mental aspects of the human person inevitably denigrates the physical and directly implies that God, and the image of God, can be related only to theoretical analysis and control (cf. 19). Identifying a specific disembodied capacity like reason or rationality as the image of God by definition implies a negative, detrimental view of the human body — a move that inevitably leads to abstract, remote notions of the *imago Dei*. In this sense substantive definitions of the image of God can rightly be seen as too individualistic, and too static.

Substantive interpretations of the *imago Dei* have subsequently been replaced largely by so-called *functional interpretations,* precisely because substantive views were seen as too static, and too strongly expressive of mind/ body dualism. A functional interpretation normally seeks to answer this kind of criticism by stressing the role of human action in a much more dynamically conceived notion of the image of God. "Functional" thus refers to what we as Christians are called to do, and is exemplified by human behavior, like our dominion over animals, as expressed by the Genesis 1 texts. On this view humans are God's representatives, and are acting as God's representatives on earth. Functional interpretations clearly represent a move away from reason and rationality to a new focus on the language of dominion in the classical biblical texts (cf. Shults 2003: 231; also Herzfeld 2002: 20f.).

Old Testament theologian Gerhard von Rad famously developed a more functional approach to the idea that humans were created in the image of God. Here the *imago Dei* was found not so much in what we are, as in what we are called to do. Rad would thus argue that the Genesis statements on the image of God do not first of all explain theoretically its nature and characteristics, but rather focus on the *purpose* for which the image is given to humans (cf. Rad 2001: 144). Against this background he rejected overly intellectualized conceptions of the image of God and argued that the original audience would have understood that the first human beings were God's sovereign emblem, placed on earth as God's representatives, enforcing God's claim to dominion of the earth. It is clear that Rad implied that the whole human person, rather than some specific quality or capacity of the person, was created in the image of God. In this holistic anthropology humans are called on to join God in imposing order on nature, a nature created in reference to humans, and thus to participate in God's saving plan (cf. Herzfeld 2002: 22f.). In this sense the purpose of the image of God refers directly to the human being's status as "lord of the world": God set the human in the world as the sign of God's sovereign authority in order for the human to uphold and enforce God's claims as lord (cf. Rad 2001: 146). In the same way that earthly monarchs set up images of themselves in their kingdom as signs of their sovereign authority, so too the Genesis texts, and Israel, thought of the human as the representative of God. Crucial for Rad's argument, however, is the idea that the image of God in humans functions in a very specific way in the nonhuman world: through the image of God in the human being, creation, in addition to being created by God and thus coming from God, is now also seen as receiving a particular ordering toward God (cf. 147).

Herzfeld has argued that this understanding of the *imago Dei* in terms of the human function of exercising dominion, and in effect acting as God's deputy on earth, in some form or another remains the favored interpretation among Old Testament exegetes (cf. Herzfeld 2002: 23). The reasons for this widespread acceptance are explicitly present in the three strengths of Rad's interpretation: (1) the functionalist approach clearly emphasizes a holistic view of what it means to be human; (2) within the context of the Genesis *imago Dei* texts, the creation in God's image is immediately followed by the charge to exercise dominion; (3) Rad consistently strove to take the historical and literary contexts of the Priestly texts into account. In addition to these specific strengths, Herzfeld has added an important argument for an updated functional interpretation of the image of God texts: in the light of the current ecological debate that is often highly critical of exploitative notions of dominion or stewardship, a functional interpretation also supports human responsibility and care for the environment precisely by positing human dominion over nature (cf. 24).

This functionalist viewpoint that "image" and "likeness" refer to a specific task or function given to humanity, namely, dominion over the earth, has indeed become very controversial, specifically as a result of feminist scholarship and ecological concerns about exploiting nature, although it certainly is still seen as an important shift away from the rather blatant anthropocentrism of classical accounts of the creation story (cf. Welker 1999: 60f.). The ascendancy of the functionalist reading had another interesting result: it made it easier for systematic theologians to acknowledge a different reading of "original sin," and therefore also to assert that the text does *not* teach that the image or likeness was lost (cf. Shults 2003: 232). Clear exegesis of these texts shows that the text does not even hint at the so-called loss of the image and likeness of God. Moreover, there is no hint even of any distortion of that image. LeRon Shults puts it rather well: "The text does not speak of 'remnants,' or a loss or distortion of the image, any more than it speaks of a 'fall' or of 'inherited' sin.

It may also come as a shock that these texts say nothing about rationality or righteousness!" (cf. 233).

Functional views have since been eclipsed by more pronounced and *relational* (cf. Herzfeld 2002: 31f.) or *existential* views (cf. Shults 2003: 217ff.) of the *imago Dei*. Certainly the most influential theologian here has been Karl Barth. For Barth the image of God does not consist of anything humans *are* or *do*, but rather of the amazing ability or gift to be in a relationship with God (cf. Barth 1958: 186ff.). For Barth the human being is never just an animal endowed with reason. On the contrary, the human being exists only in a definite history grounded in God's attitude to humans, and as such the human's relationship to God is an essential part of its being (cf. Barth 1960: 77). Theologically the argument for this relational interpretation is conceptually embedded in God's nature as Trinity. Here the *imago Dei* is not just the capacity for relationship, but the relationship itself: first our relationship with God, and then our relationships with each other, most clearly exemplified in Jesus, who alone is directly the image of God. Shults has argued that these developments have provided a conceptual space for exploring the possibility that the ideal of a creaturely imaging of God is related not just to the past, but to the transhistorical "present" (cf. Shults 2003: 233). An existential or relational interpretation has always been closely associated with twentieth-century neoorthodox theology. Some now argue that engaging existentialist philosophy brought a new depth to the theological analyses of the human condition, as theologians began to apply the biblical language directly to current human existence rather than focusing on the first parents in paradise (cf. 233).

It is interesting to note that Barth does talk about the "phenomenon of human distinctiveness" quite specifically (cf. Barth 1960: 76). In his rather positive discussion of the anthropology of Arthur Titius, he focuses on Titius's conviction that humans are to be classed with the animals, specifically the primates, as their "most developed member." Humans, according to Titius, show an incomparably greater power of adaptation: they dress, use fire, manufacture tools and weapons, adorn themselves with ornaments, play with things and copy them. Humans have a natural urge for culture, and therefore for the unlimited, for that which cannot be confined by natural instinct. Barth did appreciate the fact that Titius ended his arguments for human distinctiveness by paralleling Barth's own approach of basing anthropology on Christology, but he quips: "What a pity that none of these apologists considers it worthy of mention that man is apparently the only being accustomed to laugh and smoke!" (cf. 82f.).

On a more serious theological note, it is clear that for Barth there was nothing arbitrary about the statement that human beings were created in the image of God. In fact, in relation to the man Jesus, it is clear and necessary as a final definition of what being human is all about (cf. 323). Moreover, human beings are not alone but were created as male and female, in fellowship with one another and with God. Barth thus finds a textual basis for the human-human relationship as part of the *imago Dei* in the fact that the original Genesis texts state clearly that being created in the image of God directly refers to being created as male and female. In fact, he finds in the relationship between man and woman a correspondence, or copy of the relationship within the triune God that then serves as a prototype for all human-human relationships. On this view a human being is fully human only insofar as he or she is in relationship with another (cf. Herzfeld 2002: 26). God therefore exists in a trinitarian relationship and fellowship, and it is in this image that humans were created. In Barth's words: God is in relationship and so too is the man created by him (cf. Barth 1960: 324). And of this basic human relationality, God is the "original."

The key to Barth's notion of the *imago Dei,* and to the relationality at the heart of this concept, can thus be found in the inseparable relationship between man and woman, which is analogical to the relationship of the three persons of the Trinity to one another. Understandably Barth's relational view was seriously criticized by various scholars, notably by James Barr in his Gifford Lectures. According to Barr, Barth's ideas on the image of God were based on an ill-judged and irresponsible piece of exegesis: there is no way the ancient writers, as historical beings embedded in the culture of their times, could have entertained this notion of relationality. Although Barth's development of the *imago Dei* was ingenious, Barr saw it as completely devoid of contextual and cultural responsibility, and ultimately derived from Barth's own modern dogmatic presuppositions and assertions (cf. Barr 1993: 161). Barr also correctly identified Barth's exegesis as ultimately fueled and motivated by his controversy with Emil Brunner over natural theology. What will become increasingly clear in our discussion of the highlights from the history of the *imago Dei* is that Barth's elaborate interpretation of human relationality as imaging trinitarian relationality, although expressing an important point about human relationality itself, is not found in the original *imago Dei* texts and therefore today comes across as increasingly speculative and abstract.

Although many theologians have differed sharply with Barth on what constitutes authentic relationship, or whether the male-female differentiation mentioned in Genesis 1:27 is an adequate model for all human relationship, the relational view certainly became the most dominant view in the late twentieth and early twenty-first centuries (cf. Herzfeld 2002: 29f.). One of the most interesting and influential earlier relational positions was that of the renowned Dutch theologian Gerrit C. Berkouwer. Berkouwer argued that although it is true that the phrase "God created humankind in God's own image" is immediately followed by "male and female he created them," this does not mean that the second clause gives a definition of the first. It does not necessarily imply, therefore, that the image of God can be exhaustively defined in terms of the relationship between man and woman (Berkouwer 1962: 73). Moreover, Barth confusingly speaks of both the man-woman relationship and other interhuman relationships, an ambiguity that can hardly be resolved by Barth's argument that the man-woman relationship is simply the most original and concrete form of all interhuman relationships. In effect Barth holds to both views: the man-woman relationship because the Genesis text demands it, and other interhuman relationships because they are implied in the broader idea of the *analogia relationis* between God and humankind. In a very interesting way Berkouwer here anticipates Barr's (1993) later critique: Barth's exegesis of the Genesis texts clearly involved constructive interpretation and theological speculation. Barth is correct in pointing to the unique importance of the man-woman relationship, but he is wrong in his further conclusion that this relationship is the specific content of the image of God (cf. 73).

Over against any kind of intellectualized notion of the image of God that focuses only on abstract or "higher qualities," Berkouwer identifies with a much more holistic notion that never excludes the human body from it (cf. 75). In fact, he argues passionately that the scriptural emphasis on the whole human being as the image of God has triumphed time and again over all objections (cf. 77). The biblical text never makes a distinction between the human being's spiritual and bodily attributes in order to limit the image of God to the spiritual alone, as if the spiritual or disembodied relation could exemplify the only possible analogy between God and humankind. Ultimately Berkouwer does agree with Barth's conclusion that the human being cannot be known completely apart from its relationship with God, but he disagrees with Barth as to the exegetical means by which to arrive at this important conclusion (cf. also Herzfeld 2002: 106 n. 107). Through Jesus Christ who became human for us, and in this embodied love, we are taken up in the renewal of the image of God and we find the analogy of love that redefines the *analogia relationis* as *analogia amoris* (cf. Berkouwer 1962: 116). For Berkouwer our human uniqueness, then, is powerfully exemplified in the fact that we image God concretely in our love for others.

Let us look briefly at another important contemporary interpretation, namely, a more eschatological view of the image of God. The recent emphasis on interpreting the image of God primarily in relation to the future is tied to the broader renewal of eschatological reflection in the late twentieth century, and understandably led to very specific eschatological interpretations of the *imago Dei*. For the *imago Dei* this implies that the ideal relationship of human beings to God, against the background of the message of Jesus about the coming kingdom of God, might not be located in the past, or in the existential, transhistorical present, but instead in the future.[14] The best-known contemporary proponents of an eschatological interpretation of the *imago Dei* are Wolfhart Pannenberg and Jürgen Moltmann. At this point I want to draw out the salient features of Pannenberg's well-known notion of the *imago Dei*, and take up Moltmann later. Pannenberg famously connects human nature and the *imago Dei* through the idea of "exocentricity," a disposition that is intrinsic to the nature of human persons, and intrinsic precisely as a natural dynamic that points human beings toward a destiny that has not yet been reached (cf. Shults 2003: 235ff.). In his own way Pannenberg developed further this basic idea of ultimate relationality and located human uniqueness in the tension between our self-consciousness as individuals and our exocentricity, our openness to others and to the world.

On Pannenberg's view it is the exocentric structure of human existence that points forward as a prolepsis of our final becoming of the image of God and our future destiny of fulfilling this quest for transcendence in fellowship with God. Shults has correctly argued that Pannenberg's interdisciplinary approach, and his taking science and anthropology seriously, makes him a very important contemporary representative of a postfoundationalist approach to interdisciplinary theology (cf. Shults 1999: 39, 71, 83). I believe, moreover, that it is exactly the anthropological locus of this exocentricity of human existence that exemplifies his interdisciplinarity par excellence. I also believe his notion of exocentricity goes far beyond Niebuhr's more abstract idea of self-transcendence. Exocentricity not only points to a human orientation to others and to the world, but in a much more holistic sense reveals a disposition of human nature itself. Humans have this *Weltoffenheit*, or openness to the world, which by far transcends the openness of all animals to their environment. This exocentricity, therefore, does not mean that the world as such is for humans as their environment is for animals (cf. Pannenberg 1970: 7f.). Connecting to

14. "Here the turn to Futurity in the doctrine of God refers not simply to the abstract temporal mode of time we call 'future,' but to the absolute future of God's reign of peace that has arrived and is arriving and will ultimately arrive through the presence of the Spirit of Christ" (cf. Shults 2003: 235).

contemporary anthropology, Pannenberg finds in this exocentricity a profound distinction between animals and humans: the "openness to the world" we share as humans differs not only in degree but also in kind from the "bondage of animals to [their] environment" (cf. 8). Exocentricity thus means that humans are always open beyond every experience and beyond any given situation, in fact beyond the world itself. We are even open beyond our own cultural constructions: as we transform nature into culture, and constantly replace earlier forms of culture with new ones, we are also open beyond culture to the future, and to our finding our ultimate destiny in the future. This restlessness of human nature forms an important root for all religious life (cf. 9).

On this view "human uniqueness" clearly points to the fact that we humans by nature reach beyond everything we experience in the world in our search for fulfillment and meaning. And Pannenberg is certainly correct in arguing that this concept of human self-transcendence, or exocentricity, summarizes a broad consensus among contemporary anthropologists (cf. Pannenberg 1985: 63). In my next chapter I will argue that this "quest for meaning" and even for "religious fulfillment" certainly plays a crucial role in the way paleoanthropologists today are arguing for human uniqueness as revealed in the complex history of *Homo sapiens*. For Pannenberg, in tightening his argument theologically, this fundamental self-transcendence and relationality of all humans to the future ultimately finds its proper identity in Jesus Christ, who fulfills the image of God in its entirety. Theologically, therefore, we find our true identity, as well as the foundation for our relationships with others, in a relationality that is centered on God. In a fascinating discussion of J. G. Herder's anthropology, where embodied biological instincts as well as the image of God interact and function to give direction to the life of each individual human being (cf. 45f.), a notion of the *imago Dei* as a source of direction emerges that shapes Pannenberg's dynamic view of the role of the image of God as directing us toward our destiny. And this destiny directly points to the fact that we are destined for fellowship with God, for "life with God." In fact, the point of imaging God is fellowship with God, and we must understand our present life, even our personalities, in terms of this future destiny (cf. Pannenberg 1991: 224). Finally, for Pannenberg our disposition for the destiny of fellowship with God is not left for us to develop on our own. On the way to our destiny and in relation to it, we are not just subjects: we are in fact the theme of a history in which we become, through Christ, what we already are (cf. 228ff.).

Pannenberg develops a rich, double-sided notion of the *imago Dei* in which the theological concept of the image of God as human destiny, which will be realized fully only in the future, is directly linked to exocentricity, and thus to the *imago Dei* as a fundamental anthropological disposition of human nature. In this rich, interdisciplinary sense one can now say that the *imago Dei* is both an original gift and a future destiny for humankind.[15] In Pannenberg's anthropology it is this disposition for fellowship that is reinterpreted as our final destiny, which theologically is manifested already in Jesus Christ and in which believers already share through the power of the Spirit, and thus already is effecting the eschatological reality of the new human being in them (cf. 220).

In his evaluation of Pannenberg's eschatological proposal, Shults argues that one of the most important values of this kind of eschatological hermeneutic is that it does not necessarily exclude other thematic interpretations of the *imago Dei*. In a more comprehensive sense, it may actually incorporate and integrate them. Especially a functional interpretation of the *imago Dei*, with its focus on dominion, may be subsumed within a more general theological presentation of the call and task of human creatures in relation to the whole cosmos: if we as humans are called to be like Jesus, then our "rule of the earth" will take the form of servanthood and humility, and not oppressive domination over the creation of which we are an integral part (cf. Shults 2003: 238). Shults develops this radical Christian motif even more forcefully: humans are created in the image of God, and in our imaging of God vis-à-vis

15. Cf. Bratt 2005. Bratt develops an interesting and very plausible argument that Pannenberg, by positing the image of God as something that humans are both endowed with on being created and yet also destined for in the eschatological future, ensures that the image of God cannot be lost by human action any more than it can be acquired by human action. The image of God must therefore be predicated of all humans, since according to Genesis all are created in the image of God, and not reserved for those with particular abilities or qualities, or denied to those with limitations, handicaps, or deficits. Whereas Barth's assertion that the *imago Dei* was effected only in relationships actually made relationships necessary for demonstrating the *imago Dei*, Pannenberg's location of the image in gift and destiny, in exocentricity, and therefore in the disposition toward, or capacity for, relationship means that all humans, regardless of the degree to which they can or do exercise that capacity in relationship with others or with God, are to be understood as sharing in the *imago Dei*. For Bratt this approach not only extricates the *imago Dei* from the exclusive union of male and female (where it was confined to some degree by Barth's interpretation), but also makes it available for those who are single and not in meaningful relationships. Also, it significantly preserves the *imago Dei* for those humans who are unable for whatever reason to be in a relation with others. Moreover, because the *imago Dei* for Pannenberg is neither a quality, such as reason or self-consciousness, nor the actualization of relationality, but is simply the disposition toward and the capacity for transcendence and fellowship, it cannot be denied that it is present in those who, for instance, live in vegetative states, are mentally or physically handicapped, are sociopathic, or are otherwise prevented from functioning in ways typical of most human beings (16f.).

our neighbors we do not seek our own glory but lay down our lives for the other in love (cf. 241).

The ethical thrust of this view reveals Shults's deep commitment to concrete social issues and an embodied understanding of the *imago Dei*. He is certainly right that from a robust Christian theological point of view, an eschatological interpretation of the *imago Dei* may be able to account for more than future goals and destinies; it may also account for the traditional Western emphasis on rationality and righteousness, and incorporate it into a more relational, eschatologically dynamic view, a true holistic interpretation of the image of God (cf. 238). Furthermore, few theologians would have a problem with his more comprehensive, theological interpretation of the notion of rationality: human persons are rational creatures who grasp for intelligibility, and this longing is ultimately oriented toward knowing and being known by the eternal God. For Shults righteousness is also intrinsic to our call to image God, and he finds the theological rationale for this in the fact that "we long to share in the goodness of the trinitarian life" (238). I would, however, raise a note of caution here, especially in light of the elaborate Barthian interpretation of human relationality as imaging "trinitarian relationality," which already in the work of Berkouwer and Barr was revealed as increasingly abstract and speculative. On my view, any overly intellectualized, abstract vision of the goal of human life endangers the scriptural emphasis on the whole human being as "created in the image of God." In Shults's work, I believe there are clearly a very conscious awareness and intent to avoid disembodied notions of the *imago Dei* that are disconnected in any way from the hermeneutical heritage of scriptural texts or from the way human beings are embedded (and embodied) in nature. It is interesting, though, that for Shults the early chapters of Genesis do not claim that humans *are* the image of God, only that they are created after it, or oriented toward it, although clearly the theme of the *imago Dei* is very much part of the central Old Testament message. For the New Testament authors the concepts of the image and likeness of God refer directly to Jesus Christ, and our "sharing in the glory of the divine image" is possible only by becoming like him (cf. 239).

Ultimately, for Shults the notion of the image of God can be understood theologically only in the light of the radical claim of the New Testament authors that God is essentially three persons in relation to one another. On his postfoundationalist view, this radical trinitarian metaphysics certainly may be of primary *intra*disciplinary importance for the development of a Christian theology. However, what is not explained is how it is not a risky move away from the transversal dialogue with other disciplines, especially for a theology that so consciously is constructed as an interdisciplinary endeavor. In his theological anthropology, however, Shults leaves an important opening for rethinking the *imago Dei* in even more concrete, embodied terms when he ultimately focuses on our specific call to *holiness* (cf. 238), which is deeply consistent with the ethical thrust of his interpretation of the *imago Dei*. He could also have strengthened this idea by incorporating the rich Pannenbergian notion of the *imago Dei* as both gift *and* destiny, which would have helped to avoid the impression that his focus was the abstract, relational understanding of the *imago Dei*. This may explain why Shults can state that what is most true about human nature is not its primordial past but its eschatological future (cf. 242). This creates the idea that instead of balancing past and future, "gift" and "destiny," for finding the proper relation between God and humanity, the Christian should look only to a future fellowship with God, a future that has been manifested in the face of Jesus Christ. Ultimately, of course, Shults does want to show how the doctrine of the *imago Dei,* when interpreted relationally and eschatologically as our "proleptic participation in trinitarian glory," provides us with a hope-filled way of being embodied humans in the world that liberates us from a preoccupation with self-preservation.

On this radical eschatological view, and in so specifically letting go of the "primordial past," one has to ask how this relates to the canonical core idea of being created in the image of God as expressed in the original Genesis texts. Shults's eschatological interpretation of trinitarian relationality not only takes us into a rather intellectualized, abstract zone with notions such as "longing to share in the goodness of the trinitarian life" and "a proleptic participation in trinitarian glory," but also seems to obscure slightly his earlier call to concrete, embodied holiness. In fact, the original biblical texts not only claim that we humans are oriented toward receiving the gift of the image of God in the future (so 239), but clearly state that we *are* the created image of God; and not only as God's walking representatives on earth, but also by imaging God in our "knowing of good and evil" (Gen. 3:22), through our amazing ability for moral awareness, with all the creative and tragic consequences this has had for the ambiguous history of our species. This enigmatic, ambivalent nature of embodied human nature, the dissonance between being granted special status by God and at the same time "falling upwards" (cf. Peterson 2003: 179) into moral awareness by "knowing good and evil," should of course be linked to the New Testament idea of Jesus as the true image of God. I would want to be more careful, however, to transpose this idea exclusively into eschatological, trinitarian language, in terms of which the *imago Dei* is then retrospectively, and radically, redefined, consequently evoking the impression of floating free from the canonical core of this rich and ancient tradition.

Within the context of a very specific Christian theology, this strategic move, first to trinitarian conceptuality and then back again to a redefinition of the *imago Dei* in terms of this trinitarian language, could certainly be subsumed within the broader doctrinal constellation of meaning of the always developing notion of the *imago Dei*. Moreover, on a postfoundationalist view, theologically this move may have powerful *intra*disciplinary relevance as it fans out from theological anthropology to other theological subdisciplines. On an *inter*disciplinary level, however, it may represent a risky move where the deeper and more original embodied theological meaning of the *imago Dei*, and a biblical call to holiness, could be severed from an interdisciplinary understanding of human uniqueness. On this view we find not only increasing abstraction, but also the threatening danger of a loss of a transversal connection to the multilayered meaning of the original texts that inspired the doctrine of the *imago Dei*.

Because of the very consciously chosen interdisciplinary approach in this challenging book, Shults correctly believes that in Christian theology's response to the diverse sciences, its illuminating explanatory power could be emphasized to demonstrate the reciprocal relationship between theology and the other disciplines. In this sense theology can be seen as stepping in and contributing in a complementary way where anthropological explanations end. Therefore, Shults can correctly state that anthropological explanations cannot exhaust the religious dimension of human existence, but they can point toward the need for fuller theological explanations (cf. Shults 2003: 91f.). For Shults this argument has further apologetic force, and includes an appeal to what he calls "the explanatory power of the Christian claim that the Spirit of Christ fulfills the inherent longing of human beings" (92). On this point I may agree with the idea that "fuller theological explanations" may be descriptive of a move to the kind of theological perspective that Niels Gregersen has called a "theological redescription" of complex interdisciplinary material (cf. Gregersen 1994: 126). This would also be consistent with the contextual nature of a postfoundationalist approach to theology, where theology retains its intellectual integrity as a discipline precisely by not attempting to mirror the world of science. Any attempt to make an even stronger theological claim, such as that "the Spirit of Christ fulfills the inherent longing of human beings," and then turn it into an interdisciplinary argument is risky, however, since it could be misinterpreted as an attempt to extend theological disciplinary borders beyond the domain of Christian doctrinal theology.

What we have learned from Shults's nuanced, careful analysis of the history of the notion of the *imago Dei,* and from his constructive use of the term, is that in exploring interdisciplinarity we should recognize not only the strengths of interdisciplinary conversation, but also its natural limitations. A postfoundationalist approach to theological methodology has already shown us that sharing transversal concerns, and having porous interdisciplinary borders, does not mean that these borders can be crossed indiscriminately. Shults has pointed us toward the strengths of an intradisciplinary constructive move for Christian theology. He explicitly wants to explain theologically the uniqueness of human beings in light of the biblical claim that our existence as human creatures has to do with imaging God. In doing this he also wants to take into account that humans are in fact differentiated from other conscious creatures by the intensification of their knowing and acting, which is precisely what makes personal identity ambiguous and gives rise to sin (cf. Shults 2003: 217). In his theological anthropology, Shults opens up an important opportunity for rethinking the *imago Dei* in more concrete, embodied terms by seeing it as a call to holiness, and it is this notion that might eventually open up a link for an interdisciplinary dialogue on human uniqueness.

The *Imago Dei* as Embodied Self

It is interesting to observe that in addition to increasingly abstract trinitarian notions of the *imago Dei,* a strong focus on it as the embodied self is also emerging in contemporary theology. In an early article Robert Jenson (1983) already argued against traditional ways of answering the "great problem of theological anthropology," i.e., trying to stipulate the difference between humans and other creatures by identifying characteristics that are supposed to fit only humans. To answer the problem of human distinctiveness, Jenson proposes a different approach that, for Christian theology at least, would unfold against the background of a modified doctrine of creation (cf. Jenson 1983: 320). The heart of this argument is the conviction that the last word about human uniqueness cannot be spoken on the basis of evolutionary development alone. What emerges in Jenson's view of the human is that our valid scientific explanations for human identity need to be complemented by a theological perspective that already presupposes that humanity must begin with an event that exceeds, and cuts across, mere evolutionary explanations. What this means for Jenson theologically is that some of God's created creatures are distinguished in that God speaks not only about them, but also *to* them. It is by this role that we are to recognize sisters and brothers among the other creatures of our world. On this theological view humans are unique in that we are addressees of the conversation that is God (321). But Jenson takes this idea beyond speculative theology: we find this true humanity not in the abstract ability to "hear" God's word, but in the fact that it is in ritual that we find that specific embodiment of our discourse with God and one another. As to the question, "what part does ritual have in the step to the specifically human?" Jenson answers: as embodied prayer, ritual is the complement to that address of God that posits our ontologically specific humanity. And as such, we humans are the praying animals (cf. 311, 323f.).

In his *Systematic Theology* Jenson refines these ideas even further. To get a biblical answer to what makes us "featherless bipeds" unique, Jenson also points to Psalm 8:5, which says that we humans are "a little lower than the Gods, crowned with glory and honor" (cf. Jenson 1999: 56). For Jenson, however, the biblical material nowhere suggests that such rank and glory consist in any superior capacity of achievement. What we find in a biblical notion of human uniqueness, and thus in a notion like the *imago Dei,* is a complex set of qualities, a specificity gained from being addressed by God's moral word, and the ability to respond, especially in prayer (58). Here Jenson repeats, and correctly so, his earlier idea that we humans are embodied beings, that in fact we are the praying animals (59). I will later argue that this religious disposition or ability is deeply embedded in our species' symbolic, imaginative behavior. What is really interesting and significant is that at this point a decidedly interdisciplinary approach emerges as Jenson reaches back to human origins to answer the intriguing question, who then were Adam and Eve? For Jenson these mythical humans were the first hominid group that in whatever form of religion or language used some form of expression that we might translate as "God." On this view Adam and Eve strikingly represent the first hominid group that by ritual action were embodied before God, and thus Christian theology is liberated from the obligation to anxiously stipulate morphological marks that distinguish prehumans from humans in the evolutionary succession (59).

In light of what will follow when we enter into dialogue with paleoanthropology, it is intriguing to read Jenson's next comments. If it is plausible for us to see "Adam and Eve" as the first hominid group who by ritual action were embodied before God, then theology need not join the debates about whether the (Paleolithic) cave paintings were attempts to control the hunt or were thanksgivings for the hunt, were "magic" or "religion" (60). More important is the fact that these painters were human, as we may know simply from the fact of their ritual. And most intriguing: by the very fact that they used material, painted images to give visibility to wishes directed beyond themselves, they in fact gave up control and worshiped (61).

In Jenson's theological anthropology we now see a quite dramatic move away from abstract, speculative thought on the *imago Dei* to embodied, contextual reflection: to be in the image of God is to be embodied before God, and to be specifically human is to be available to one another. And with shades of Pannenberg, Jenson now speaks of the mystery of transcendence: the human person is "self-transcendent," a "future-open" entity that now is itself only as it projects what it is not yet (64). To be human, therefore, is to have a body, and as this embodied person to be open and available to God and to one another (cf. 59). The image of God thus consists in the action of prayer, but it is faith that performs this action through love for the other. Ultimately it is in *love*, then, that we find the true *imago Dei*, thus weaving together all the complex historical components of the history of ideas behind this powerful symbol (72).

As is clearly implied in Jenson's theological anthropology, in much of contemporary theology it is also now acknowledged that the human being has emerged within the process of biological evolution as a dynamic person, exemplified by the emergence of the human brain and consciousness, creating culture in its symbolic, ritual interaction with the world. On this view the human person has emerged *biologically* as a center of self-awareness, religious awareness, and moral responsibility. This concept of embodied human distinctiveness is developed in an even stronger sense in the theology of Philip Hefner. Hefner has argued that the image of God in humans refers to that which portrays or sets forth God in the world (cf. Hefner 2000: 88). To be created in the image of God, therefore, means that humans are destined to be a portrayal, an image, or a representation of God in creation. From a Christian theological perspective, Hefner finds in the idea of the image of God the purpose of being human. Our being created in the image of God carries a statement of our purpose to set forth the presence of God in the world. In this sense the notion of the *imago Dei* can be seen to ground personhood, and also the necessity to which the human person is accountable (cf. 73).

In his important interdisciplinary work on the human person, Hefner has also reached out to biology and to the work of Richard Dawkins, and calls the *imago Dei* a meme, a complex and powerful cultural symbol that indicates how much we become persons precisely through our relationship to the world and to God. This personhood is deeply embedded in our genetic and neurobiological nature and proceeds within us along Darwinian lines. "Person" is therefore a symbiosis of genes and culture, an emergent within evolutionary processes, but also a construction on a cultural level, because it is culture that carries the biological level in new directions. In this kind of distinctiveness we are not superior or of greater value than animals, but as God's *created cocreators,* we have the specific task and purpose to set forth the presence of God in this world. In this quite specific theological sense *Homo sapiens* are God's created cocreator, whose task and purpose is the "stretching and enabling" of the systems of nature so that they can participate in God's purposes for this world, for which Jesus Christ is the paradigm. It is in this sense, then, that the notion of the human being as God's created cocreator in the world also opens up the possibility of relating Christian theology to scientific understandings (cf. Hefner 1998: 185).

What is most interesting for this project is that Hefner goes beyond Jenson's important interdisciplinary reference to prehistoric human origins and uses the notion of the human being as God's created cocreator to link human origins directly to mythmaking (cf. Hefner 1993: 175). In Hefner's work human uniqueness is defined by the fact that humans, by virtue of their very existence, seek meaning to both understand and guide their behavior. And it is this quest for meaning that guides behavior that ultimately defines what human culture is about. Culture is here defined as the behaviors we humans choose, together with the interpretations by which we give meaning and justification to those behaviors, which is precisely what we humans need to supplement our genetically based information system (cf. 158). What really sets Hefner's work apart, however, is that in addition to linking this notion of *Homo sapiens* as created cocreator to prehistoric human origins, he quite specifically, albeit briefly, turns to prehistoric art and the question of how myth and ritual emerged within the context of the celebrated Paleolithic cave paintings in France and Spain. Hefner's brief foray into the much neglected challenge of an interdisciplinary dialogue between theology and paleoanthropology thus very meaningfully anticipates the central focus of my research project. Moreover, his major assumption, that cave wall art and some prehistoric portable art are linked directly to the emerging religious myth and ritual praxis of our earliest Cro-Magnon ancestors in Europe (cf. 166), will be confirmed by the most recent research in contemporary paleoanthropology. I will later argue that it is precisely in contemporary paleoanthropological notions of human uniqueness that theology may find a transversal link to a revisioned notion of an embodied *imago Dei.*

*　　　*　　　*

From this all too brief and selective overview of the history of ideas in which the notion of the *imago Dei* has been embedded, it is clear that the meaning of the canonical notion of "being created in the image of God" has shifted — sometimes radically — in the constant tension between the ongoing evolution of the Christian tradition and the gravitational pull of this central, canonical idea. The ongoing evolution of this notion thus reveals rather strikingly that our theological traditions also exhibit both change and continuity, and that at its heart the "behavior" of a tradition is fundamentally pragmatic (cf. Brown 1994: 26ff.). It now is clear that also the identity and integrity of the tradition of the *imago Dei* have been preserved, despite very diverse and multilayered interpretations. This canonical core of the *imago Dei* tradition was revealed in the centrality of the God-human relationship, and the resulting central position of humans in creation, that in its many interpretations has functioned, and still functions, as an authoritative narrative and conceptual framework that have shaped and molded continuity and change in the interpretative history of this canonical concept. We have seen that the *imago Dei* texts from Genesis are certainly normative for the Jewish-Christian tradition, and as such have always functioned as an orientation for knowledge and reflection on what it means to be human, and uniquely so, even as theologians have greatly differed in their interpretations of anthropology. I have now argued that a rereading of the Genesis texts, and a careful analysis of important examples from the history of theological ideas following these canonical texts, reveals some of the predominant interpretations of the *imago Dei* to be creatively diverse, but often also increasingly abstract and problematical. When compared to the deepest intentions of the biblical texts, they could in fact be misleading, distorting definitions of what it means to be human (cf. Welker 1999: 6). These abstract ways of looking at the *imago Dei* have resulted in interpretations that are often so exotically baroque, and so removed from the biblical texts, nature, and our embodied existence in nature, that it is tempting to judge the esoteric, speculative interpretation of the meaning of this central concept as metaphysical pyrotechnics of the first degree. As has become clear, this kind of move to "high theology" may facilitate a theological program with coherent *intra*disciplinary consequences, but as an *inter*disciplinary project, it has to fail. From a postfoundationalist perspective, therefore, the overly abstract, highly a-contextual nature of some of the dominant and influential Christian interpretations of the *imago Dei* will have to be addressed. Secondly, this critical deconstructive process will be aided by a rereading of the central biblical texts, and by transversally linking this revisioning process to insights provided on human uniqueness by the interdisciplinary dialogue with the sciences (in this specific case, paleoanthropology). This will enable me, thirdly, to seek more satisfactory answers to what human uniqueness, and the *imago Dei*, might mean in theology today. Or, as Michael Welker has phrased it, can the transformed abstractions of the museum pieces of theological history present themselves differently, so that they may again radiate and provide orientation for Christian reflection today (cf. 20)?

For Christian theology the classical biblical accounts of creation in Genesis 1 and 2 not only function as the standard orientation point for understanding the creation of the primal humans, but also grant to the creation of human beings the central position in the whole process of creation. For a long time this unquestioned central position seemed simply to be a fact, perhaps a privileged distinction, that came with certain moral responsibilities like caring for nature (cf. 60). In the last three decades of the twentieth century, an important shift away from this rather blatant anthropocentrism occurred. Welker has suggested two important reasons for this: (1) an awareness of the major ecological crises of our times that are destroying nature and also costing countless human beings their lives each day, and (2) strong and influential feminist voices that have unmasked the systematic underprivileging and oppression of women in diverse human cultures (cf. 60f.). As we saw earlier, feminist theologians have argued persuasively that the long-standing anthropocentrism of our cultures has manifested itself quite openly as blatant androcentrism.

For similar reasons Welker has proposed a radical critique of the anthropocentrism of the biblical creation accounts and of theologies and doctrines of creation that are deeply anchored in these accounts, and in doing so has significantly advanced discussion of the *imago Dei* issue. Central here should be a critique of anthropocentric dominance of those functionalist interpretations of the *imago Dei* that manifests itself as ecological imperialism, as well as the fact that the older creation account (Gen. 2:4bff.) clearly seems to support a typically androcentric and patriarchal anthropocentrism by presenting the creation of man and woman as a hierarchy of domination in which the man obviously holds the superior position. Welker orients himself to these two classical biblical traditions and then tries to clarify the thorny interconnection between the image of God and the mandate of dominion, the connection between the *imago Dei* and the *dominium terrae*, as that to which human beings are ordained (cf. 61). To do this he has provided important insights into the complex interconnections between the classical biblical creation accounts of the idea of the image of God, the so-called mandate of dominion, and the sexual differentiation of human beings. He also argues that important theological treatments of this problem by prominent theologians like Karl Barth and Jürgen Moltmann have actually sidestepped important difficulties in their attempts to rethink these important issues. An important question to ask will be whether the idea of the *imago Dei* and its seemingly direct connection to ruling the earth, or the *dominium terrae* (Gen. 1:28), can be clarified within the broader context of the process of creation as expressed in the classical texts (cf. 61).

Welker's argument for a strong contextual understanding of the *imago Dei* within the broader conceptual network of its connections to the anthropocentrism of Genesis 1 and the so-called mandate of dominion now clearly emerges as what I have called a postfoundationalist strategy: a strategy for revisioning these important issues in ways that would resonate with a close reading of the core biblical texts, even as it converges with the public understanding of these core issues in contemporary culture. Most importantly, this is a move away from speculative abstraction, and helps to lay the groundwork for the kind of public, interdisciplinary theology that I have been arguing for. Exactly this move can then, as a next methodological step, bring the theological idea of the *imago Dei* into direct conversation with notions of human uniqueness in other disciplines.

As a first step toward developing this kind of argument, Welker focuses on three basic theological questions:

1. Does the image of God refer to the relation of created humankind as male and female (Gen. 1:27)?
2. Does the image of God refer to the so-called mandate of dominion (Gen. 1:26)?
3. Does the image of God rather refer to the connection of both these aspects, i.e., the connection of the relation of man and woman with the mandate of dominion (Gen. 1:28)?

If the image of God refers to only the relationship between man and woman, we would be back to a typically Barthian, abstract interpretation that concentrates only on relationality or partnership. For Barth the face-to-face existence of the I and Thou is first constitutive for God, and then for "man" as created by God (cf. Barth 1958: 207) — so much so that to move out of this relationship would be tantamount to removing the divine from God and the human from "man" (cf. Welker 1999: 65). According to Welker, Barth gives a surprisingly brief treatment of the explicit emphasis on sexual differentiation in the Priestly creation account. Barth does initially emphasize that sexual differentiation is something humans have in common with animals ("the beasts . . ."), and that humans are not first of all created to exist in groups and species, or in races and peoples. The only real differentiation and relationship is that of "man" to "man," and in its original and most concrete form of man to woman and woman to man (cf. Barth 1958: 186). Barth does not go beyond the formal likeness to animals, and although he ascribes a "peculiar dignity to the sex relationship," he primarily is interested in, or as Welker would say, is fixated upon, the abstract partnership of the I-Thou relation (cf. Welker 1999: 65).

In contrast to Barth, Moltmann has argued in his Gifford Lectures that the true likeness of God is to be found not at the beginning of God's history with humankind, but in true eschatological fashion at its end (cf. Moltmann 1985: 225-27). Taking his cue from the particular interconnection of plurality and singularity within God and between human beings, Moltmann defines the *imago Dei* as *unity in community*. Here the image of God is found in the temporal life of women and men, parents and children, as constituted by the eternal life of the Father, the Son, and the Spirit. This socially open companionship between people is the form of life that most corresponds to, or images, God, or more specifically, the nature of God (cf. 223ff.). In this way Moltmann wants to mediate his interpretation of the image of God with what he calls the "social doctrine of the Trinity," and he interprets the triune God as a perichoretic communion, with the image of God in humans corresponding to this "internal" plurality of God (cf. Moltmann 1981; 1992; also Welker 1999: 65). Welker now argues that, as in Barth's exclusive focus on relationality, Moltmann's emphasis on sociality as the root and form of the image of God also clearly abstracts from the core message of the Priestly creation account (cf. 67). Moltmann does explicitly say that it is primarily in the sexual relationship between men and women that the true likeness to God and human uniqueness can be found (cf. Moltmann 1985: 22). Welker is right, however, that this does not help him escape from a formal abstraction of this relationship. In a way that is formally similar to Barth's I-Thou model, the sexual relationship between men and women is here defined in the abstract and sublimated form of sociality and sociability, and not tied to what I would call embodied sexuality or, in Welker's words, fertility (cf. Welker 1999: 67) at all. Moreover, Moltmann specifically separates the "social" image of God from the mandate of dominion (cf. Moltmann 1985: 223f.). God's charge to humans to "rule over the animals" and to "subdue the earth" is therefore not tied to the image or likeness of God at all, but is identified specifically as an addition to it. This means that the image of God is specifically not found in the given task to rule (cf. 224).

Welker has also shown, referring to the influential work of Phyllis Bird, what a difference it makes if one moves beyond some of these well-known abstractions. In her landmark article Bird focused on Genesis 1:27b ("in the divine image God created them [humankind], male and female [God created them]") and argued convincingly that it is precisely sexual differentiation and biological reproduction that are the decisive aspects of the partnership and image of God as focused on by the Priestly creation account. In what I would see as a highly concrete, contextual move, Bird argues that Genesis 1:27 describes the very specific biological couple, not merely an abstract social partnership (cf. Bird 1981: 129ff., 155). Furthermore, in an interesting move, Bird holds this text against the general anthropology of the Priestly writings (P), which she argues are strongly androcentric because they comprise the genealogies and the establishment of the cult, which are so important to them, in a thoroughly androcentric manner. Because the egalitarian statements of Genesis 1:27b are clearly incompatible with the basic androcentric mood of the rest of the Priestly writings, the emphasis on the communion of man and woman can be properly understood only if the verse screens out, as it were, cultural and social perspectives, and should therefore be seen to be restricted entirely to the primary biological function of man and woman (cf. Welker 1999: 67). In this way the text can be seen to actually point beyond the androcentric conception of the Priestly writings and also beyond patriarchal structures of hierarchy. From then on both man and woman had to be recognized as created in the image of God, and defining the image of God inclusively as both masculine and feminine also destroys all hierarchical interpretations of the *imago Dei*. For Bird, then, a contemporary insistence that woman images God as fully as man and that she is consequently as essential as he is to an understanding of humanity as God's representative in the world is therefore exegetically sound even if it exceeds exactly what the Priestly writer intended to say or was able to conceive at the time. This idea that the full implication of the Priestly statement lies beyond the author's ability to comprehend, can now easily be linked to Paul's affirmation in Galatians 3:28 that in Christ there is no more male or female (cf. Bird 1981: 159).

Welker's response to this focused, highly contextualized and embodied account of the *imago Dei* expresses exactly my sentiments for moving the *imago Dei* discussion out of the twilight zone of abstraction. Clearly the great strength and advantage of Bird's approach is, first of all, that she concretizes the implicit meaning of the text in terms of sexual differentiation. In models of relationality or sociality this emphasis is effectively submerged, despite assertions to the contrary. Over against an abstract I-Thou relationality, or a trinitarian metaphysics that constructs a correspondence between the relationship of the sexes and a relationship within the Godhead, or even a recourse to general sociality, Bird holds on to the very concrete, tangible sexual differentiation between men and women, and between humans and God. And she is right: the Priestly theologian seems to guard carefully the mystery and distance of God from all God's creatures (cf. 156). For Welker, however, the greatest advantage of Bird's approach is that she also connects the idea of the image of God as man and woman directly to the so-called mandate of dominium. Bird has, correctly, not felt forced to let Genesis 1:26b fall away and let 1:27 and 1:28 go their separate ways. On this view one can emphasize that both being fruitful and multiplying, on the one hand, and subduing the earth and having some form of responsibility for it, on the other hand, really stand in close connection with one another (cf. Welker 1999: 68).

The image of God, therefore, is not simply human beings in relational dialogue or in plural sociality. It is found in men and women of flesh and blood who exercise responsible care as they multiply and spread over the earth. This obviously includes the fact that at the same time they also live in relationships with one another in ways that are dialogical and socially open. For Welker, Bird's highly concrete and contextualized interpretation, when compared to, for instance, the relationality and sociality models of Barth and Moltmann, does seem to reveal these theological views as conveying a certain abstract harmlessness (cf. 68). I, on the other hand, would argue that this move into abstraction is much more than that: it is both philosophically problematical and theologically harmful. It is *philosophically* problematical because of the foundationalist move first to isolate exotic constructions of God's nature as trinity, and then use that in a "top-down" way as a basis for analogously defining what it might mean for humans to be created in that image. It is *theologically* harmful because it leaves us with a generic, abstract, and impoverished notion of what the *imago Dei* might mean for us today. Any move into speculative abstraction thus represses the deep resources of the classical biblical texts on the full reality of the embodied human condition, and at the same time, as will become clear in later chapters, ignores the powerful fact that we also create models of God in our own image. Moreover, ignoring this basic anthropological given ultimately aids in effectively isolating theology from interdisciplinary reflection. And finally, in this way our theological constructions are artificially alienated and effectively isolated from ways we construct images of human uniqueness in other disciplines.

As for Bird, in spite of the important step she takes in getting closer to the classical text and thus doing greater justice to the richness of the meaning of the *imago Dei*, it does seem problematical that she insists that *only* the biological couple and *only* biological reproduction are intended here. In this way she seems to move into a dichotomization of "nature" and "culture" that would be foreign to the classical creation accounts. And Welker is right: a focus on the sexual nature of humans and the mere physical reproduction of human beings might not be enough to fulfill and revision the so-called mandate of dominion (cf. Welker 1999: 69). Therefore, if Bird's interpretation were linked to the insight that biological *and* cultural development are necessarily connected, and that our human cultural identities are always embedded in our biological natures, it would be enriched and would also include — even as it critically corrects — the elements of truth in Barth's and Moltmann's interpretations of the *imago Dei*. And it could do so without surrendering its own superior insight that in Genesis 1 biological reproduction, equality of the sexes, and powerful domination are indissolubly connected. Human beings become so powerful precisely because they connect biological reproduction and cultural development (cf. 69).

Clearly, then, a rereading of the classical creation texts compels us to see that the image of God is not found merely in humans as dialogue partners, or as plural participants in open communication, or exclusively in our future eschatological destiny, or, I would add, in analogies to abstract trinitarian language. According to Genesis 1, the image of God is found in men and women who are embodied beings, with deeply ambivalent natures, even as they exercise dominion as they multiply and spread over the earth. Welker correctly asks, though: Should this image that implies so much dominating power not leave us horrified for what it seems to impart on us humans? Is the connection between the *imago Dei* and *dominium terrae* in Genesis 1 about nothing other than the sad and brutal truth of the human species that always powerfully asserts its strength to prevail biologically as well as culturally (cf. 69)? Could we revision the idea of the *dominium terrae* without a power-centered and violent anthropocentrism? Earlier we analyzed Gerhard von Rad's influential functionalist interpretation of the *imago Dei*, and now the question is raised whether the mandate to "subjugate the earth and rule over the animals" does not compromise everything that may be found and envisioned in the notion of the image of God in terms of relationality, sociality, embodied transcendence, and solidarity among human beings and with other creatures.

On Welker's view the so-called mandate of dominion can be revisioned in a twofold manner: first, it is God's will that human beings stand in a community of solidarity with animals, because they have to live with the animals of the earth and air in a common realm of nourishment; second, as the image of God, human beings stand over against animals, and should extend God's solidarity and care to what is creaturely (cf. 70). I would phrase this somewhat differently: the amazing fact is that, because of our animal nature and our extreme closeness to the animal world, we are still for some reason *theologically* designated to exemplify the image of God and represent God's presence in this world. This explains our solidarity with the animal world, and also the responsible care we are to afford to nature and to animals of all kinds. This care should not be motivated by hierarchical dominion, but precisely by the kind of solidarity that as embodied beings we have with nature and the animal world. Or, as Welker puts it, humankind, created in God's image, must cultivate this community and preserve it in a specific form, namely, one that bears responsibility for those who are weaker (cf. 73).

In his important recent work on the *imago Dei* in Genesis 1, J. Richard Middleton has developed further a notion of the *imago Dei* that closely resonates with Welker's central idea and argues that precisely an interdisciplinary conversation between theologians, biblical scholars, ethicists, and other scholars can make the notion of the image of God more accessible as a resource for theological reflection on human identity and ethics, especially in a world increasingly characterized by brutality and dehumanization (cf. Middleton 2005: 10). In an exegetical pattern closely reminiscent of the arguments discussed by biblical scholars Dexter Callender, Sibley Towner, Patrick Miller, and James Luther Mays earlier in this chapter, Middleton argues that careful exegesis of Genesis 1:26-28, in conjunction with an intertextual reading of the symbolic world of Genesis 1, does indeed suggest that the *imago Dei* refers to human rule, that is, the exercise of human power on God's behalf in creation. For Middleton this could be articulated in two different but complementary ways: seen from one perspective, humans are *like* God in exercising royal power on earth; seen from another perspective, the divine ruler delegated to humans a share in his rule of the earth (cf. 88). The first perspective suggests the image of God as "representational," indicating a *similarity* or *analogy* between God and humans. The second perspective suggests the image as "representative," designating the responsible *office* and *task* entrusted to humanity in administering the earthly realm on God's behalf. Middleton has argued persuasively that these two perspectives on, or expressions of, the *imago Dei* should not be seen as alternatives, but are in fact integrally connected. It is precisely because the representational aspect of the image consists in a functional similarity between God and humanity, specifically concerning the exercise of (royal) power, that the image can be articulated also as representative, referring to the human office of representing God's rule in the world (cf. 88). Against the background of the diverse and many-layered readings of the texts as discussed earlier in this chapter, I believe that Middleton's reading of the connection between the *imago Dei* and *dominium terrae* in Genesis 1 indeed confirms, for this specific aspect of the *imago Dei* texts, what he has called a "royal-functional" reading of the texts.

He has also argued, however, that the meaning of "rule" in these texts goes well beyond our contemporary hermeneutical preconceptions. The royal metaphor, and thus also the *imago Dei* as "rule over the earth," does not exclude but rather integrally includes wisdom and artful, creative construction. The God who rules the creation by his authoritative word is also the supreme artisan who constructs a complex, beautiful, and habitable cosmic structure (cf. 89). Stunningly, humans are now called to imitate or continue God's two-fold creative activity by populating and organizing the unformed and unfilled earth ("fill the earth and subdue it"). In a strong statement that essentially affirms Philip Hefner's highly original designation of humans as "God's created co-creators" (cf. Hefner 1993: 23-51), Middleton now argues that humans, as God's earthly delegates, are to continue the process of creative forming and filling that was started by God. Importantly, then, the human task of exercising power over the earth is modeled on God's creative activity. By implication the human calling as *imago Dei* is itself developmental and transformative, and the human task thus reflects in significant ways the divine artisan portrayed in Genesis 1 as artfully constructing a world.

Importantly, however, the *imago Dei* also includes a priestly or cultic dimension. In the cosmic sanctuary of God's world, humans have pride of place and supreme responsibility, not just as royal stewards and cultural shapers of the environment, but also as "priests of creation," actively mediating divine blessing to the nonhuman world and directing a fallen world toward God's purposes for justice and redemption. Instead of a more traditional picture of the *imago Dei* as a mirror reflecting God, this canonical notion now becomes more like a *prism* refracting the concentrated light of God's glory through a multitude of human sociocultural activities, as we interact with our earthly environment (cf. Middleton 2005: 89f.). Furthermore, Middleton has argued impressively that Genesis 1 portrays God's relationship to the created order in fundamentally nonviolent terms (cf. 235). In fact, the text depicts God's founding exercise of creative power in such a way that we might appropriately describe it as an act of generosity, even of love (cf. 278f.). The human responsibility as the *imago Dei* to imitate the creative act as an act of generosity and love also directly conflicts with any reading of these texts that may want to find in the original text a justification for a scientific or technological conquest over nature, or for violence against women and the environment. On the contrary, Genesis 1 depicts God as a generous creator, sharing power with humans and inviting them to participate in the creative, historical process with responsibility and care. Middleton strikingly sees this nonviolent reading of the original texts as directly implying an ethic of interhuman relationships and ecological practice, which now is fundamentally rooted in the liberating character of the *imago Dei*. Theologically, then, our vision of God's redemptive love can never again be artificially separated from our understanding of God's creative power (cf. 279).

In his vision for an intercultural theology, George Newlands has recently argued in similar fashion for the radical ethical dimension of all interdisciplinary work in theology and science. By linking Christology directly to human rights (cf. Newlands n.d.), Newlands develops the same strong ethical dimension implicit in the idea of humans created in the image of God, and applies it directly to theological anthropology and interdisciplinary theology. On this view, now enhanced by Christology, he can argue that a theology (and science, for that matter) that does not build communities in ways that enhance humanity, and the possibility of exercising full human capacities in ways consonant with the promise of Jesus Christ to bring life more abundant, fails as Christian theology (cf. also Newlands 2005). Newlands is able to go even further, and in an argument parallel to Middleton's rooting of ethics in the liberating character of the *imago Dei*, claims that an ethics of care and solidarity implies care for and solidarity with the marginalized at a fundamental, interdisciplinary level. Thus Newlands opens up a creative way to help us recognize that the issue of human rights belongs at the heart of a discussion of the *imago Dei*.

The doctrinal tradition of the *imago Dei* is of course embedded within the broader context of the rich and complex history of ideas of the Christian faith. In the widest sense of the word one could indeed say that the tradition of the *imago Dei* goes beyond the interpretation of biblical texts: it includes a history of worship, reflection, prayer, and social action. What Newlands therefore has argued for the tradition of the Christian gospel, is also directly true for the tradition of the *imago Dei*: this tradition is complex, multi-leveled, and richly diverse, and insofar as it also is a tradition of relationality, it is a tradition of relationality transformed, and as such points to reconciliation, justice, and liberation (cf. Newlands 2005). This definition of relationality points away from speculative abstraction and toward embodied human persons challenged by the ethical dimensions of interhuman and ecological responsibility.

Conclusion

In my first chapter I argued that any worldview that implies that the domain of religious faith and the domain of scientific thought in any sense exemplify rival or opposing notions of rationality illustrates a rather narrow and highly reductionist perspective on human rationality. Against such a fragmented view of rationality I argued instead for a more holistic, embodied way of thinking about human rationality. On this view it quickly became clear that different and seemingly incompatible reasoning strategies actually share what I have called "the resources of human rationality." For this reason a postfoundationalist notion of rationality, rightly conceived, enables us to leave behind abstract, overgeneralized "blueprints" for engaging in interdisciplinary research and, furthermore, helps us focus on developing, first *contextually* and then *transversally,* the merits of specific interdisciplinary problems. It is in this sense that I hope to show that a multidisciplinary approach to a quite specific problem may actually yield interdisciplinary results.

For this specific case study in interdisciplinarity I have focused my research on the problem of human uniqueness. To stay true to my argument for a postfoundationalist approach to interdisciplinary studies, it was necessary to first identify human uniqueness contextually as a very specific theological problem. Only against the background of the disciplinary identity of it as a theological problem will it be possible to, secondly, apply this contextual approach to paleoanthropology and ask what human uniqueness, in this specific discipline, might mean in terms of human origins. And only against the background of these initial two necessary steps in an interdisciplinary methodology will it be possible to take the third and final step of moving from disciplinary contextuality to a transversal inquiry about the challenges and possible merits of human uniqueness as an interdisciplinary problem.

In Christian theology the problem of human uniqueness, or human distinctiveness, has always been associated directly with the powerful biblical claim that humans are created in the image of God. In this chapter I have turned to the discipline of theology and, against the background of the vast literature on this problem, have analyzed specific trends and themes in the work of a selected number of theologians. In the development of my argument I have tried to show that the canonical core of the ever evolving doctrine of the *imago Dei* has shifted and changed as theologians responded to cultural pressure. However, in the self-critical evolution of the interpretation of the idea of the image of God as defining what the problem of human uniqueness might mean in theology, there is also remarkable continuity as theologians again and again return to the original biblical texts in search of better interpretations. This should not be surprising, given that this kind of disciplinary contextuality always and necessarily implies the embeddedness of all our theological knowledge claims in quite specific disciplinary traditions. This fact alone should inspire us to reflect critically on exactly those traditions that underlie our knowledge claims. In this chapter this has proven to be especially challenging, and it has revealed the alleged sacrosanct core of the tradition of the *imago Dei* as dynamic, pluriform, and multi-interpretable.

In this chapter I have therefore argued:

1. That the concept of the *imago Dei*, in its many incarnations and interpretations, has always in some broad sense functioned to express the relationship between Creator and creatures, God and humans. What we have learned from the history of this canonical tradition is that the idea that humans are created in the image of God never should be argued in abstraction from the concrete historical and social ways we find ourselves situated in today's world. On a postfoundationalist view this also calls for a very consciously pluralistic and interdisciplinary approach to theological reflection.

2. At the heart of the idea of being created in the image of God we found as the deepest intention of the Genesis texts the conviction that the mythical "first humans" should be seen as the significant forerunners of humanity that define the special relationship between God and humans. Being created in God's image in a very specific sense highlights the extraordinary importance of human beings as walking representations of God, in no sense superior to other animals, and with an additional call to responsible care and stewardship to the world, also to our sister species in this world. The multileveled meaning of the notion of the *imago Dei* in the ancient biblical texts was however transversally integrated into the dynamics of one crucial text, Genesis 3:22a: "Then the Lord said, 'See, the human being has become like one of us, knowing good and evil. . . .'" Clearly, in this important text is embedded the most comprehensive meaning of the biblical notion of the *imago Dei*. Here, in the emergence of an embodied moral awareness, and a holistic, new way of knowing, lies the deepest meaning of the notion of the image of God. Also, the theme of the image of God in the texts of the New Testament reflects a remarkable continuity with the Old Testament texts, where Jesus is now identified as the one who, like the primal human before him, defines the relationship between humanity and God. Furthermore, this notion of

the *imago Dei* is as contextual and embodied as that of the "first Adam": what we know of God, we know only through the story of the suffering and resurrection of the embodied person of Jesus, the Jew. Against this background the notion of the *imago Dei* still functions theologically to express a crucial link between God and humans, and should give Christian theologians *intra*disciplinary grounds for redefining notions of evil, sin, and redemption within Christian theology.

3. An analysis of the many diverse incarnations of the notion of the *imago Dei* in recent theological history reveals the danger of disembodied, abstract interpretations of some of the most important and influential substantialist, functionalist, relationalist, existentialist, and eschatological interpretations of this canonical concept. On the other hand, finding a transversal connection between the best of intentions of these many models for imaging God can take it out of the twilight zone of abstraction and reveal it as a powerful symbol and a source of direction for human life. An imaginative, embodied interpretation of the *imago Dei* specifically directs us toward recognizing that our very human disposition or ability for ultimate religious meaning is deeply embedded in our species' symbolic, imaginative behavior, specifically in religious ritual as that specific embodiment of discourse with God and with one another. This view presupposes that the embodied human person has biologically emerged in history as a center of self-awareness, religious awareness, and moral responsibility.

4. Feminist theology has crucially influenced any contemporary rethinking of the idea of the *imago Dei* and has unequivocally shown that this doctrine has traditionally also functioned as a source of discrimination against and oppression of women. Any attempt to revision its powerful resources should therefore specifically uncover the fact that this important theological symbol does indeed give rise to justice, and thus exemplifies a root metaphor for understanding the human person. Such an understanding should ground further claims to human rights, because all humans are equally created in the image of God. On such a theological reading the *imago Dei* implies a liberating ethic of interhuman relationships and ecological responsibility and becomes a source of direction that can guide us beyond imperialist behavior against nature, against our sister species in the animal world, and against those who are different from us. On this view the liberating character of the *imago Dei* is revealed as a theological move away from speculative abstraction and toward embodied human persons, and as a powerful symbol that points to justice, liberation, and reconciliation.

5. Finally, a postfoundationalist approach to the problem of human uniqueness in theology not only reveals a more holistic, embodied way to think about humanness, but also argues for the public voice of theology in our rather complex contemporary culture. As we find ourselves deeply embedded in the very specific research traditions of our disciplines, an interdisciplinary awareness may now help us also to realize that a particular disciplinary tradition, in this case Christian theology, may also generate questions that cannot be resolved by going back to the resources of that same tradition alone. And it is precisely this kind of interdisciplinary awareness that should lead us across disciplinary boundaries in search of intellectual support from other disciplines. In the discipline of paleoanthropology, to which we now turn, we will discover a startlingly similar question to the one that has led us to theology and the *imago Dei*, namely, what does it mean to be human?

The defining notion of the *imago Dei* in theology, when seen in its deepest sense as embodied human uniqueness, will turn out to be an interesting, and even tempting, link to various notions of human uniqueness in the sciences. Reflections on evolutionary epistemology in chapter 2 already revealed the evolution of human cognition as a deeply embodied process, functioning interactively in a real world of challenges and opportunities. What will we now find as we take our theological notions of embodied human uniqueness to paleoanthropology and ask what kind of human beings were behind the symbolizing minds of our distant ancestors, so stunningly revealed in the prehistoric cave art of the Upper Paleolithic? What do these prehistoric artifacts, among the oldest created by *Homo sapiens* in the world, tell us about embodiment and symbolic behavior, about moral awareness, and even about the emergence of religious awareness? It is to these interdisciplinary questions that I turn in the following chapters.

four Human Uniqueness and Human Origins

"To my way of thinking, there is no greater archaeological enigma that the subterranean art of the Upper Palaeolithic western Europe. Anyone who has crouched and crawled underground along a narrow, absolutely dark passage for more than a kilometre, to be confronted . . . by a painting of an extinct wooly mammoth or a powerful, hunched bison will never be quite the same again. Muddied and exhausted, the explorer will be gazing at the limitless *terra incognita* of the human mind."

David Lewis-Williams, *The Mind in the Cave*
(London: Thames and Hudson, 2002), 11

In the first chapter I argued that only in a transversal, interdisciplinary dialogue do we find an adequate vehicle for studying the case before us. Moreover, I argued that only a carefully defined interdisciplinary discourse could help us determine whether what theologians mean by human uniqueness even remotely relates to what scientists mean when they talk about *human origins* and *human uniqueness.* This sets the stage for developing critically both themes so strongly implicit in Lord Gifford's original charge: that of an integrative and interdisciplinary praxis for "theology and the sciences," and the basic theological conviction that there is something about being human, even uniquely human, that is constituted by the relationship of ourselves and our world to God.

In fleshing out an interdisciplinary dialogue on human uniqueness, I have now picked up threads from different discourses and, one by one, woven them into the emerging pattern of this conversation. Recasting Lord Gifford's charge in terms of a postfoundationalist epistemology opened the way for developing a theory of traditions that provides new ways of looking at the origin, the canonical core, and the evolution of scientific and theological traditions. Against this background I argued in my second chapter that Charles Darwin's notion of human identity and human nature still functions as the canonical core of the ongoing discourse on *human evolution,* and that the powerful galaxy of meaning surrounding this Darwinian canon is still forcefully shaping our views of the evolution of *human cognition.* The epistemic implications of these views are most clearly represented today in contemporary evolutionary epistemology, which emerged as an important new discourse to be woven into our interdisciplinary conversation. Finally, teasing out the interesting evolutionary route from Darwin to evolutionary epistemology also set the interdisciplinary stage by creating the necessary transversal space to begin a dialogue between theology and the sciences on human origins and human uniqueness. The different voices of the sciences and theology on human uniqueness can, as I argued, be transversally connected only through the multileveled interaction of this kind of interdisciplinary discourse. Having also woven the complex thread of the textual origins and the theological history of the notion of the *imago Dei* into this emerging interdisciplinary conversation in chapter 3, I now turn to the sciences for a very different perspective on human uniqueness.

In this chapter I will, first, introduce to this interdisciplinary conversation a discipline much neglected in the theology and science dialogue, namely, paleoanthropology. I will argue that there are remarkable methodological links between a postfoundationalist approach to theology and some of the most important voices in contemporary paleoanthropology. Precisely for this reason paleoanthropology, by focusing on human origins and modern human behavior, may intersect transversally with theological arguments and help to redirect our theological understanding of what it might mean to talk about human uniqueness today. At this point it will become important to ask what we encounter when we "sail upstream toward our origins" and look at the spectacular cave art in southwestern Europe, dating from the end of the last Ice Age. Does it make any sense to ask about the "meaning" of prehistoric imagery, or, even more challenging, what might have made these images meaningful for our remote ancestors from a distant and vanished culture? Furthermore, does the remarkable imagery from the Upper Paleolithic help us in any way to isolate any specific features or characteristics of humanness that may justify the fact that scientists today are also talking about "human uniqueness"?

Secondly, I will turn to the research of two prominent scientists, Ian Tattersall and Steven Mithen, who have focused on this Paleolithic material. Their different, sometimes even opposing views have contributed to the discussion of the possible links between the emergence of the cognitively fluid minds of the first humans and the emergence of symbolic and religious behavior. Thirdly, against the background of this discussion of modern human behavior in paleoanthropology and archeology, I will ask whether provocative recent theories that want to link at least some of the prehistoric imagery to shamanism, and thus possibly to the origins of religion, are in any way justified or plausible.

Human Uniqueness and Paleoanthropology

Not only the voices of Charles Darwin and of contemporary evolutionary epistemologists, but also the history of ideas surrounding the theological notion of the *imago Dei,* have now clearly shown that science and theology, each in its own way, are struggling to come to terms with the fact that there is only one kind of human being left on earth today. From our own insular human standpoint we may feel that it is somehow inevitable, or maybe even appropriate, that we are alone in the world. But the living world, in contrast, is so amazingly diverse, and its message seems to be one of variety rather than continuity, which may reasonably lead us to expect some diversity when it comes to our own species. However, our existence as the "last of the hominids" does seem to imply that there is something rather different and distinctive about *Homo sapiens.* Perhaps our being alone in the world today may just be a hard evolutionary and historical fact, with no further scientific or really special theological implications. Then again, what if being alone in the world does have a deeper meaning? If it does, can we know what that is, and would it be possible to have interdisciplinary access to this level of meaning?

Whether theologians or scientists, however, we will certainly never properly understand how we became what we are without first identifying our links to other earlier hominids in a normal biological context, and asking about our origins as a species. On a scientific level, of course, this task falls to paleoanthropologists and archeologists, scientists involved deeply in uncovering evidence of the human past. In this chapter I will weave a new transversal thread into our emerging interdisciplinary conversation by introducing the discipline of paleoanthropology, and the crucial questions it raises about human uniqueness. "Paleoanthropology" is an umbrella term for the diverse group of sciences contributing to the knowledge of human evolution, including studies of extinct and living humans and their exclusive ancestors and relatives, and also the wider biological framework within which the hominid family exists.[1] Paleoanthropology, in focusing on human origins and ancient human behavior, will fulfill a crucial bridging function in our quest for what it might mean to talk about human uniqueness today.

We humans often have no great difficulty interpreting each other's motives, but what about interpreting the motives of other species, even species who are our close relatives? Or, most intriguingly, the motives and intentions of our own remote, prehistoric ancestors? As Tattersall points out, we humans are almost incapable of imagining states of consciousness other than our own (Tattersall 2002: 56f.). We know we share the bulk of evolutionary history with lemurs, monkeys, and the great apes, and we know equally well that, as a result, we also share most of our brain structures with them. It seems to be evident, however, that the way even our closest relatives process information from the outside world differs from our own. Just how large that difference is, and how it impacts the subjective consciousness of those relatives, remains one of the great mysteries of biology and of philosophy. None of this means that nonhuman animals necessarily lack "intelligence," or do not in some way possess "consciousness." Precisely the fact that many other animals clearly have so much in common with humans has led some to conclude that it is more important to understand what unites us with rather than what divides us from closely related species. Yet others feel strongly that it is precisely the fact of human uniqueness that we need to define carefully. In reality, of course, these two interests are effectively identical, since we cannot understand whether we really are unique, and how unique we may be, without also knowing the full extent of what we share with our closest relatives (cf. 57).

In all sciences, prevailing theories are the result of a process of continual testing and the reformulating of ideas and hypotheses, for instance, about the mechanisms of evolution. New discoveries may influence the interpretation of existing evidence, or theories may progress or emerge even in the absence of new evidence. In paleoanthropology, as in anthropology in general, there is a third contributing factor to the status of prevailing theory. This factor is rather unique and has direct epistemological implications, since it concerns the perception of the subject of this kind of study, which turns out to be *ourselves* (cf. Lewin 1993: ixf.). The Copernican and Darwinian revolutions, for example, fa-

---

1. At the core of paleoanthropology are paleontologists who study human fossils and archeologists who study the behavioral record of ancient humans; cf. Tattersall 2003: 223, 637.

mously dislodged humans from a position of centrality in the universe, resulting in a revisioning of what it means to be human. Yet even when accepting our own species, and therefore ourselves, as the product of an evolutionary process, is it still possible to think of ourselves as a rather special product of this process? How should science, and ultimately theology, inform our self-perception on this controversial issue, and what will the influence of this interdisciplinary perception be as we try to discern how humans came to be the way they are?

An interesting part of our self-perception is that it is often the less material aspects of the history of our species that fascinate us most in the evolution of modern humans. We seem to grasp at an intuitive level that language, self-awareness, consciousness, and mythology are probably the defining elements that really make us human (cf. Lewin 1993: 4). Yet exactly these elements are often the least visible in the prehistoric record. For this reason paleo-anthropologists have correctly focused on more indirect but equally plausible material pointers to the presence of the symbolic human mind in early human prehistory. Arguably the most spectacular of the earliest evidences of symbolic behavior in humans are the Paleolithic cave paintings in France and Spain, painted toward the end of the last Ice Age. The haunting beauty of these prehistoric images, and the creative cultural explosion they represent, should fascinate any theologian interested in human origins. Furthermore, at first blush there seems to be a rather remarkable convergence between the evolutionary emergence of *Homo sapiens* and Christian beliefs about the origins of the human creature. In a sense the famous "cultural explosion" of the Upper Paleolithic, more or less 40,000 years ago, although in no historical or evolutionary sense the beginning of a new species, does exemplify some of the most distinctive traits of our species, much as the creation myths of the Abrahamic religions refer to the emergence of a new species, created in the "image of God." But easy comparisons stop here, for as we saw in chapter 3, in the classic religious texts of the ancient Near East the "primal human being" is seen as the significant forerunner of humanity, and as such defines the emerging relationship between humanity and the deity. The theologian, therefore, needs to be aware that the Genesis 1 texts are meant as very distinct religious expressions of the uniqueness of the primal human being, who occupies a position between the deity and humanity, and who is the only one who can lay claim to this distinction (cf. Callender 2000: 206f.). Theologically, then, being created "in the image of God" highlights the extraordinary importance of human beings: human beings are in fact walking representations of God, and as such of exquisite value and importance (cf. Towner 2001: 26), a tradition that was augmented centuries later by a very specific focus on the rational abilities and moral awareness of humans.

Over against more than two thousand years of complex but fairly transparent, conceptual evolution in the history of ideas of theological thought, the prehistoric treasures from the Upper Paleolithic are still strangely inaccessible and seem to have become almost impossible to interpret, their "true meaning" so enigmatic and elusive that it is virtually impossible to re-create any "original" context of meaning in which they were created. Yet we join paleoanthropologists in sensing that these products of ancient imagery may hold the key to what it means to be human, which for theology may significantly broaden and enrich what is meant today by "human uniqueness," especially if we shift our focus of inquiry to accommodate more contextual and particularist interpretations.

Of crucial importance for understanding human uniqueness within the broader context of human evolution, then, is the European prehistoric record, specifically in southwest France and in the Basque Country of northern Spain, where an abrupt and rather stunning transition occurred between 40,000 and 30,000 years ago. Stone tool technologies, essentially unchanged for almost 200,000 years, were suddenly replaced by more sophisticated, stylish artifact tradition, and for the very first time body images (in the form of beads, pendants, and possibly necklaces) and artistic expression (in the form of engraved and painted images on objects and especially on cave walls) appeared. In this era, also called the Upper Paleolithic, the modern human mind was clearly, intensely, and impressively at work.

One of the most important and challenging questions that arises is whether a similar and obvious pattern of cultural change should be expected in other parts of the world too. The still incomplete archeological record seems to give no final answers to this question. Are we dealing here with a process of gradual, cumulative change in the total range of human cultural expression? Or was there some kind of radical shift in the innate biological capacities of the human brain that suddenly led to a rather dramatic and imaginative cultural expression only (or first) in the west European Upper Paleolithic?

Another way of posing this important and fascinating question would be to ask whether we have in the Upper Paleolithic a remarkable evolutionary shift in human *capacities,* or rather a shift in *performance* (cf. Soffer and Conkey 1997: 5f.). Is this a biological change or a shift in social and cultural organization? A real biological, evolutionary event, or rather a cultural revolution? If a real evolutionary event underlies the origin of modern human behavior, then our earlier ancestors were archaic because they lacked the cognitive capacities to perform more complex behaviors. If cultural revolution initiated modern types of human behavior, however, then these ancestors of ours were archaic only because they had yet to launch that revolution. A more balanced view would take a middle ground on this controversial issue and accept that modern human behavior is a complex, pluralistic phenomenon, and that specifically its origins are likely to be as complicated, related to diverse times and spaces, and would certainly include the complex interaction of biological and cultural determinants (cf. Lewin 1993: 116).

As we saw in chapter 2, the Out of Africa hypothesis, with its two waves of emigration to the Middle East and Europe, is currently dominant in paleoanthropology (cf. Lewis-Williams 2002: 189). In addition to the archeological pattern left behind by modern human behavior, there are also the patterns of anatomy and of genetics. For supporters of the Out of Africa hypothesis, then, a remarkable consonance between these different patterns can now be discerned. From anatomical evidence, modern humans appear to have arisen first in Africa, some 100,000 years ago, and then expanded to the rest of the Old World over the next 60,000 years, replacing at least some existing archaic populations. Genetic evidence from mitochondrial and nuclear DNA can be interpreted to give the same overall pattern, even implying complete replacement of archaic populations (cf. Lewin 1993: 117).

The arrival of the Upper Paleolithic in western Europe, which began with the Aurignacian tradition some 40,000 years ago, included a truly unprecedented variability and sophistication in artifact assemblages. This state of affairs is almost universally accepted to be an emergence of more complex and highly structured cognitive systems, and is also associated directly with the appearance of fully developed language abilities. Also, if it is true that modern humans came into Europe from elsewhere, the Aurignacians represent that first wave, and they must have encountered established Neanderthal populations. For many anthropologists the appearance of modern humans in Europe was a true revolution, both qualitatively and quantitatively. In the broad sweep of European prehistory, the Upper Paleolithic people were the first people for whom archeology clearly implies the presence of both "culture" and "cultures" in the classic anthropological sense (cf. Klein 1999: 514ff.). If this kind of characterization is accepted, then in Europe the anatomical and archeological patterns do indeed match, and modern human behavior accompanies the arrival of anatomically modern humans. Because of this, most scholars in the field (but not all) would take the Upper Paleolithic as the standard for recognizing symbolic behavior in *Homo sapiens*.

One thing that is unequivocally clear, however, is that when Upper Paleolithic or Cro-Magnon people started to use pendants and beads as body ornamentation and to paint spectacular paintings on cave walls, they were opening up a dramatically new chapter of human prehistory in western Europe. Between 35,000 and 10,000 years ago, for a period of at least 25,000 years, people were carving, engraving, and painting a wide range of images, sometimes in spectacular assemblages and often in deep, inaccessible sites. In fact, some of these remarkable paintings have been called "deep art," that is, art located in utter darkness, far from daylight and twilight zones and living places, sometimes painted on wide expanses of wall, sometimes hidden in caves within caves, almost like secrets within secrets.[2] The painted caves of Lascaux (in the Périgord region of France) and Altamira (in the Cantabrian region of the Basque Country, or northern Spain), arguably the best examples of this remarkable prehistoric imagery, are both the product of peoples who lived just under 20,000 years ago. And most paleoanthropologists would agree that, although the prehistoric imagery of this remarkably creative period in early human history may not be directly relevant to questions about the *origin* of modern humans, it certainly is overwhelmingly relevant to the question of what it *means to be human* (cf. Soffer and Conkey 1997: 1ff.), and to what it therefore reveals about humanness as such.

During this early period, both portable and parietal prehistoric art (i.e., images painted or engraved on the walls and ceilings of caves) became part of the uniquely human repertoire, a distinct element of the human social and cultural context. Examples include exquisitely carved horses and other animals in ivory; enigmatic rock sculptures like those at Cap Blanc in the Dordogne, France; mammoths and other animals painted on cave walls; carved reindeer antlers; and carnivore teeth as pendants. Recognized today as possibly the very first examples of this kind of prehistoric art are the exciting finds from recent excavations at the cave site of Hohle Fels in Swabia in southwestern Germany. This discovery has bolstered the belief of archeologists and paleoanthropologists that the origin of symbolic figurative art is a crucial threshold in human evolution. Nicholas J. Conard reported the discovery there of three figurines carved from mammoth ivory in the journal *Nature* as recently as December 2003, providing new evidence for the appearance of figurative art more than 30,000 years ago (cf. Conard 2003: 830). These findings are part of the oldest body of figurative art in the world (cf. Sinclair 2003: 774), and include the oldest known representation of a bird, a remarkable therianthropic

2. Cf. John E. Pfeiffer, in García-Rivera 2003: 2.

sculpture (only the second *Löwenmensch*, a small half-human half-lion figure, ever found), and an animal that most closely resembles a horse. For Conard the discovery of a second *Löwenmensch* clearly lends support to the growing hypothesis that Aurignacian or Cro-Magnon people might have practiced some form of shamanism (cf. Conard 2003: 831). These figurines are clearly not "art" as we know it today, but seem to have been personal possessions, and almost certainly the evidence of very discreet, possibly ritual, activities (cf. Sinclair 2003: 774).

Certainly one of the most spectacular examples of early figurative artwork outside of Germany comes from the Grotte Chauvet in the Ardèche region of southern France, discovered in 1994, where rock paintings date as far back as 32,000 years. However, concrete evidence for cultural modernity and symbolic communication, in the form of numerous figurative depictions, regular manufacture of ornaments, and the presence of musical instruments, can rarely be dated earlier than those found in the Swabian region of Germany (cf. Conard 2003: 832). For a scientist such as Anthony Sinclair, these recent findings destroy the idea that the first examples of human art would necessarily be simple and crude. On the contrary, all evidence points to the fact that behaviorally modern humans were astonishingly quick in developing their creative artistic skills over the shortest period of time (cf. Sinclair 2003: 774).

Above everything towers the enigmatic ordering of spectacular painted images in a great number of prehistoric caves in France and the Basque Country: animals of many kinds, rare human images, signs, and mysterious chimeras, part human, part beast. By now more than 330 prehistoric sites have been discovered in Europe (cf. Clottes and Lewis-Williams 1998: 60), and also more than 10,000 decorated objects, or so-called portable art (cf. Lewin 1993: 139). It is this wide-ranging imagery from the Upper Paleolithic that will be central to our interdisciplinary quest for what it means to be human. Many paleoanthropologists strongly believe that the images of Upper Paleolithic art were deeply meaningful in some mythological, even religious sense to the people of the time. The crucial and difficult question is how we, as viewers of these ancient images from a distant (and now vanished) culture, could know whether religious motivation was indeed expressed in these spectacular paintings. Religious and mythological symbols are often cryptic: they speak volumes to members of the culture concerned, but to an outsider they may be merely baffling, strange images. However, the cognitive ability to create these highly sophisticated images requires these early humans to possess the facility to manipulate objects in a remarkable symbolic manner. In addition, some paleoanthropologists point to the important fact that images that become symbols often move in a medium of power.[3] The Upper Paleolithic people did not emphasize a single beast in the same way the south African San reified the eland, but their art was dominated by horses and bison, which raises the question whether these animals also were connected with the potencies of spirit worlds, as the eland was (and still is) for the San. These challenging views are now being taken up directly by scientists like David Lewis-Williams and Jean Clottes.

Parietal art, i.e., images painted or engraved on the walls and ceilings of caves, was made by diverse techniques, some of which were combined in a single image. Some painted images, such as those in the Hall of Bulls in Lascaux (pl. 12 and 13), are as long as 2 meters (6 feet 7 inches) and executed in a number of brilliant colors (cf. Lewis-Williams 2002: 28). Others are only a few centimeters in length and made in one color only. Some were engraved or scratched into the surface, without the use of paint, while others were not just engraved but deeply cut into the walls to create bas-reliefs. One of the most intriguing techniques is the use of a natural rock fold or crack to provide the outline of an animal's body. Only a few strokes of paint were then used to suggest the missing parts, and in some cases such images were visible only when a light source was held in a certain position. This implies that the presence of a human being with a lamp or torch was always necessary for bringing these images to view, and thus to life. This reveals a fascinating and important instance of the interaction between image-maker and cave wall, a form of creative interaction true not only in a metaphorical, interpretative sense, but even in the most literal sense of the word: in some instances it is human presence itself that interactively calls forth the mysterious images from the face of the rock. Contemporary interpretations of these cave paintings, therefore, embody a very distinct holistic, interactive approach for viewing and interpreting them. Against this kind of background it will be abundantly clear that the cave wall itself was given profound significance for the meaning or function of prehistoric "artwork," and was never meant to be only neutral support for the images (cf. 28, 37).

The motifs of parietal art include animals, such as bison, horses, aurochs, woolly mammoths, deer, and felines. In chapter 5 we will discuss the occasional and rare anthropomorphic figures that may or may not represent human beings. Some of these are clearly therianthropes (part-human, part-animal figures; pl. 11), and may have a human body and an animal head. Some

3. For instance, the way the eland symbolizes potency for the San people of southern Africa, both in its living form and when crafted as images by shamans (cf. Lewin 1993: 143).

of the most important and ubiquitous images in Upper Paleolithic caves, however, are handprints: some of these are *positive prints,* i.e., paint was applied to the palm and fingers of the hand and then the hand was pressed against the rock; others are *negative prints,* where a hand was placed against the rock wall and paint was then blown from the mouth (or through a hollow bone) over the hand, so that when the hand was removed, its outline remained imprinted on the rock surface (pl. 1 and 2). Finally, there are also a large number of very diverse and mysterious "signs," geometric forms such as grids, dots, and chevrons that seem almost always to be an intrinsic part of prehistoric "art" (cf. 29; pl. 7).

More than one hundred years of paleoanthropology have given rise to a wide range of comprehensive interpretations of this ancient imagery, ranging from Bruil's hunting magic and Leroi-Gourhan's structuralism to a diversity of new interpretations (cf. Clottes and Lewis-Williams 1998: 61-81; Lewis-Williams 2002: 41-68). Especially important today, however, are arguments for more local and contextual interpretations of Paleolithic imagery, and it is precisely these more contextual approaches that will resonate with my postfoundationalist approach to interdisciplinary discourse. As a serious advocate of such a radically contextual approach, Margaret W. Conkey has warned against too glibly calling Upper Paleolithic image-making "art," since this superimposes a contemporary Western aesthetic perspective onto our evaluation of these mysterious images. A more contextual approach would also imply that rather than asking what the *enduring meaning* of these images may be, we should try to understand what made them *meaningful* for our early modern ancestors (cf. Conkey 1997: 343ff.). What is undoubtedly clear is that a full century of the study of Paleolithic imagery has not produced any definite or final theory about this "art," but rather has brought forth a number of truly conflicting claims. This is why Conkey and Soffer recently suggested that our understanding of prehistoric imagery will be greatly advanced by decoupling this body of archeological evidence about past lifeways from its categorization as "art" (cf. Soffer and Conkey 1997: 1f.). These scientists believe that the initial understanding of this material as "art" was based precisely on unwarranted Western aesthetic assumptions that have greatly constrained our subsequent understanding of the subject matter. For this reason they propose to term this corpus of Paleolithic data *prehistoric imagery* and, when using the term, put "art" in quotation marks.

This growing dissatisfaction with past approaches to prehistoric imagery should be seen as a direct result of an insufficient attention to concrete times and places when the images were actually produced and used. Soffer and

Conkey's views therefore embody a strong reaction against unwarranted uniformitarian assumptions, and broad ahistoric, abstract, and often decontextualized frames of reference (cf. 1f.). For Soffer and Conkey there are various problematic assumptions at work behind the generally used term "art" for prehistoric images. As defined in the past century, art is a cultural phenomenon assumed to function in what we recognize, and even carve off separately, as the so-called aesthetic sphere. It is exactly this Western notion of an aesthetic function that we cannot assume to have existed or functioned similarly in prehistory, and so we cannot assume that the so-called artists of 30,000 years ago discovered something enduring and true for all humans at all times in all places (cf. 2). The deeper and more abstract assumption, then, that a transhistoric level of the meaning of this prehistoric "art" may exist, and that this may be "true for all humans at all times and at all places," does seem to be troublesome and highly a-contextual in its own right.

Soffer and Conkey strengthen this argument by cautioning against seeing prehistory and its accomplishments too simplistically as a "modernity marked by painting," akin to what Bakhtin has called an *epic chronotope*, i.e., an entire period of human life, evoked through the trope of the origins of art, an "absolute past" with a fixed meaning separated by an unbridgeable gap from the real time of today (cf. Bakhtin 1981: 218). Soffer and Conkey also caution against seeing prehistory too simplistically as part of a linear, evolutionary trajectory. The idea that we can explain human prehistory only as part of (or the beginning of) a progressive evolutionary trajectory has now been weakened considerably. As Soffer and Conkey nicely put it, we have to recognize and accept that the ground on which we stand when trying to represent the viewpoints of others in the distant, prehistoric past is not firm, but is rather tectonic and shifting (cf. Soffer and Conkey 1997: 3). The archeological record, therefore, reveals that the past is a complex mosaic rather than a linear trajectory: anatomically modern humans may have been in Australia before they were in France; some would even argue that Neanderthals cohabited with modern humans, using similar tool kits in the Middle East and moving into the same sites and valleys, and that early image making occurred in many places in the world. Such a "catholic," or comprehensive, view that takes location and context absolutely seriously is indeed crucial in reorienting the entire field of inquiry (cf. 3). For the theologian entering into interdisciplinary dialogue with paleoanthropology, this will be crucial. Our view of this fascinating but enigmatic period of early human history will necessarily be fragmentary and pluralist, and might leave us with a mosaic of possibilities when we start asking questions about human uniqueness.

1. The Cave of Gargas: two red hands and two black hands

2. The Cave of Gargas: three red hands with bent fingers

3. The Cave of Cougnac:
the wounded man

4. The Cave of Cougnac:
the wounded man

5. The Cave of Niaux: the bison (Salon Noir)
6. The Cave of Niaux: the ibex (Salon Noir)

7. The Cave of Pech-Merle: the Dotted Horses
8. The Cave of Lascaux: the "Chinese Horse" (the Painted Gallery)

9. The Cave of Lascaux: the "Swimming Stags" (the Main Gallery)
10. The Cave of Lascaux: the Unicorn (Great Hall of the Bulls)

11. The Cave of Lascaux: the Bird Man (The Shaft)
12. The Cave of Lascaux: the Great Hall of the Bulls

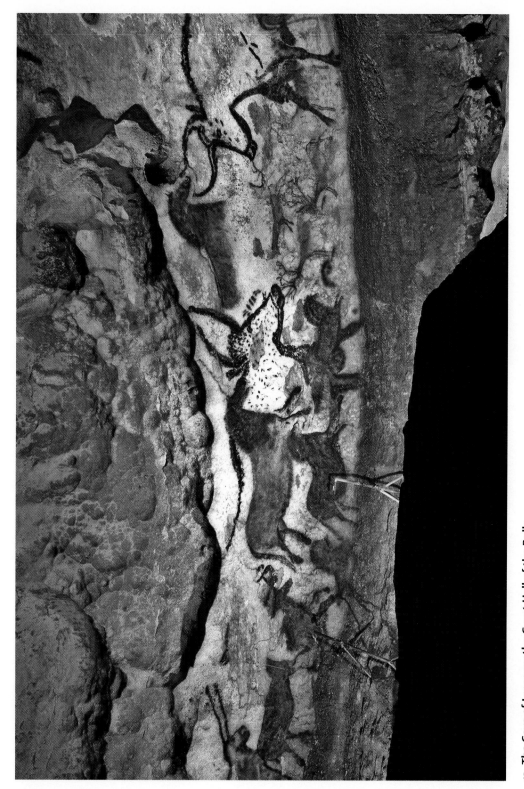

13. The Cave of Lascaux: the Great Hall of the Bulls

14. The Cave of Lascaux: the Black Cow Panel (the Main Gallery)
15. The Cave of Lascaux: the Red Cow (the Painted Gallery)

The question that remains to be answered, I believe, is, what is it about the highly exceptional prehistoric imagery that still speaks to us in such a profound way? Surely, the spectacular prehistoric imagery could at least be expected to exhibit some aesthetic or communicative *intent* to which we can bear witness. Even if we are careful not uncritically to impose contemporary Western aesthetic notions onto these images, they possess a recognizable beauty, and, we sense, a possible symbolic, even if elusive, narrative meaning that may have some cross-cultural, transversal intelligibility and appeal. This would not necessarily be the same as saying that those distant image-makers "discovered something that is true for all humans at all times in all places." Soffer and Conkey do seem to be right, that we cannot assume that the primary function of prehistoric imagery was aesthetic in any modern, Western sense of the word. We must be nuanced, and careful not to claim, for instance, that Lascaux (pl. 8-15) represents the origins of art as the "first masterpiece" of human art history, a mistake recently made by Alejandro García-Rivera in his *Wounded Innocence: Sketches for a Theology of Art* (2003). We also have to be careful, I would argue, and for the same reasons, not to see the spectacular prehistoric imagery as "art in its very infancy" (Sullivan 2002: 11). This reveals more about our cultural categories and constructions than about the complex contexts of prehistoric social action within which these images were created and carried very specific meaning(s). Classifying prehistoric imagery exclusively as art, or as the origins or beginnings of art, does seem to limit deeper and more contextualized understandings and often reveals a highly Eurocentric view of human evolution. On this point Soffer and Conkey rightly warn us against getting tangled up in the self-congratulatory history of the achievements of "the West" (cf. Soffer and Conkey 1997: 3).

Yet all symbolic Paleolithic images, whether they are supposed to function in the aesthetic domain or not, certainly evoke beauty, and as such values and beliefs, and all of them carry emotionally charged meanings that are readily apparent to specific individuals and groups of people, while remaining opaque, at best, to others. What does seem to be universal to all of us as humans is that we mark durable objects with symbols, a behavior strongly associated with anatomically modern humans and a modern human way of life that is embedded in, and expressed through, culture. We make sense of our worlds by producing symbolic ones that include real and imaginary creatures, myths, and beliefs. Therefore, and importantly, it is in part this association of modern humans and material symbolization that makes this phenomenon a historical one, something that came into existence at some specific time and appears not to have existed prior to it (cf. 4). And as a historical phenomenon, created symbolically by people like us, our direct ancestors, these images also become accessible to us, even if in a tentative, ambiguous way. Soffer and Conkey's promosaic, contextual approach with clear transversal intent now seems to resonate extremely well with my own postfoundationalist approach, as argued in chapter 1. In the end we will have to judge whether this postfoundationalist approach to interdisciplinary dialogue will allow us to bring the mosaic of current interpretations in paleoanthropology into direct dialogue with the equally checkered and fragmented history of human uniqueness in Christian theology.

*   *   *

As discussed in chapter 2, all humans alive today are classified in a single subspecies, *Homo sapiens sapiens,* anatomically modern human beings, whose direct ancestry as such, in various parts of the world, dates back to between 125,000 and 40,000 years ago. Remarkably, this species, and this species alone, is firmly and unequivocally associated with the habitual and patterned symbolic marking of objects. It is in this very specific sense that most paleoanthropologists would argue for a distinct species uniqueness that can also be translated as "human uniqueness." It is the practice of a symbolic organization and mediation of life that finally signals the advent of a fully modern way of life: a way of life embedded in and shaped by culture, and thus dependent on the making of meaning (cf. Soffer and Conkey 1997: 4).

A crucial question that we should ask is: Why do we have prehistoric "art" from around 40,000 years ago and not before? The answers to this difficult question have been varied and diverse, but come down to hypotheses about the advent of some form of modern capacity for symboling among anatomically modern people that focuses on the invention of symbol-based language and accompanying neurological changes of some sort. Conkey and Soffer, to bolster their argument for a highly contextual, pro-mosaic, pluralist approach in paleoanthropology, argue that these explanations are intriguing but ultimately unsatisfactory. By equating the proliferation of image making with the advent of the capacity to do so, such explanations disregard at least three things: (1) the presence, albeit sparse and ambiguous, of some images considerably prior to 40,000 years ago; (2) the spatial discontinuity in image making across regions occupied by equally modern humans (e.g., the abundance of Upper Paleolithic images in the Franco-Cantabrian regions versus their sparseness in the Levant, Africa, and Asia); (3) the temporal and even spatial discontinuities in the production of images within the different regions (e.g., the virtual disappearance of image making in the Franco-Cantabrian region with the advent of the Holocene, the last 10,000 years, versus its proliferation in the Levant at the same time). It is also clear that this image making cannot simplistically and directly be equated with the mere biological phenomenon of *Homo sapiens sapiens*. Furthermore, our anatomically modern ancestors were clearly present in Africa and the Middle East as long as 60,000 years before prehistoric imagery appears in the western European archeological sites (cf. 5).

The troubling question remains, of course, why such an unusual and spectacular revolution in human symbolic behavior happened in the southwest European Upper Paleolithic. In Asia the neat concordance of patterns begins to fragment, and there is no clear Middle to Upper Paleolithic transition. In Africa the burning question is, does the scarcity of artifacts of explicit modern human behavior definitely imply the relative absence of the modern mind? Alison Brooks and Sally McBrearty, in a well-known paper, have strongly argued against this viewpoint (McBrearty and Brooks 2000). In this interpretation of modern human behavior, they argue against the viewpoint that modern human behaviors arose suddenly, and nearly simultaneously, throughout the Old World around 40,000 to 50,000 years ago. Moreover, for them the "human revolution" model creates a time lag between the appearance of anatomical modernity and perceived behavioral modernity, and thus creates the impression that the earliest modern Africans were behaviorally primitive. In a rather strong statement the authors claim that the unusual developments in western Europe represent a remote cul-de-sac with a somewhat anomalous prehistoric record. Furthermore, they argue that models derived from the unique record of European prehistory do not explain events in Africa where modern people actually originated (cf. 545). McBrearty and Brooks thus want to warn against a profound Eurocentric bias and a failure to appreciate the depth and breadth of the African archeological record. What should be remembered is that significant modern human behavior — as in blade technology, bone tools, increased geographic range, specialized hunting, the use of aquatic resources, the systematic processing and use of pigment, art, and decoration — is found in the African Middle Stone Age thousands of years earlier. Moreover, these items do not occur suddenly together as predicted by the "human revolution" model, but at sites that are widely separated by space and time. This indeed suggests a much more gradual assembling of the "package" of modern human behaviors in Africa.

For those of us who still want to talk of the amazing "creative explosion" of the western European Upper Paleolithic, and thus of the suddenness with which this new "package" of consciousness appeared in western Europe and the comparative speed with which it replaced the old Neanderthal way of life, it is very important to remember that in Africa and Asia we find important precursors of the "creative explosion." It is certainly in Africa that we must seek the earliest evidence for what we might later want to call the "human revolution," and theologians who are engaged in interdisciplinary dialogue with paleoanthropologists have to be careful not to prolong a Eurocentric bias even beyond the disciplinary boundaries of Paleolithic research. One way to achieve a less biased account of the west European transition is to distinguish between what scientists call (a) the anatomically modern features of the human body and (b) the behaviorally modern features of human life. Furthermore, in trying to understand "human uniqueness," whether anatomically or behaviorally, it is important to realize that not all early *Homo sapiens* communities made bone tools, ate fish, or used paint to make images in caves (cf. Lewis-Williams 2002: 97).

David Lewis-Williams has argued for the importance of this point by also pointing to the African evidence for the emergence of modern human anatomy and behavior. As became clear in chapter 2, most researchers today accept the so-called Out of Africa hypothesis. They believe that the fossil evidence has conclusively shown that the precursors of anatomically modern human populations evolved in Africa and left the continent in two waves. This hypothesis explains why western Europe was occupied by Neanderthals for thousands of years before the *Homo sapiens* communities made their way west from the Middle East and through eastern Europe. What it does not confirm is that those modern populations that left Africa did not yet have fully modern behavior and acquired it only some 40,000 to 50,000 years ago. It now seems that the shift to behavioral modernity started in Africa as long as 250,000 to 300,000 years ago. Like McBrearty and Brooks (2000), Lewis-Williams makes the important point that we should not speak of "modern human behavior," but rather of "modern human behaviors": modern human behavior did not appear suddenly in the prehistoric world as a complete package, and in this sense there indeed was no "revolution" (cf. Lewis-Williams 2002: 98). Good examples of this include the fact that blade making and pigment processing using grindstones date back to 250,000 years ago; bone tools are about 100,000 years old. Probably the most sensational new find was made by Chris Henshilwood and his team on the southeastern coast of South Africa in a cave called Blombos: remarkable seashell ornaments, and a piece of ocher, carefully engraved with crosses and a central line, have been dated to 77,000 years ago, more or less. Though not a representational image, this is now the oldest dated "art" in the world, and it shows indisputable modern human behavior at an unexpectedly early date. In light of this and related discoveries, Henshilwood and his team have also argued powerfully for a more gradual emergence of modern human behavior in Africa (cf. Henshilwood et al. 2004: 404f.). This clearly shows that modern human behavior was appearing piecemeal in Africa as a stepwise progress and a gradual assembling of the modern human adaptation, before the Upper Paleolithic transition in western Europe (Lewis-Williams 2002: 99). Precisely for this reason the Middle to Upper Paleolithic transition in western Europe should never be confused with the origin of *Homo sapiens*. Lewis-Williams puts it well: the African evidence shows that innovations were often ad hoc and their dissemination sporadic. But western Europe still remains a special case that saw an efflorescence of certain components of modern human behavior (cf. 99).

In one sense, then, there was indeed an "Upper Paleolithic Revolution," a creative explosion and a sudden burst of symbolic activity. But this explosion was not universal, nor was it an indivisible package deal. Lewis-Williams is right: this cautionary note in no sense diminishes the importance of what happened in western Europe; it merely places it in a wider perspective, one that opens up new lines of explanation. If the modern mind and modern behavior evolved sporadically in Africa, it follows naturally that the symbolic activities we see in Upper Paleolithic western Europe could have occurred before *Homo sapiens* communities reached present-day France and the Iberian Peninsula (cf. 99). For Lewis-Williams this also means that we should not seek a single neurological event as the triggering mechanism for the west European "creative explosion."

Scholarly opinion, therefore, is as divided over the interpretation of the archeological evidence as it is over that of the fossils. The themes are the same: Gradual behavioral change or abrupt change? Continuity or replacement? These themes have been central to the debate over the origins of modern human populations throughout the greater part of the twentieth century (cf. Lewin 1993: 129). In light of this ongoing discussion, it is again important to note that Soffer and Conkey have consistently warned against conflating *capacity* and *performance* when trying to explain the advent of image making as a result of the advent of some new capacity for this behavior; while capacity is necessary for performance, performance need not follow the capacity to perform (cf. Soffer and Conkey 1997: 5). Further, when performance does follow capacity, its appearance may depend entirely on contextual circumstances. The capacity for image making, then, may have been present among the ancestors of fully modern people, but prior to the Upper Paleolithic or its African equivalent, the Late Stone Age, it was not regularly or routinely exercised. What was absent was *performance,* the habitual use of the capacity in imaginative, patterned behavior. And why it was absent points to the social and cultural contexts within which such a material practice normally would have been efficacious and would have had appropriate meanings. Therefore, this kind of contextualized approach requires us to examine the kinds of circumstances under which image making becomes habitual, an approach that can help us understand the temporal and regional discontinuities in the global record (cf. 6).

Many of the past searches for the meaning of prehistoric "art," therefore, began with unjustified uniformitarian or metatheoretical assumptions that some meanings are universal or transcendent. It is now clear, however, that this kind of generic claim is totally negated by the very essence of symbols and symbol making, namely, that their meaning is always historically shaped, and therefore rather arbitrarily and culturally determined. For exactly this reason the "broad approaches," looking for metatheories and single overarching accounts to interpret the meaning of the cave paintings, are now rightly discredited. Soffer and Conkey would rightly argue for using the images in their local and historical contexts to understand the wider, and what I would call *transversally* linked, phenomena of human material symbolization and image making, as a practice that was clearly always accomplished in very specific settings but at the same time revealed a transcontextual intent and meaning.

Soffer and Conkey's postfoundationalist argument is at its strongest when they reflect on the interactive mode of our continuing interpretation. Nothing can arrest the continual transformation of our ongoing interpretations of the ancient imagery into what I would call "frozen meanings." Specific "codes of recognition" constantly circulate through the famous ancient imagery; the viewer is an interpreter, interpretation changes, and we can never lay claim to absolute knowledge of our object of study. The interpretation of Paleolithic art on this view is therefore truly postfoundationalist, and always fallibilist and provisional. As interpreters we constantly construct ourselves through the others we study. Interpretations change because there are new finds, new data, new facts, but our stories also change because of new assumptions, new theories and hypotheses, precisely because new interpreters have taken up the topic (cf. 8). Also in my interdisciplinary reinterpretation for these Gifford Lectures, I hope to redefine, and reconceptualize, the accessibility to what we now may see as the meaning of Paleolithic "art." In terms of my approach, the ongoing interactive process of interpreting Paleolithic imagery might reveal the transversal opening up of often radically diverse perspectives, and these perspectives circulate around the gravitational pull of the elusive, deeper historical meanings or "canons" of these spectacular achievements bequeathed to us by our ancient Cro-Magnon ancestors.

Conkey and Soffer are certainly correct, then, in warning us to be wary of attempts to use the terms "Ice Age" and "Upper Paleolithic" as suggesting any uniformity of expression. There was indeed a great and quite stunning diversity in Paleolithic art, both in space and in time. During the Upper Paleolithic, especially during the era 18,000 to 10,000 years ago, there was a real escalation in the importance of cave painting. For this reason Roger Lewin can argue that 88 percent of all Ice Age images come from this late era of Lascaux and Altamira, which has led some scholars again to question the idea of an "explosion of artistic expression" at the beginning of the Upper Paleolithic (cf. Lewin 1993: 146). To this general caution should be added the often neglected presence of music making and instruments, notably flutes, in Upper Paleolithic cultures. A truly spectacular find happened at Geissenklösterle in Germany, where a fragment of a bone pipe or flute, made from the radius bone of a swan, with three clear finger holes, was discovered. Such is the evidence of complexity of these earliest prehistoric flutes that they cannot possibly have been the first musical instruments, even though they certainly are the oldest in the archeological record (cf. Sinclair 2003: 774). For a scholar like Lewin the richness of prehistoric painting, musical instruments, and other portable art clearly indicates that a picture may gradually be constructed of Upper Paleolithic hunter-gatherers with a rich mythology, who engaged in widespread social and political alliances enhanced by trade and exchange (cf. Lewin 1993: 146ff.).

The existence of Paleolithic art was first established and accepted through the discovery, in the early 1860s, of engraved and carved bones and stones in a number of caves and rock shelters in southwest France. In some areas, such as the Basque Country, superstitions and religious traditions associated with caves are probably extremely ancient, perhaps extending back all the way to the period of the actual creation of Paleolithic art. Certainly there is some evidence that rituals associated with the prehistoric imagery may have survived in certain areas until quite recently. In an interesting anecdote Paul G. Bahn and Jean Vertut refer to an incident in 1458 when Pope Calixtus III forbade Spaniards from performing rites in the "cave with the horse pictures." It is not clear exactly which cave he meant, but from this description he was likely referencing pictures dating back to the Ice Age (Bahn and Vertut 1997: 16).

What is fascinating is that no cave art, as far as we know, was ever mentioned in print before the nineteenth century. According to Bahn, this is quite understandable, since prehistory, at least as a concept, did not "exist" until

then, and so the pictures had no significance. However, once prehistoric studies got under way and portable art from the Ice Age had been discovered and
authenticated, a few scholars began to notice what had been staring them in
the face for so long. It took archeology a long time to recognize the spectacular
nature and value of cave art. In the famous discovery of Altamira in Spain, it
was claimed that the paintings were far too good to be so ancient, and that a
modern artist had faked them (cf. 18). After the discovery of a Paleolithic lamp
in the cave of La Mouthe, in the Dordogne, France, in 1899, the age and credibility of cave art could no longer be opposed and acceptance came at last. On
August 14, 1902, a number of prehistorians attending a congress of the French
Association for the Advancement of Science made an excursion to the Les
Eyzies area and visited the painted caves there. According to Bahn, this event
marked the official recognition by science of the existence of prehistoric cave
art (22).[4] Toward the end of the Pleistocene, artistic activity was under way all
over the world. The technical, naturalistic, and aesthetic qualities of European
Paleolithic images remain almost unique to date, but it is nevertheless true
that, at this period in other parts of the world, especially in Africa, one can see
traces and intimations of the same phenomenon. Nevertheless, the European
sites do seem to remain rather unique, for the moment, in the quantity and
quality of their surviving Paleolithic art (cf. 41).

Like Margaret Conkey, Bahn warns against the construction of all-
embracing metatheories to explain the complex phenomenon of Paleolithic
art, theories that bend the facts to fit an imposed overall explanation — or ignore them. The reason is quite simple: we are faced here with two-thirds of
known art history, covering at least twenty-five millennia and a vast area of the
world.[5] Paleolithic art is so complex and varied that most scholars now agree
that it would be futile to try to include all of it within one overall theory. In the
same sense, not all Paleolithic art is necessarily mysterious or religious, although some of the cave paintings are almost certainly tied to ritual and ceremony (213). Some of the art is overtly public, some very private. And although
there is a certain thematic unity in the depictions especially of animals, most
of the recent studies emphasize that each cave has its own unique decorative
program. For this reason one can study the complex phenomenon of
Paleolithic art on at least three principal levels: (1) the individual sites (either a

4. Cf. Bahn and Vertut 1997: 23-27, for a discussion of Lower Paleolithic art as "proto-
art."

5. For the same reason it is rather ironic that so many books about the origin of art begin with a token picture of Lascaux, since these famous paintings actually stand at the halfway
mark in the history of art (cf. Bahn and Vertut 1997: 212).

cave, an object, or a group of objects); (2) regional groupings (of motifs, complex signs, dominant animal species, styles, etc.); (3) as a whole, seeking homogeneity and regularity. As we saw with Conkey and Soffer's proposal, this last option is quickly losing favor, and efforts are now focused on the first two directly contextual options.

It is also now generally agreed that Paleolithic art contains hidden messages, no doubt of many kinds, such as signatures, ownership, warnings, exhortations, demarcations, commemorations, narratives, myths, and metaphors (cf. 213). Their basic function was probably to affect the knowledge and behavior of those who could read them. We, alas, do not know how to read them. We can certainly analyze their content, their execution, their locations, but the way everything was combined into a meaningful experience is gone forever. Without direct information from the bygone age, we can today use the imagery only as a source of hypotheses, never as definite confirmation of them. Nevertheless, we are constantly learning, and despite frustrations, the study of Paleolithic art is extremely rewarding, not only because of the unique experience of visiting the caves as the very places where the artists worked, but also because it still represents our most direct contact with the beliefs and preoccupations of our direct ancestors, and therefore constitutes one of the most fascinating episodes of prehistory (213).

*   *   *

When we begin to ask about the meaning and purpose of Paleolithic art, the postfoundationalist argument for discovering transversal links from within a radically contextual study of the prehistorical imagery is bolstered if we focus on what we see in some of the most famous caves. Also, in trying to understand and interpret the prehistoric imagery in the caves of southwest France and the Basque Country, it is important to keep in mind that none of the Paleolithic caves represents the entire evolution of Paleolithic "art." This spectacular phenomenon stretched over a period of roughly two hundred centuries (20,000 years). Some of the oldest and most schematic images are found in Grotte Cougnac, where human forms pierced with strange arrows, a rare depiction I will discuss in chapter 5, are almost 25,000 years old (pl. 3 and 4). Also, for instance, the exaggerated proportions and perspectives of the beautiful "dotted horses" in Grotte Pech-Merle reveal their age (pl. 7); they were painted more than 20,000 years ago, at a time when our ancestors had already been practicing graphic art for nearly 10,000 years (cf. Plassard and Marie-Odile 1995: 26). As time went by, progress was inevitable. This is most evident in the world-famous cave of Lascaux, painted around 17,000 years ago. In Lascaux the paintings are more stylistic, and through the skillful use of paint the artists seem to get closer to an exact, though ethereal, representation of their subjects (pl. 8-15). It was perhaps only with the images of Font-de-Gaume, painted around 15,000 years ago, that prehistoric "art" entered its classical period; the harmony in the shapes of the bodies, the exactness of proportions, and the deep respect for perspective with highly evolved painting techniques give the figures realism and life. In the cave of Niaux, in the French Pyrenees, French paleoanthropologist Jean Clottes has established that in the cave's famous Salon Noir sanctuary, most of the animals were first sketched in charcoal, with manganese paint then added on top (pl. 5 and 6). This clearly indicates a special place where the images were carefully planned, especially in contrast to the other drawings in the cave, which were done without any preliminary sketches (cf. Bahn 1998: 156). For the same reason Roger Lewin has argued that the Salon Noir in Niaux can definitely be regarded as an important sanctuary since the outline sketch of the panels, followed by their full execution, speaks of a premeditation absent from most of the other images, often deeper in the cave. Such premeditation is consistent with a ritual ceremony of considerable importance (cf. Lewin 1993: 146ff.).

By the time the Magdalenians discovered Rouffignac, one of the most famous caves near Les Eyzies in the Dordogne, and painted around 13,000 B.C.E., they had acquired such mastery over perspective and such skill in the use of synthesis that it took them only a few lines to sketch their subject matter. In Rouffignac the so-called Patriarch, the Rhinoceros Frieze, and the bison and horses on the Great Ceiling all prove their superior craftsmanship and the result of 200 centuries of technical inventiveness. Here all the compositions are well balanced, and everything indicates the know-how of true professionals. The work is also markedly more austere, a foretaste of the pure symbolism of later years, with less emphasis on display, and with a push toward abstraction (cf. Plassard and Marie-Odile 1995: 28). The difficulty of answering questions of meaning and purpose is demonstrated clearly by a visit to Rouffignac, famous for its "great ceiling." What is interesting, however, is that at the time the ceiling was painted, the cave floor was so high, so close to it, that there was no space for the prehistoric "artist" to stand back and look at the drawings and paintings. Unlike today, now that the floor space has been dug out and cleared and we can look up at the entire spectacular ceiling, the ceiling at the time could never have been seen in its entirety by the painter. This certainly poses deep and serious questions as to the purpose of prehistoric cave imagery, and we have no final answers to questions like: If the artists could not see their work, who could? And what was the most important feature of the prehistoric imagery: the act of painting itself, or the end product and its visual attraction, however constrained (cf. 20)? The cave at Rouffignac, with its famous "cave bear holes," has been attracting animals and people for many thousands of years. But while for animals it provided shelter and a safe place to raise their young, for *Homo sapiens* it must have had a different, more enigmatic purpose. Scholars seem to agree that at Rouffignac the general uniformity of style and technique shows that the art was completed within a very short period of time and that it could have been the work of a small number of artists (cf. 22). At Rouffignac, as with other Paleolithic caves in the Dordogne region like Bernifal, Font de Gaume, Combarelles, Lascaux, others farther south like Cougnac and Pech-Merle, and in the Pyrenees, Niaux and Gargas, there is clear evidence that in spite of enormous diversity in time and space between the cave sites, the artists desired to depict detail in a rather exact way, with a very specific and clear attempt at stylization.

While it is easy to describe the imagery one sees when visiting the Paleolithic caves in the southwest of France, it is almost impossible to understand some sense of deeper meaning. What does seem to be clear is that this prehistoric imagery was never intended to be merely descriptive. Paleolithic "artists" never depicted their animal (and rare human) figures in their natural surroundings (pl. 11 and 12). So, for instance, in the background against which the artwork was composed, there clearly is no attempt to depict the sky, the sun, the moon, water or vegetation, not even the ground, or any horizontal lines suggesting the ground or a landscape. In the great ceiling at Rouffignac, the tips of the horses' tails are considerably lower than their hooves. Sometimes the lower parts of the mammoths' bodies merely suggest a long coat hanging down into empty space. Many of the animals are depicted by a mere outline of some prominent feature of their anatomy (pl. 9). Despite the accuracy of certain anatomical details, however, everything suggests that the aim was not to depict animals with any sense of realism. In an atmosphere steeped in an aura of serenity (pl. 13), the subject seems to be immaterial and floating on air (cf. 23). The ancient and remarkable work of these Paleolithic artists seems to depict some idea, some principle, possibly even some narrative concept, but what exactly this was we may never know for sure, even as scholars come forward with new and highly plausible theories.

It took the world a long time to acknowledge cave painting and prehistoric imagery as a true cultural, aesthetic achievement, as a witness to the creative spirit and genius of our ancestors from the last Ice Age. Today, however, thanks to this spectacular imagery, we are indeed invited to "sail upstream towards our origins" (cf. Fanlac 1994: 10). In addition to the paintings (cf. Lascaux, Altamira, and Font-de-Gaume), engravings (especially Combarelles and Rouffignac), and sculptures (Cap Blanc), many caves also display mysterious signs and symbols like "tectiforms" that are painted or engraved on cave walls. These signs are in almost all the caves, and although the mystery of their meaning remains unsolved, their intriguing presence is playing an increasingly important role in new shamanistic interpretations of some of the Paleolithic "art."

Most pressing, therefore, is the question whether the images, especially the images of animals and, more rarely, humans, represented some form of symbolism, and a possible imaginative, symbolic world. Some scholars do refer explicitly to what they call "the durability of this coded system," i.e., the broadly defined similarity of style, though often strikingly different at different times and in different caves, that nevertheless links together this rich treasure in western Europe over several thousand years as Paleolithic "art." One thing seems certain: this ancient imagery was of great importance to hunting people during the Magdalenian era. This makes it very tempting to ascribe beliefs or rituals to these humans, based especially on what we know today of groups of humans still living under roughly similar conditions. As we will see, some paleoanthropologists are looking carefully at the possibility that the prehistoric imagery might suggest forms of early religious behavior, even shamanism.

Even though these material works of "art" strongly suggest a spiritual mind-set, we actually know very little about our distant ancestors. These magical, elusive works suggest questions like: What were the beliefs of the Cro-Magnon peoples? What were their customs? What were their legends? How were their social structures organized? It is difficult to escape the implication that the Paleolithic paintings suggest a definite narrative frame of mind that might have led directly to the painting of these figures. Although we will never know, and although we should be careful not to project our own categories onto these ethereal expressions, there might be good reasons for arguing that these drawings, paintings, and etchings could have functioned as links between the natural and the supernatural worlds. But how would we know? Which scientists are arguing this position, and how plausible is their argument for seeing the artwork as symbolic, possibly even religious artifacts? And if this argument could be made plausibly, what would it mean for the way we perceive what it means to be uniquely human today?

I will contend that if there are plausible arguments for the symbolic, or even just tentative religious, meaning of some of these paintings, this symbolic heritage of our distant ancestors may reveal something about the emergence of the earliest form of religion, and thus support the naturalness and rationality of religious faith. If this were the case, however, would there be any way to intelligently link our much more recent theological traditions of human uniqueness to this ancient heritage from a distant, vanished culture? Put differently, could contemporary theological traditions of human uniqueness learn anything from these ancient traditions? Of course, all this would first of all presuppose a successful interdisciplinary dialogue between paleoanthropology and theological anthropology.

Imagination and Prehistoric Art

Against this background we now have to ask: What do paleoanthropologists and archeologists really mean when they talk about the evolution of "human uniqueness"? To answer this question I want to turn to the very different, sometimes even opposing views of two prominent scientists who have incorporated this Paleolithic material into their work on human uniqueness, Ian Tattersall and Steven Mithen.

In his intriguing book *Becoming Human: Evolution and Human Uniqueness* (1998), Tattersall takes his cue for analyzing human uniqueness directly from the amazing mural work and rock art of our ancient ancestors in the caves of southwest France. He argues that our Cro-Magnon ancestors exhibited a distinctly human need for symbolic expression of values and beliefs, and from the beginning the most important leitmotif of his book is the question: What kind of evolutionary history led to the appearance of this symbol-making creature? Tattersall unveils a scenario that traces hominid evolution from its origins some 5 million years ago in Africa, with the appearance of the australopithecines, through the emergence of various species of the genus *Homo* (*Homo habilis, Homo ergaster, Homo erectus, Homo neanderthalensis,* etc.), right through to us, *Homo sapiens,* in whom symbolic behavior appeared explosively about 40,000 years ago.

Tattersall also examines chimpanzees and other primates that offer the best comparative models for understanding the cognitive capacities of early hominids. Where Darwin and most neo-Darwinians have held that the anatomical and cognitive traits of modern humans gradually arose in tandem, and faint beginnings would be ascribed to our remote ancestors and greater capacities to our more proximate relatives, Tattersall distances himself from this gradualist position and argues that the emergence of human uniqueness was achieved in one quantum leap. He finds theoretical support for this belief in Stephen Jay Gould and Niles Eldredge's punctuated equilibrium model of hominid evolution. This theory suggests that hominid evolution was punctuated by rapid speciation events, usually caused by dramatic changes in climate or geography, during which groups split from one another, creating new species that might then remain morphologically and behaviorally stable for hundreds and thousands of years. It is certainly clear that we share various behaviors, propensities, and physical structures with other kinds of animals, and through these similarities we know we are an integral part of nature. What Tattersall wants to do, however, is look carefully at the question of *human uniqueness,* and what exactly sets us apart from our closest relatives in nature. Consequently, much of his argument is devoted to mapping the size of the cognitive gulf that separates us from the great apes, leading him to the conclusion that, as far as we know, we are indeed alone in nature in being able to contemplate our place in it. Early on in his book Tattersall clearly highlights this kind of human uniqueness: "We human beings are indeed mysterious animals. We are linked to the living world, but we are sharply distinguished by our cognitive powers, and much of our behavior is conditioned by abstract and symbolic concerns" (3).

Human beings, in all their uniqueness, are certainly the result of a long evolutionary process, but about 40,000 years ago we find a remarkable creative surge in Europe. At this time Europe was inhabited by only the Neanderthals, a distinctive and now extinct group of humans belonging to the species *Homo neanderthalensis.* These important ancestors were certainly complex beings and talented users of the landscape in which they lived, and had diverged sharply from the brutish image with which generations of cartoonists have endowed them (cf. 5). Even so, Tattersall argues that they left no evidence of the creative, innovative spark that is so conspicuously a characteristic of our own kind.[6] They were also quite rapidly displaced by the first European *Homo sapiens,* who arrived at that time, fully equipped with modern behaviors. These

6. Tattersall plausibly argues that *Homo neanderthalensis* provides us with the best yardstick we have for assessing the degree of our own uniqueness but also — and more importantly — the crucial differences, including a discussion of burial rites, and their ambiguous significance (cf. 1998: 161ff.). Symbolic behavior may be absent here, but these rites certainly expressed some sense of grief and loss. Also crucial here is Tattersall's discussion of whether or not the Neanderthals shared in the evolution of speech and language (cf. 166ff.). Tattersall's final conclusion remains: it is only with the arrival of *Homo sapiens* that we find true innovation: a radical departure from the pattern of sporadic improvement on existing themes that had characterized the rest of human evolution (cf. 173).

"new Europeans" are often known as Cro-Magnons. Tattersall is sharp and to the point here: exactly where the first Cro-Magnons arrived *from* is still not completely clear, but there is no doubt that they were *we* (6). In fact, physically they were indistinguishable from living *Homo sapiens,* and in its richness and complexity the surviving material evidence of their lives indicates unequivocally that they were our intellectual equals.

While the Neanderthals sporadically practiced burial of the dead (cf. 161), with the Cro-Magnons we see for the first time evidence of regular and elaborate burial, with hints of ritual and a belief in an afterlife. Tattersall argues convincingly that this represents the earliest and most compelling evidence for the existence of something like religious experience, since burial of the dead with grave goods is a widely accepted indication of belief in an afterlife; the goods are there because they will be useful to the deceased in the life to come (cf. 11). In this restless, innovative spirit we see our modern selves mirrored, and the principal lesson to be learned from Cro-Magnon burials is this: while we will never know exactly what rituals accompanied them and what exact sets of beliefs they embodied, these burials, taken overall, reflect not only the fundamental human urge to adorn and decorate, but also the multifaceted subtlety and complexity of living human societies the world over (cf. 13).

The aspect of Cro-Magnon life that speaks to us most directly as human beings lies in the evidence of art and symbolic representation: the astonishing art of the caves in southwestern France, evidence for music, notation, musical instruments, as well as clear evidence of highly complex symbolic systems (cf. 14ff.). For Tattersall all this dramatically bolsters the conclusion that the first modern people arrived in Europe equipped with all the cognitive skills that we possess today. With the appearance on earth of *Homo sapiens,* a totally new kind of being had arrived on the scene. This clearly implies, I believe, that we are still warranted to ask today: Just how special are we really? Exactly what are the attributes that give us this acute sense of being so different from all other living species? It seems clear that any consideration of what human distinctiveness or uniqueness might mean today will have to account carefully for significant and outstanding attributes that paleoanthropologists like Ian Tattersall are lifting up, attributes like *human intelligence, rationality,* but more importantly, the ability to construct *symbolic* and ultimately *religious meaning.* The question remains, however, how and why were these attributes acquired in the course of our evolutionary past? And, most importantly, can we usefully seek evolutionary explanations for our complex and often unfathomable behaviors?

In a sense we are not simply *more* intelligent than other species, we are also *differently* intelligent: intelligent in a manner that allows us not only to view ourselves and thus be self-aware, but also to manipulate the environment around us in a qualitatively unique way. In both of these forms of self-reflection our linguistic abilities are crucially important, and almost all the literature in this field acknowledges the central role that language plays in human intelligence. As far as we humans go, language is intimately tied up with our complex symbolic capacities, and is in fact the medium through which we explain those capacities to ourselves. I will return to the central role of language in chapter 5, but Tattersall is in full agreement with the majority view in paleoanthropology today: universal among humans, language is the most evident of all our unique abilities (cf. 58). It is not surprising, then, that almost all the unique cognitive attributes that so strongly characterize modern humans are associated in some way with language. Language both permits and requires an ability to produce symbols in the mind, which can then be reshuffled and organized by the generative capacity that seems to be unique to our species (cf. 186).

For Tattersall the important question is whether apes possess any of those aspects of cognition that predisposed our ancestors to acquire language (cf. 59ff.). He concludes that chimpanzees do *not* have language or any linguistic abilities. Human beings are truly unique in having language and in possessing the apparatus that permits them to acquire and express it. Naturally, all this ties in with that most mysterious of organs, the human brain, an organ with its own evolutionary history, which is directly linked with the dramatic evidence for art, music, and symbol very early on in the history of our species. It is precisely this symbolism that lies at the very heart of what it means to be human. In fact, if there is one single thing that distinguishes humans from all other life-forms, living or extinct, it is the capacity for symbolic thought, the ability to generate complex mental symbols and to manipulate them into new combinations. Tattersall correctly argues that this is the very foundation of *imagination* and *creativity*, of the unique ability of humans to create a world in the mind and then re-create it in the real world outside themselves (cf. 177f.).

Tattersall's main point, however, is well taken: *Homo sapiens* is not simply an "improved version" of its ancestors, but is in fact a new thing altogether, qualitatively distinct from them in highly significant if limited respects (cf. 188). What has been called the distinctly "human capacity" is therefore not at all just a further development of earlier trends in our lineage, but is in fact a huge leap away from our ancestors, if not genetically, then at least culturally. On an everyday level, of course, we human beings are so different because we *feel* so different. What Tattersall is describing here is the amazing human ability for introspection and self-awareness that we call *consciousness*. This is exactly, from a more philosophical point of view, what Nicholas Rescher means when he argues that in humans the intellectual, reflective dimension of our thought processes can be properly apprehended only in terms of our own experience. Having a causal account of the biological origins of our mental processes will therefore differ markedly from having experiential access to what we are thinking about. Coming to grips with cognitive issues like meaning, symbol, intention, and purpose means understanding them. And understanding them means also performing them, and performing them requires having the kind of mind that has the ability to access those particular mental experiences (cf. Rescher 1990: 122). The most telling quality of our human consciousness and self-awareness is therefore *inner experience;* it is the filter through which we view and interpret the environment around us. From this fact we can rightly conclude that this capacity for self-awareness and consciousness, inextricably related to our linguistic capacities, is our most conspicuously unique human characteristic.

Consciousness thus reflects a unique property of the mind, a self-reflexivity that allows the brain to observe itself at work. Without this capacity for self-reflective insight, the depth, complexity, and biological importance of human interpersonal relationships, which far exceed those of any other animal, would be impossible (cf. Tattersall 1998: 193). For a strict Darwinian this simply means that human consciousness has inevitably resulted from the reproductive advantage conferred by natural selection, generation after generation, on individuals with even greater powers of reflective insight. For Tattersall, however, the evolutionary process is clearly much more complex than this: the history of the brain suggests that evolutionary change has not merely consisted of gradual improvement over the ages. In his own words: "Brain evolution has not proceeded by the simple addition of a few more connections here and there, finally adding up, over the aeons, to a large and magnificently burnished machine. Opportunistic evolution has conscripted old parts of the brain to new functions in a rather untidy fashion, and new structures have been added and old ones enlarged in a rather haphazard way" (194).

Many levels of the natural process were involved in getting us to where we are today. First, the modern human brain arose within a local population of early humans, through developmental alterations we do not yet understand, from a precursor form that possessed a variety of necessary exaptations. Next, natural selection worked within that local population to establish this new variant as the norm. Then speciation intervened to establish the historic individuality of this new entity. And finally, the new species competed successfully with its relatives, in a process that eventually left *Homo sapiens* as the sole remaining hominid. For Tattersall, then, human consciousness is typically and simply one more effect of the routine and random emergence and fixation of innovations that occurs in the evolution of all lineages. Well over 3 billion years after life established itself on earth, we humans, alone among the millions of descendants of our ancient common ancestor, somehow acquired not just a large brain — the Neanderthals had that too — but a fully developed mind. For Tattersall "this mind is a complex thing, not in the sense that an engineered machine is, with many separate parts working smoothly together in pursuit of a single goal, but in the sense that is the product of ancient reflexive and emotional components, overlain by a veneer of reason. The human mind is thus not an entirely rational entity, but rather one that is still conditioned by the long evolutionary history of the brain from which it emerges" (234).

But how does all this relate to the emergence of religion and religious belief? On exactly this issue Tattersall makes an important point: precisely because every human society, at one stage or another, possesses religion of some sort, complete with origin myths that purportedly explain the relationship of humans to the world around them, religion cannot be discounted from any discussion of typically human behaviors (201). More importantly, what we already saw in our discussion of evolutionary epistemology now seems to be confirmed in paleoanthropology too; in a very specific sense religious belief is one of the earliest special propensities or dispositions that we are able to detect in the archeological record of modern humans. In this sense, then, there is indeed a naturalness to religious imagination that challenges any viewpoint that would want to see religion or religious imagination as esoteric, or as an isolated faculty of the human mind that developed later. Even if we are not certain what exactly the artistic productions of the Cro-Magnons represented to the people who made them, it is nonetheless clear that this early "art" reflected a view held by these people of their place in the world and a body of mythology that explained that place. One of the major functions of religious belief has always been to provide explanations for the deep desire to deny the finality of death, and the curious reluctance of our species to accept the inevitable limitations of human experience. This is exactly the reason it is possible for us to identify so closely with Cro-Magnon rock art, and to recognize that it goes beyond mere representation and as such embodies a broadly religious symbolism (cf. 201).

Tattersall goes on to argue that it is ironically in our notions of God that we see our human condition most compactly reflected. Human beings, despite their unique associative mental abilities, are incapable of envisioning entities that lie outside their own experience or that cannot be construed from what they know of the material world. For Tattersall the notion of God is just such an entity. And even with our dramatic increase in knowledge about the unimaginably vast expanse of our universe, our concepts of God — even when expanded commensurately — remain resolutely anthropomorphic (cf. 202). We continue to imagine God in our own image simply because, no matter how much we may pride ourselves in our capacity for abstract thought, we are unable to do otherwise. Importantly, however, this does *not* imply the illusory character or nonexistence of God, but in fact might actually reveal the only intellectually satisfying way to believe in a God with whom we can have a humanly comprehensible personal relationship. In his words: "Perhaps we will one day be able to at least admit of a God possessing sufficient majesty and expansiveness to transcend the limits of our own imaginations and experience. But meanwhile, although we need not literally heed Wittgenstein's admonition not to speak whereof we do not know, we might do well to look upon the inadequacy of our concepts of God as the truest mirror of those limitations that define our condition" (203).

Does this intriguing comment by Tattersall suggest possible boundaries and limitations for scientific language? And if it does, do our intellectual limitations and "the inadequacy of our concepts of God" also suggest limitations for an interdisciplinary dialogue between theology and paleoanthropology? This is the question we will have to return to after considering the possible religious implications of the paintings from the Upper Paleolithic. But first we need to turn to Steven Mithen's very different approach to the prehistory of the human mind.

*   *   *

British archeologist Steven Mithen, in his influential book *The Prehistory of the Mind: A Search for the Origins of Art, Religion, and Science* (1996), also recently took on the challenge of coming to grips with the intangible human mind, the mind as an abstraction that eludes definition and adequate description, let alone explanation. As was argued earlier, we as human beings are almost always haunted and fascinated by questions like: What is intelligence? What is consciousness? What happened to the human mind that allows it to create art, do science, and creatively symbolize religion and religious faith, when not a trace of any of these is found even in the chimpanzee, our closest living relative? Mithen believes that many disciplines can contribute toward an understanding of the complex human mind, and as an archeologist he can contribute to answering these difficult, multidisciplinary questions. In this sense, it clearly is time for a "cognitive archeology" (cf. 11). It will be especially challenging, however, to see whether his interdisciplinary approach leaves any room for religious/theological contributions to the multidisciplinary conversation.

Mithen, forcefully and with good reasons, rejects all kinds of "super-naturalistic" theologies that may still hold that the human mind suddenly sprang into existence fully formed as a product of divine creation. On the contrary, the mind has a long and fascinating evolutionary history that can be explained without recourse to supernatural powers. In understanding Mithen's work, it is important to note why he regards a study of chimpanzees as so limited a venture for understanding the human mind. Although chimpanzees are our closest living relatives, a full 6 million years of evolution separate the minds of modern humans and chimpanzees. We indeed shared a common ancestor about 6 million years ago, but after that date the evolutionary lineages leading to modern humans and apes diverged. And it is precisely on this *prehistory of the mind* that Mithen wishes to focus in his book.

Mithen begins by explaining how his approach will differ from the so-called commonsense view of the mind, which generally sees the mind as a general-purpose learning mechanism, some sort of powerful computer. Mithen feels closer to those evolutionary epistemologists who oppose this view and argue that the mind should rather be seen as a series of specialized "cognitive domains" or "intelligences," each of which is dedicated to some specific type of behavior, such as specialized modules for acquiring language, or tool-using abilities, or engaging in social interaction. On this view the mind is constituted by a series of specialized cognitive processes, each dedicated to a specific type of behavior — almost like the blades of a Swiss army knife. Mithen is convinced that this view holds the key to unlocking the nature of both the prehistoric and modern mind — although in a very different way than evolutionary psychologists currently believe (cf. 13ff.). If the mind is constituted by numerous specialized processes, each dedicated to a specific type of behavior, we still have not accounted for one of the most remarkable features of the modern mind — its capacity for an almost unlimited imagination. For Mithen the answer to this issue lies in exposing the prehistory of the mind.

Mithen sets out to find what he calls the "cognitive foundations" of art, religion, and science; by exposing these foundations he intends to demonstrate that we share common roots with other species — even if the mind of our closest living relative, the chimpanzee, is fundamentally different from our own. It is in this process that Mithen wants to provide hard evidence for finally rejecting "the creationist claim that the mind is a product of supernatural intervention" (16). Ultimately, his argument will be that the modern human mind has an architecture built up by millions of years of evolution, which finally yielded a mind that creates, thinks, and imagines. Mithen also highlights recent efforts in psychology to move beyond thinking of the mind as running a general-purpose program, or as a sponge indiscriminately soaking up whatever information is around. A new analogy for the human mind has taken its place: the Swiss army knife, a tool with specialized devices, designed for coping with very special types of problems (cf. 37). This is found especially in Howard Gardner's important book *Frames of Mind: The Theory of Multiple Intelligences* (1983). In this well-known work we are presented with a Swiss-army-knife architectural model for the mind, with each "blade," or cognitive domain, described as a specialized intelligence. Gardner initially identified seven intelligences: linguistic, musical, logical-mathematical, spatial, bodily-kinesthetic, and two forms of personal intelligence (one for looking at one's own mind, one for looking outward toward others).

Mithen's thesis moves beyond this model and is built on his suggestion that three broad stages for the evolution of the human mind can be identified, which helps him formulate his most important metaphor for the complex, creative human mind: *the mind as a cathedral* (Mithen 1996: 65ff.). Mithen argues that we can think of the mind of each individual as a new cathedral being built as he or she develops from an infant to a mature adult. It is built according to the architectural plan encoded in the genetic constitution of that individual, as inherited from parents, and under the influence of the particular developmental environment. Our minds are therefore as unique as our genetic constitutions and our developmental environments, although as members of the same species, we share substantial similarities in the architectural plans we inherit, and thus the minds we develop as well. This situation has been the same for all our ancestors, but the architectural plans have been constantly tinkered with by evolution. Random changes were brought about by evolution; the environment was also changing; and our ancestors constantly faced new types of problems, requiring new types of thought processes for their solution. The architectural plan of the human mind, under the joint effects of genetic inheritance, random mutations, and constant environmental change, was thus shaped by natural selection.

Mithen fills out the three stages in the historical development of the human mind as follows:

In *Phase One* human minds were dominated by a central "nave" of generalized intelligence.

Phase Two adds multiple "chapels" of specialized intelligences, including the cognitive domains of language, social intelligence, technical intelligence, and natural history intelligence.

Phase Three brings us to the modern mind in which the "chapels" or cognitive domains have been connected, resulting in what Mithen calls *cognitive fluidity* (cf. 70). This creative combination of the various cognitive domains of the mind would ultimately have profound consequences for the nature of the human mind. With this cognitive fluidity, the mind acquired not only the ability for, but also a positive passion for, metaphor and analogy. And with thoughts originating in different domains engaging one another, the result is an almost limitless capacity for imagination (71). It is exactly this amazing ability that would make our species so different from early humans who shared the same basic mind — a Swiss-army-knife mentality of multiple intelligences, but with very little interaction between them. Mithen's useful model here, again, is a cathedral with several isolated chapels, within which unique services of thought were undertaken, each barely audible elsewhere in the cathedral. In Mithen's words: "Early humans seem to have been so much like us in some respects, because they had these specialized cognitive domains; but they seem so different because they lacked a vital ingredient of the modern mind: cognitive fluidity" (146).

As we saw in our discussion of Ian Tattersall's view of human origins, from 60,000 to 30,000 years ago, in the final prehistoric phase of the drama of our past, there was a very significant cultural explosion, a "big bang" of human culture that would finally lead to the origins of art and religion. The final, sole survivor *Homo sapiens sapiens* had already entered the scene around 100,000 years ago. This new actor appears to have immediately adopted certain forms of behavior never seen before, and identifies the Middle/Upper Paleolithic transition as the setting for this big bang of human culture. Mithen's explanation for this explosion of culture is that it coincides with the final major redesign of the human mind. This is when "doors and windows were inserted between chapel walls" (153), when thoughts and information began flowing freely among the diverse cognitive domains or intelligences. Specialized intelligences no longer had to work in isolation, but a "mapping across knowledge systems" now became possible, and from this "transformation of conceptual spaces" creativity could now arise as never before. Mithen thus appropriates some of the work of cognitive psychologists, to make the related point that in both development and evolution the human mind undergoes (or has undergone) a transformation from being constituted by a series of relatively independent cognitive domains to a situation in which ideas, ways of thinking, and knowledge now flow freely between such domains (cf. 154). This forms the basis for the highly plausible hypothesis that during this amazing emergent period of transition, the human brain was finally hardwired for cognitive fluidity, yielding imagination and creativity.

Most importantly, however, the rise of a complex human mind, literally hardwired for cognitive fluidity, is also directly related to the rise of religion. Many of the new types of behaviors, such as anthropomorphic images in cave paintings and the burial of people with grave goods, suggest that these Upper Paleolithic people were the first to have beliefs in supernatural beings, and possibly also in an afterlife. These behaviors mark the first appearance of what Mithen calls religious "ideologies" (cf. 174). Creative religious and symbolic ideas could arise from only a cognitively fluid mind. At exactly this point one could pose a critical question of Mithen: After tracing the development of cognitive fluidity from general intelligence through language, technical intelligence, natural history intelligence, and social intelligence, why does he stop short of acknowledging a new kind of "symbolic intelligence" that would explain, or at least accommodate, the origins of art, of religion, and of science? It is already clearly implied in his argument that this new cognitive fluidity thoroughly transformed the human mind and all aspects of human behavior. It is in this sense, then, that we see the appearance of concepts and beliefs that no single cognitive domain could create by itself, concepts such as art and religion.

Of critical importance here is also a marked change in *the nature of consciousness.* Mithen has argued that reflexive consciousness evolved as a critical feature of social intelligence, as it enabled our ancestors to predict the behavior of other individuals. He then makes the point that there is now reason to expect early humans to have had an awareness about their own knowledge and thought processes concerning the nonsocial world. Via the mechanism of language, however, social intelligence began to be invaded by nonsocial information, and the nonsocial world becomes available for reflexive consciousness to explore. This new consciousness/cognitive fluidity now enabled an integration of knowledge from separate domains that was impossible before (cf. 190ff.).

The seeds for cognitive fluidity were sown with the increase of brain size that began 500,000 years ago. This was also directly related to the evolution of a grammatically complex social language. The utterance of this language, however, carried snippets of nonsocial information as well, and those individuals who were able to exploit such nonsocial information gained a reproductive advantage. And as social language switched to a general-purpose language, individuals acquired an increasing awareness about their own knowledge of the nonsocial world. Consciousness then adopted the role of a comprehensive, integrating mechanism for knowledge that had previously been "trapped" in separate specialized intelligences (cf. 194). The first step toward cognitive fluidity appears to have been an integration between social and natural history intelligence in early modern humans around 100,000 years ago. The final step to full cognitive fluidity, the potential to entertain ideas that bring together elements from normally incongruous domains, occurred at different times in different populations between 60,000 and 30,000 years ago. This involved an integration of technical intelligence, and led to the cultural explosion we are now calling the appearance of the human mind (cf. 194).

Ultimately this important step in the evolution of the human mind was what enabled our species to design complex tools, to create art, and to discover religious belief. This switch from a specialized to a generalized type of mentality between 100,000 and 30,000 years ago was a remarkable "about-turn" for the evolutionary process to have taken. The previous 6 million years of evolution had seen an ever-increasing specialization of the mind: natural history, technical, and then linguistic intelligence had been added to the social intelligence that was already present in the mind of the common ancestor to living apes and humans. As soon as language started acting as a vehicle for delivering information into the mind, carrying with it snippets of nonsocial information, a transformation of the nature of the mind began (cf. 208ff.). Language now switched from a social to a general-purpose function, consciousness from a means to predict other individuals' behavior to managing a mental database of information relating to all domains of behavior. Thus a *cognitive fluidity* arose within the mind, reflecting new connections rather than new processing power. And consequently, this mental transformation occurred with no increase in brain size. As with Tattersall, so too with Mithen we find that in essence it is the origins of symbolic capacity that are unique to the human mind.

Mithen has plausibly argued that knowing the prehistory of the human mind provides us with a more profound understanding of what it means to be human. It also helps us understand a little better the origins of *art* and of *religion*. But what about *science* and our amazing ability for scientific reflection? Mithen sees science as the third of the unique achievements of the modern mind, and the most important feature of our cognitively fluid minds (cf. 213). He says science has three critical properties: the ability to generate and test hypotheses, something that has proven to be fundamental to any form of specialized intelligence; the ability to develop and use tools to solve specific problems; and the ability to use metaphor and analogy, which he sees as no less than the "tools of thought" (cf. 214). Mithen's most interesting point here is that *some metaphors and analogies can be developed by drawing on knowledge within a single domain, but the most powerful ones are those that cross domain boundaries.* By definition these kinds of metaphors can arise only within a cognitively fluid mind.

It has become abundantly clear that in contemporary paleoanthropology and archeology much debate surrounds the origin and development of hominid symbolic behavior. For scholars like Tattersall and Mithen the emergence of this capacity is closely associated with the transition from Middle to Upper Paleolithic in Europe (cf. Mithen 1996; Mellars 1989; 1991). According to most scholars, anatomically modern humans arriving in Europe expressed this remarkable capacity for symbolic behavior by developing the use of body ornaments, and especially a complex repertoire of abstract and depictional art. These behaviors implied the rather dramatic use of symbols for the very first time (cf. d'Errico and Nowell 2000: 123). An alternative view is that the emergence of symbolic behavior is a more gradual process whose roots can be traced back to the Lower and Middle Paleolithic. We encountered these two viewpoints, the discontinuist and the gradualist approach, in chapter 2. These approaches, also so clearly evident in the work of Tattersall and Mithen (who both have stressed discontinuist views on the emergence of symbolic minds, although Tattersall more so than Mithen), represent two very distinct and dominant paradigms to the emergence of symbolic behavior.

It is important, however, to heed voices that criticize a too rigid distinction between discontinuist and gradualist approaches. Mithen, in an article in the *Cambridge Archeological Journal* (1997), was very critical of the division of work in this area into the two camps, and saw the distinction as overly simplistic. His own work (cf. 1996) is normally placed in the discontinuist camp, even though it explicitly argues that the building blocks for symbolic thought were gradually laid down throughout the earlier Paleolithic. Mithen has always strongly claimed that without the gradual evolution of human cognitive capacities, any seemingly sudden appearance of symbolic behavior could not have been possible. He says it is more appropriate to characterize his position as gradualist with regard to the cognitive capacities that allow for symbolic behavior and discontinuist as regarding the manifest and spectacular appearance of such thought, even if it arises as a further step in the gradual evolution of such capacities (cf. Mithen 2000: 149). This is significantly different from the type of discontinuist position defended by Tattersall, which argues that symbolic behavior emerged from one chance mutation, which suddenly and dramatically transformed the human mind.

Mithen also stresses that each person's neural networks are being continually remolded in the light of experience. In other words, changes in cultural behavior can actually change our biology. The resulting positive feedback between changes in culture and biology is potentially immense, and one might expect there to be periods of rapid behavioral and cognitive change (cf. 149). As for the possibility of a gradual evolution of protosymbolic behavior, Mithen cautions us to keep two important issues in mind. The first is the compelling idea or possibility that the origin of symbolic behavior would have been like throwing on a light switch — once something is symbolic, everything is potentially symbolic. On this view any phase of protosymbolism is likely to have been so rapid as to be archeologically invisible. A second issue concerns the cognitive basis for symbolism and whether this is necessarily the same in archaic and modern humans (cf. 150). This directly implies the question whether similarities in observed behavior actually reflect similarities in cognition. The point Mithen wants to make here is that the interpretation of artifacts from the early Paleolithic record as possessing symbolic status does not automatically lead to the conclusion that such objects were made using the same cognitive processes used by modern humans for symbolic thought, or indeed even an early version of those processes (cf. 150ff.).

Mithen[7] also agrees with William Noble and Iain Davidson (1996) that linguistic communication changed the nature of self-consciousness in the human mind and hence created the world of symbols. Mithen also agrees with Tattersall and Noble and Davidson that Neanderthals lacked symbolic thought, and that bipedalism was of immense significance for cognitive evolution because it released constraints on brain size and enabled new foraging patterns. But Mithen strongly disagrees on a few other issues: he finds it impossible to accept that language could not have appeared in a gradual fashion, and that there can be no such thing as a "protolanguage." What a gradualist wants to talk about and reconstruct is not language "as we do not know it," but *proto*language, which might have had symbols while lacking syntax, and might have had a more restricted content than language today. Mithen puts it rather forcefully: modern human language could not have just popped into existence out of nothing, or from the type of vocalizations we find in modern apes or monkeys (cf. Mithen 2000: 271).

Mithen also strongly critiques the idea that there can be no mind without language, as argued by Noble and Davidson, and to which we will return in the next chapter. Clearly monkeys and apes exhibit without language a range of communicative behaviors that can only be understood by appreciating that

7. "Pulling the Mind Apart," *Cambridge Archeological Journal* 7, no. 2 (1997): 269-86.

a complex mentality underlies them. Similarly, premodern humans who may have possessed various types of protolanguage had sophisticated and complex minds that were like ours today in some ways, and radically different in others. As Mithen puts it, the emergence of fully modern language transformed those minds but did not create them (275). Here again we see why Mithen argues that without the gradual evolution of human cognitive capacities any seemingly sudden appearance of symbolic behavior could not have been possible. Clearly modern human cognitive abilities and symbolic behavior emerge as indicative of what human uniqueness might mean in a paleoanthropological sense.

I think we can now safely conclude that explicitly symbolic behavior should be seen as the hallmark of the behavioral transition from the Middle to the Upper Paleolithic in Europe (cf. Mellars 1989; 1991). Importantly, Paul Mellars has also argued that this new symbolic component is reflected not only in spectacular cave art and personal ornamentation, but also in the design and form of stone tools, and perhaps even in features such as the organization of living structures (cf. 1991: 63-76). It is therefore these behavioral changes, and their general features, that most typically signify the transition from Middle to Upper Paleolithic in Europe, and bring us closer to a paleoanthropological definition of human uniqueness. These general features of "human uniqueness" can now be summarized as follows:

1. a general shift in the pattern of stone tool technology from predominantly "flake" technologies to more regular and standardized forms of "blade" manufacture;
2. a simultaneous increase in the variety and complexity of stone tools;
3. the appearance of relatively complex and extensively shaped bone, antler, and ivory artifacts;
4. a generally increased *tempo* of technological change (in both bone and lithic technology), as well as an increased regional diversification in tool forms produced in different geographical areas;
5. the appearance of a wide range of beads, pendants, and other ornaments, from simple forms to elaborately carved examples;
6. the appearance in certain contexts of sophisticated and, in many respects, highly complex forms of representational or "naturalistic" art;
7. a strong hint of closely related associated changes in both the economic and social organization of human groups. There seemed to be a clear trend toward (a) a much more specialized pattern of animal exploitation and systematic hunting; (b) a sharp increase in the overall density of hu-

man population; (c) an apparent increase in the maximum size of local residential groups; and (d) the appearance of more highly "structured" forms of human settlements, frequently including regular and well-defined huts, tents, and other living structures (cf. 63ff.).

We clearly find at least two strong suggestions in the contemporary paleoanthropological literature. First, we find that these explicit behavioral transitions from the Middle to the Upper Paleolithic should be seen as the reflection of an "explosion," or at least a dramatic change, in human symbolic behavior; and second, that this "symbolic revolution" can be seen to reflect the emergence of new and higher patterns of linguistic and symbolic communication. The question is therefore whether we are dealing with a symbolic as well as a linguistic revolution in the Middle to Upper Paleolithic transition.

The issue of the origins and development of language in prehistory raises an enormous range of very difficult questions, and I will return to aspects of this issue in chapter 5. Noble and Davidson (1996) have argued strongly that the production of many kinds of Upper Paleolithic symbolic art would seem inconceivable without the ability to communicate in relatively complex verbal ways. Mellars also argues, in tandem with Tattersall and Mithen, that the possibility remains that the emergence of fully complex language systems was indeed one of the hallmarks of Upper Paleolithic culture throughout large areas of Europe and western Asia. Language must therefore be seen as one of the most fundamental components of human culture in the fullest sense of the word, ultimately indispensable to the highly complex patterns of human behavior of the Upper Paleolithic times, and crucial therefore for any paleoanthropological definition of human uniqueness. Mellars states it well: "In short, if one were to look for one single behavioural development which could, potentially, explain almost the whole of the transition from the Middle to the Upper Palaeolithic — technological, economic, social and demographic — the emergence of complex, highly-developed and highly structured linguistic systems would seem the obvious candidate to choose" (1991: 69).

The tying of language and linguistic ability so closely to symbolic behavior allows an even clearer paleoanthropological definition of human uniqueness to emerge.

In terms of a more *anatomical* or *morphological definition* of typically modern humans, only a small number of unique anatomical characteristics stand out (cf. Mellars 1989; 1991; Tattersall and Mowbray 2003).

1. *Homo sapiens* is the only surviving member of the family Hominidae, a group anatomically committed to terrestrial bipedalism.
2. Members of this species have (not uniquely) relatively large brains, but with the most complex neocortex of all primates.
3. Their chin-bearing faces are small compared to their neuro-crania.
4. They have a brow region structured into two parts.

In terms of a more *behavioral definition,* modern humans are identified by the unique presence of

1. a spoken language;
2. the cognitive capacity to generate mental symbols, as expressed in art and religion;
3. explicit symbolic behavior, i.e., the ability to represent objects, people, and abstract concepts with arbitrary symbols, vocal or visual, and to reify such symbols in cultural practices like painting, engraving, and sculpture (cf. Lewis-Williams 2002: 96f.);
4. the capacity for abstract thinking, the ability to act with reference to abstract concepts not limited to time and space;
5. planning depth, or the ability to formulate strategies based on past experience and to act on them in group context;
6. behavioral, economic, and technological innovation; and
7. a bizarre inability to sustain prolonged bouts of boredom (cf. Tattersall and Mowbray 2003: 298).

The question that remains is how these characteristics for human uniqueness combine in the undeniable capacity for explicit symbolic behavior, and how the emergence of religion and religious belief might actually help us to understand the mysterious treasures and haunting images from the Upper Paleolithic.

Human Imagination and Religious Awareness

It is exactly on the issue of the emergence of human imagination and religious awareness that Ian Tattersall has made an important point. He said precisely because every human society, at one stage or another, possessed religion of some sort, complete with origin myths that purportedly explain the relationship of humans to the world around them, that religion cannot be discounted from any discussion of typically human behaviors (cf. Tattersall 1998: 201). More importantly, what we saw in our discussion of evolutionary epistemology in chapter 2 now seems to be confirmed in paleoanthropology. In a very specific sense religious belief is one of the earliest special propensities or dispositions that we are able to detect in the archeological record of modern humans. In this sense, then, there is a naturalness to religious imagination that challenges any viewpoint that would want to see religion or religious imagination as esoteric, or as an isolated faculty of the human mind that developed later. Even if we are not certain what exactly the artistic productions of the Cro-Magnons represented to the people who made them, it is nonetheless clear that this early "art" reflected a view held by these people of their place in the world and a body of mythology that explained that place. This resonates closely with a central theme in Tattersall's work: one of the major functions of religious belief has always been to explain the deep desire to deny the finality of death, and the curious reluctance of our species to accept the inevitable limitations of human experience. This is one of the most important reasons why it is possible for us to identify so closely with Cro-Magnon rock art, and to recognize that it goes beyond mere representation and as such embodies a broadly religious symbolism (cf. 201).

We have also learned from paleoanthropology, even if indirectly, that religious thought, and certainly Christian theology, in a sense still has to come to terms with the enormous vistas of time revealed by Darwinian evolution. What Tattersall has argued for the broadly religious symbolism of Cro-Magnon rock art is true for religion in the broadest sense of the word. Today we can look back and see even the historical religions as expressions of an ambivalent urge inherent in human nature to limit and unlimit, to define and explore, and as such as a need for ultimate meaning rooted in humankind's very biopsychological constitution as beings in the world (Krüger 1995: 179). From an evolutionary point of view, religion certainly appears to be continuous with the most elementary forms of creative adaptation to the vast world around us. It is in this sense that it could be suggested that institutional animal behavior such as territoriality, ritualization, play, and the unmistakable capacity for feelings of meaning and loss (death) may be seen as precursors of the human sense of sacred place and time, of ritual and myth, ecstasy and mysticism. Scholars like J. S. Krüger have argued that religion should be seen as a dialectic between the synthesizing faculty of the human mind operating at its most inclusive level and the urge to radically transcend the given. Krüger takes it even further and states that, in the sense that humans are driven by their very nature, by their very being in the world, to experience the world as a meaningful gestalt, one could speak of a religious imperative. And in this broadest sense of the word, religion co-emerged with humanity itself (147ff., 163f.). It is in this sense that I argued, in terms of evolutionary epistemology, for the naturalness of religion (cf. chap. 2). In this wider sense of the word, religion, like art, can be seen as a radically human phenomenon. This also allows us to assume that the symbolic religious expressions of Upper Paleolithic Europeans, of southern African Stone Age San, of the classical religions of India and the Levant, and of us modern humans stem from the same "panhuman consciousness" (cf. 159).

We have seen how carefully constructed arguments by scientists like Tattersall, Mithen, and Mellars have focused on the emergence of symbolic behavior and language as typifying that which is most unique about the evolution of humans from a paleoanthropological point of view. We have also seen how these scientists agree on the remarkable and crucial role of Paleolithic imagery as exemplifying this unique form of symbolic behavior. However, from a more philosophical point of view we are still left with the postfoundationalist challenge to pursue more contextual, even if highly tentative, answers to what the prehistoric images in their different chronotopes (times and spaces) might have meant. We are left with a mystery, and we have to ask whether there is any way we can possibly get closer to what these images might have meant to Upper Paleolithic people. For instance, one of the great enigmas of Upper Paleolithic art is the presence of mysterious geometric patterns — grids, lines of dots, nested curves, chevrons, rectangles, etc. — scattered among the realistic images of animals. These abstract "signs" are a constant component of Upper Paleolithic art. Complex interpretations of them have now made way for a new interpretation, not only of the signs themselves, but also of important examples of Upper Paleolithic imagery as such. David Lewis-Williams, a South African paleoanthropologist and archeologist who also is an expert in the art of the southern African San, has suggested that some of the images could actually be expressions of minds in states of hallucination, and thus a sure sign of shamanistic art. In conjunction with French scholar Jean Clottes, Lewis-Williams has developed a theory for interpreting south African San art as shamanistic, and then retroactively explaining the much older Paleolithic art in the decorated caves of western Europe as similarly emerging out of shamanistic practices. Clottes and Lewis-Williams are convinced that shamanism, both in terms of the concept of the universe and the practices it engenders in so many regions of the world, resonates more completely than any other theory with certain highly contextual particulars of the art of the deep caves (cf. Clottes and Lewis-Williams 1998: 9).

Shamanism, in the sense of intense religious experiences accompanied by states of ecstasy, is found all over the ancient world. Clottes and Lewis-Williams argue that ecstatic revelations and visions actually form an integral and important part of the Judeo-Christian tradition that stretches back to Old Testament times. Moreover, they maintain that this tradition goes even further back, to the very first emergence of the fully modern human being (cf. 12). At all times and in all places people have entered ecstatic, frenzied, altered states of consciousness and experienced hallucinations. They also argue that the potential shift, voluntary or involuntary, between different states of consciousness in humans is a function of the universal human nervous system. In fact, all people have to cope with different states of consciousness in one way or another. Some people, however, became shamans (cf. 12).

The induction, control, and exploitation of altered states of consciousness are at the heart of shamanism the world over. In chapter 5 I will explore the broader set of questions that Lewis-Williams (2002) has raised for the issue of evolutionary origins of religion, and for understanding the phenomenon of shamanism by linking it directly to research in neuroscience and neuropsychology. For this chapter it is important to point to the crux of this hypothesis for a broadly religious interpretation of the imagery of the Upper Paleolithic. In fact, for Clottes and Lewis-Williams recent neuropsychological research on altered states of consciousness provides the principal access to the mental and religious life of the people who lived in western Europe during the Upper Paleolithic. The deepest reason for this is that these Cro-Magnon ancestors of ours were *Homo sapiens sapiens,* and as such had the same brain and nervous system as all humans have today. Contrary to what is normally thought, these scientists argue that we may actually have better access to the religious experiences of Upper Paleolithic people than to many other aspects of their lives (cf. Clottes and Lewis-Williams 1998: 13). Religious mystics and visionaries around the world have always exploited all these ways of changing their consciousness and achieving states of ecstasy. For Clottes and Lewis-Williams shamanism is just one of the ways people through the ages have induced, manipulated, and exploited deep altered states of consciousness (cf. 14). If shamanic practices are rooted in innate human behaviors, then it should not be surprising that those kinds of behaviors manifest themselves in somewhat similar ritual practices around the world.

Clottes and Lewis-Williams also argue that there are three stages to shamanism that seem to be universal, and that are also wired into the human nervous system. In chapter 5 we will analyze these claims in greater detail, but for the argument of this chapter it is important to know that, in the first or lightest stage of trance, people "see" geometric forms, dots, or lines; in the second stage subjects try to make sense of these geometric perceptions by construing them as objects of religious or emotional significance; the third stage is always reached via a vortex, or tunnel. When subjects emerge from the far end of the tunnel, they are in the bizarre world of trance: monsters, people, and settings are intensely real. One of the most frequently reported experiences of the third stage of altered consciousness is transformation of the self into animal forms. The vividness of that sort of experience is captured by southern African San rock art images of shamans turned into antelope, having antelope heads and hooves but human bodies (cf. Clottes and Lewis-Williams 1998: 16ff.). Although these three neurological stages are universal, it is also clear that the meanings given to the geometrics of stage one, the objects into which they are illusioned in stage two, and the hallucinations of stage three are always culture- and context-specific (a San shaman may see an eland antelope, whereas an Inuit may see a polar bear or a seal). Even allowing for such cultural diversity, however, the three stages provide a framework for understanding shamanistic experiences.

Clottes and Lewis-Williams also point out that altered states of consciousness shade into one another, and the various stages are notoriously hard to define. They may however be thought of as ranging along a continuum. At one end of the continuum is what we may loosely call "alert consciousness"; at the other end is "deep trance," a state often observed by early explorers of the world. Alert consciousness is the condition in which people are fully aware of their surroundings and are able to react rationally to them. "Inward looking" or reflective states move a little further along the continuum. On this view people in a "light" altered state of consciousness are in the state we often call daydreaming, sometimes so much so that they are almost oblivious to their surroundings. Dreaming is another altered state of consciousness, one still further along the continuum. At the far end are the deep states that are an essential part of shamanism. In these states people perceive things that are not really there; in other words, they hallucinate. These hallucinations may be blissfully ecstatic, or terrifying. In deep states all the senses hallucinate; people not only see visions, they also smell, hear, and taste nonreal things and experience strange sensations in their bodies. These deep states include the condition generally known as *trance*, the actual state that shamans enter and value so much (cf. 13f.).

In their work Clottes and Lewis-Williams[8] restrict their use of the con-

8. Cf. also David Lewis-Williams, "Vision and Shamanism in Upper Paleolithic Western Europe," in Soffer and Conkey 1997: 321-43; cf. Lewis-Williams 2002.

cept "shaman" to ritual practitioners in hunting-and-gathering societies who enter altered states of consciousness to achieve a variety of ends that include healing the sick, foretelling the future, meeting spirit-animals, changing the weather, and controlling real animals by supernatural means. They want to be particularly careful not to create the impression that they are projecting uncritically the present onto the past so as to make it seem that Upper Paleolithic people were nothing more than exact replicas of Siberian, American, or southern African shamans. But they are concerned to point out the remarkable similarities that exist among shamans in various parts of the world and at various times. The similarities among these very different situations are both striking and puzzling. Clottes and Lewis-Williams's argument to explain and justify them derives from the ways in which the human nervous system behaves in altered states. It is these commonalities, more than anything else, that enable us to form some idea of the social and mental context out of which Upper Paleolithic religion and art came, and to explain why people braved the depths of the caves to make pictures, or sometimes simply to touch the wet limestone walls. In this sense, also, shamanism is not just an unimportant addendum to a society; it should always be seen as an all-embracing way of life and thought (cf. 19ff.).

One of the most important aspects of the shamanic experience is the "spirit possession" or "soul loss" that accompanies deep altered states of consciousness. Hunting-and-gathering societies usually interpret the effects and hallucinations of stage three of the shamanic experience as soul loss, i.e., they believe that a shaman's spirit leaves his or her body. It is frequently experienced as either *flight* or *traveling underground.* All over the world shamans speak of flying to distant places and other realms, and very often the feeling of flight is expressed by reference to birds (cf. 26).

The opposite of flight, descent into the ground, is a related shamanic experience and is of particular importance for the discussion of Upper Paleolithic art. This descent into the underworld is part of a complex ceremony; spurred on by insistent drumming, singing, and dancing, the shaman believes that he travels through a vortex to an underground world of spirits. This kind of descent — out-of-body travel to the underworld — is often part of shamanic initiation. Clottes and Lewis-Williams argue that the ubiquity among shamanic groups of beliefs regarding such a descent into the earth may be explained by the neurologically generated sensations of the vortex that draw people into the third and deepest stage of trance, the stage in which they experience hallucinations (cf. 28f.). The vortex creates sensations of darkness, constriction, and occasionally difficulty in breathing. Entry into an actual hole in the ground or a cave replicates this neuropsychological experience. During the Upper Paleolithic, entry into a cave may therefore have been seen as virtually the same thing as entry into a deep trance via the vortex. The hallucinations induced by entry into and isolation in a cave probably combined with the images already on the walls to create a rich and animated spiritual realm. It also resonates well with the fact that throughout the world the shamanistic cosmos is always tiered, i.e., organized into three levels: the level of everyday life, the realm above, and the realm below. This kind of three-tiered cosmos provides an effective framework for a discussion of the caves, where the underground world — both real, as in the physical caves, and hallucinatory — was certainly one of the levels of the Paleolithic cosmos. It is in this sense that Clottes and Lewis-Williams claim that a complex link between caves and altered states seems undeniable today.

Against this background they analyze the specific shamanic rock art of the San of southern Africa and argue that when compared to the much older Paleolithic art, it illuminates the earlier art in a very striking way. It shows how the elements and underlying stages, of a neurological origin, are expressed in a unique culture, and it also illustrates the way in which animals take on a symbolic meaning in shamanistic societies. The images of animals, after all, constitute a major element in Upper Paleolithic art (cf. 31ff.). Like the rock art of the southern African San, which Lewis-Williams considers the best-understood rock art in the world, the cave paintings of the Upper Paleolithic clearly were no mere descriptive pictures. More than simple, decorative pictures, these paintings were gateways to the spirit world, panoramas that, in their trance experience, shamans could enter and with which their own projected mental imagery could mingle in three animated dimensions. In San culture the rock paintings became reservoirs of potency. As shamans danced in rock shelters, they turned to face the paintings when they felt the need to increase their potency. Then, like electricity, the potency flowed from the paintings into them, and they were catapulted into the spiritual realm. In this sense the rock face was like a veil suspended between this world and the spirit world. This was particularly important where handprints were made, because it seems that this was not done so much to make pictures or mere images of human hands. Rather, the potency-filled paint created some sort of bond between the person, the rock veil, and the spirit world that seethed behind it. Ultimately, for Clottes and Lewis-Williams, both San rock art and Upper Paleolithic cave paintings demonstrate how the universal aspects of shamanism are expressed quite contextually within a specific local, cultural community (cf. 35).

We saw earlier that European Paleolithic art has become famous the world over for both its antiquity and its complexity, and that 95 percent of these painted caves are in France or on the Iberian Peninsula. We also discussed the fact that Paleolithic art, from the beginning to the end, is an art of animal forms, even if some human forms and geometric shapes are also found. In Paleolithic imagery horses dominate, although sometimes they are outnumbered by bison, deer, even rhinoceroses and felines in the beginning (Chauvet Cave), and much later by the mammoths at Rouffignac. Paintings of humans exist in small numbers, and the famous painted hands (cf. Gargas Cave; pl. 1 and 2) belong exclusively to the most ancient period of Paleolithic art (cf. 45).

To their arguments that the potential of the human nervous system to enter altered states and to generate hallucinations is of great antiquity, and that shamanism is ubiquitous among all hunter-gatherer communities, Clottes and Lewis-Williams now add the important contextual argument that the cave itself should be seen as an ensemble, not so much of images (although they are of primary importance), but of spaces differentiated by the performance of different rituals. What this means is that the walls, ceilings, and floors of the caves were in some way very significant; they were in fact little more than a thin membrane above the creatures and happenings of the underworld. In their own words: "The caves were awesome, liminal places to be: literally, they took one into the underworld" (86).

On this view the paintings could have been visions with which shamans interacted, and in this sense they did not just depict realistic pictures. The way many of the images were made and conjured out of the rock face suggests that the artists were re-creating, or in a sense redreaming, their visions and fixing them on the membrane through which they had materialized. A richly painted cave therefore did not simply contain a number of pictures of animals. It contained many visions made manifest and fixed by painted and engraved lines (cf. 92).

On this view the best explanation of Upper Paleolithic prehistoric imagery seems to be that the caves were believed to be passages leading into the lowest tier of the shamanic cosmos. People who crawled and walked through these passages were completely surrounded by the underworld. It is important to realize, though, that shamanism is a multicomponent belief system. It comprises healing techniques, control of animals, weather-changing rites, prediction, vision quests, sorcery, out-of-body journeys, and other activities, each with its own appropriate rituals, symbols, and myths. Clottes and Lewis-Williams are not arguing that each and every Upper Paleolithic image was the product of shamanistic practices and beliefs. There might have been other conceptual currents and practices of which we know nothing (cf. 112). Yet, despite all the diversity of the art, there is a long-term unity that testifies to some sort of common framework. It is this broad framework that Clottes and Lewis-Williams have tried to uncover in terms of a shamanistic worldview. By arguing for this worldview, it becomes possible to bring the diverse and often extremely puzzling evidence into a coherent, flexible pattern.

It is interesting that as recently as 1997, close to the publication of Clottes and Lewis-Williams's important work on Upper Paleolithic artistic imagery and shamanism, a scholar like Paul Bahn was still very critical of the shamanism hypothesis. Bahn acknowledged that it does seem likely that beliefs of this kind existed and played a role in the production of Paleolithic art. But he was very wary of any blanket explanations or a metatheory that would leave no room for discussion, and especially of any attempt to retrospectively explain Ice Age behavior and art entirely in terms of recent research on southern African rock art (cf. Bahn and Vertut 1997: 181f.). As we saw, however, Clottes and Lewis-Williams are not arguing that each and every Upper Paleolithic image is the product of shamanistic practices and beliefs, but only that certain caves suggest ritual practices (Grotte Niaux and Lascaux), and that certain mysterious signs and enigmatic painted figures (like the so-called sorcerer in Grotte des Trois Frères, and the famous scene of a wounded bison confronting a bird-headed ithyphallic man lying on his back with outstretched arms, from the Shaft in Lascaux) very strongly suggest shamanism. I will specifically return to the shamanistic interpretations of some of the rare human figures in Upper Paleolithic imagery, especially the bird-headed ithyphallic man from the Shaft in Lascaux and the "wounded men" from Cougnac and Pech-Merle, in chapter 5.

As we saw earlier in this chapter (cf. 170f.), the very latest evidence to support this shamanistic hypothesis is the exciting results from recent excavations at the cave site of Hohle Fels in Swabia in southwestern Germany, which not only seem to bolster the belief of archeologists that the origin of figurative art is a crucial threshold in human evolution, but are also recognized as the very first examples of this kind of prehistoric art (cf. Conard 2003: 830). These findings include the oldest known representation of a bird, a remarkable therianthropic sculpture (only the second *Löwenmensch*, a small half-human half-lion figure, ever found), and an animal that most closely resembles a horse. For Conard the discovery of a second *Löwenmensch* very explicitly lends support to the hypothesis that Aurignacian or Cro-Magnon people practiced some form of shamanism (cf. 831). Moreover, these figurines are clearly not just "art" as we know it today, but seem to be personal possessions, and may be evidence of very discreet activities (cf. Sinclair 2003: 774).

Whichever way we look at Upper Paleolithic "art," it is certainly much more than one archeological puzzle among many others. In it we are dealing with the remarkable expression of something that is quintessentially human, something that sets us apart from other animals, and even from our closest prehuman ancestors. In an important sense, therefore, this is not about only the remote past. It concerns our images of ourselves and what we see as our own humanness. The Upper Paleolithic art of France and Spain offers unique and rich data on how, in that region, people became recognizably human, even if today we have only tentative, and even competing, suggestions about what this art, and the creation thereof, might have meant to them.

Conclusion

What can we now conclude from the insights gained from the sciences of paleoanthropology and archeology on the evolution of human uniqueness, and how will these conclusions affect the already complex dialogue between the very diverse reasoning strategies of theology and the sciences?

In this interdisciplinary conversation it has become clear that:

1. Transversal lines of argument between evolutionary epistemology and paleoanthropology converge and intersect on the fact that the very first modern humans were distinct in the evolution of their symbolic, cognitively fluid minds that directly led to symbolic, creative behavior as witnessed, most importantly, by the remarkable cave art of the Upper Paleolithic.

2. What we learn from the sciences of paleoanthropology and archeology, then, is that human uniqueness emerged as a highly contextualized and physically embodied notion, where the symbolizing minds of our distant ancestors are stunningly revealed today in the materiality of prehistoric cave art. The emergence of these symbolizing minds, revealed in the cave art, is also linked to the unique ability of spoken language, and a remarkable cognitive fluidity as expressed in the ability to generate mental symbols, to think, to feel, to reason, to imagine, and to plan.

3. Paleoanthropologists, like evolutionary epistemologists, have linked this emergence of consciousness and of symbolic behavior directly to the emergence of religious awareness. What we have here, then, are two transversal lines of argument converging in support of the plausibility and integrity of the presence of religious awareness in our earliest, mod-

ern human ancestors. This obviously is not an argument for the truth of any religion, nor for the existence of God. It is, however, an argument for the integrity of the earliest forms of religious awareness and behavior, and points to evolutionary reasons for the naturalness and the integrity of religious faith, and the possibility of ritual behavior in our earliest human ancestors.

4. These convergent arguments from evolutionary epistemology and paleoanthropology for the presence of religious awareness in our earliest Cro-Magnon ancestors are strengthened by recent arguments in paleoanthropology for linking shamanistic explanations not only to this early form of religious awareness, but also to possibly deeper forms of meaning for much of the painted prehistoric imagery of the Upper Paleolithic.

5. Therefore, transversally intersecting arguments from evolutionary epistemology and paleoanthropology support the plausibility of the larger argument that since the very beginning of the emergence of *Homo sapiens,* the evolution of those characteristics that made humans unique from even their closest sister species, i.e., characteristics like consciousness, language, symbolic minds and symbolic behavior, is directly related to religious awareness and religious behavior. And it is precisely because every human society, at one stage or another, possessed religion of some sort, complete with origin myths and rituals that purportedly explain the relationship of humans to the world around them, that religion cannot be discounted from any discussion of typically human behaviors.

Looking at these magical, elusive works of art will always suggest questions about the enigmatic beliefs of the Cro-Magnon peoples, about what their customs and their legends were, and how their social structures were organized. It is difficult to escape the implication that the Paleolithic paintings suggest one or another definite narrative, and in some cases even a ritualistic mind-set that might have led directly to the painting of these figures. Although we will never know, and should be careful not to project our own categories onto these ethereal expressions, there might be good reasons for arguing that these drawings, paintings, and etchings could have functioned as spiritual links between the natural and the supernatural worlds. In the next chapter I will take up this question, and will explore linguistic, neuroscientific, and neuropsychological arguments that might support this thesis. I will argue that if there are plausible arguments for the symbolic, or even just tentative religious meaning of some of these paintings, this symbolic heritage of our distant ancestors may reveal something about the emergence of the earliest form of religion, and thus support arguments for the naturalness and rationality of religious faith as a uniquely human predisposition.

In Upper Paleolithic "art" we are dealing with the remarkable material expression of something quintessentially human, something that sets us apart from other animals, and even from our closest prehuman ancestors. In an important sense, therefore, this quest for meaning in human prehistory is not about only the remote past. On the contrary, it directly concerns our images of ourselves and what we see as our own distinctive humanness. The Upper Paleolithic art of southwestern France and the Basque Country of northern Spain, however enigmatic and mysterious, does offer us unique and rich data on how, in that specific region, people became recognizably human.

I argued in the first lecture that there is no clear philosophical blueprint or timeless recipe for relating the bewildering complexity of contemporary theologies to the increasingly complex spectrum of contemporary sciences (cf. van Huyssteen 1999: 235-86). This does not mean that we cannot develop focused dialogues between theology and the sciences on issues of shared concern, on issues that seem to be quite specific, and that resonate with both partners in this dialogue. I do believe that the evolution of "human uniqueness," so much highlighted now by current paleoanthropological research, has presented us with an outstanding and exciting case study for precisely this kind of interdisciplinary dialogue.

Christian theology, as became clear in chapter 3, has traditionally assumed a radical split between human beings, created "in the image of God," and the rest of creation. This split was mostly justified by cognitive traits like human rationality or intelligence, by problematic notions of stewardship, or by abstract notions of relationality that served to define what was meant by "human uniqueness," even as it floated free above nature and the human body. Crucial to the prehistory of the human mind, from a paleoanthropological point of view, however, is the amazing emergence of what Steven Mithen has called cognitive fluidity. Science, art, and religion are all deeply embedded in the cognitive fluidity of the embodied human mind/brain. As such, they rely on psychological processes that originally evolved in specialized cognitive domains and emerged only when these processes could actually work together. Of perhaps even greater significance, the cognitive fluidity of our minds allowed for the possibility of powerful metaphors and analogies, without which science, religion, and art could not exist. What became clear, as we saw in the work of Ian Tattersall, is that *the potential arose in the mind* to undertake science, create art, and discover the need and ability for religious belief, even though there were no specific selection pressures for such abstract abilities at any point during our past. In this sense we cannot understand early human behavior unless we take this fundamental religious dimension into account.

At the end of the first chapter I suggested that a theological appropriation of these rich and complex results of science at the very least should inspire the theologian to carefully trace and rethink the complex evolution of the doctrine of the *imago Dei*. As became clear in my third lecture, interpretations of the *imago Dei* have varied dramatically throughout the long history of Christianity. Theologians are now challenged to rethink what human uniqueness might mean for the human person, a being that has emerged biologically as a center of embodied self-awareness, identity, and moral responsibility. This notion of personhood, when reconceived in terms of embodied imagination, symbolic propensities, and cognitive fluidity, will now enable theology to revision its own notion of the *imago Dei* as emerging from nature itself, an idea that does not imply any superiority or a greater value over other animals or earlier hominids, but might express, from a theological point of view, a specific task and purpose to set forth the presence of God in this world (cf. Hefner 1998: 88). Now supported by voices from paleoanthropology, I would call for a revisioning of the notion of the *imago Dei* in ways that would not be overly abstract and exotically baroque, that instead acknowledge our embodied existence, our close ties to the animal world and *its* uniqueness, that deeply respect those hominid ancestors that came before us, while at the same time focusing on what our symbolic and cognitively fluid minds might tell us about the emergence of an embodied human uniqueness, consciousness, and personhood, and the propensity for religious awareness and religious experience.

five Human Uniqueness and Symbolization

"One point of dwelling on human nature is to stress that the arrow of human history, though awe-inspriring, is not mystical or uncanny. Technological evolution, and cultural evolution more broadly, are not alien forces, visited on the human species from the great beyond. . . . Technology and other forms of culture come from within. The directionality of culture, of history, is an expression of our species, of human nature."

Robert Wright, *Nonzero: The Logic of Human Destiny* (New York: Pantheon Books, 2000), 27

In earlier chapters my research into evolutionary epistemology (chap. 2) and paleoanthropology (chap. 4) yielded not only challenging but also converging results on the issue of human uniqueness. It seems that both philosophically and scientifically it can be argued that the potential arose in the human mind to create art, to discover the need and ability for religious belief, to invent technologies, and — much later — to undertake science. In my second chapter I argued that what is distinctive about human beings is precisely this evolution of cognition, imagination, and religious awareness. This is the reason why one can argue that human behavior is imperfectly understood if we do not take into account the very early emergence of religion, and then ask about the plausibility of religious and theological explanations for human nature as such. In an interdisciplinary conversation such as this one, theologians especially are challenged to take seriously the fact that our ability to respond religiously to ultimate questions through worship and prayer is deeply embedded in our species' symbolic, imaginative behavior, and in the cognitively fluid minds that make such behavior possible.

In the second chapter we also saw that the evolutionary epistemologist Franz Wuketits argues that the need for metaphysics, and metaphysical explanations, seems to be a universal characteristic of all humans (cf. Wuketits 1990: 117). In the fourth chapter, on paleoanthropology, we saw that even our earliest ancestors, the Cro-Magnons of the Upper Paleolithic, who were "us" in every anatomical and behavioral way, seem to have had metaphysical systems or first religions, which almost certainly included notions about meaning, survival, beauty, life after death, and the "other world." Evolutionary epistemologists explain the persistence of this kind of religious awareness as the result of the particular interactions between early humans and their external world, and thus as resulting from the specific life conditions in prehistoric times (cf. 118). This, however, raises two questions: Why should we, so suddenly and only at this point, distrust the phylogenetic memories of our direct ancestors, and should the emergence of religious consciousness be explained only in terms of specific life conditions in prehistoric times? Might there not be something about being human, something about the human condition itself, that could offer us a slightly different perspective on the enduring need for religious faith?

We also saw that an evolutionary epistemologist like Wuketits, after arguing for the propensity for religious belief in humans, and thus for the naturalness of religion, proceeds reductionistically to classify religious beliefs as giving rise to irrational worldviews (cf. 118). I argued in chapter 2 that this seems to conflict with his own careful distinction between biological and cultural evolution. He specifically argues that there are biological constraints on cultural evolution, but that culture is not reducible to biology. Cultural evolution, once started, obeys its own principles, giving the evolution of human cognition an entirely new and unprecedented direction (cf. 130f.). Wuketits seems to be inconsistent, therefore, in using evolutionary arguments to curtail the scope of cultural evolution, interpreting all religious beliefs as irrational and determined solely by the way they are embedded in the way our prehistoric ancestors coped with their worlds.

Against this background theologian Tomáš Hančil was correct to use evolutionary epistemology's own argument ("instead of asking what kind of mind is required to know the world, we should rather ask what kind of world the world must be to have been able to produce the sort of minds we have") to expose some of the reductionist and inconsistent antirealist conclusions often singled out for religious worldviews only. What also became clear earlier is that a proper theological answer to this kind of reductionism can be very difficult. Hančil was right to argue that this kind of scientism is possible only if one assumes that God does not influence our world in any meaningful way. He was less successful in his attempt to fuse evolutionary epistemology and theology by arguing that if God does influence the world, God's influence should be part of the data we work with (cf. Hančil 1999: 240). I believe that evolutionary epistemology does challenge theology to take seriously the implications of the biological origins of human cognition and rationality, and of the embodied history of the evolution of this capacity. In the interdisciplinary conversation between theology and the sciences, the boundaries between our disciplines and reasoning strategies are porous, but that does not mean that deep theological convictions can be easily transferred to philosophy, or to science, to function as "data" in a foreign system. In the same manner, transversal reasoning does not imply that scientific data, paradigms, or worldviews can be transported into theology, to there set the agenda for theological reasoning. Transversal reasoning means that theology and science can share concerns, can converge on commonly identified problems such as the problem of human uniqueness. We will see later that the argument from evolutionary epistemology, when transversally interwoven with the central paleoanthropological argument about human uniqueness, resonates critically with some core theological claims about human uniqueness. But I will also argue that precisely by recognizing the limitations of interdisciplinarity, the disciplinary integrity of both theology and the sciences should be protected. On this view the theologian can caution the scientist to recognize the reductionism of scientistic worldviews, even as the scientist can caution the theologian against constructing esoteric and imperialistic worldviews.

These mutually critical tasks presuppose the richness of the transversal moment in which theology and paleoanthropology can find a plausible interdisciplinary connection on the issue of human uniqueness. In chapter 3 I argued that the most responsible Christian theological way to look at human uniqueness requires, first of all, a move away from esoteric and baroquely abstract notions of human uniqueness, and second, a return to embodied notions of humanness where our embodied sexuality and moral awareness are tied directly to our embodied self-transcendence as believers who are in a relationship with God. In chapter 4 I argued that, from a paleoanthropological point of view, human uniqueness also emerges as a highly contextualized and embodied notion and is directly tied to the embodied, symbolizing minds of our prehistoric ancestors, as materially manifested in the spectacularly painted cave walls of the Upper Paleolithic. This opened up the possibility not only for converging arguments, from both evolutionary epistemology and paleo-anthropology, for the presence of religious awareness in our earliest Cro-Magnon ancestors, but also for the plausibility of the larger argument: since the very beginning of the emergence of *Homo sapiens,* the characteristics that made humans uniquely different from even their closest sister species, i.e., characteristics like consciousness, language, symbolic minds, and symbolic behavior, always included religious awareness and religious behavior.

In this chapter I want to extend this argument and take a closer look at the symbolizing minds of our Cro-Magnon ancestors. First, I will ask about the role of culture and language in the evolution of symbolic and imaginative human behavior. A discussion of paleoculture will reveal adaptability and versatility as a remarkable human capacity in which the role of symbolic language was a crucial factor. This will reveal the prehistoric material "art" from the Upper Paleolithic as exemplifying a profound dimension of imagination and symbolic meaning, in which the presence of spoken language has to be presupposed. In fact, the painting of images on cave walls could have emerged only in communities with shared systems of meaning, mediated through language. Second, I will focus on some of the current discussions in neuroscience and neuropsychology and explore the possibility of transversal links to paleo-anthropological perspectives on the symbolic propensities of the human mind. This will reveal the cave paintings from the Upper Paleolithic as a reliable window through which we can glimpse the symbolic minds of our prehistoric, Cro-Magnon ancestors. Moreover, a neuroscientific perspective on the embodied human mind and human consciousness will yield the possibility not only of a neurological bridge to the Upper Paleolithic but also that our universal human capacity for altered states of consciousness may provide a link to the spectacular scope of prehistoric human imagination as well as reveal a form of shamanism as a plausible interpretation of the earliest forms of religious imagination. Third, religious imagination will emerge as central to any paleoanthropological or theological definition of human uniqueness. This proposal will challenge the ability of neuroscience and cognitive psychology to effectively explain religious experience; although biological origins have directly shaped human origins and human understanding, the genesis of religions, so unique to humans, is not something that we can unproblematically extrapolate from earlier explanations in biology or neuroscience.

Human Uniqueness and Language

In chapter 4 we saw that Steven Mithen has argued that seeds for the cognitive fluidity of the human mind were sown with the increase of brain size that began around 500,000 years ago. This was directly related to the later evolution of a grammatically complex social language. On Mithen's more gradualist view, as social language switched to a general-purpose language, individuals acquired an increasing awareness about their own knowledge of the nonsocial world. Consciousness then adopted the role of a comprehensive, integrating mechanism for knowledge that had previously been "trapped" in separate specialized intelligences (cf. Mithen 1996: 194). The first step toward cognitive fluidity appears to have been an integration between social and natural history intelligence in early modern humans around 100,000 years ago. The final step to full cognitive fluidity — the ability to entertain ideas that bring together elements from normally incongruous domains — most probably occurred at different times in different populations between 60,000 and 30,000 years ago. This involved an integration of technical intelligence, and led to the cultural explosion we now call the appearance of the human mind (cf. 194). In chapter 4 we also saw clear differences of opinion as scholars in paleoanthropology and archeology approached this rather spectacular emergence of the human mind differently. From a theological perspective, however, irrespective of differences in scientific interpretation and perspectives, it was this important step in the evolution of the human mind that ultimately enabled our species to design complex tools, to create art, and to discover religious belief.

This, of course, leads to the broader question of what we can reconstruct today about the evolution of culture, and any unique cultural capacities, in humans. In his most recent work Rick Potts discussed this question in depth and pointed out that scholars in primatology and paleoanthropology today generally assume that a common ancestry of culture exists among at least the great apes and humans, including the oldest human ancestors (Potts 2004: 249; also 1996). This means that the concept of culture, normally exclusively applied to human beings, is now also applied to chimpanzees by primatologists who have demonstrated geographic variation in the behavioral repertoires of these apes. These variations are described as "cultural" because these apes are able to invent new customs and then pass them on independently within different social groups, where neither ecological nor genetic factors can account for the behavioral differences manifested between groups. The most well-known example here is differences in termite feeding. At Gombe, Tanzania, chimpanzees practice termite fishing with slender twigs that are prepared and then inserted into termite nests; by contrast, chimpanzees in Equatorial Guinea use stout digging sticks to break open termite nests in their termite digging (2004: 249).

A very different concept of culture is employed when Paleolithic archeologists and paleoanthropologists speak of culture, in which they almost always refer to stone tools. Here different artifacts and manufacturing techniques are equated with different, distinct cultures and are considered indicative of cultural change. It is in this sense that archeologists then speak of Oldowan culture, Acheulean culture, and Mousterian culture. In applying these terms, scientists assume that change in toolmaking methods and the proportion of distinct artifact types over time and space reflects the development of new bodies of cultural information, which evolving hominids became capable of inventing and sustaining.

In spite of these differences in using the concept of culture, Potts has argued persuasively that the quest for a common ground between primate culture, hominid culture, and human culture is scientifically sound and defines a way of studying the continuities between human and nonhuman primate behavior. On this view paleoanthropologists and primatologists agree on at least four elements of what constitutes cultural behavior (251ff.).

1. Culture is a system of nongenetic information transfer, which occurs across generations and among individuals of the same generation.
2. Cultural behavior is manifested in discrete forms, i.e., specific activities, implements, or systems of belief.
3. Geographic differentiation in behavior, i.e., differences between separated populations, is an important and distinctive common ground for cultural behavior, and has been well documented in chimpanzees, orangutans, and humans.
4. The potential for change across generations is a final hallmark of primate cultural behavior. In modern humans, cultural variations are cumulative: the inventions of many generations are stockpiled, creating vast repositories of social information. In nonhuman primates there is less evidence for such accumulation.

The really interesting question is how this shared concept of culture fares when compared to the behavioral deposits, or artifacts, left behind by early humans. Here too Potts's answer is persuasive and to the point. He has argued that the oldest material record of hominid behavior is about 2.5 million years old and consists of assemblages of precisely and repetitively chipped and battered rocks that define Oldowan toolmaking. It used to be thought that Oldowan cores (the sharp-edged rocks that bear multiple flake scars) represented purposeful tool designs that were in the minds of *Homo habilis* toolmakers. Detailed studies have now shown, however, that these idealized forms were mainly "stopping points" in a continuous process of knocking sharp flakes from rocks of different original shapes. In fact, over a span of 800,000 years (from ca. 2.5 million to 1.7 million years ago) the Oldowan largely consists of continuously varying artifact forms that resulted from the repetitive process of flaking stone, making sharp edges, and using rounded stones or the cores themselves to hammer and crush other objects (252f.). The earliest Acheulean, around 1.7 million years ago, reflected an apparent breakthrough in the process of stone flaking. Hominid toolmakers were able, for the first time on a regular basis, to detach very large flakes, and when this was done and the piece then flaked around the perimeter, the first hand axes, or large cutting tools, were made. What is important, as well as fascinating, is that the enormous distance between Africa and East Asia did not prohibit or hinder the making of very similar tools; the tools certainly point to similar cognitive and technological capabilities in Africa and East Asia. For Potts this clearly implies that even on this large geographic scale, and across long stretches of time, cultural differentiation of hominid populations is not as apparent as once believed (259f.).

When we compare the rich body of archeological evidence to the common ground of modern ape and human culture, intriguing differences become apparent. Potts has argued that over the first 2 million years of the archeological record, early humans manifested a behavior system that differed from great ape and human culture. Potts has called this a *paleocultural system,* which was indeed characterized by the transmission of nongenetic information, yet the artifacts and inferred behaviors of early humans, until roughly 500,000 years ago, exhibited continuous variation, which points to ecological factors for an explanation of some of this variation (260). At the same time, Paleolithic toolmaking was also marked by long periods of stasis, hundreds of thousands of years over which stone flaking did not change in any systematic manner. In other words, separation in space and time did not necessarily imply distinct behavioral packages, or "cultures," as the term is used by anthropologists and primatologists. What this means is that while nongenetic transmission of culture exists in all great apes, other commonalities of ape and human culture are not homologous. Although bonobos and gorillas, for instance, exhibit complex social learning, tool-assisted behavior in the wild and consistent geographic variations in social behavior have yet to be demonstrated in these species. It would still be possible to argue, however, that a greater capacity for innovation and geographic differentiation of discrete behavioral variants emerged independently in chimpanzees and orangutans during the Pleistocene, parallel to the pattern in the human record (261).

This finally leads us to the crucial question: When did modern human cultural behavior emerge, and under what conditions did this process of emergence take place? Potts has argued that vast environmental fluctuations have characterized the past several million years and provided the critical context in which humans evolved. This is especially true of the past 700,000 years (cf. Potts 1996), which have constituted one of the most turbulent periods of environmental instability in the earth's history. As a consequence, the Pleistocene was a period of high species extinction, and lineages that did not become extinct seemed to have one of two options: either mobility and wide dispersal, which allowed these creatures to keep up with geographic shifts in their preferred climatic zone or food resources, or a greater degree of versatility or adaptability to a wider range of environmental conditions (Potts 2004: 261).

It is precisely this capacity for versatility that Potts has identified as the "astonishing hallmark of modern humanity" (Potts 1996; 2004). Never before has a single species of such ecological adaptability evolved, at least among vertebrates. *Homo sapiens* thus emerged because its ancestral lineage persisted and changed in the face of dramatic environmental variability. It is in this dynamic prehistoric environment that a suite of anatomical and behavioral shifts occurred: not only did the fastest rate of increase in brain size relative to body size take place over the past 700,000 years, but around 500,000 years ago the stone tools made by early hominids became more diversified with increasingly standardized forms (2004: 262). At the same time, social interactions also intensified. Although it has been suggested that home bases existed earlier in time, it was only around 400,000 to 300,000 years ago that the primary signals of modern human home-base behavior, namely, hearths and shelters, became apparent in the prehistoric record.

As for symbolic behavior, it became clear earlier that a few artifacts between 250,000 and 70,000 years ago indicated that symbolic behavior began to be reflected in the things hominids made. The presence of pigment at least 230,000 years ago in central Africa suggests decorative capabilities in some early human populations (cf. McBrearty and Brooks 2000: 524). However, as we saw in chapter 4, a tremendous expansion of symbolic behavior occurred 50,000 to 30,000 years ago, manifested in body ornamentation, cave paintings, sculpture, and the first musical instruments (bone flutes). Innovation started to soar, exemplified by the routine use of new materials such as antler and bone, in addition to stone, to create new kinds of implements and aesthetic objects (Potts 2004: 263).

Most important for understanding the symbolic minds of these ancestors of ours, however, is language — one of the most elaborate forms of symbolic coding imaginable. Language, and the ability to refer to distant sources of water, food, and other "nonvisible" aspects of the natural and social environment (263f.), may have made the difference between survival and extinction in a challenging environment. Symbolic language enables humans to create complex mental maps, to imagine "what if . . . ," to think in terms of contingencies, and to plan and create strategies for events in the future. And exactly relevant to this point, Hauser, Chomsky, and Fitch, in a recent article analyzing the evolution of the language faculty, have argued that the unique ability of *recursion* lies at the heart of uniquely human language, i.e., the ability to turn a finite set of elements (phonemes, words, syntactical rules, mental activities) into a potentially infinite array of discrete expressions and representations (cf. Hauser, Chomsky, and Fitch 2002: 1569ff.). Most scholars would also agree that animal systems of communication lack precisely the rich expressive and open-ended power of human language. Against this background Potts has argued that although it is difficult to see how it might have evolved via habitat-specific, directional selection, this infinitely inventive aspect of language does make sense as an evolved response to the type of complex, inconsistent settings in which *Homo sapiens* emerged (Potts 2004: 261; 1996).

It is clear that a highly specific view of human uniqueness emerges in the work of Rick Potts. The origin of language, and of cultural capacities so distinctive to living humans, greatly enhanced the chances of adapting to environmental instability, and this enhancement decoupled the early modern humans from any single ancestral milieu (Potts 2004: 265). Trying to understand humanness from a paleoanthropological and archeological point of view inevitably reveals the overarching influence of symbolic ability, and thus the means by which humans create meaning. Clearly, then, human cultural behavior involves not only the transmission of nongenetic behavior, but also the coding of thoughts, sensations, things, times, and places that are not empirically available or visible. In this way Potts's work becomes invaluable for an interdisciplinary dialogue with theology, because his is an argument from science that not only the material culture of prehistoric imagery as depicted in the spectacular cave "art" of France and Spain, but the heights of all human imagination, the depths of depravity, moral awareness, and a sense of God also must depend on this human capacity for the symbolic coding of the "nonvisible." This "coding of the nonvisible" through abstract, symbolic thought enabled also our early human ancestors to argue and hold beliefs in abstract terms. In fact, the concept of God itself follows from the ability to abstract and conceive of "person" (265f.).

I believe that Potts has made a convincing argument that this paleo-cultural system of early human behavior would not have made sense as a response to a world of certainty and stability. But it does make sense as a psychological and social response to a world of contingency: the need to create meaning, whether religious, ethical, philosophical, aesthetic, is part of the "tool kit" that *Homo sapiens* has evolved in its long journey of physical and spiritual survival. However much humans share with primate or hominid culture, we cannot avoid acknowledging the emergence of distinctive cultural properties that highlight both the evolutionary continuities and discontinuities in the cultural behavior of *Homo sapiens,* earlier humans, and other primates. And the most distinctive discontinuity is the emergence of language and the symbolic capacity of the human mind. It is language that engages the interactive minds of the social group, and that enables the social world beyond an individual's own lifetime to be defined symbolically. It is this astonishing dimension of human cultural behavior that is unique to modern humans and that suggests the origins of a spiritual sense. A sense of the ineffable, the sacred, the spiritual is part and parcel of how human beings have coped with their personal and social universe (270), and in this coping process the role of language in the evolution of the uniquely human mind was crucial. Steven Mithen has argued that as soon as language started acting as a vehicle for delivering information to the mind, carrying with it snippets of nonsocial information, a rather dramatic transformation of the nature of the mind began (cf. Mithen 1996: 208ff.). At that point language switched from a social to a general-purpose function, and consciousness from a means to predict other individuals' behavior to managing a mental database of information relating to all domains of behavior. Thus a *cognitive fluidity* arose within the mind, and consequently a mental transformation occurred, which physiologically implied no increase in brain size. This move, in essence, was the origin of the kind of symbolic capacity that is unique to the human mind.

Consequently, as we saw in chapter 4, scholars like Steven Mithen, Ian Tattersall, and Paul Mellars have argued that knowing the prehistory of the human mind will provide us with a more profound understanding of what it means to be uniquely human. It certainly helps us understand a little better the origins of art and of religion, and how these cultural domains are inescapably linked to the ability of the cognitively fluid human mind to develop creatively powerful metaphors by crossing the boundaries of different domains of knowledge. By definition this kind of symbolic language use can arise only within a cognitively fluid mind.

However, Mithen's archeological perspective on the evolution of language still leaves us with important questions regarding the symbolic capacities of our human minds. In particular, scholars still wrestle with these: When did modern human language arise, and what exactly was its function in an evolutionary context? Here, too, answers are given along the two well-known lines of current evolutionary and paleoanthropological debates: Did language arise rather suddenly, in a punctuated leap at the very threshold of modern human existence, perhaps at the Middle to Upper Paleolithic boundary (cf. Lewin 1993: 162)? Or did linguistic abilities develop gradually, reaching modern levels through steady, cumulative increments? It is obviously very difficult to address the timing of language origins since language does not fossilize or impress itself directly on the archeological record. Paleontologists therefore have to look for indirect products of language capability, or for evidence from the anatomical structures that produce language, namely, the brain and the vocal tract (163).

What seems to be clear is that the potential for language was fully realized when Upper Paleolithic people for the first time were neurologically equipped for language. An increasing number of scholars have also pointed to various areas of archeological evidence that point, directly or indirectly, to a dramatic enhancement of language abilities that seems to have coincided with the Upper Paleolithic: (1) deliberate burial of the dead, which almost certainly, at least in a basic sense, had already begun in Neanderthal times; (2) artistic expression, especially bodily adornment and image making (notably the painting of caves), which began only with the Upper Paleolithic; (3) a clear and sudden acceleration in the pace of technological innovation and cultural change; (4) the development of real regional differences in culture, an expression and product of social boundaries; (5) evidence of long-distance contact and trade; (6) a significant increase in size of living sites, for which complex language is a prerequisite for planning and coordination; (7) the addition to the predominant use of stone technology of other raw materials, such as bone, antler, and clay (cf. 163).

This combination of "firsts" in human activity looks impressive, and seems increasingly to define the uniqueness of *Homo sapiens* from a paleoanthropological perspective. Although some scholars question the punctuational appearance of some of these elements, most find the evidence of these historically meaningful shifts persuasive support of the appearance of a complex, fully modern spoken language (cf. Klein 1999: 590f.). In light of the latest evidence, it is tempting to infer that the Upper Paleolithic was ushered in by a major enhancement of language abilities. What is most interesting for our purposes, however, is that the same kind of pattern is to be seen in that major area of archeological evidence, namely, prehistoric art or imagery. As was argued in lecture 4, activities such as engraving, sculpting, and especially painting appeared late in the prehistoric record, and coincided with the sudden emergence of innovation and rapid change that defines Upper Paleolithic tool technologies. If the ability to produce representational and symbolic images and decorative objects does relate to language abilities, the evidence of the archeological record would indeed point to dramatic enhancement late in human prehistory (cf. Lewin 1993: 166).

It is exactly for this very close link between creative prehistoric imagery and language that scholars like Iain Davidson and William Noble have argued. In his argument for a very direct link between language and symbolic abilities, Davidson takes a comparative approach that juxtaposes data from Europe with that from Australia, and then argues that the similarities in the development of early image-making clearly show the universal use of art to reflect the negotiation of environmental (i.e., both natural and social) relationships. He also argues, rather impressively, that the most significant European influence on the cultural development of modern humans is not to be found in the sculpture of the classical Greeks, the paintings of the Italian Renaissance, the plays of Shakespeare, or the musical tradition of Mozart and Beethoven, but in the paintings and engravings of the Upper Paleolithic (cf. Davidson 1997: 125).

Davidson also argues that early humans worked out their relationship with their environment and with each other through this "art," and sees the burst of image making after 40,000 B.P. as reflecting the way these ancestors of ours explored the limits and possibilities of the power of their recently discovered symbolically based communication. Because of this, most scholars in the field would take the Upper Paleolithic as the standard for recognizing symbolism, even if in a sense it is anomalous, because symbolism did not emerge elsewhere in the world populated by *Homo sapiens* at that time (cf. 125). For Davidson this symboling power is tied directly to the origins of language: it would have been impossible for creatures without language to hold opinions about the making or marking of surfaces that make them art. For this reason Davidson argues that it is precisely these supremely important artistic artifacts from the Upper Paleolithic that give us unique insights into evolutionary processes, into the evolution of human behavior, and into the very nature of what it might have meant to be a modern human.

Davidson takes as his fundamental assumption throughout that language emerged fairly late in human evolution (cf. 126; also Noble and Davidson 1996). He recognizes that the vocal apparatus evolved gradually over the course of human evolution, but argues that the actual transition between language absence (although certainly including vocal and other communication) and language use involved the recognition of symbols. What is crucial is that language is distinguished from other forms of communication not only by modes of communication like speech, signs, or writing, but also by the use of symbols in any or all of these modes of communication (cf. Davidson 1997: 126). In this sense the emergence of language goes hand in hand with the recognition of symbols. This means we could not have art without language, but it does not mean that the origins of language can be identified with the origins of art. Davidson argues that the earliest evidence that requires an interpretation that there were people who must have had language is the colonization of Australia around 60,000 years ago. This seems to be 20,000 years earlier than the Upper Paleolithic of Europe. The important question now is, what does the rather late origin of language mean for our understanding of prehistoric art? For Davidson one of the most distinctive features of language is the arbitrariness of symbols, and how that necessarily results in inherent ambiguity, especially when compared to prelinguistic communication systems (cf. the complex calls of vervet monkeys) that have no possibility of ambiguity because they have been honed by natural selection. One way to cope with the proliferation of this kind of ambiguous creativity was to produce emblems or signs that we, even today, can recognize as in some sense *iconic*. Successful communication, therefore, requires means of identification that the utterances are trustworthy. We should not be surprised to find these kinds of emblems among early language users (cf. 126f.). We should also not be surprised, I think, that we are still fascinated by the enigmatic character of these symbolic images and signs.

This argument, that Paleolithic art is symbolic, not just decorative, is considerably strengthened by what was discussed in chapter 4, namely, Margaret Conkey's persuasive arguments *against* trying to capture the generic "meaning" of Paleolithic art as a single, inclusive, empirical category or metatheory of our inquiry, and *for* a more contextual understanding of the "meaning" of this art as enmeshed in the social context of its time. On this view the original meaning can be said to exist only through the contexts in which it was first produced as individual paintings or parts of paintings (cf. 128). What this really means is that "meaning" is a property not of Paleolithic art in itself, but of the interaction, then and now, between the human agents and the material. We also, in our relational, interactive interpretations of this art, discover and produce meaning. Therefore, the meaning we find in the earliest art produced by people like us clearly is a product of our interpretative interaction with this art. What again emerges here is an important convergence between theological and paleoanthropological methodology, a truly post-foundationalist argument for meaning that, as I argued in chapter 1, implies that we relate to our world(s) through interpreted experience only.

When viewed like this, the Upper Paleolithic tradition of prehistoric "art" emerges as an evolving tradition (or traditions) that has had, and still has, the capacity to reveal distinct regularities, and not just western European particularities, about the evolution of human behavior (cf. 133).[1] Davidson has also argued that personal ornamentation is earlier in the surviving evidence than the "making of places" (cave paintings). In the evolutionary process of "art" in the Upper Paleolithic era, this does not imply that there was an inevitability of "progress" from personal decoration to the painting of the caves. But personal decoration was indeed an early part of the complex of symbolic representation in the Upper Paleolithic of Europe. Davidson is suggesting that, although the earliest language, and hence symbolism, may have left no material trace, on both continents the newly arrived humans had only recently discovered language and its symbolic properties. And in this context they also discovered personal decoration and cave painting (cf. 138, 147f.).

But what more can be said about language and symbolism in prehistoric cave paintings, that most famous manifestation of Upper Paleolithic "art"? One of the most fascinating examples of the way prehistoric cave art reveals distinct regularities is found in the so-called hand stencils, or handprints. The earliest images in Upper Paleolithic cave art are indeed the famous handprints, especially those from Gargas in the French Pyrenees, now confirmed by the early dates from those in Cosquer, the famous "cave beneath the sea" (cf. Clottes and Courtin 1996). The production of handprints on cave walls is one of the truly universal features of expressive human behavior, produced all over the world and at almost all times since there have been humans (cf. Davidson 1997: 148f.). Although Davidson has maintained that we have no way of ever knowing exactly what they meant, Jean Clottes and David Lewis-Williams have now persuasively argued for an interpretation that sees them as shamanistic "touchings of the other world," and thus for an unmistakable ritualistic, religious interpretation of these mysterious, ubiquitous signs.

1. Davidson insists he is not arguing this from a Eurocentric view, but rather from a view that sees Europe as a rather isolated little peninsula far away from the scenes of most of the major events of prehistory. The people in western Europe, though, were subject to the same sorts of evolutionary pressures as other evolving humans elsewhere in the world. The story can be told, then, from the perspective of the spectacular archeological record of western Europe because it is also confirmed by the record of Australian prehistory (cf. 1997: 138f.).

From a paleoanthropological point of view, symbolism should therefore be seen as part and parcel of turning communication into language, *but the use of symbols separate from language, as in cave paintings and abstract signs, could only have been a product of language* (cf. 153). What this implies is that whatever symbolic, expressive quality those spectacular prehistoric cave paintings had in southwestern France and in the Basque Country of northern Spain, they owed to the linguistic context in which they were created. Hence the imagination, productivity, and creativity we associate with humans is very much a product of language, which makes language and symbolic abilities central to a definition of embodied human uniqueness.

In their *Human Evolution, Language, and Mind* (1996), Iain Davidson and William Noble have made an even more detailed case for this close relation between language and prehistoric art. At the heart of this argument is the conviction that the making of images to resemble things can have emerged historically only in communities with shared systems of meaning, and shared systems of meaning are mediated through language. Davidson and Noble's main argument, however, is that the development of language and the development of image making are interdependent, each facilitating the other. In this sense representational images in prehistory should be seen as the imprint of language in a tangible, material form (cf. also Lewin 1993: 166). For Noble and Davidson human "mindedness" and "minded" behavior arise only within the socially constructed context of linguistic communication, which is why the appearance of symbolic behavior like cave paintings is so directly related to language, and why both language and symbolic behavior are very late developments, appearing no more than 50,000 years ago (cf. Mithen 1997: 269ff.).

What I see emerging here is an interpretation of the embodied human mind functioning as a "mindedness of behavior in context," especially in its very specific historical, social, and paleocultural context. Crucial to Noble and Davidson's argument is how communication between humans came to be unquestionably intentional, and they answer by seeing language as social interaction where those practices that happen to be unique to humans interactively recruit the structures of the brain, rather than being determined by them. Such practices obviously depend on prior structural evolution, but it is these cultural *practices* that interact with brain structures (cf. Noble and Davidson 1996: 18). It is in this sense that minded human behavior is linguistic and essentially interactive, and that human minds are socially constructed. Against this background it can be argued that in early humans, the physical acts of throwing and pointing actually led to iconic gestures, which in turn made possible the transformation of communication into language. The fact that a gesture could be a meaningful object for perception facilitated the remarkable symbolic discovery that one thing can stand for another. This discovery, for Noble and Davidson at least, was an all-or-nothing event that cannot be explained in gradualist terms (cf. also Corbey and Roebroeks 1997: 917ff.). This radical position leads them to reject a gradualist approach to the evolution of language, and along with that the possibility of "protolanguage": if a form of communication was not language as we actually know it, it would be misleading to refer to it as language at all (cf. Noble and Davidson 1996: 8ff.).[2]

On this view the discovery or emergence of language was more a matter of behavior than of evolutionary changes in biology alone. Language as a symbolic communication system created mindedness, being aware of experience and knowledge, being able to judge and plan and thus better control the future. This ability finally released early humans partially from the immediate contingencies of a specific natural environment, enabling them to plan logistically in all kinds of environmental settings, to abstract, to differentiate between "us" and "them," to construct notions about the supernatural, and to reflect on past, present, and future (cf. Corbey and Roebroeks 1997: 917ff.). Noble and Davidson thus effectively argue that Upper Paleolithic tools, art, shelters, burials, and especially the colonization of islands are the first valid indicators of the kind of planning that depended on language. This view is consistent with majority views today about the late origin of the modern human adaptation (cf. Parker 1997: 579).

By now it should be clear that throughout the history of paleoanthropological research, one of the primary questions has always been when humans began to think, feel, and act like humans. Central to this question has always been the issue of cognition or awareness, and how it might be recognized in its initial stages (cf. Simek 1998: 444f.). Mithen's answer to this question was an evolutionary approach to the origins of the human mind, and the development of a three-stage typology of cognition that follows the evolution of domains of intelligence from the earliest members of the genus *Homo* through to their final integration in modern humans. Only in the final phase, in *Homo sapiens*, do we find a dramatic behavioral break, a "big bang" of cognitive, technical, and social innovation with the rise of cognitive fluidity, the final phase of mind development. Noble and Davidson, on the other hand, see one development, namely, language, as pivotal in the evolution of human cognition. Here social context is seen as a primary selective force, and language, symbol-

2. For a strong and opposing view that argues for the slow, gradualist evolution of human linguistic abilities, cf. Lieberman 1999: 549ff.

ization, and mind are integrated into an explanatory framework for the evolution of human cognition, centered on the human ability to give meaning to perceptions in a variety of ways. Ultimately Noble and Davidson see language as emerging out of socially defined contexts of communication, encouraged as a more efficient form of gesture, with the selection of language occurring precisely because of its efficiency and flexibility (cf. Simek 1998: 444f.).

My discussion in this chapter of the important work of Rick Potts, Steve Mithen, and William Noble and Iain Davidson, against the background of our earlier analyses of human origins and human uniqueness, has shown how extremely complex and interdisciplinary the field of paleoanthropology has become. For a philosophical theologian like myself, who normally lives and works outside of this field, it has at least become clear that the origin of human consciousness and cognition, like most aspects of human behavior, was part of the complex mosaic of evolution and in fact a convergence of many evolutionary trajectories. Jan F. Simek puts it persuasively: over time elements of the brain itself may have evolved in different ways, and at different rates. Various human behaviors, including the capacity for symboling and communication, also developed in distinctive ways along particular pathways. These pathways were subject to diverse selective forces over time and space, and may ultimately have converged in different areas in different forms. Thus the late Pleistocene relationship between biology and behavior in the Near East may well have differed from that in Europe, and art could "explode" in one area and not (yet) in another (cf. 444f.). What should be increasingly clear for the theologian in dialogue with these sciences is that the diverse, and sometimes conflicting, voices in paleoanthropology are all adding importantly to an emerging mosaic of what it means to be distinctively human.

Human Uniqueness and the Symbolic Mind

The important discussion in paleoanthropology and archeology on language and the symboling mind is enhanced if we transversally connect this dialogue to voices from the neurosciences and neuropsychology, where the focus has quite specifically been on the symbolic propensities of the human mind. A specific focus on the human brain may add different perspectives to this discussion and also the argument that language can be seen as the major cause, not just the consequence, of human brain evolution. Some would see this as indicating a gradual increase in language competence throughout human prehistory (at least post-*Homo*), which prepared the human brain for the cognitive leap that occurred with the appearance of behaviorally modern humans.

In *The Symbolic Species* Terrence Deacon takes up the theme of human uniqueness and quite deliberately links it to the paleoanthropological discussion on the unparalleled cognitive ability of our Cro-Magnon ancestors in the Upper Paleolithic. For Deacon it is clear that as humans we think differently than all other creatures on earth, and we can share those thoughts with one another in ways that no other species even approaches. "Hundreds of millions of years of evolution have produced hundreds of thousands of species with brains, and tens of thousands with complex behavioral, perceptual, and learning abilities. Only one of these has ever wondered about its place in the world, because only one evolved the ability to do so" (Deacon 1997: 21).

As humans we very consciously inhabit a world full of abstractions, impossibilities, and paradoxes. We alone brood about what did not happen, and we alone ponder what it will be like not to exist. We tell stories about our real experiences and invent stories about imagined ones, and we even make use of these stories to organize our lives. In a very real sense, then, we live our lives in this shared virtual world (cf. 22). For Deacon this remarkable ability has everything to do with language, and with the absence of language in other species. The doorway into this virtual world was opened to us alone by the evolution of language. The human brain is different, not just in size, but precisely in our unique and complex mode of communication, language. In a very specific sense only humans communicate with language, and this unique form of communication is special and far more precise and rapid than any other kind of communication. No other form of animal communication has the logical structure and open-ended possibilities that language has, and the underlying rules for constructing sentences are so complicated that it is hard to explain how they could ever be learned. Therefore, although other animals communicate with one another, this communication resembles language only in a very superficial way (for example, by using sounds), and there is no evidence that these modes of communication have the equivalent of anything like words, much less nouns, verbs, and sentences (cf. 12f.). Deacon also investigates how language differs from other forms of communication, and why other species encounter virtually intractable difficulties in learning even simple language. The human brain, however, has evolved to overcome these difficulties. There is an unbroken continuity between human and nonhuman brains, and yet at the same time there is a singular discontinuity between human and nonhuman minds, between brains that use this form of communication and brains that do not.

But language is not only a highly unusual form of communication, it is also the outward expression of a highly unusual mode of thought, namely, *symbolic representation* (22). We seem to be the only species that has evolved the ability to communicate symbolically. The questions about human origins that so deeply fascinate us cannot therefore be answered only in a paleontological way by inquiring about who were our ancestors, how they came to walk upright, or how they discovered the use of stone tools. For Deacon the broader question should be a neuroscientific one: *Where do human minds come from?* Thus the missing link that we hope to fill in by investigating human origins is not so much a gap in our own family tree as a gap that separates us from other species in general. Deacon rightly argues that this is a Rubicon crossed at a specific time and within a specific evolutionary context. If we could identify what was different on either side of this divide — differences in ecology, behavior, anatomy, and especially neuroanatomy — perhaps we could find the critical change that catapulted us into this unprecedented world full of abstractions that we call human (cf. 23).

It is therefore not just the origins of our biological species that we are trying to explain; rather it is especially the origin of our novel form of mind that we are trying to understand. The most critical piece of missing information regarding the origin of humans is the ancestral hominid brain, because the internal microarchitecture of these brains left no fossil trail (cf. 24). Therefore the point is not that we humans are better or smarter than other species, or that language is impossible for them. The differences are not due to incommensurate *kinds* of languages, but rather, these nonhuman forms of communication are something quite different from language. In fact, of no other natural form of communication is it legitimate to say that "language is a more complicated version" of it. This kind of analogy would ignore the sophistication and power of animals' distinctive nonlinguistic communication. At the same time, increased cognitive abilities do not necessarily represent some form of "progress" in evolution. According to Deacon, the idea of progress in evolution is an unnoticed habit left over from a misinformed sense of seeing the history of the living world in terms of *design*. Evolution certainly is an irreversible process, a process of increasing diversification — but only in this sense does evolution exhibit a consistent direction (29ff.).

The most important issue in defining the difference between language and other modes of communication is not the complexity of language as such. The most salient difference between language and nonlanguage communication is the common everyday miracle of word meaning and reference. This is why it was not grammar, syntax, or vocabulary that has kept other species from evolving languages: it is the simple problem of figuring out how combinations of words refer to things. This uniquely human form of communication/mode of reference can be called *symbolic reference.* "Somehow, despite our cognitive limitations, our ancestors found a way to create and reproduce a simple system of symbols, and once available, these symbolic tools quickly became indispensable. Because this novel form of information transmission was partially decoupled from genetic transmission, it sent our lineage of apes down a novel evolutionary path — a path that has continued to diverge from all other species ever since" (45).

Therefore, if the human predisposition for language has been honed by evolution, then our unique mentality must also be understood in these terms. The implications for brain evolution are profound: the human brain should reflect language in its architecture the way birds reflect the aerodynamics of flight in the shape and movements of their wings. Moreover, what is most unusual about language, i.e., its symbolic basis, should then correspond to that which is most unusual about human brains, i.e., a radical reengineering of the whole brain, and on a scale that is unprecedented. In the co-evolution of the symbolic brain and language, then, two of the most formidable mysteries of science converge. Basically, though, if symbol learning is the threshold that separates us from other species, then there must be something unusual about human brains that helped to surmount it. We have to ask, therefore, what other changes in brain organization correlate with this global change in brain size, and what are their functional consequences (cf. 148)?

On this point Deacon has moved close to Ian Tattersall's point of view, discussed in chapter 4, and the statement that we humans are not just more intelligent than other species but are differently intelligent (cf. Tattersall 1998: 58ff.). The difference between human and nonhuman brains may be far more complex and multifaceted than simply an increase in extra neurons over and above the average primate or mammal trend (cf. Deacon 1997: 224). Deacon also closely approaches Steven Mithen's idea of cognitive fluidity. Individual linguistic symbols are not exactly located anywhere specific in the brain, but the brain structures necessary for their analysis seem to be distributed across many areas. Deacon suggests that the first use of symbolic reference by some distant ancestors changed the way natural selection processes affected hominid brain evolution. In a very real sense this means that the physical changes that make us human are the incarnations of the process of using words. This is explained further by a subtle modification of the Darwinian theory of natural selection, as outlined more than a century ago by James Mark Baldwin, and often called "Baldwinian evolution," although there is nothing non-Darwinian about the process. Baldwin suggested that learning and behavioral flexibility can play a role in amplifying and biasing natural selection. What his theory explains is how behaviors can affect evolution, which is not the same as the Lamarckian claim that responses to environmental demands acquired during a lifetime could be passed on directly to offspring (cf. 322).

What this means is that the remarkable expansion of the brain that took place in human evolution was not the *cause* of symbolic language but in a sense rather a *consequence* of it. Each assimilated change enabled even more complex symbol systems to be acquired and used, and in turn selected for greater prefrontalization (cf. 340ff.). More than any other species, hominids' behavioral adaptations have determined the course of their physical evolution, rather than vice versa. For instance, stone and symbolic tools, which were initially acquired with the aid of flexible ape–learning abilities, ultimately turned the tables on their users and forced them to adapt to a new niche opened by these technologies. The point of origin of "humanness" can now be defined as that point in our evolution where these tools became the principal source of selection on our bodies and our brains, and in this sense is the "diagnostic trait" of what Deacon has called *Homo symbolicus* (345). On this view it is clear that the importance of toolmaking as a learned skill, not a physical trait, was passed on not genetically but behaviorally. We cannot assume that all tool users were our ancestors, of course, but the introduction of stone tools and the ecological adaptation they indicate mark the presence of a socioecological predicament that demanded a symbolic solution. For Deacon stone tools and the use of symbols must both be seen as the architects of the *Australopithecus-Homo* transition, and not just as its consequences. As a result, the large brains, stone tools, reduction in dentition, better opposability of thumb and fingers, and more complete bipedality found in post-australopithecine hominids can now be seen as the physical echoes of a threshold already crossed (cf. 348).

What is interesting to observe in this highly plausible argument is a very clear convergence between Deacon's views and the views of evolutionary epistemologist Franz Wuketits on the evolution of human cognition. For Deacon, as for Wuketits in his hypothetical realist approach to evolutionary epistemology, the evolutionary interactive dynamic between social/environmental and biological processes was the architect of modern human brains. For Deacon it was also the key to understanding the subsequent evolution of an array of unprecedented adaptations for language. Closely echoing Mithen's views in cognitive fluidity, Deacon can therefore conclude that once symbolic communication became essential for one critical social function, it became available for recruitment to support dozens of other functions as well. And as more functions came to depend on symbolic communication, it would have become an indispensable adaptation (cf. 352).

However, if the primary mystery of language is the origin of symbolic abilities, the second mystery is how most symbolic communication became dependent on one highly elaborated medium, namely, speech (cf. 352f.). For Deacon the development of skilled vocal ability was almost certainly a protracted process in hominid evolution, not a sudden shift. The incremental increases in brain sizes over the last 2 million years progressively increased cortical control over the larynx, and this was almost certainly both a cause and a consequence of the increasing use of vocal symbolization. In this sense, then, early symbolic communication would not have been just a simpler form of language; it would have been different in many respects as a result of the different state of vocal abilities. Thus it becomes highly plausible that our prehistoric ancestors used languages that we will never hear and communicated with symbols that have not survived the selective sieve of fossilization. As for prehistoric "art," Deacon seems to be in complete agreement with Iain Davidson: we can reliably expect a society that constructed complex tools and spectacular art to also have a correspondingly sophisticated symbolic infrastructure. Moreover, a society that leaves behind evidence of permanent external symbolization in the form of paintings, carvings, and sculpture, most likely also included a social function for this activity. And that is why material archeological artifacts are one of the few windows through which we can glimpse the workings of the "mental" activity of a distant prehistoric society (cf. Deacon 1997: 366). And that is why, I would add, the cave paintings of the Upper Paleolithic might be the only reliable window through which we can get a glimpse of the minds of our prehistoric, Cro-Magnon ancestors. This rather spectacular phase in modern human behavior should therefore be seen as a source of evidence for the first use of symbols, the origin of speech, and the origin of religion. And even if scientists differ, sometimes markedly, about the timing, the pace, the impact of the evolution of the human mind, about its symbolic propensities and its close ties to language, as theologians in an interdisciplinary dialogue on human origins we can move beyond the details of the controversies and glean important facts about human uniqueness and the origin of a religious capacity from these diverse sciences. The challenging task will be to identify those shared concerns, and those transversal moments, that will enable us to translate from theology to science, and back to theology.

For a neuroscientist like Deacon, it is clear that as far as Paleolithic art goes, the first cave paintings and carvings that emerged from the Upper

Paleolithic period do give us the very first direct expression of the symbolizing human mind. "They are the first irrefutable expressions of a symbolic process that is capable of conveying a rich cultural heritage of images and probably stories from generation to generation. And they are the first concrete evidence of the storage of such symbolic information outside of a human brain" (cf. 372).

What has now become clear in our discussion of the work of Mithen, Tattersall, Potts, Noble and Davidson, and Deacon is that human mental life includes biologically unprecedented ways of experiencing and understanding the world, from aesthetic experiences to spiritual contemplation. The origins of many of these most distinctive human traits are deeply intertwined with the origins of language. Language is without doubt the most distinctive human adaptation. In fact, both the special adaptations for language and language it-self have played important roles in the origins of human moral and spiritual capacities (cf. Deacon 2003: 504ff.). Assessing the origins of these abilities, however, is complicated by the fact that no direct consequences of language use are preserved in the fossil record. In a recent article Deacon makes the im-portant point that the spectacular Paleolithic art and the burial of the dead, though not final guarantees of shamanistic or religious-like activities, do sug-gest strongly the existence of sophisticated, symbolic reasoning. And, impor-tant for the gradual, piecemeal evolution of human symbolic capacities in Af-rica that scholars like Potts and David Lewis-Williams have argued for, these earliest examples of expressive symbolism in southwestern Europe can be un-derstood as evidence not so much for the initial evolution of symbolic abili-ties, but rather for their first expression in durable media (cf. Deacon 2003).

Like most of the voices from evolutionary epistemology and paleo-anthropology I discussed earlier, it is significant that a neuroscientist such as Terrence Deacon can also conclude that the symbolic nature of *Homo sapiens* explains why mystical or religious inclinations can be regarded as an essen-tially universal attribute of human culture (cf. Deacon 1997: 436). As we saw earlier, there is no culture that lacks a rich mythical, mystical, and religious tra-dition. The co-evolution of language and brain not only implies that human brains have been reorganized in response to language, it tells us that the conse-quences of this unprecedented evolutionary transition for human religious and spiritual development must be understood on many levels as well. Deacon argued recently that there are reasons to believe that the way language can symbolically refer to things provides the crucial catalyst that initiated the tran-sition from species with no inkling of the meaning of life into a species where questions of ultimate meaning have become core organizers of culture and consciousness. These symbolic capacities are ubiquitous for humans, and largely taken for granted when it comes to spiritual and ethical realms. For Deacon this is precisely where crucial differences in ability mark the boundary that distinguishes humans from other species. In this sense one could say that the capacity for spiritual experience itself can be understood as an emergent consequence of the symbolic transfiguration of cognition and emotions (cf. Deacon 2003).

Against this background it again becomes clear why one can argue that no culture lacks a rich mythical, mystical, and religious tradition, and that mythology and imagination are the mark of the modern human mind, the creation of worlds shared in the medium of language (Lewin 1993: 177). The predisposition to religious belief is one of the most complex and powerful forces in the human mind, one of the universals of human behavior. The question, of course, is how this kind of force might spring from the font of consciousness. When humans became aware of themselves as individuals with feelings and motivations, they imaginatively attributed similar feelings not only to other humans, but also to other animals and to inanimate objects of the world. From the moment of consciousness there has been a universal urge to account for the rest of the world, to tell stories of how things came to be, which forces were good, which evil, and how they might be influenced. And with awareness of self comes awareness of death. Therefore, as had the cave paintings with their symbolic and enigmatic nature, so also the practice of burial and the death awareness that must have gone along with it offer the paleoanthropologist and archeologist the possibility of gleaning from the past something of the level of conscious imagination in our distant ancestors' minds (cf. 177). And it is this conscious imagination that seems to have naturally, and unambiguously, included symbolic, religious imagination.

*   *   *

Deacon's argument that the spectacular cave "art," as well as the burial of the dead that accompanied it, strongly suggests shamanistic or religious-like activities (cf. Deacon 2003) resonates remarkably well with Jean Clottes and David Lewis-Williams's intriguing proposal for a shamanistic interpretation (cf. chap. 4) of at least some of the imagery from this important prehistoric period. In his most recent work, *The Mind in the Cave* (2002), Lewis-Williams has returned to this theme and developed a much stronger argument for seeing neuroscience, as well as neuropsychological research on altered states of consciousness, as providing the principal access to what we might know today about the mental and religious life of the humans who lived and painted in western Europe during the Upper Paleolithic. I now will not only argue for the plausibility of this interpretation, but will also illustrate how it enhances the interpretation of a select number of the most famous cave paintings from the Upper Paleolithic in Europe. In the process, a remarkable consonance with the postfoundationalist methodology I have proposed for interdisciplinary dialogue in chapters 1 and 4 will emerge and further solidify my attempt to find transversal connections between paleoanthropology and theology.

As has become abundantly clear, in spite of the remarkable progress in paleoanthropology and archeology, it often seems that we are still very far from knowing why the people of the Upper Paleolithic penetrated the deep limestone caves of France and Spain to make spectacular images in total darkness. We still do not really know what the images meant to those who made them and those who viewed them, and the great mystery of how we became human, and in the process began to make art, continues to tantalize us. In spite of this, Lewis-Williams believes that a century of research has given us sufficient data, the "material conditions," to attempt a persuasive, general explanation for a large amount of Upper Paleolithic art. Moreover, we are now in a position to explain some hitherto inexplicable features of the imagery and its often bizarre contents. It is in this sense that Lewis-Williams has argued that what is needed is not more data, but rather a radical rethinking of what we already know (cf. Lewis-Williams 2002: 7f.).

In developing his methodology for approaching this interdisciplinary problem, Lewis-Williams, echoing Margaret Conkey's rejection of meta-theories for the interpretation of prehistoric imagery (cf. chap. 4), shies away from overly generic explanations, while at the same time avoiding the overcontextualization of some relativist forms of interpretation. His sensitivity for contextuality will emerge as a focus on the social and historical context of our ancestors from the Upper Paleolithic. A keen sense for embodied materiality also drives him to seriously consider the role of intelligence and consciousness in prehistory. He argues that most researchers have consistently ignored the full complexity of human consciousness and have then presented us with a one-sided view of what it is to be an anatomically and cognitively fluid modern human being (cf. 9). It is against this rich background that he examines the interaction of mental activity and social context.

Lewis-Williams has argued that for scientific work to present us with "better" explanations, it has to be focused on verifiable, empirical facts, and any hypothesis must relate explicitly to the observable features of specific data. A hypothesis also has to be internally consistent, with no part of it contradicting another. Most importantly, though, any hypothesis that *covers diverse fields of evidence* is always more persuasive than one that pertains to only one narrow type of evidence. In this sense complementary types of evidences that converge to address the complex problems posed by Upper Paleolithic "art" can in fact produce persuasive hypotheses. This points directly, I believe, to the superiority of an interdisciplinary approach to issues in paleoanthropology and, by implication, in theology. It is in this sense too that useful hypotheses have strong heuristic potential, and as such lead to further creative questions and research. Lewis-Williams also argues that for us to understand the historical trajectory of Upper Paleolithic research, we have to be especially alert to the social embeddedness of scientific work and research (cf. 49). I believe this lends strong support to the fact that in our interactive relationship with Paleolithic imagery, even if the "original meaning" of these images is lost forever, a sense of patternedness reveals enigmatic narrative structures, even if the original narratives are lost forever.

A key epistemological principle emerges for Lewis-Williams: to allow for the effects of social contexts while emphasizing a real historical past and the possibility of constructing hypotheses that may approximate this past. With this in mind, we can now address the enigma of what happened to the human mind in the caves of Upper Paleolithic western Europe. To try to unlock the enigma of these images, we must look more closely at the human brain, the mind, intelligence, and what Lewis-Williams has called the shifting, mercurial consciousness of human beings (cf. 68). As a first step he wants to distinguish between human intelligence and consciousness and examine how this distinction may help to clarify what was happening to the Upper Paleolithic mind at this time. We saw earlier that the amazing behavioral changes that culminated in the Upper Paleolithic were slowly and sporadically assembled in Africa. This history clearly points to the presupposition of a kind of human consciousness that was alien to Neanderthals and that quite specifically allowed for symbolic conceptions of an "alternate reality" (cf. 101). This leads directly to questions as to the evolution of intelligence and the very specific role of human consciousness in this process. For Lewis-Williams this directly implies what I have called a transversal approach to interdisciplinary research, precisely by incorporating "strands of evidence" from neuroscience and neuropsychology into paleoanthropology. This kind of transversality is exemplified by his "cabling" method of weaving together perspectives and arguments from different disciplines so as to sustain a specific hypothesis about the relationship between brain, mind, and the earliest forms of art (cf. 103).

Lewis-Williams is rightly critical of any overemphasis on intelligence, and the evolution of intelligence, that has marginalized the importance of the full range of human consciousness in human behavior. This reveals a one-sided focus on a "consciousness of rationality and intelligence," and has marginalized the fuller spectrum of human consciousness by suppressing certain altered states of consciousness as irrational, marginal, aberrant, or even pathological. This is especially true of altered states of consciousness, which in science and even within mainstream religion normally have been eliminated from investigations of the deep past. In a move closely reminiscent of Antonio Damasio's work, Lewis-Williams now refines his earlier discussion of altered states of consciousness (cf. chap. 4) and suggests that we think of consciousness not as a state but as a continuum, or *spectrum,* of mental states (cf. 121ff.). Following the work of Colin Martindale (1981), he describes the spectrum of states of consciousness that encompasses a trajectory from being fully awake to a state of sleeping. On this trajectory, as we drift into sleep we pass through the following six phases:

- waking, problem-oriented thought
- realistic fantasy
- autistic fantasy
- reverie
- hypnagogic (falling asleep) states
- dreaming

In waking consciousness we are concerned with problem solving, usually in response to environmental stimuli. We then become disengaged from those stimuli, and different states of consciousness begin to take over. First, in realistic fantasy we are oriented to problem solving. These realistic fantasies grade into more autistic ones — ones less connected to external reality. In this state our thoughts are far less directed, and image follows image in no narrative sequence. These then shade over into hypnagogic states that occur as we fall asleep. Sometimes the hypnagogic imagery is startlingly vivid and leads to what is called hypnagogic hallucinations, where someone would start awake and believe the imagery is real. These hypnagogic images may be both visual and aural. And finally, in dreaming, a succession of images appears, at least in recall, as a narrative. Focusing on the first part of this sequence, Lewis-Williams also speaks of *fragmented consciousness:* during the course of any day we are repeatedly shifting from outward-directed to inward-directed states (cf. 123). What this means is that sometimes we are fully attentive to our environment, and at other times we withdraw into contemplation and are less alert to our surroundings.

In addition to this spectrum of consciousness from shifting wakefulness to sleep, Lewis-Williams also suggests another trajectory that passes through the same spectrum but with different effects. He calls this an *intensified trajectory* of consciousness, and it is more profoundly concerned with inward-direction and fantasy. He argues that dreamlike autistic states may be induced by a wide variety of means other than normal drifting into sleep — for instance, fatigue, pain, fasting, and the ingestion of psychotropic substances are all means of shifting consciousness along the intensified trajectory toward the release of inwardly generated imagery. At the end of this trajectory emerge pathological states, such as schizophrenia and temporal lobe epilepsy, that take consciousness to the far end of the intensified trajectory. Hallucinations may thus be deliberately sought, or may emerge unsought (cf. 124). For Lewis-Williams this second trajectory has much in common with the one that takes us into sleep and dreaming, but there are also important differences. Dreaming gives us an idea of what hallucinations are like, but the states toward the far end of the intensified trajectory — visions and hallucinations that may occur in any of the five senses — are generally called "altered states of consciousness" (cf. 125). Lewis-Williams argues that this phrase can equally be applied to dreaming and to "inward" states on the normal trajectory, even if some prefer to restrict its use to extreme hallucinations and trance states. More importantly, however, this kind of description reveals an essentially Western concept of the "consciousness of rationality," and thus implies that there is an "ordinary consciousness" that is considered genuine and good, and then perverted, or "altered," states. For Lewis-Williams, less focus on rationality should reveal that all parts of the spectrum of consciousness are equally important, and equally genuine (cf. 125).

Importantly, all the mental states described here are generated by the neurology of the human nervous system, and are thus part and parcel of what it is to be fully human. In this sense they are literally "wired into the brain," although we have to remember that the mental imagery humans experience in altered states is overwhelmingly, although not entirely, derived from memory and thus culture-specific. This is why Inuits will see polar bears in their visions, the San see eland, and Hildegard from Bingen experienced the Christian God (cf. 126). The spectrum of consciousness, therefore, is indeed wired, but its content is mostly cultural.

For Lewis-Williams the concept of a spectrum of consciousness will ultimately help us explain many specific features of Upper Paleolithic imagery by linking it directly to shamanistic experiences that are remarkably consonant with experiences along the intensified spectrum of consciousness. In fact, it provides us with a neurological bridge that leads back directly to the Upper Paleolithic, especially if we look carefully at the visual imagery of the intensified spectrum and see what kinds of percepts (the representation of what is perceived) are experienced as one passes along it. In chapter 4 we saw that Lewis-Williams identified three stages, each characterized by particular kinds of imagery and experiences (cf. 126).

- In the first, or "lightest," stage people may experience geometric visual percepts that include dots, grids, zigzags, and meandering lines. Moreover, because these percepts are wired into the human nervous system, all humans, no matter what their cultural background, have the potential to experience them. They flicker, scintillate, expand, contract, and combine with one another, and importantly, they are independent of an exterior light source. Lewis-Williams also argues that such percepts cannot be consciously controlled; they seem to have a life of their own. These entopic phenomena (from the Greek, meaning "within vision") may originate anywhere between the eye itself and the cortex of the brain. Entopic phenomena should be distinguished from hallucinations, the forms of which have no foundation in the actual structure of the optic system. Unlike neurologically "wired" entopic phenomena, hallucinations include iconic imagery of culturally controlled items such as animals, as well as somatic (bodily), aural (hearing), gustatory (taste), and olfactory (smell) experiences (cf. 126f.).

- In stage two of the intensified trajectory, subjects try to make sense of entopic phenomena by elaborating them into iconic forms, i.e., into objects that are familiar to them from their daily life. In addition, in altered states of consciousness the nervous system itself becomes a "sixth sense" that produces a variety of images, including entopic phenomena (cf. 128).

- As subjects move into stage three, marked changes in imagery may occur. At this point many people experience a swirling vortex or rotating tunnel that seems to surround them and draw them into its depths. There is a progressive exclusion of information from the outside as the subject becomes more and more autistic. This tunnel hallucination is often associated with near-death experiences, and sometimes a bright light in the center of the field of vision creates this tunnel-like perspective (cf. 129). In non-Western cultures shamans typically speak of reaching the spirit world via this kind of vortex or hole in the ground. From this Lewis-Williams can conclude that the vortex and the ways in which its imagery is perceived are clearly universal human experiences (cf. 129). Furthermore, in this stage iconic images derive from memory and are often associated with powerful emotional experiences. Subjects may also enter and participate in their own imagery during stage three, and it is in this sense that people sometimes feel themselves turning into animals and undergoing frightening or exalting transformations.

All anatomically modern people, not only from the Upper Paleolithic but also from our own time, had, or still have, the same nervous system and therefore cannot avoid experiencing the full spectrum of human consciousness, refrain from dreaming, or escape the potential to hallucinate (cf. 130). And exactly because our Paleolithic ancestors were fully human, we can confidently expect that their consciousness was as shifting and fragmented as ours, though the ways in which they regarded and valued various states would have been largely culturally determined, which Lewis-Williams strikingly refers to as the "domestication of trance" (cf. 131). These people were as capable as we are of moving along both trajectories of consciousness as described by Lewis-Williams, although the content of their dream and autistic imagery would have been different. And it is in exactly this sense that Upper Paleolithic, prehistoric imagery becomes accessible to us through this neurological bridge to the Upper Paleolithic.

Various scholars have concluded that the capacity to experience altered states of consciousness is a universal psychobiological capacity of our species. The patterning of these altered states, however, is always culturally determined, but ecstatic experience is certainly a part of all religions (cf. 130ff.). Among hunter-gatherer communities, this sort of experience is called *shamanism*. Lewis-Williams uses this controversial term carefully, and argues that shamanism usefully points to a universal in the makeup of the human mind — the need to make sense of shifting consciousness. The term "shamanism" need not be a generic label, however, and certainly need not obscure the diversity of worldwide shamanism any more than "Christianity" obscures theological, ritual, and social differences between the Russian Orthodox, the Greek Orthodox, the Roman Catholic, and the many Protestant churches (cf. 133).

Since the people of the Upper Paleolithic were all hunter-gatherers, Lewis-Williams is very specific by what he means by "shamanism," and identifies some of its most important characteristics. In all states of "deep trance," shamans are believed to have direct contact with the spiritual realm. But we must beware stipulating some naively-simple altered state of consciousness as *the* shamanistic state of mind. Lewis-Williams puts it well: the shamanistic mind is a complex interweaving of mental states, visions, and emotions (cf. 135). At the heart of this argument lies the deeper conviction that altered states of consciousness are directly related to the genesis of religion. The practice of shamanism, although we could never prove it today, seems to be related to the very origins of human religious practices and beliefs. James McClenon has also persuasively argued that shamanism, the result of cultural adaptations to a biologically based capacity for altered states of consciousness, is the origin of all later religious forms (McClenon 1997: 349; 2002). In this specific sense some have even called it the de facto source of all forms of religious revelation, and thus of all religions (cf. Lewis-Williams 2002: 135).

What has become clear from this discussion is that however important human intelligence is, it is in the way people understand the rich dimensions of their own forms of shifting consciousness that religious experience, experiences of cosmology, concepts of supernatural realms, and the aesthetic dimensions of art/image-making all come together. This consciousness, however, is always embedded in specific social and historical contexts. As far as the Upper Paleolithic goes, it is clear that the driving mechanism for the so-called "creative cultural explosion" can be found in social diversity and historical change. Against this background Lewis-Williams can plausibly argue that even if we know almost nothing about the vanished culture of these distant ancestors of ours, Upper Paleolithic communities were clearly history-making people par excellence (cf. 188). It seems clear to me, therefore, that their "art" in southwestern France and the Basque Country should never be seen as simply an idyllic expression of contentment, or as only the efflorescence of some higher aesthetic sense, but in a much more comprehensive, holistic sense the spectacular prehistoric cave paintings were the material results of a struggle to find a dimension of meaning in the struggle to survive the challenges of everyday prehistoric life.

To understand how image making could be born in this historical contextuality of everyday social life, Lewis-Williams develops further his rich notion of human consciousness. This is going to be important as we try to understand why the Cro-Magnon peoples selectively decided to paint certain images only; there must have been some distinct presuppositions in the minds of the people of the Upper Paleolithic, and they were most probably "looking for" certain things and not for others. Lewis-Williams takes this to mean that a vocabulary of motifs must have existed in people's minds *before* they made images (cf. 185). Moreover, Upper Paleolithic society at large would have needed good reasons for wanting to make more images in the various caves, and, closely resembling Iain Davidson's position on prehistoric art presupposing linguistic capacities as discussed earlier in this chapter, Lewis-Williams now argues that these images would directly flow from a predetermined vocabulary. It follows, then, that the images as we see them today must have had some preexisting, shared meaning and value for groups of people for them, first, to notice them at all, and secondly, to want to go on making them. In this sense, images of specific sets of animals must have had some a priori value for people to take such an intense interest in them (cf. 185). This is also Lewis-Williams's answer to the question, how did these prehistoric people invent two-dimensional images? The people from the Upper Paleolithic did *not* invent two-dimensional images of things in their material environment; on the contrary, a notion of these images *and* the vocabulary of specific motifs *were part of their experience* before they made parietal or portable images (cf. 185).

This crucial point is explained by the spectrum of human consciousness we discussed before. To deepen his understanding of human consciousness Lewis-Williams follows Gerald Edelman (1992) and moves away sharply from any Cartesian dualism in the understanding of body and consciousness: mind and consciousness are the products of matter, the matter we call the brain. Consciousness has evolved biologically, but to try to understand human consciousness we have to move beyond Edelman's focus on only the "alert" end of the spectrum of consciousness and focus also on the more autistic end. Edelman's methodology enables us to do this when he identifies two kinds of consciousnesses, namely, *primary consciousness* and *higher-order consciousness* (cf. Lewis-Williams 2002: 186). Primary consciousness is experienced to some degree by some animals, such as (almost certainly) chimpanzees, (probably) most mammals, and some birds, but (probably) not reptiles. For Edelman primary consciousness is a state of being aware of things in the world, of having mental images in the present, but it is unaccompanied by any sense of being a person with a past and future. Primary consciousness is a kind of "remembered present," a mental picture of ongoing events. Creatures with primary consciousness, while possessing mental images, have no capacity to view those images from the vantage point of a socially constructed self (cf. Edelman 1992: 117-23).

Humans, however, have higher consciousness; this involves the recognition by a thinking subject of his or her acts or affections. It embodies a model of the personal, of the past and future, and means that we humans are actually conscious of being conscious. We also have developed symbolic memory, and the long-term storage of symbolic relations is critical to our self-concepts (cf. 124ff.). Moving close to the views of Damasio, Lewis-Williams argues that this higher-order consciousness sits, as it were, on the shoulders of primary consciousness. This means we are the only species that can remember better and use that memory to fashion our individual identities in mental "scenes" of past, present, and future events. This is a crucial point for human consciousness. It also goes without saying that a fully modern language is a sine qua non for higher-order consciousness. And language, of course, makes possible auditory hallucinations: it is only when they have language that "inner voices" can tell people what to do, which gives a deeper dimension to visual dimensions, so that not only do shamans "see" their animal spirits, the spirits also "talk" to them (cf. Lewis-Williams 2002: 188f.).

Lewis-Williams believes it would be reasonable to assume that higher-order consciousness developed neurologically in Africa before the second wave of emigration to the Middle East and Europe. This is the reason the pattern of modern human behavior, made possible by higher-order consciousness, was put together piecemeal and intermittently in Africa. It certainly was impossible to have higher-order consciousness without language (cf. 189). What this means for the transition from Middle Paleolithic to Upper Paleolithic in western Europe, is that the Neanderthals, descendants of the first Out of Africa emigration, must have had a form of primary consciousness, while the *Homo sapiens* communities had higher-order consciousness. Precisely the shift from primary to higher-order consciousness facilitated a different kind of experience and a socially agreed-upon apprehension of the spectrum of human consciousness. Improved memory made possible the long-term recollection of dreams and visions, and the reconstruction of those recollections into a spirit world.

Importantly, for Lewis-Williams the wider range of consciousness also afforded a new instrument for social discrimination that was not tied to either strength or gender, namely, shamans, or mystics, that could now explore the autistic end of the spectrum of consciousness and thereby set themselves apart from others (cf. 189). Thus, not only do we humans socialize our dreaming, and talk about what it might mean, but we also have no option but to socialize the autistic end of the spectrum. Humans place value on some of these experiences in accordance with socially constructed notions of dreaming, and of the intensified, induced trajectory, namely, visions and hallucinations. Dreams and visions are thus inevitably drawn into the socializing of the self and into concepts of what it is to be human, concepts that change through time. It is in this sense that the worlds of *Homo sapiens* were already invested with two-dimensional images, images that were the product of the functioning of the human nervous system in altered states of consciousness and within the context of higher-order consciousness. Lewis-Williams proceeds to present an intriguing argument: at a given time, and for unknown social reasons, the mentally projected images of altered states were insufficient, and prehistoric humans developed the need to "fix" their visions on cave walls. They reached out to their emotionally charged visions and tried to touch them, to hold them in place. In this sense they were not inventing images on cave walls, but were painting what was already present in their minds (cf. 193). Of course, this does not mean that all Upper Paleolithic paintings and engravings are images fixed in altered states of consciousness.

Higher-order consciousness allowed a group of people within a larger community to commandeer the experience of altered consciousness and set themselves apart from those who, for whatever reasons, did not have those experiences. The far end of the intensified spectrum of consciousness in this way became the preserve of those who mastered the techniques necessary to access visions. This is how the spectrum of human consciousness became an instrument of social discrimination, and its specific importance lay in the way the socializing of the spectrum gave rise to image making. More important for my argument, however, is that because image making was related, at least initially, to the fixing of shamanistic visions, "art" and religion were simultaneously born in this creative process (cf. 196).

It is important to keep in mind that image making did not originate in only one specific place and then spread throughout the world. On the contrary, once higher-order consciousness evolved, it emerged differently in different places. Lewis-Williams does not present this shamanistic view of the origins of image making and religion as a universal explanation for the origins of all human image making. This explanation nevertheless highlights certain universals in human neural morphology, in shifting consciousness, and in the fact that people have no option but to rationalize and socialize the full spectrum of human consciousness (cf. 203). We should be aware of the ancient, universal, human neurological inheritance that includes the capacity of the nervous system to enter into altered states and the need to make sense of the resultant dreams and hallucinations within a foraging way of life. There seems to be no other explanation for the remarkable similarities among shamanistic traditions worldwide (cf. 206). In the Upper Paleolithic, the socializing of the autistic end of the spectrum of higher-order consciousness certainly seems to have resulted in spectacular image making.

Within a shamanistic context the Upper Paleolithic subterranean passages and chambers were therefore places that uniquely provided the opportunity for close contact with, and even penetration of, a very specific spiritual tier of the cosmos. And this hallucinatory, spiritual world, exemplified by its painted and engraved imagery, was thus invested with materiality and was precisely situated cosmologically. It certainly did not exist merely in human minds; the spiritual world was there, tangible and material, and some could empirically verify it by entering the caves and seeing for themselves the "fixed" visions of the spirit animals that empowered the shamans of the community (cf. 210). But entering the caves, and the sensory deprivation generated by remote, silent, and totally dark chambers (like deep and remote parts in the caves of Lascaux, Altamira, and the *salon noir* in Niaux), and experiencing the enigmatic painted images on the walls could certainly also induce visions and altered states of consciousness. In Lewis-Williams's striking words: it is as if the rock surface were a living membrane or veil, and behind the veil lay a realm inhabited by spirit animals and spirits themselves, and the passages and chambers of the caves penetrated deep into that realm (cf. 214).

Finally, I want to turn to three outstanding examples of prehistoric imagery that on my view best exemplify the profound role of shamanism and altered states of consciousness in the Upper Paleolithic. These are (1) the positive and negative handprints in the deep caves, (2) the ithyphallic "Bird Man" from the Shaft in Lascaux, and (3) the "Wounded Men" from Cougnac and Pech-Merle.

A. Handprints in the Deep Caves
(Plates 1 and 2)

There are two distinct kinds of handprints: *positive prints* made by placing paint on the palm and fingers and then pressing the hand against the rock wall, and *negative prints* made by placing the hand against the rock and then blowing paint over the hand and the surrounding rock, leaving an image of the hand after it was removed. These amazing and ubiquitous handprints are found in many Upper Paleolithic caves, but some of the most famous prints, and in my experience the most striking, are found in the caves of Gargas and Pech-Merle. While Gargas presents us with some of the oldest prints known today, the six handprints in Pech-Merle are remarkable for being part of the magnificent and mysterious composition of the famous "Dotted Horses" tableau (pl. 7). The challenging question, of course, is why people would have wanted to leave their handprints in the deep caves. If we take seriously Lewis-Williams's proposal that some of the cave imagery was shamanistic, and the resulting tiered cosmos of this prehistoric world revealing an interpretation of the rock wall as a membrane or veil between people and the spirit world, then the answer might have more to do with touching the rock surface than with actual image making (cf. 217). Touching the rock wall would then literally imply a touching of the veil that separated humans from the spiritual world, and I find it tempting, at least from a contemporary point of view, to see this ritual as a deeply sacramental moment.

Scholars consider the negative handprints in the "Dotted Horses" tableau to be integrally related to the representational horse images, and as such they constitute one of the most stunning and meaningful compositions from the Upper Paleolithic (cf. 219). What is fascinating about this composition is that not only are the handprints negative, i.e., created by blowing paint onto a hand pressed against the rock surface, but even parts of the horses were made by blowing paint onto the rock. It is clear, then, that in a variety of ways people touched, respected, painted, and ritually treated the walls of caves because of what they were and what they believed existed behind their surfaces. The cave walls were never just meaningless background: they were part of a highly charged metaphysical context, a context that provides for us today some of the earliest material evidence available for the origin of the first religion(s) (cf. 220).

We can never reconstruct the rituals that surely must have been performed in the cold, silent, and dimly lit passages and chambers, nor can we reconstruct the narratives and even tentatively guess at what each image and geometric sign might have meant to the people who saw them. But we can know that the minds of the people who entered these caves were working with faith and illusion (cf. 227). Most importantly, especially in trying to understand parietal art, we have to go beyond generalities to the very empirical specifics of images and caves, as Margaret Conkey has also argued (cf. Conkey 1997: 343ff.). Lewis-Williams discusses in detail how to approach these differences between individual images in individual caves, particularly the caves of Gabillou and Lascaux, which powerfully suggest a shamanistic world. This is especially true of the spectacular Axial Gallery in Lascaux, which was clearly carefully planned and communally executed as a remarkable evocation of the neurological vortex. In fact, for Lewis-Williams the parallelism between the physical entry into the subterranean passages and the psychic entry into deeply altered states of consciousness is nowhere better seen than in the Axial Gallery (cf. Lewis-Williams 2002: 236-52).

B. The Ithyphallic "Bird Man" from the Shaft in Lascaux
  (Plate 11)

The Shaft is the most enigmatic section of Lascaux, and although the human figure there was painted in a "stick" style not found elsewhere in the cave, and although the Shaft may originally have been part of another cave that was related to Lascaux, most researchers believe the Shaft itself, as well as the famous human and "wounded bison" figures, is part of Upper Paleolithic Lascaux. The Shaft is on a markedly lower level than the rest of the cave, and Lewis-Williams finds it hard not to conclude that it was a special "end" area, a narrow cleft to which people went and possibly conducted rituals (cf. 262).

But it is the images in the Shaft that have been most discussed. On one wall is the image of a black horse, but opposite this image we find probably the most discussed group of all Upper Paleolithic images. On the left is a rhinoceros with a raised tail, and beneath the tail are two rows of three black dots each. Beyond a slight curve in the rock wall is the famous man and wounded bison. Lewis-Williams describes the image as follows: the bison was drawn around a darker, ocher patch of rock that extends in some places beyond the image. Here, as in so many of the caves, an Upper Paleolithic artist used a natural rock formation and created an image around it. The bison's head is markedly lowered and it seems to be charging, while its tail is raised and bent back over its rump in anger. Furthermore, its entrails seem to be hanging from its belly, and there is what appears to be a spear across its body (cf. 264).

In front of the bison, drawn in black, is a comparatively crudely drawn ithyphallic man who appears to be lying on the ground but may be falling backward.[3] What is truly remarkable about this figure is that it has a bird's head and also four-fingered birdlike hands. Some scholars see the replacement of each human hand with a four-fingered bird's foot as a deliberate and sophisticated ploy of the artist to make the image more birdlike (cf. Davenport and Jochim 1988: 560). What is very clear is that the artist has portrayed this humanoid figure as half-bird and half-man, bird from the waist up and man from the waist down. The avian theme is expanded further by what seems to be a staff with an effigy of a bird on its top, which makes it impossible to see these images as only a historical, tragic hunting incident. Moreover, the bird on the staff is virtually identical to the man's head. Against this background Davenport and Jochim, following various other scholars including Mircea Eliade, unequivocally see the Lascaux humanoid/bird-man as a shaman. They also suggest that it could be a shaman being transformed into the bird-spirit at the moment of death, and that his erect phallus suggests the role some shamans play in the fertility of their communities (cf. 561). In fact, sexual arousal

3. According to French paleoanthropologist Jean Clottes, the bird-man is clearly falling backward in a state of hallucinatory ecstasy. Clottes, oral communication, Les Eyzies, France, May 2004.

and penile erections are directly associated with both altered states of consciousness and sleep, while sexual arousal certainly was a metaphor for altered states of consciousness (cf. Lewis-Williams 2002: 176, 264).

All of this leads Lewis-Williams to put forth an even stronger interpretation based on specific aspects of Upper Paleolithic art. First, the images do not suggest a real-life tragedy, but that the image maker fashioned a spirit bison out of the stain on the rock, thus "fixing" the *spirit* animal. Secondly, its hooves are shown to be cloven, and its position suggests that it is not standing on the ground in any realistic sense but is rather "floating" in a spiritual space. Thirdly, the man's erection suggests death in a very specific sense; "death" in shamanistic thought implies traveling to the spirit world in an altered state of consciousness. Fourthly, then, "death" in this sense is seen as a portal to shamanistic status. Shamans are said to die, and to be resurrected with a new persona and a new social role (cf. 265).

What we have in the Shaft in Lascaux, then, is not a hunting disaster as it was commonly interpreted. Instead this remarkable image expressed a transformation by death: the "death" of the man paralleling the "death" of the eviscerated bison. As both "die," the man fuses with one of his spirit helpers, a bird. Lewis-Williams also argues that, as in many shamanistic societies, this kind of symbolic transformation into a shamanistic world would almost certainly have been woven into some mythical narrative or series of myths. And those who descended into the Shaft certainly did not simply view pictures, but they saw real things, real spirit animals and beings, real transformations. Lewis-Williams puts it succinctly: they saw through the membrane and participated in the events of the spirit realm (cf. 266). In this sense these paintings in the Shaft capture the essence of Lascaux shamanism, and support arguments that the roots of Upper Paleolithic cave art in general lie deep in the shamanic tradition (cf. Davenport and Jochim 1988: 561).

C. The "Wounded Men" from Cougnac and Pech-Merle (Plates 3 and 4)

Although the images in Lascaux that are arguably linked to shamanism are chiefly concerned with visual hallucinations, Lewis-Williams suggests some fascinating examples of parietal art that may clearly indicate that when human consciousness moves to the autistic end of the intensified spectrum, all the senses can hallucinate, not just vision. This is a key element in trying to understand the so-called wounded men in Upper Paleolithic imagery, and is most notably in the images found in the caves of Cougnac and Pech-Merle. To further this argument, he focuses on somatic hallucinations, especially sensations of pricking and stabbing (cf. Lewis-Williams 2002: 270ff.). Somatic hallucinations can occur in various ways and to different degrees, and may be induced by the ingestion of psychotropic drugs, sensory deprivation, or pathological conditions like temporal lobe epilepsy or schizophrenia. Less painful somatic hallucinations are more common and occur in various in-duced altered states, and may include tingling, pricking, and burning sensa-tions. In a fascinating and provocative argument, Lewis-Williams points to remarkable examples of intense, heightened religious experiences in contem-porary charismatic Christianity and its experience of "showers of blessing" and other somatic hallucinations, especially including the phenomenon known as glossolalia, or "speaking in tongues," which is also known among Native American shamans (cf. 273).

As far as the enigmatic wounded men in Upper Paleolithic cave paintings are concerned, it is important to know that Leroi-Gourhan had estimated that there are only seventy-five anthropomorphic figures in Upper Paleolithic pari-etal art, a number that certainly constitutes a very small percentage of the (un-known) total number of images (cf. Lewis-Williams 2002: 277). Some of the most enigmatic, mysterious images come from the caves of Cougnac and Pech-Merle in France, and are known as the "wounded men," although the sex of the figures is fairly undecided. These images are of human figures with three or more lines radiating from their bodies. The Cougnac figure is painted in black and appears to be running toward the right while three lines emanate from its lower back and buttocks. Its forward-leaning posture also gives it a sense of movement, perhaps of fleeing. The second Cougnac figure has seven or eight lines emerging from various parts of its body and has short arms with no hands, and a birdlike head. A third example is from Pech-Merle. This "wounded man" is more erect than the others and has nine lines protruding from it, one of which may be a penis. Lewis-Williams suggests that the posture of these figures may represent a physical response to the prickings and con-tractions induced by some altered states of consciousness (cf. 279). As in the case of the bird-man in the Shaft of Lascaux, Lewis-Williams argues against interpreting these figures in any realistic sense. Although most writers accept that the emanating lines of the wounded men probably depict spears of some kind, they are most probably not meant realistically. In fact, two key factors — the universality of the human nervous system and the shamanistic hunter-gatherer setting — suggest that the artists who painted the Cougnac and Pech-Merle figures probably experienced the pricking sensations of trance and hallucinated them as multiple stabbings with sharp spears. Therefore, although the radiating lines may represent spears, they are not literal spears; the images do not record violent incidents from daily life but should rather be seen as representing spiritual experiences (cf. 281).

Moreover, a specific context in which piercing is commonly reported is that of shamanistic initiation. As Lewis-Williams puts it, shamans must suffer before they can heal, "die" before they can bring life to their people (cf. 281). For this reason it seems highly plausible that the wounded men represent a form of shamanistic suffering, "death," and initiation that was closely associated with somatic hallucinations. For Lewis-Williams the neurological and ethnographic evidence suggests that, in these subterranean images, we have an ancient and unusually explicit expression of complex shamanistic experience that was given its primary form by altered states of consciousness. He even suggests that the distinctive wounded men images were probably also an answer, even a challenge, to the general scarcity of anthropomorphic images in the Upper Paleolithic parietal art (cf. 282f.).

*　　　*　　　*

There obviously are a number of remarkable images from prehistoric painted caves in southwestern Europe that strongly suggest shamanistic practices, but these three examples, on my own view, best exemplify the possible role of shamanism and altered states of consciousness in some of the caves from the Upper Paleolithic era. They also confirm that Lewis-Williams has successfully and plausibly argued for linking shamanism directly to some of the most well-known Upper Paleolithic cave paintings. In doing so he has not only risen to the methodological challenge that Margaret Conkey has posed for nongeneric, highly contextual interpretations of prehistoric imagery, but he has also made an important contribution to the kind of naturalness of religious imagination that emerged in my dialogue with evolutionary epistemology (chap. 2). He has thus not only developed further the depth of the earliest of human propensities for religious imagination, but has also argued forcefully for seeing shamanism as one of the very first, primordial forms of religion.

In an interesting move, he also supports his argument by briefly referring to the work of neuroscientists Eugene d'Aquili and Andrew Newberg and their attempt to develop a "neurotheology" that would give a neuroscientific explanation of religious experience (cf. 289f.). "Neurotheology," a term first used by James Ashbrook, is used today in various imaginative, interdisciplinary attempts to integrate neuroscience and theology, and in the search for specific brain structures that correlate with religious or mystical experiences (cf. Oomen 2003: 617f.). In their attempt at a neurotheology, d'Aquili and Newberg take precisely the kinds of mental features that Lewis-Williams pinpointed as most typical of shamanism and try to further the neurology of all religions by explaining that our sense of transcendence and ecstatic, mystical experiences seems to be grounded in the human brain and nervous system. In *The Mystical Mind* (1999) and *Why God Won't Go Away* (2001, also with Vince Rause), d'Aquili and Newberg have tried to explore what happens in the human brain when people are overcome by the kinds of ineffable feelings they ascribe to mystical or other religious experiences. It is exactly these kinds of experiences that are in effect altered states of consciousness. For Lewis-Williams neurotheology may therefore be a valuable tool for understanding the neurological basis of the whole spectrum of religious experience ranging from prehistoric shamanism to what he has called contemporary "urban shamanism," those kinds of dubious attempts that try to resurrect a supposed primordial religiosity through the sentimentality of New Age spirituality or through other bizarre, cultic sectarian movements of our day (cf. Lewis-Williams 2002: 289).

But how helpful is the neurological work of d'Aquili and Newberg really for Lewis-Williams's central hypothesis? In these neurobiologists' recent work, they explore what happens in the human brain when people are overcome by intense, ineffable feelings that they ascribe to divine visitation or an ecstatic, aesthetic oneness with the universe. These religious experiences are, I believe, correctly seen as altered states of consciousness, and the authors have focused on complex neurobiological processes that evoke these responses. In doing so, they have developed a model for religious experiences that involves the entire brain, and is based on noninvasive neuro-imaging of the working brain during actual ritual behavior and meditation. In this attempt to explain how religious mental states, and even God, are experienced by the human brain and mind, their research revealed that during meditation and worship, the level of activity in those parts of the brain that distinguish between the self and the outside world is radically diminished, or even cut off, in a process they call *deafferentation* (cf. d'Aquili and Newberg 1999: 41f., 165f.).

Presupposed in d'Aquili and Newberg's attempt to incorporate all the elements of religion into one rational, neuroscientific explanatory scheme is our biological necessity to seek out causality, and the fact that our brain functions in such a way that it always tries to find the cause of all the things it experiences (cf. d'Aquili and Newberg 2001). In this context the authors speak of the *causal operator* that has often led to the development of myth formation and particular, religious beliefs. In this sense all religions offer an answer to what ultimately causes things to happen in the universe, like natural forces, spiritual powers, and in the higher religions, God. The causal operator is that area of the brain that explains reality for us when our senses cannot. In this sense, then, God, spirits, etc., are automatically "generated" by the propensity of our brains for ultimate explanations. And even if we cognitively reject the existence of God or gods, this neural disposition is still a universal trait in all humans — believers and nonbelievers alike (cf. d'Aquili and Newberg 1999: 150ff.).

Other cognitive operators work in tandem with the causal operator. The *holistic operator* leads to the development of integrative concepts, like the concept of God. The *reductionistic operator* involves the primary intuition and existential sense that the whole is made up of the sum of the parts, i.e., an intuition for a deeper underlying reality like transcendence, and as such often combines with the holistic functions of the brain. The *quantitative operator* quantifies the various objects in the external world. The *binary operator* allows for opposing concepts like good and evil, justice and injustice, humans and God. The *abstract operator* creates general concepts from larger groups of objects, especially by using certain specific objects to symbolize certain more abstract concepts (cf. in Christianity the cross, or the Eucharist). And finally, the *emotional value operator* deepens personal religious feelings (cf. 166-73). Of these seven cognitive operators, the causal and holistic operators are the most important for understanding religious experiences. Where the causal operator permits reality to be viewed in terms of causal sequences, the holistic operator allows us to view reality as a whole, or as a gestalt. This operator is therefore also involved with the perception of spatial relations. For d'Aquili and Newberg it is ultimately the holistic operator that might allow us to apprehend the unity of God or the oneness of the universe.

For Lewis-Williams these brain processes or "operators" are especially important for understanding prehistoric forms of shamanism. The causal operator helps us understand that the brain automatically generates concepts of gods, powers, or spirits, in attempts to control the complexity of an often threatening environment. Also, this causal component of religious experience is closely linked to the more holistic and emotional components, where emotional states and altered states of consciousness, for participants at least, verify the existence of spiritual entities that cause things to happen (cf. Lewis-Williams 2002: 290). It is this sense of transcendence, or ecstatic experience, that d'Aquili and Newberg have called the sense of *Absolute Unitary Being*, and it is in this extreme altered state of consciousness that a breakdown of the distinction between the subject and the external world occurs (cf. d'Aquili and Newberg 1999: 109ff.).

It thus becomes clear why this neurological approach to religious experience is so attractive to Lewis-Williams; it also dovetails exactly with his arguments that the essential elements of religion are thus "wired into the brain" (cf. Lewis-Williams 2002: 290). Cultural contexts may differ and therefore advance or diminish the effect of this neurological bridge to the past. But we modern humans all share this neurological disposition, which is precisely, in d'Aquili and Newberg's provocative phrase, why "God won't go away" (d'Aquili, Newberg, and Rause 2001), and why the neurology of religious experiences and its remarkable persistence directly link the Upper Paleolithic to the present. In both *The Mystical Mind* and *Why God Won't Go Away*, d'Aquili and Newberg have tried to forge an integrated approach toward understanding religious experience.

Lewis-Williams has — wisely, I believe — not followed the much more problematic and controversial aspects of d'Aquili and Newberg's proposal. Crucial to their work has been the argument for a neurological account of the nature and origin of religion in terms of each of the cognitive operators. From this, however, they have also deduced a metatheology, and even a megatheology, that they claim contains the essence of all religions and theologies (cf. d'Aquili and Newberg 1999: 195ff.). They believe that their neurophysiological, neuropsychological, or neurotheological understanding of religions and theologies can actually bring us to understand all religious experiences in terms of a metatheology and megatheology. *Metatheology* is seen as that most overarching approach to fundamental reality comprising the general principles that regulate and constrain the construction of any and all specific theologies. *Megatheology* points to the most overarching content available in terms of current knowledge, derived specifically from neurotheology. This megatheology could be adopted by all the world's great religions without prejudice to their individual doctrinal content, and the authors' mystifying conclusion is that not only the general structures of religion but also the general structures of theology itself necessarily arise from the functioning of the human brain (cf. 207). The confusing notions of meta- and megatheologies are meant to function as overarching approaches that claim to explain the essential features of any theology arising out of any specific religious tradition. Clearly, if this is only meant *neurologically,* it would be highly reductionist and a rather naive, scientistic violation of the disciplinary boundaries between neuroscience and theology. If it is seriously claimed to be a *philosophical* position, it would be naively modernist, if not foundationalist, in its disregard for the specificity and integrity of the world's very diverse religions.

D'Aquili and Newberg's proposal for a neurological disposition for religious experience in the human brain does give valuable cross-disciplinary support to Lewis-Williams's hypothesis for seeing certain specific cave paintings from the Upper Paleolithic as indicative of shamanism. However, their speculations on the kind of meta- and megatheologies that might be derived from this is bad science as well as bad theology. Ultimately biology or neuroscience cannot explain religious experience completely. Only the human person experiencing something within a highly specific cultural context, and his or her interpretation or identification of this experience as religious, qualifies an experience as a religious experience (cf. Proudfoot 2000: 1159f.).

In her extensive study "Sacred or Neural? Neuroscientific Explanations of Religious Experience" (2004), Anne Runehov reached similar conclusions. Runehov argues persuasively that d'Aquili and Newberg's goal not only was to develop a neuroscientific theory for understanding religious experiences, but also to push beyond these disciplinary boundaries and draw quite specific implications for theology, philosophy, and the sciences. From their studies of meditation techniques, Newberg and d'Aquili have concluded that there is an invariant element across all religions, that all experiences are neurologically similar, and that the structure of religious experiences may point to the existence of God(s) (cf. Runehov 2004: 177ff.). In answering her core question, i.e., *in what way,* and *to what extent,* neuroscientists can explain religious experiences, she has shown that for d'Aquili and Newberg there must be more to religious experiences than can be neurally accounted for. For this reason d'Aquili and Newberg maintain that religious experiences are not illusory, and that God or divine reality actually exists in such a way that religious experiences can be explained in terms of a correlation with specific neural activities. Against this background Runehov correctly argues that the aspects of religious experiences that can be studied by contemporary scientific methods are indeed limited. Moreover, contextualizing religious experiences within very specific religions, doctrines, and traditions is methodologically of primary importance, and it is exactly these specific contexts that point to dimensions of religious experience that neuroscientific explanations alone cannot reach (cf. 193ff.). Lifting up the limitations of scientific explanations certainly points directly to the methodological need for a truly interdisciplinary approach for the understanding and explanation of religious experiences.

However, d'Aquili and Newberg initially focused on exploring what happens in the brain when people are overcome by ineffable feelings that they ascribe to mystical, ecstatic religious experiences. These experiences are in effect altered states of consciousness, and an explanation for the sense of transcendence and ecstasy, and for all other mystical experiences, indeed seems embedded in the human nervous system. It is for this "naturalness of religious imagination" that I have argued, and transversally intersecting arguments from evolutionary epistemology, paleoanthropology, and now neuroscience have shown that the essential elements of religious imagination are thus "wired into the brain." Cultural contexts may advance or diminish their effect, but these elements are always there (cf. Lewis-Williams 2002: 291). It is this fact that has finally provided us with a neurological bridge to the first behaviorally modern humans of the Upper Paleolithic in southwestern Europe.

Human Uniqueness and Religious Imagination

The idea that religious imagination might not be an isolated faculty of human rationality but that the predisposition to religious belief and mystical or religious inclinations can be regarded as an essentially universal attribute of the human mind and human culture, has recently also been taken up in interdisciplinary discussion by some theologians. In a recent paper Niels Gregersen argues that imagination, and also by definition religious imagination, is not an isolated faculty of human rationality but can be found at the very heart of human rationality. Thus the "naturalness" of imagination also applies to religious imagination, and religious imagination should not be seen as something esoteric that can be added to, or subtracted from, other mental states (cf. Gregersen 2003: 1f.). Rather, the process of human imagination opens itself up to more generalized images, some of which might be seen as "religious" according to our current cultural usage.

In fact, scholars like Steven Mithen, Ian Tattersall, Jean Clottes, David Lewis-Williams, Rick Potts, and Terrence Deacon have all argued that religious imagination emerged naturally and spontaneously in the course of the evolution of human cognitive systems. This same theme was addressed by cognitive anthropologist Pascal Boyer in his *Religion Explained: The Evolutionary Origins of Religious Thought* (2001). In this work, however, Boyer presents an openly reductionist application of cognitive psychology for the study of religion, and argues that the human mind receives and processes information through the functioning of innate predispositions ("modules") to perceive, feel, think, and act in distinctive ways that have contributed to our adaptive fitness as a species through evolutionary history. These hardwired cognitive abilities are clearly advantageous to our species, but Boyer believes they also get us into cognitive trouble. Because our powers of social cognition are so strong, we are very quick to see everything in the world in terms of agency and volitional behavior, and sometimes this innate perceptual tendency leads us to make mistakes. Our agency detective systems are biased toward overdetection, and our evolutionary heritage is that of organisms that must deal with both predators and prey. In either situation it is far more advantageous to overdetect agency than to underdetect it. The expense of what Boyer calls "false positives" (seeing agents where there are none) is minimal, if we can abandon these misguided intuitions quickly. In contrast, the cost of not detecting agents when they are actually around (either predator or prey) could be very high (cf. Boyer 2001: 145). Although our background as predators and prey is rather remote to most of us today, Boyer thinks it is still crucial to understanding some features of how our minds work.

Basing his argument on this evolutionary reasoning, Boyer asserts that religion is in effect a cognitive "false positive," i.e., a faulty application of our innate mental machinery that unfortunately leads many humans to believe in the existence of supernatural agents like gods that do not really exist. This also leads Boyer to describe religious concepts as parasitic on ordinary cognitive processes; they are parasitic in the sense that religion uses those mental processes for purposes other than what they were designed by evolution to achieve, and because of this their successful transmission is greatly enhanced by mental capacities that are there anyway, gods or no gods (cf. 202). Boyer judges the puzzling persistence of religion to be a consequence of natural selection designing brains that allowed our prehistoric ancestors to adapt to a world of predators. A brain molded by evolution to be on the constant lookout for hidden predators is likely to develop the habit of looking for all kinds of hidden agencies. And it is just this kind of brain that will eventually start manufacturing images of the concealed actors we normally refer to as "gods." In this sense, then, there is a natural, evolutionary explanation for religion, and we continue to entertain religious ideas simply because of the kinds of brains we have (cf. Haught 2002a: 12). On this view, the mind it takes to have religion is the mind we have.

The argument here is that religious inclinations are more a by-product than a direct consequence of our cognitive evolution, a spin-off from the hardwired cognitive inference systems characteristic of our species. To inquire into the evolved function of religion is therefore rather quixotic: what we need to be looking for are the deep cognitive processes that have (accidentally, as it were) given rise to religion. In a sense our disposition toward religion is the price we pay for our specific mental architecture.[4] Even so, Boyer

4. Cf. David Livingstone Smith, review of *Religion Explained*, by Pascal Boyer, *Metapsychology Online Book Reviews*, December 16, 2002.

does offer a model for understanding how religious concepts, often amaz- ingly counterintuitive and even baroquely exotic (cf. Boyer 2001: 65), have their natural place in the contexts of the ordinary workings of the brain (cf. Gregersen 2003: 12). Religious concepts are natural both in the phenomeno- logical sense that they emerge spontaneously and develop effortlessly, and in the natural sense that also religious imagination belongs to the world of na- ture and is naturally constrained by genes, central nervous systems, and brains (cf. Boyer 2001: 3f.).

Most scholars of religion would not find Boyer's description of reli- gion(s) as counterintuitive and of only subjective, existential importance satis- factory, for so are fairy tales and science fiction stories (cf. Gregersen 2003: 11). Also, the characterization of religious concepts as being about supernatural beings is equally unsatisfactory, for the distinction "natural/supernatural" is certainly not relevant to all religions. Niels Gregersen has correctly argued that religious faith is not in fact confined to nonobservable, supernatural entities, but instead comprehensively redescribes the observable world as well in the light of the particular faith (cf. 12). Boyer thus leaves us with a too narrow, and too reductionist, view of religion, but he valuably contributes to the idea that religious imagination uses the same inference systems as the human brain and the mind in general. His theory also seems to be stuck in examples from so- called primitive societies, and complex and vastly important shifts in religious perception in the different religions of the world as well as specific develop- ments in human cultural evolution are not reflected in his work (cf. Gregersen 2003: 15). In fact, Boyer admits that his theory functions at a highly general level and does not explain the particular shape of particular religions (cf. Boyer 2001: 319).

Gregersen is correct, therefore, in stating that the evolutionary psycholo- gist, on this point at least, cannot succeed in evaluating or explaining the inter- nal rationality of religious belief. In that sense Boyer's claim to have "explained religion" is certainly premature, or is at the very least a very limited claim. More importantly, though, a theory about the emergence of religious imagina- tion and religious concepts does not at all answer the philosophical question about the validity of religion, or the even more complex theological question whether, and in what form, religious imagination refers to some form of real- ity. Gregersen phrases it well: as a matter of principle, the reasons that may un- dergird the unreasonable effectiveness of religious belief and thought may just transcend the scope of evolutionary psychology and evolutionary epistemol- ogy (cf. Gregersen 2003: 16). Boyer has certainly not attempted to answer the theological question of how religious faith could be addressed or explained on its own terms. On his view evolution makes all of us likely worshipers in much the same way that it makes all of us likely language users. We are innately disposed for both, so such disparate religious traditions as Christian theology, Islamic law, and Buddhist metaphysics are merely different forms of baroque ornamentations added on to an evolutionary edifice (cf. Griffiths 2002: 54). Boyer, therefore, fails to consider the acceptability or unacceptability of the religious believer's explanations for his/her religion(s). His attempt, in spite of its rather grand claim to explain religion, offers only a limited explanation for the naturalness of religion in terms of evolutionary psychology.

Boyer's work in evolutionary psychology, reminiscent of the work of some contemporary evolutionary epistemologists, on whom I focused in lecture 2, has made a case for explaining the psychological plausibility of religious belief, the naturalness of religious imagination, and the ease with which religious ideas are spread socially. However, both evolutionary psychology and evolutionary epistemology cannot explain, or explain away, the rationality or irrationality of religious belief, nor can they discuss the plausibility or implausibility of the reality claims intrinsic to most lived religions. For Gregersen this means that evolutionary psychology, like other sciences, should be seen as neutral to the validity and reality claims of religious belief (cf. Gregersen 2003: 20). On a postfoundationalist view I would contextualize this statement and argue that in an interdisciplinary conversation like the one before us, we identify the issues and shared concerns that theology may learn from, but we also may run into the distinct limitations of this specific interdisciplinary conversation. Only in the transversal context of an interdisciplinary conversation does it become clear that explanatory models from the pluralistic network of the sciences, and from philosophy of religion and theology, cannot be reduced to one another. Only in this kind of transversal interaction can we discover where exactly our interests overlap, and where they inevitably are in conflict, or where they just go their separate ways once the transversal moment of shared interest has passed and the scientist and theologian return to the boundaries of their disciplines to consider the interdisciplinary results of the multidisciplinary conversation.

In our present conversation we can at least reach an interdisciplinary agreement that religious imagination and religious concepts should be treated equally with all other sorts of human reflection. In this sense religious imagination is to be treated as an integral part of human cognition, not separable from our other cognitive endeavors (cf. 23). Religious imagination can also not be treated as a generic given, however, but can be discussed and evaluated contextually only within the specific context of specific religions. This should in fact be the starting point for a discussion on this difficult interdisciplinary issue.

When discussing the problem of human uniqueness in paleoanthropology, we encountered similar arguments for the naturalness of religion. Various scientists see the cognitively fluid human mind as blending and recombining templates of understanding used for other purposes and domains of cognition as well. Steven Mithen has also argued that there exists no specialized religious module in the human brain, and no distinct borderline between religious and nonreligious imagination. The emergence of religion is in fact an intrinsic part of the liberation of human rationality from the constrained and enclosed structure of "Roman chapels" to the open and fluid structures of the Gothic cathedral-like cognitive fluidity. Ian Tattersall has argued that we construct our religious images (also our images of God) in terms of our everyday, human experiences. In this sense, then, religious imaginations are natural phenomena, and are deeply embedded in the brain's cognitive capacities. The *fact* of religious imagination is no final argument for its credibility or implausibility as part of the human condition. It suggests neither that there is something true about religious imagination nor that religion is basically prerational and, as useful fiction, worked well for our ancestors.

In this chapter we have looked at various arguments by Tattersall, Mithen, Noble and Davidson, Potts, Deacon, and Lewis-Williams, and in spite of their different and even opposing views on human origins and the timing of the evolution of language, they do converge in their conclusions on the unique but natural nature of human imagination, consciousness, and our symbolic linguistic abilities. Tattersall, Mithen, Potts, Lewis-Williams, and Deacon would also agree with Boyer on the emergence and naturalness of religious imagination, although they approach the issue very differently. Tattersall, Lewis-Williams, Potts, and Deacon in particular are less reductionistic and more open toward the specific emergence not just of a propensity for religious belief, but of spirituality, and they all seem to leave room for the possibility that the symbolic human mind, because of its vast neural complexity, might be an emergence of newly integrated capacities for perception, knowledge, and awareness that go beyond the biological nature of the brain. These arguments converge strikingly with those of Holmes Rolston in his Gifford Lectures (1997/1998), published as *Genes, Genesis, and God* (1999). In this work Rolston pointed far beyond sociobiological explanations in his argument for gene-culture co-evolution. If human minds are not completely controlled by genes, then a more plausible possibility for gene-mind co-evolution is that a certain kind of mind, produced with certain sets of genomes, will be disposed to certain sorts of cultural practices. But even if we are genetically disposed to certain behaviors, human minds have evolved with amazing flexibility and imagination. Humans, of course, do have behavioral dispositions of some kinds, like fearing snakes, seeking mates, avoiding incest, protecting our children, reciprocating for mutual benefits, obeying parents, or following leaders. For sociobiologists like E. O. Wilson, this would clearly reveal that genes hold culture on a leash, even if it is a long leash, so that even if there are many options in culture, genetic constraints always circumscribe and overrule human behavior. Rolston, however, convincingly argues that natural selection is greatly relaxed in great areas of cultural activity. There may therefore be numerous nonbiological beliefs that are not at all coded into our genes, not even dispositionally, and have to be discovered and constructed in another way (cf. 1999: 124).

On this view, then, natural selection clearly is relaxed, even superseded, on a cultural level. And though culture is superimposed on biology, the leash here is not just loose, but there is in fact some release from biological determinism. In a sense, then, biological evolution cannot limit what may happen on a cultural level. The leash is broken and biology and culture are two dramatically different events — even though culture is superimposed on and embedded in biology, and even though they can both be subsumed under a formal selection theory. Against this background Rolston can advance the argument, closely resonating with that of Anthony O'Hear (chap. 2), that science, ethics, and religion importantly transcend their biological frameworks, even as they simultaneously understand and evaluate their biological origins.

This obviously leads us to the important question: What would Rolston consider a plausible account of the genesis of religion? Can we trace a pathway along which religion might have appeared, especially since it is clear that with the emergence of religion something entirely new appeared in the evolutionary process of humankind? For Rolston the emergence of religion may actually represent the achievement of an entirely new level of insight. The fact that our conceptual and perceptual facilities have evolved does not mean that nothing true appears in them, nor that nothing new can ever arise in them (cf. 293). This leads to a highly intriguing suggestion that goes far beyond Boyer's "explanation" of religious belief: although biological origins clearly contribute to our human understanding, the genesis of religion, so unique to humans, is not something one can extrapolate from earlier explanations in biology. For Rolston, then, *biology does not generate religion; it is the phenomenon of life, rather, that evokes religious response* (cf. 294). And it is exactly this fact that Rolston connects directly to human uniqueness: the real surprise is that human intelligence can be religious and philosophical, something we do not find anywhere else in animal life (299).

Conclusion

I have woven together in this chapter arguments from evolutionary epistemology, paleoanthropology, neuroscience, and evolutionary psychology that support the emergence of the cognitive, fluid, symbolic human mind; of imagination and religious awareness; and of the crucial role of language in this process. In fact, in many ways language without doubt can be seen as the most distinctive human adaptation. We have also seen arguments for why both the special adaptations for language and language itself have played important roles in the origins of human moral and spiritual capacities, and why mystical or religious inclinations can indeed be regarded as an essentially universal attribute of human culture. In fact, for a scientist like Terrence Deacon the capacity for spiritual experience can be understood as an emergent consequence of the symbolic transfiguration of human cognition and emotions. This has now led to important conclusions for the interdisciplinary dialogue between Christian theology and the sciences.

1. Theologians are now challenged to take seriously the fact that our very human ability to respond religiously to ultimate questions, through various forms of worship and prayer, is deeply embedded in our species' capacity for symbolic, imaginative behavior, and in the embodied minds that make such behavior possible. This valuable perspective offered by various sciences converges well with my theological argument in chapter 3: the most responsible Christian theological perspective on human uniqueness requires a distinct move away from esoteric and overly abstract notions of human uniqueness and a return to embodied notions of humanness where our embodied imagination, sexuality, and moral awareness are directly linked to the fully embodied self-transcendence of believers who are in a relationship with God.
2. This strong interdisciplinary convergence between theology and the sciences on human uniqueness presupposes arguments from both evolutionary epistemology and paleoanthropology for not only the presence of religious awareness in our earliest Cro-Magnon ancestors, but also for the plausibility of the larger argument: since the very beginning of the emergence of *Homo sapiens,* the evolution of those characteristics that

made humans uniquely different from even their closest sister species, i.e., characteristics like consciousness, language, symbolic minds and symbolic behavior, always included religious awareness and religious behavior. Presupposed in this argument, however, is the remarkable degree of adaptability and the versatility of our species. *Homo sapiens* emerged as a result of its ancestral lineage having persisted and changed in the face of dramatic environmental variability. It is this versatility that Rick Potts has called the "astonishing hallmark of modern humanity" (cf. Potts 2004), and which also gives new depth to human symbolic capacities.

3. In fact, not only can the material culture of prehistoric imagery as depicted in the spectacular cave "art" in France and Spain be seen as the first large-scale evidence of the storage of symbolic information outside the human brain, but the heights of all human imagination, the depths of depravity, moral awareness, and the sense for transcendence depend on the symbolic ability of humans to "code the nonvisible" through abstract thought. The need to create meaning, whether religious, ethical, philosophical, or aesthetic, is part of the mental "tool kit" that *Homo sapiens* has evolved in its long journey of physical and spiritual survival.

4. It is this mental tool kit that some scientists have helpfully called "higher-order consciousness." Precisely because we humans are conscious of being conscious, we have developed a high degree of self-awareness and symbolic memory. This means that we are probably the only species that has remarkable memory, and that can use that memory to shape our own identities through mental images of past, present, and future events. And at the heart of this is the human capacity for language.

5. Part of the remarkable tool kit of the modern human mind is what I have called, following Niels Gregersen, the "naturalness of religious imagination": the neurological disposition or capacity for religious awareness and religious experience. The emergence of this capacity, and of the uniquely human ability to exist in a dimension of meaning, has given valuable cross-disciplinary support for David Lewis-Williams's important hypothesis that certain very specific cave paintings from the Upper Paleolithic strongly suggest shamanistic beliefs and practices. Although the neurological capacity for altered states of consciousness opens the door for regarding early forms of shamanism as the very first forms of human religions, this neurological bridge to our distant prehistoric past does not legitimize complete neurological explanations of contemporary religious experiences and theological convictions. Ultimately the inter-

disciplinary dialogue with the sciences runs up against distinct limitations: neither biology nor neuroscience can explain religion or religious experiences adequately. Only the religious person, experiencing his or her faith within a highly specific cultural context, can interpret or identify an experience as religious, and that as such qualifies an experience as a religious experience. Such an awareness of the limitations of scientific explanations points directly to the methodological need for an interdisciplinary approach for the understanding and explanation of religion and religious experiences.

6. Because religion and religious faith are not confined to nonobservable, "supernatural" entities, they also redescribe the observable world, and our place in it, in the light of a particular faith commitment. For this reason science cannot be expected to successfully explain the internal rationality of religious belief. Only within the transversal context of interdisciplinary dialogue does it become clear that explanatory models from the pluralistic network of the sciences, from philosophy, religion, and theology, cannot be reduced to one another. One of the most remarkable facts about human uniqueness is the stunning ability of the embodied human mind to be philosophical and religious.

But what does all of this imply for theology? Our ongoing interdisciplinary conversation about human uniqueness has now pushed the boundaries of theology and leads the interdisciplinary theologian to an enriched appropriation of facts and information about our origins as humans, and about what humanness may mean today. The important questions that still remain are: How can theology possibly be enriched by the insights gained from the sciences on the evolution of human uniqueness, and how will these insights affect the already complex dialogue between these very diverse reasoning strategies? I argued in the first chapter that there is no clear philosophical blueprint or timeless recipe for relating the bewildering complexity of contemporary theologies to the increasingly complex spectrum of contemporary sciences. This did not mean, as has hopefully become clear by now, that we could not develop a focused dialogue between theology and the sciences on issues that are quite specific, and that resonate with both partners in this dialogue. I do believe that the evolution of "human uniqueness," so highlighted now by the sciences of consciousness, evolutionary biology, and paleoanthropology, has presented us with an outstanding and exciting case study for precisely this kind of interdisciplinary dialogue. In the final chapter I will ask what is it about the embodied human mind that we have now encountered in evolutionary epistemology, in paleoanthropology, neuroscience, and cognitive psychology, that might actually have a transversal impact on theological anthropology and help us to revision humanness, and "human uniqueness," in theology.

However, what have also surfaced in this postfoundationalist dialogue between theology and the sciences are the very specific limitations of interdisciplinary work. Very diverse disciplines like theology and specific sciences converge and share creative transversal moments that have the potential to enrich critically both partners in the conversation. Scientists certainly would want to back away from overzealous theologians who might want to uncritically transport scientific facts across disciplinary borders into theological paradigms. But philosophical theologians also have a critical task: not only to back away from reductionistic explanations in science, but also to critique and expose the philosophical problem behind any kind of reductionist scientism.

The focus on context, so much a part of any postfoundationalist approach to interdisciplinary dialogue, should also alert theologians and scientists that partners in dialogue on carefully identified shared problems, after initially sharing important research trajectories, can very consciously decide to move beyond these intersecting, interdisciplinary transversal moments to return to their own specific domains of research, now enriched and even changed by the dialogue, and with agreements, conflicts, and different worldviews firmly in place. On a more positive and constructive note, in the dialogue with the sciences an interdisciplinary theologian should ideally make two moves: take the interdisciplinary results from specific multidisciplinary conversation back into his or her own intradisciplinary context to enrich current research in theology; and at the same time keep the interdisciplinary conversation going with scientists who are interested in the broader religious, or specific theological, perspectives that theology might bring to the table.

six Human Uniqueness in Science and Theology

"Looking at myself from the perspective of society or thinking comparatively, I am an average person. Facing myself intimately, immediately, I regard myself as unique, as exceedingly precious, not to be exchanged for anything else. I
would not like my existence to be a total waste, an utter ab-
surdity. No one will live my life for me, no one will think my
thoughts for me or dream my dreams. My own being, placed
as it is in the midst of many beings, is not simply being here
too, being around, being part of the environment. It is at the
very center of my consciousness that I am distinct."

Abraham J. Heschel, *Who Is Man?*
(Stanford: Stanford University Press, 1965), 34f.

My previous five chapters have revealed various interdisciplinary arguments
from both the sciences and theology for moving away from abstract, esoteric
notions of human uniqueness and toward revisioning the issue more concretely in terms of embodied personhood. From evolutionary epistemology
we have learned that theologians also should take seriously the epistemic implications of the biological origins of human cognition, and of the embodied
history of this remarkable and defining human capacity in the long process of
human evolution. Both from evolutionary epistemology and the science of
paleoanthropology we have learned the importance of rediscovering our very
close connection to the animal and hominid worlds. This obviously implies
that we cannot afford to think of human distinctiveness in terms of value su-

periority over other animals, or over the rest of nature, nor conceive of ourselves in a superior, disembodied position at the "center of the universe." Rather, the evidence compels us to revision the notion of human uniqueness solely in terms of species specificity and concrete embodiment.

As for Christian theology, in my third chapter I argued that the complex and checkered history of ideas of the *imago Dei* clearly revealed the failure of overly abstract and speculative theological constructions for expressing what it might mean to be created in the image of God. At the same time, exciting new developments in theological anthropology demonstrate the remarkable fluidity and powerful ability of this central idea to be reconnected with classical biblical texts and from there to shape more concrete, embodied notions of what it means to be human. In addition, in my fourth chapter a transversal connection to contemporary paleoanthropology revealed that prominent scholars in this field already work with radically revisioned notions of human uniqueness by focusing on the historical and material context of human origins, and the emergence of the embodied symbolic, mythical minds of our earliest ancestors, as exemplified in the spectacular cave art of the Upper Paleolithic. In a similar fashion, voices from the neurosciences are presenting an important interdisciplinary challenge for refocusing theological anthropology on the emergence of the symbolic human mind.

As someone who has argued rather passionately for developing a truly interdisciplinary theology, it now remains as my task in this final chapter to search for ways to integrate into a wide reflective equilibrium these diverse, intersecting transversal lines of argument. Two important questions have to be dealt with in this chapter, and with these we return one last time to my own revisioning of Lord Gifford's original charge in his last will and testament:

> I having been for many years deeply and firmly convinced that the true knowledge of God . . . and the true and felt knowledge . . . of the relations of man and of the universe to Him, and of the true foundations of all ethics and morals — being, I say, convinced that *this knowledge, when really felt and acted on, is the means of man's highest well-being, and the security of his upward progress,* I have resolved . . . to institute and found . . . lectureships or classes for the study and promotion of said subjects. (Jaki 1986: 71f., my italics)

As we saw in my first chapter, the very explicit and well-known statement here is that *in knowing God, and in knowing the world, our relationship to the world in relation to God, and the true foundations of all ethics and morals, we may actually find and achieve something unique, i.e., our highest well-being as humans.* Implicit in this statement are two important themes that can be revisioned to reach out to us transversally across time: one is a direct challenge to a form of multidisciplinary reflection in theology and science that may actually lead to interdisciplinary insights; the other is a clear and unambiguous relational statement on what is unique about our human species, which as such can be optimally understood only in terms of our broader connection to the universe and to God. Lord Gifford seemed to be making a theological statement about how we humans might achieve the moral goal of our "highest well-being" and "upward progress" by acting on the comprehensive knowledge of God and of our relationship to God and the world. He might just as well have said that what is truly unique about us as humans is to be found in exactly this remarkable ability we have to know God through our relationships to this God, and how this knowing of the relationship of the universe to this God may inspire us to moral, ethical behavior, and thus to the achievement of a distinctive human uniqueness as our highest "well-being."

In light of these revisioned interpretations of the Gifford statement, two questions remain for us to deal with in this final chapter: What have we learned about the possibilities and the epistemic range of interdisciplinarity in this research project on human uniqueness? And what have we learned about human uniqueness in this interdisciplinary project in science and theology? I hope to show that the achievement of interdisciplinarity through the interweaving of diverse lines of transversally intersecting arguments is not about the mere fact that diverse disciplinary voices have been brought to the same table, as it were. In this case it is rather about how interdisciplinary dialogue provides for us an accumulating argument for radically rethinking the theological notion of the *imago Dei* as a move away from sterile abstractions toward radical embodiment and ethically responsible action, a move that should resonate transversally with disciplines of both theology and paleoanthropology.

In my earlier critique of the many interpretations of the *imago Dei* in the history of Christianity, I tried to highlight the continuity of the core ideas of this central Christian doctrine, and how they functioned as the gravitational pull of this powerful doctrinal tradition. At the same time, I tried to show how many of these notions lured us into a "twilight zone of abstraction" where disembodied theological notions of human uniqueness could easily float free above text, body, and nature in exotically baroque, overly abstract, metaphysical speculations. I also argued, however, that exciting recent developments in theological anthropology point to a retrieval of exactly the earthy, embodied dimensions of humanness that we encountered in the ancient texts. In a striking image Robert Jenson sees *Homo sapiens* as the praying animal, and Adam and Eve as the first hominid group that, in whatever form of religion or language, by ritual action were embodied before God (cf. Jenson 1999: 59). In Philip Hefner's work the human being, as a product of biocultural evolution, emerges within the natural evolutionary processes as a symbiosis of genes and culture, as a fully embodied being, as God's created cocreator (cf. Hefner 1993: 277). In the writings of Phyllis Bird and Michael Welker there is a very conscious move away from theological abstraction toward interpretations of the *imago Dei* in a highly contextualized, embodied sense that respects the sexual differentiation between men and women, even as they exercise responsible care and multiply and spread over the earth (cf. Welker 1999: 68). And in Richard Middleton's and George Newlands's recent work was found a creative new way to take seriously the ethical and moral dimensions of Lord Gifford's charge, and thus to recognize that human rights and solidarity with the marginalized belong at the heart of any discussion of human uniqueness (Middleton 2005; Newlands 2005).

But we also know that our embodied existence confronts us with the realities of vulnerability, affliction, and deprivation, and that this vulnerability is deeply embedded in our bodily existence. For this reason the image of God is not found in some narrow intellectual or spiritual capacity, but in the whole human being, "body and soul." In fact, the image of God is not found *in* humans, it *is* the human, and for this reason the *imago Dei* can be read only as *imitatio Dei:* to be created in God's image means we should act like God, and so attain holiness through our compassionate care for the other and for the world. What we find, then, is a rediscovery of the meaning of embodiment for theological anthropology, and the beginnings of a revisioning of notions of human uniqueness and the *imago Dei* that resonate powerfully with the embodied, flesh-and-blood humans we encounter in the Genesis texts. But what happens if we connect transversally these conclusions about theological notions of human uniqueness with some of the results gleaned from the sciences on human uniqueness?

The most important aspect of my interdisciplinary conversation with the sciences on human uniqueness was the attempt to establish transversal links with those sciences that deal directly with human origins, i.e., paleoanthropology and archeology. Here we saw that those characteristics that make us really human, i.e., language, self-awareness, moral awareness, consciousness, imagination, mythology, are often the least visible in the prehistoric record. What is available to us for interpretation, however, is some of the most spectacular and earliest material evidence of symbolic behavior in humans — the Paleolithic cave paintings from France and the Basque Country in northern Spain, all painted toward the end of the last Ice Age. Various scholars argued that the explicitly symbolic behavior of our Cro-Magnon ancestors should be seen as the hallmark of the behavioral transition from the Middle to the Upper Paleolithic in western Europe. This spectacular cave art, along with portable art, personal ornamentation, and the design and form of advanced stone tools, reflects the newly arrived human symbolic disposition that in time would come to define what it means to be fully human. Furthermore, the fact that human uniqueness also emerges in paleoanthropology as a highly contextualized and embodied notion, where the symbolizing minds of our distant ancestors are stunningly and physically revealed in material, prehistoric cave art, also revealed why many paleoanthropologists have linked the emergence of consciousness and of symbolic behavior directly to the emergence of religious awareness. These convergent arguments were strengthened by recent contextualized arguments for linking early shamanistic explanations to the possible meaning and religious dimensions of some of the prehistoric imagery.

As became clear in chapter 5, some paleoanthropologists have argued that symbolic behavior should be seen as part of turning communication into language. Even more importantly, though, the use of symbols separate from language, as in the famous imagery from the Upper Paleolithic, could have been the product only of a creature that already possessed a fully developed language (cf. Davidson 1997: 153). Exactly this idea was developed further by Terrence Deacon in his argument that we are the only species to have evolved the ability to communicate symbolically. Having symbolic minds, therefore, includes biologically unprecedented ways of experiencing and understanding the world, from aesthetic experience to spiritual contemplation. Precisely the symbolic nature of *Homo sapiens* also reveals language as our most distinctive human adaptation, and of crucial importance for the origins of moral and spiritual capacities. This also suggests why mystical or religious inclinations can be regarded as an essentially universal attribute of human culture (cf. Deacon 1997: 436).

Human Uniqueness and Embodiment

As a final point of entry into the question, what have we learned about human uniqueness so far? I would like to pursue further intersecting lines of argument from my second, third, fourth, and fifth lectures, and explore the important idea that human uniqueness can be adequately addressed only if we take our own animality and embodied personhood seriously in both theology and the sciences. In this final chapter I would like to enter into a final round of conversations on interdisciplinary notions of embodiment with a set of important but rather diverse scholars, namely, Edward Farley, Gordon Kaufman, Alasdair MacIntyre, Christian Smith, and Abraham Heschel. I will attempt to show that in each case the strong focus on embodied personhood that we already encountered in the theological anthropologies of Robert Jenson, Philip Hefner, Phyllis Bird, and Michael Welker (chap. 3) will be enhanced by a dialogue with this group of scholars.

However, one of the earliest and most important philosophical influences on the development of holistic notions of embodiment during the last century, and specifically on the work of Farley and MacIntyre, has been French phenomenologist Maurice Merleau-Ponty. In his *Phenomenology of Perception* (1962) Merleau-Ponty consciously set out to develop a "phenomenology of lived existence" that would overcome the opposition, characteristic of traditional metaphysics, between the thinking, rational human subject and its objects in the world. In this approach he famously saw the human body as a relational mode of being, as the most fundamental form of existing-in-the-world. "I cannot understand the function of the living body except by enacting it myself, and except in so far as I am a body which rises toward the world" (Merleau-Ponty 1962: 75).

To be human, then, is to be embodied consciousness, for "I am not in front of my body, I am in it, or rather, I am it" (150). Or phrased differently, to exist as a human being is to be a body-in-the-world. In fact, the human body is the vehicle for being in the world, and having a body is to be interactively involved with a definite environment, and we are conscious of the world only through the medium of the body (82). More specifically, the body is our general medium for having a world (146), and as embodied consciousness the human body is a focal point of living meanings, or what Merleau-Ponty calls "a grouping of lived-through meanings which moves towards its equilibrium" (151, 153). Finally, for Merleau-Ponty all our talk about embodiment is a way of examining the concrete, interactive relationality of the self and its world within which each coconstitutes itself and the other. And importantly, it is in language and speech that we find the primary human form of self-world cocreation (175ff.).

In Merleau-Ponty's highly concrete "phenomenology of the flesh," the human body in all its forms of behavior, not merely in speech, becomes the carrier of meaning, and as such the carrier of tradition, passing on its culture, its history, its life (cf. Brown 1994: 102f.). Against this background it is revealing to engage briefly with scholars from different disciplines on issues of embodiment and its crucial role in theology and science. One of the most important recent American voices speaking out against speculative, abstract ideas on human nature, and for embodiment, is theologian Edward Farley. In his *Good and Evil: Interpreting a Human Condition* (1990), Farley warns against interpreting human distinctiveness on a level so theoretically abstract and a-contextual that whatever is seen as true humanness inevitably floats free from the immediate realities of nature and the human body. As we saw in chapter 3, Christian theology has used the history of philosophy to distinguish the *imago Dei* as reason, or rationality, for the largest part of its history, and by implication to assign human bodies and biological networks of natural causality to the margins of the human condition. This ironically would "free" theology to abstractly formulate its revelational or scriptural versions of human nature as if they had no relation whatsoever to the awe-inspiring realities being studied by evolutionary biology, neurophysiology, and evolutionary psychology (cf. Farley 1990: 77f.).

While this kind of disciplinary isolation does seem to protect the domain of faith, and of theology, from the reality of the world of the sciences, it should by now be clear that it also forces us to some very unfortunate, and reductionist, choices. For Farley these reductionist choices can be phrased as follows: The first option would be that the human being, as described by specifically the sciences, is in fact the "real" human being. On this view a human trait like aggression, for instance, is seen as the scientifically demonstrated depiction of what some religious traditions have rather vaguely called "sin." Here the "true" scientific (read: genetic) view of human nature quickly replaces any more comprehensive religious accounts of human nature. A second option would be to see theology as describing the "real" human condition, with what the sciences say having little or no bearing on the issue. Here the "real human being" would be something spiritual and mental that floats above earth and body, and also above physical and genetic causality. The third option would be some form of dualism, which states that the causal networks studied by the sciences and the realities attested by faith are both real but have nothing to do with each other (cf. 7f.). Any theologian wishing to choose this dualist option would find it almost impossible not to fall back into the second option, giving only lip service to the biological and embodied aspects of what it means to be human. This kind of theological view acknowledges our biological and evolutionary dimensions, but what is argued further is that we have developed so far beyond our animal and instinctual natures toward something spiritually unique, that we have virtually no biological nature to take into account at all when talking about humanness. On this view human agency is interpreted as whatever transcends the biological, and therefore focuses almost exclusively on the "spiritual," or on culture, language, freedom, history, and the personal (cf. 79). Clearly, all three of Farley's options show that theology pays a high price for any self-imposed isolation from the sciences.

More importantly, I think we can conclude from this that any *intra*disciplinary attempt at a theological anthropology, no matter how well intended, will always be incomplete, if not seriously impaired, if the more holistic approach of interdisciplinary theology is not allowed to complement, and contribute to, the issue of defining the human condition. Against this background Farley presents his own rather modest thesis: the condition of human persons, whatever else it is, is first of all the condition of living animals (cf. 79). This clearly and correctly implies that the features that constitute life, animality, and being a mammal and a primate are not eliminated or left behind by whatever eventually constitutes human distinctiveness. The biological, the organic and phylogenetic do not just constitute possibilities for theoretical hypotheses about our human condition, but they in fact constitute important aspects of that condition itself. In this sense one could certainly argue that the biological is a fact of individual human reality along with the givenness, on another level, of our intersubjective and social relationality, and it is these various dimensions of being human that ultimately define the embodied human condition (cf. 79).

But how can we unpack this notion of embodied humanness a little more clearly? As *biologically* specific, we human beings occupy a niche in the hundreds of thousands of species of living things on this planet. As *animals* rather than plants, we are mobile and perceptual. As *vertebrates* distinguished from nonvertebrates, we have a backbone and other features of vertebrate lifeforms. As *mammals,* we are warm-blooded and live-bearing, and nurse our young. In contrast to marsupials and felines, we share many physiological, genetic, and even behavioral features with *primates.* As the one remaining hominid on the planet, we have an erect posture and are bipedal. In this concrete, bodily sense human uniqueness can never be defined as an abstract, intellectual, or spiritual capacity alone, for it is precisely these kinds of taxonomical observations that add up to the fact that *human specificity is the specificity of a species* (cf. 80). And this kind of embodied specificity, I would add, should be of direct relevance for a theological interpretation of human uniqueness. Whatever our most unique features as human beings may be today, they can only be exemplifications of our biological condition, and never evidence that we have somehow managed to surpass our biological natures. As Farley puts it, even with our outsized cerebral cortex, our relatively long lives, and our complex facial expressions, we are still also organic, living animals (cf. 81).

Therefore, whatever our degree of difference from other animals, it is our evolutionarily developed bodies that are the background and bearers of human uniqueness — our bodies, and our embodied brains, that we use to experience and act in a typically human fashion.[1] It is in this sense that biology is a dimension of the human condition, and as such it also explains those pre-aware physiological operations that constitute ongoing life processes and make possible all human acts and sensations including thinking and feeling.

Another prominent North American theologian who has developed strong and holistic anthropological ideas for seeing *Homo sapiens* as fully embodied persons, deeply embedded in evolutionary, natural history, is Gordon D. Kaufman. At the heart of his approach is a *biohistorical* understanding of human life, and of humans as biohistorical beings (cf. Kaufman 2004: 42f.). In this interdisciplinary approach to human distinctiveness, Kaufman, like myself, and like the contemporary theologians whose work on the *imago Dei* I analyzed in chapter 3, takes for granted the basic evolutionary account of the origins of human life. Similar to philosophers like Henry Plotkin, Franz Wuketits, and Anthony O'Hear, whose work was discussed in chapter 2, Kaufman wants to move beyond biology for an interpretation of what is distinctive about human nature: although the consensus today is that humankind emerged out of less complex forms of life in the course of evolutionary developments over many millennia, and that humans could not exist apart from this living ecological web that continues to nourish and sustain them, an evolutionary explanation alone is still too vague, and thus insufficient, to provide an adequate understanding of the sorts of beings that humans actually are today. For Kaufman this ultimately means that a biological conception of human beings still says nothing about the importance of the uniquely historical features of human existence. And it is, in fact, through their historical, sociocultural development over many thousands of years, and not their biological evolution alone, that humans have acquired some of their most distinctive and significant characteristics (cf. 43).

This historical development over many millennia, and the gradual emergence of human culture, human activities and projects, has been as indispens-

---

1. In Farley's words: we cannot listen to symphonies or fall in love without our bodies and our brains, but what constitute our distinctive human condition are the aesthetic and intellectual activities that bodies and brains make possible (cf. Farley 1990: 82).

able to the creation of humans as biohistorical creatures as were the biological and evolutionary advances that preceded our appearance on planet earth today. And this human history, with its eventual development of highly complex cultures, its diverse modes of social organization, and its exceedingly flexible and complex languages and behaviors, turns out to be the only context within which biological beings with self-consciousness, with great imaginative powers and creativity, and with freedom and responsible agency have appeared (cf. 44). In this holistic sense Kaufman can argue that in our distinctively human existence we are not only biological beings or animals but also biohistorical beings, beings shaped by both biological evolution and historical, cultural developments. But Kaufman wants to push even further in developing our embeddedness in biology and nature: it is precisely these biohistorical processes that have transformed our relationship to nature within which we have emerged. In the course of human history we have gained a "kind of transcendence" over nature unequaled by any form of life we know, and as such have transformed the face of the earth. Against this background Kaufman can define human uniqueness as our *historicity*, our being shaped decisively by an evolution and history that have given us power to shape future history in significant ways (cf. 45).

With this explicit focus on historicity and creativity Kaufman adds a valuable dimension, often implied in the work of other scholars who have developed the notion of humanness in terms of biocultural embodiedness. Kaufman has developed this central idea against the background of what he calls an "ongoing cosmic serendipitous creativity" (45f.) that manifests itself through various evolutionary trajectories over time. The evolutionary story of the human animal is a striking example of such an evolutionary trajectory; human existence, its purposiveness, its complexes of social/moral/cultural/religious values and meanings, its virtually unlimited imaginative powers and creativity, but also its horrible failures and horrendous evils, has come into being in the trajectory that finally led to beings with historicity. Another striking way to phrase this would be as follows: with the emergence of historical modes of beings, explicitly purposive or teleological patterns appeared on this planet as human intentions, consciousness, and actions began to become effective. Thus a "cosmic trajectory" gradually developed increasing directionality, ultimately creating a context within which deliberate purposive action could emerge and flourish (cf. 46).

Kaufman explicitly wants to relate our embeddedness in this evolutionary trajectory to our human responsibilities toward ecological concerns. What is unfortunate, however, is that he also sees the traditional Christian under-

standing of humans in relationship to God, so closely associated with the belief that humans are created in the image of God, as obscuring and diluting
ecological ways of thinking about our human place in the world (cf. 41). Not
only that, but he writes that the notion of the image of God has strongly influenced unfortunate and damaging traditional anthropological dualisms like
"body and soul (or spirit)," mind and matter, and those beings that are created
in the image of God and those that are not (cf. 47). This leads him beyond the
Christian tradition to retrieve from the history of human evolution a new holistic notion of humanness. As an interdisciplinary, strategic move, this has
proven to be a valuable moment in our rethinking of the notion of the image
of God. However, as I argued in chapter 3, the complex history of this concept
in Christian theology has clearly shown that there is really no possibility of
even talking about "being created in the image of God" in such a generic, abstract way. It is certainly true that damaging disembodied, dualistic, and oppressive interpretations of the *imago Dei* resulted from an excessive focus on
ideas of rationality, functionality, relationality, and futurity. Importantly, however, various biblical scholars, and theologians like Michael Welker, Robert
Jenson, Phyllis Bird, Wolfhart Pannenberg, and Philip Hefner, have all argued
that a more holistic idea of humanness can be revisioned, not by leaving the
rich and complex tradition of the *imago Dei* behind, but by rethinking this
very fluid notion within an interdisciplinary context, while at the same time
basing it on a responsible, interdisciplinary rereading of the original biblical
material.

At the heart of Kaufman's argument, of course, is his proposal for moving beyond the idea of God as a kind of "cosmic person" who should be im-
aged by human persons. He wants to move beyond the long and complex history of the notion of God as being or person to seeing God as the creativity
manifest throughout our cosmos. This creative activity, or more specifically
God as "serendipitous creativity" (cf. 53ff.), generates the web of life on our
planet earth, a serendipitous creativity we humans are deeply embedded in
and sustained by, and live through (cf. 48). This problematical move is motivated by the fact that God has traditionally been understood in personlike
terms, while we now know that agential personhood has emerged only fairly
recently in the history of our cosmos. Kaufman notes that, as far as we know,
personal agential beings did not exist, and could not have existed, before billions of years of cosmic evolution, and then further billions of years of biological evolution. Kaufman goes on to ask how we can today think of a personlike
creator God before and apart from the history of evolution (cf. 48).

This is not the place to ask about the compatibility of theistic notions of

God with the theory of evolution, but I do believe that Kaufman makes two very problematical moves here: first, his argument that the notion of personhood is a too recent concept to be taken seriously in light of the immense span of evolutionary history not only abstractly denies the place and role of the idea of God as person in the complex history of ideas in theology, but refutes his earlier claim for what it means for us humans to be embedded in biology and nature. For Kaufman it is precisely these biohistorical processes that have transformed our relationship to nature within which we have emerged. In the course of human history we have gained a "kind of transcendence" over nature unequaled by any form of life we know, and as such have transformed the face of the earth. Against this background, then, Kaufman could define human uniqueness as our *historicity.* If it is true that the biocultural process has transformed our relationship to nature, then the products of our cultural evolution (like our ideas of personhood, God, and humanness) cannot be definitively shaped by biological evolution. It thus becomes confusing why he would think that whatever happened in the vast trajectory of *natural* history before we humans arrived, could in any sense shape or determine whether, in the *cultural* evolution of ideas, we could use the idea of personhood for what we call "God."

Secondly, therefore, in terms of a postfoundationalist approach to interdisciplinary reflection, the idea that biological evolution may completely determine what may or may not be achieved on a cultural level reveals a serious interdisciplinary failure. If one were to take Kaufman seriously on this point, science (in this case biology) would be able to force theology not only to minimize the philosophical influences of its own history of ideas, but to push it beyond its own heritage (and disciplinary identity) from naming God in terms of the metaphors and symbols of its ancient tradition, to a post-Christian and generic, abstract notion of God, now resurfacing as "serendipitous creativity." Kaufman's very helpful vision of humans as embodied, biohistorical creatures, I believe, does not necessarily have to lead to this covert scientistic conclusion about possible ways for theologians to talk about God.

His idea that the metaphor of serendipitous creativity may help us to move beyond personal, anthropomorphic notions of God is therefore problematical. It is highly questionable whether all forms of anthropomorphism would be avoidable in the way that humans conceptualize God. In chapter 4 I discussed paleoanthropologist Ian Tattersall's valuable comments on this issue. He argued that it is ironically in our notions of God that we see our human condition most compactly reflected. Human beings, despite their unique associative mental abilities, are incapable of envisioning entities that lie outside their own experience or that cannot be construed from what they know of the material world. For Tattersall the notion of God is just such an entity. The contrast to Kaufman's argument is rather striking: even with our dramatic increase in knowledge about the unimaginably vast expanse of our universe, our concepts of God — even when expanded commensurately — remain resolutely anthropomorphic (cf. Tattersall 1998: 202). We continue to imagine God in our own image simply because, no matter how much we may pride ourselves in our capacity for abstract thought, we are unable to do otherwise. Importantly, however, this does *not* imply the illusory character or nonexistence of God, but might actually reveal the only intellectually satisfying way to talk about God if we wish to believe in a God with whom we can have a humanly comprehensible personal relationship. In Tattersall's words: we might do well to look on the inadequacy of our concepts of God as the truest mirror of those limitations that define our condition (203). Kaufman's option to reject the notion of personhood for God is therefore not the only option. From an interdisciplinary perspective, not only the notion of the *imago Dei* but also the notion of God itself could be revisioned and enriched in terms of contemporary understandings of personhood.[2]

In spite of my reservations regarding Kaufman's concept of God, his important contribution to a holistic understanding of human existence as biohistorical, shaped by both biological evolution and radical historicity, is of great significance for a refining of an understanding of embodied human existence. In his intriguing work *Dependent Rational Animals: Why Human Beings Need the Virtues* (1999), Alasdair MacIntyre has pushed the ideas of embodied being and species specificity even further by arguing why it is important for us also to understand what human beings have in common not only with other humans, but specifically also with members of other intelligent animal species. Although he never considers evolutionary epistemology directly, his position converges very closely with my argument in chapter 2, where I reasoned that it would be a serious mistake to think that the evolution of human cognition could be possible independent of human embodiment, and consequently, that one could conceive of an epistemology independently of biology. Only by also taking the history of our biological origins into account can we understand the kinds of abilities or dispositions that we see as fairly unique to humans.

Human embodiment has another serious implication, however, and directly points to our vulnerability as embodied beings. MacIntyre argues that

---

2. I am much indebted to Anna Case-Winters, and to Kevin Hector, for their insightful contributions to conversations about Gordon Kaufman's work. Cf. also Case-Winters n.d.

acknowledging this kind of embodiment is the only way to come to grips with the nature and extent of human vulnerability and disability as central features of human life. He understands this vulnerability in the broadest possible sense, but especially as a vulnerability to physical and mental dangers and harms, to bodily illness and injury, mental defect and disturbance, and human aggression and neglect (cf. MacIntyre 1999: xff.). What this implies further is a very particular dependence on others for protection and sustenance, something that in our species is most obvious in early childhood and old age. And it is exactly the facts of *vulnerability and affliction* and the related fact of *dependence* that he wants to take seriously as central to an understanding of the human condition (cf. 4). I believe this rich understanding of human embodiment, now broadened to include vulnerability, affliction, and dependence, will provide a challenging and all-important theological link to less abstract, more nuanced notions of human uniqueness in theology.

In chapter 3 I argued that precisely in theological anthropology, and even more specifically when we reflect on the meaning of the *imago Dei,* there often is a refusal to acknowledge adequately the bodily dimensions of our existence. Resonating closely with Edward Farley's views, MacIntyre argues persuasively that this refusal is deeply rooted in, and reinforced by, the extent to which we conceive of and imagine ourselves as other than animal, and as exempt from the hazardous condition of "mere" animality. The kind of cultural prejudice that divorces the human present from the human past often finds support in philosophical theories about what distinguishes members of our species from other species. MacIntyre's views now converge exactly with Farley's: we easily forget our bodies and think that our rationality as thinking beings is somehow independent of our animality, while in reality it is the thinking of one species of animal. For MacIntyre, then, in a specific reference to Merleau-Ponty, we have to recognize that we are our bodies (cf. 5f.). Human identity is primarily bodily, and therefore animal, identity. While acknowledging our animal nature and bodies, we must also realize that even when we transcend some of the limitations of our animal ancestors, we never completely separate ourselves from what we share with them. In fact, our ability to transcend those limitations depends in part on certain of those animal characteristics, among them the nature of our identity (cf. 8).

In my second chapter it became clear that what we have learned from Darwin is precisely that human history, in spite of unique human abilities like imagination, reason, and moral awareness, is the natural history of one more animal species. This fact should alert us to the dangers of a cultural tendency that is reinforced by too exclusive an attention to, and even an exaggeration of, those characteristics and propensities that do seem to define human species specificity and therefore distinguish human beings from members of other species. This is most problematical when a particular human capacity is selected and made the object of inquiry, like the capacity for rationality, which normally includes having thoughts, or beliefs, or the ability to act for reasons, or the power to frame and use concepts, and then often is tied directly to the use of language. For MacIntyre a focus on the embodied human condition really challenges the narrow claims of this position to define humanness. It would be a serious problem, for instance, to conclude that since animals do not have our kind of language ability, they obviously also lack the other capacities so closely linked to language (cf. 12). For MacIntyre an understanding of our intelligence, perception, and feelings would only be enhanced if philosophical attention is paid to the perceptions, feelings, and intelligent activities of certain nonhuman animal species too. Although he does not draw on paleontology or linguistics for this argument, I believe he is making an important philosophical point: we cannot deal with, or adequately understand, what is unique or different about human beings if we draw a single dividing line between humans on the one hand, and nonhuman animals on the other (cf. 13).

In fact, our ability to recognize and respond to prelinguistic signals from other human beings precisely enables us to recognize the intentions embodied in responses from other intelligent nonhuman animals, especially dolphins, which in his *Dependent Rational Animals* are of special significance to MacIntyre. Honed by evolution, our relevant responses and recognitions enable us to respond accurately to signals sent by other humans and nonhuman animals that are closely related to us on the evolutionary scale. In a very interesting way, then, MacIntyre seems to be extending my earlier argument for tentatively understanding our prehistoric ancestors, to understanding intelligent animals. In my fourth and fifth chapters I concluded that if we have inherited from the co-evolution of nature and culture a dependable framework of mind by which to credibly recognize the intentions of others, why would this cognitive and emotive ability let us down when we tried to relate to the material signals and symbolic messages communicated by our Paleolithic ancestors through paintings, carvings, and ritual practices? In fact, we are of exactly the same species as our Cro-Magnon ancestors, with the same symbolic minds and the same religious propensities. No wonder some of us feel compelled to interpret the cave paintings of the Upper Paleolithic as embodied expressions of the religious and aesthetic imagination of our direct, but distant, ancestors.

MacIntyre seems to be suggesting some form of pretheoretical, embodied, practical knowledge, a prelinguistic, almost instinctive knowing of how to interpret and read one another, a know-how that arises from a history of complex social interactions with others, in which our responses to them, and their responses to us, generate a recognition of the thoughts and feelings to which each is responding (cf. 14). In the relationship of human being to human being this is fairly uncontroversial. What MacIntyre is suggesting, however, is that there is no significant difference in the relationship of human beings to members of certain other animal species (cf. 15). This gives us a way of characterizing the kinds of interactive, interpretive experiences without which we would not be able to ascribe thoughts and feelings to others, whether human infants, dogs, or dolphins. Obviously these interpretive experiences are not the same in these different cases. The interpretive experiences through which we acquire these abilities are certainly honed by evolution, and are in a significant measure species-specific (cf. 18). MacIntyre has also argued that there is no obstacle to ascribing reasons for their actions to certain members of a nonhuman intelligent species, even if they do not possess the linguistic resources for articulating and uttering those reasons (cf. 12f.). What we do need to be able to identify, to ascribe reasons for action to the members of a different species (like dolphins), are a set of goods at the achievement of which the members of that species aim ("eating fish is among the goods of dolphin life": 25), a set of judgments about which actions are or are likely to be effective in achieving those goods, and a set of conditions that enable us to connect the goal-directedness and the judgments about effectiveness. MacIntyre can therefore conclude: so it is with humans and so it is also with dolphins (cf. 25). To this I would add, and so it also is with our prehistoric human ancestors, who are much closer to us than dolphins.

MacIntyre thus wants to reveal the fatal flaw of using, for instance, the language ability to create a rigid and absolute distinction between humans and intelligent animals. Heidegger did this by seeing all nonhuman animals in a homogenous way as *qualitatively other* than humans, and understanding them only *in contrast to* humans (cf. Heidegger 1995: 264; also MacIntyre 1999: 45). This allows a single sharp line to be drawn between human beings and members of all nonhuman species — the line drawn between those who possess language and those who do not. MacIntyre may be right, of course, but it is important to focus also on the important differences between language-possessing and non-language-possessing animals. What should not be obscured by the quest for human uniqueness, however, is the significance of the continuity and resemblances between some aspects of the intelligent activities of nonhuman animals and the language-informed practical rationality of human beings (cf. MacIntyre 1999: 50). I believe this is true irrespective of the actual evolutionary route and the timing of the evolution of language, which we examined in some detail in chapter 5. It is exactly the powerful expressive powers of animal communication through recognition, belief, and correction of belief, and by intentions carried out in communal action, that place in serious question any single sharp line between language users and those who do not use language. In fact, even if the evolution of language is our most powerful and distinctive adaptation as a species, it is still true that human language, and the language ability, ultimately is deeply embedded in the communicative structures of the prelinguistic history of our animal past.

MacIntyre also would affirm the important point that human distinctiveness, and the specificity of our species, is marked not merely by language, but also by the imaginative ability to put language to all kinds of reflective uses. This remarkable ability does distinguish us, but it does not remove from us what we share with other animal species. MacIntyre puts it well: our kinship to the dolphin and the chimpanzee is a kinship not only with the animality of the body, but also with respect to forms of life like the skills and social behaviors of our sister species in the animal world (58). Like dolphins and chimpanzees, we humans need social relationships to flourish. MacIntyre answers his original question, whether we can in some sense ascribe to members of other intelligent species goal-directed action, by arguing that we are right to ascribe to members of at least some of those species intentions and reasons for action, and also that in our own beginnings as rational agents we are very close to their condition, and that as such our identity remains an animal identity.

Human embodiment, however, has yet another serious implication: the only way we can come to grips with the nature and extent of human vulnerability and disability is through our embodied identity as human beings. This central feature of human life, with one important exception, has not been mentioned in any of the scientific discussions of human uniqueness so far. In my discussion of Rick Potts's work in chapter 5, it became clear that the human capacity for versatility and adaptability to a wide range of environmental conditions can rightly be seen as the "astonishing hallmark of modern humanity" (cf. Potts 1996; 2004). Against this background Potts could argue that human cultural behavior involves not only the transmission of nongenetic behavior, but also the coding of thoughts, sensations, things, times, and places that are not empirically available or visible. It is an argument from science that not only the material culture of prehistoric imagery as depicted in the spectacular cave "art" of France and Spain, but in fact the full range of all human imagination, the depths of human depravity, our distinctive moral awareness, our vulnerability and disability, and finally even our religious quest for ultimate meaning must all relate to the deeply human capacity for the symbolic coding of the "nonvisible." In fact, for Potts our concepts of God themselves follow from the ability to abstract and imaginatively conceive of personhood (cf. Potts 2004: 265f.).

The facts of vulnerability and affliction, the related fact of dependence on others, and the ambivalence of our moral natures should also be taken seriously as central to the embodied human condition, and should be added to the interdisciplinary discussion of human uniqueness by theology and philosophy. Moreover, I believe that this more holistic understanding of human embodiment will provide an all-important theological link to less abstract, more nuanced notions of understanding human uniqueness in theology. An important discussion of some of these themes, this time from a social scientific viewpoint, is found in Christian Smith's recent *Moral, Believing Animals: Human Personhood and Culture* (2003). In this work Smith has similarly stressed human animality, but he also argues that human beings have a peculiar set of capacities and propensities that distinguishes them significantly from other animals on this planet. But what is it about being human that makes this crucial difference? Smith argues that despite the vast differences in humanity between diverse cultures and across history, and no matter how differently people narrate their lives and histories, there does seem to emerge an underlying structure of human personhood that helps to order human culture and history, and our narration of it. Drawing on various interdisciplinary resources, Smith argues that humans are animals with an inescapable moral and spiritual dimension. This is a very specific focus on moral awareness as an intrinsic feature of the distinctively human mind, and in arguing that we humans cannot avoid a fundamental moral orientation to life, Smith resonates closely with the positions of MacIntyre and Farley. He also argues that, in addition, this moral orientation of all human beings is intellectually embedded in broader paradigms of thought, which more often than not function as sacred narratives. In this sense, then, humans are "moral, believing animals" whose lives, actions, and institutions are constituted, motivated, and governed by narrative traditions and moral orders on which they inescapably depend.

When I refer to "human nature" or "the human condition" in this final chapter, I certainly do not want to imply any essentialist claim about what it might mean for us to be human beings. As we have seen throughout these lectures, there is no single trait or characteristic that adequately captures the notion of human uniqueness. However, there is also no point in denying that we human beings do share an identifiable and peculiar set of capacities and propensities that clearly distinguishes us from other animals on this planet. My interdisciplinary approach, then, attempts a descriptive anthropology of human personhood that might help us understand, and reveal, the theological relevance of our own species specificity. For Smith, as a social scientist, the most adequate approach to theorizing human culture is a normative one that conceives of humans as moral, believing animals and of human social and cultural life as consisting of moral orders that constitute and direct social action. If Smith is right about this, then exactly this point, however much concealed in the mists of prehistory, could be claimed to be true of our earliest human ancestors too. In fact, precisely because our Cro-Magnon ancestors, in a biological and anthropological sense, were undeniably *us*, I would argue that we cannot understand their nature and behavior unless we presuppose the same moral dimension to their prehistoric beliefs and actions. Human culture always implies moral order, and human persons are inescapably moral agents (cf. Christian Smith 2003: 7). Human actions and behaviors, as well as those of our remote ancestors, are therefore necessarily morally constituted and propelled practices. And this is the dimension of the human condition that is difficult, if not impossible, for the sciences to grasp and include in a comprehensive understanding of human nature. It thus becomes clear that neither anthropological nor scientific explanations as such can exhaust the religious dimensions of human existence. For the interdisciplinary theologian, in fact, they point toward the need for fuller theological explanations (cf. Shults 2003: 91f.).

Therefore, what would certainly have to be true also for our Paleolithic ancestors is that one of the most central and fundamental motivations for human action is to act out and sustain moral order, which helps constitute, directs, and makes significant human life itself. Human persons nearly universally live in social worlds that are thickly webbed with moral assumptions, beliefs, commitments, and obligations. The relational ties that hold human lives together are glued together with moral premises, convictions, and obligations. In this sense Smith is correct: there is no way to be human except through moral order (cf. Christian Smith 2003: 8).[3] Human animals are moral animals in that we possess a capacity and propensity unique among all animals: we have not only desires, beliefs, and feelings, but also the ability to form strong evaluations about our desires, beliefs, and feelings that hold the potential to actually transform them (cf. 9). Humans, for instance, have the ability

3. Smith defines "moral" as an orientation toward understandings about what is right and wrong, good and bad, worthy and unworthy, just and unjust, that are not established by our actual desires, decisions, or preferences, but are believed to exist apart from them, providing standards by which our desires, decisions, and preferences can themselves be judged (cf. Christian Smith 2003: 8).

not only to hate, but also to judge that our hatreds are wrong, and to decide that we do not want to be hateful anymore. As far as human personhood is concerned, the consciousness and self-consciousness that place moral belief at the center of human action also give rise to capacities for human creativity and discrimination that help to constitute human persons as active subjects with agency (cf. 28). As self-conscious animals, we are able to "step back" from and develop alternative and creative perspectives on moral orders and institutions.[4] We are therefore able to consider critically, to evaluate, and to judge. For as moral and believing animals, humans are also necessarily *creative* and *discriminating* animals that find themselves with sufficient (but not absolute) "distance" in consciousness from both their own selves and that around them that is not their selves, a distance that enables them to exercise their wills in the making of meaningful choices about the moral order or orders to which they will commit their lives (cf. 28).

For Smith the question now is, what is it about humans as moral animals that makes them unique among all other animals? Christians, of course, would answer that humans are uniquely moral animals because they are made "in the image" of a personal, moral God, who created them uniquely to reflect, know, and obey God (cf. 33). Others will say that humans are moral animals because of the relatively large brains their species acquired through evolutionary history, which are therefore neurologically capable of depths and complexities of evaluation and emotion unavailable to smaller-brained animals. On my point of view, both views incorporate important truths and should connect transversally to complement one another on different levels. As humans, then, we are morally aware beings because humans are not only conscious creatures but also self-conscious creatures. In our moral awareness as embedded in self-consciousness is found the source for our uniqueness, for our understanding life in rational and moral terms (cf. also O'Hear 2002: 49ff.). We are indeed self-conscious animals, and as such we not only have experiences, pleasures,

---

4. Smith has argued against confusing this deeper sense of morality with something like "altruism," and against reducing morality to "altruism" (as a willingness to sacrifice one's own interest for the welfare of others). Altruism, among humans at least, is a particular attitudinal and behavioral expression of a certain kind of moral commitment that becomes relevant in specific situations within systems of moral order. Morality, as argued for by Smith, is much bigger, thicker, and more complex than mere altruism. There are all kinds of moral beliefs, judgments, and actions that are not particularly altruistic. One's actions can be normatively directed in many ways without being self-sacrificial. To suppose, then, that taking morality seriously essentially means a closer attention to altruism, both unrealistically raises the bar on, and drastically narrows the range of, what might count as moral (cf. Christian Smith 2003: 14f.).

pains, and beliefs, but we are also aware that we have them. Humans are unique among animals because they are uniquely self-conscious animals. This self-consciousness gives rise to reflective distances between the self and its cognitions, emotions, and desires. And those epistemic distances provoke the quest for standards above and beyond the self's cognitions, emotions, and desires by which they might be evaluated as worthy of thinking, feeling, and believing or not. Therefore humans are moral animals not primarily because morality serves some instrumental interest. Rather, humans are moral animals because they experience, in part as a result of their self-consciousness, a particular relationship to themselves and the world that evokes a search for standards beyond themselves by which they may evaluate themselves (cf. Christian Smith 2003: 34).

Against this background one should ask: What is religion, and what do we mean when we say people are religious? Smith correctly argues that we should not be thinking about religion in essentialist terms, as if we were positivist scientists discovering the natural laws of religion (cf. 96). Religions could rather be seen as sets of beliefs, symbols, and practices about the reality of superempirical orders that make claims to organize and guide human life (cf. 98). In this sense religion is not always about belief in the supernatural or only about things considered sacred. Smith correctly finds the concept of the supernatural too confining for interpreting religion, for humans treat many things in life as sacred that are arguably not very religious. Rather, religions are moral orders rooted in beliefs about superempirical realities (cf. 105).

Smith develops further his model of the moral, believing animals by focusing on what he has called the centrality of human transcendent consciousness. Moral, believing animals are the kinds of creatures about whom it is not odd to think that they would develop beliefs, symbols, and practices about the reality of a superempirical order that makes claims to organize and guide human life. Humans, therefore, must look beyond themselves for sources of moral order that are understood as not established by their own desires, decision, or preferences, but are instead believed to exist apart from them, providing standards by which their desires, decision, and preferences themselves can be judged. As believing animals, human faith in superempirical orders that make claims to organize and guide human life is not categorically different from the fundamental and continual acts of presupposing and believing all the other assumptions and ideas that make the living of life even possible (cf. 118f.).

Smith's argument for the centrality of moral awareness and the openness to religious fulfillment as ultimately defining human uniqueness clearly intersects with and enhances Wolfhart Pannenberg's theological arguments (chap. 3) and Alasdair MacIntyre's philosophical arguments for human uniqueness. It also converges with my earlier arguments for the naturalness, rationality, and plausibility of religious belief, as supported by evolutionary epistemology and paleoanthropology. Moreover, in this sense one can indeed argue that for humans to be religious is epistemologically in continuity with the living of the ordinary human life as a whole. In this sense it would be "normal, natural, and rational" to be religious, and although it will never succeed as an argument for the existence of God, on this view the human condition and the character of religion quite naturally fit, cohere, complement, and reinforce each other (cf. 153).

Human Uniqueness in the Jewish Tradition

Before we return to Edward Farley's view of human nature and ask how that might move us forward theologically on the issue of human uniqueness, I would like to ask what would be revealed about human uniqueness theologically if we looked more closely at another faith tradition, Judaism, with which Christians share deep historical, textual, and theological roots. Religions and theologies, of course, have always formed an important framework in which to search for and formulate answers to questions about human nature, human destiny, suffering, and evil. In Western civilization Christianity still provides an important source of meaning for many of us, even though the centuries-old cultural monopoly of Christianity is certainly under increasing pressure today. The fact is, even on an issue like the doctrine of the *imago Dei,* Christianity, and the history of Christian theology, does not provide a uniform system of answers, as was clearly shown by the pluriformity of the changing Christian viewpoints discussed in lecture 3.

In that lecture I worked with a theory of traditions that enabled me not only to trace the complex history of ideas behind the notion of the *imago Dei,* but also to go back to the classical Genesis texts to establish whether there is some continuity to this crucial theological tradition, some canonical meaning that reaches back through history to connect us to its distant origins. I now want to argue that our notion of human uniqueness will be enriched precisely if we return also to a parallel faith tradition that is closely connected to the origins of Christianity, and with whom Christians share the classical *imago Dei* texts. Moreover, Judaism has also been part of what we call Western civilization for centuries now, and its often-threatened existence not only reminds one of the origins of the Christian religion, but also reveals profound and fundamentally different views on the idea of humans being created in the image of God (cf. Kemp 2002: 613). Clearly, whatever we see as the deepest theological meaning of being human, of being created in the image of God, and, I would add, therefore, as human uniqueness, directly relates to how we deal with questions of evil and suffering. For this reason alone, any attempt to define the meaning of the *imago Dei* in Christian theology would also have to ask about its meaning in classical Judaism, and for contemporary Jewish thinkers (cf. 614).

One way of capturing what Jewish theology is about in a broad sense, is to realize that in it doctrine and life are inextricably linked, and everything, including doctrine, is about living life (cf. 620). Theology in Judaism is not just about knowledge, but constitutes a living interaction of worship, the gathering of knowledge, and conscientious moral accountability for all human acts. In Judaism the Torah has always been an object of study; it is both perfect and perpetually unfinished, and was created more as a process than as a complete system. In Marcel Kemp's words, the Torah is both a complete whole and an eternal source of new interpretations, because it has been given to humans with a view toward *acting*, which actually moves humans and creation toward fulfillment (cf. 620).

Within the Jewish tradition there also is no unanimity about the explanation of the central words of Genesis 1:26a, *tselem* (image) and *demut* (likeness), although this text is normally read against the background of Psalm 8:

> What are human beings that you are mindful of them,
>   mortals that you care for them?
> Yet you have made them a little lower than God,
>   and crowned them with glory and honor.
> You have given them dominion over the works of your hands.
>
> (vv. 4-6 NRSV)

In fear of speaking of God too anthropomorphically, the word *tselem* is treated with great reticence. But the fact that Genesis 1 nevertheless describes humans as made in God's image has been a continuous source of reflection for the rabbis. They normally use this idea to strongly underline the sacredness and irreplaceable value of each individual human (cf. 620). The idea is also seen in the broader context of the imitation of God, the *imitatio Dei*. Here the knowledge that we are created in God's image brings with it the obligation to show oneself worthy of God's love by acting in accordance with that love. So, being made in God's image generally means having the capacity to act like God by thinking, planning, and formulating intentions. On this broader view the *imago Dei* stands for humankind's rational capacity to grasp the order of creation and to imitate God's creative work (cf. 621).

Many rabbis also believed that God's image can be found in humankind's intellectual abilities, an idea also put forward by Jewish scholars like Philo, and later by Moses Maimonides. The latter states in his *Guide for the Perplexed* that "a man's distinction consists in a property which no other creature on earth possesses, viz. intellectual perception. . . . On this account, i.e., on account of the Divine intellect with which man has been endowed, he is said to have been made in the form and likeness of the Almighty." A little later he speaks of Adam's "great perfection which is the peculiarity of man, viz., the power of distinguishing between good and evil, the noblest of all the faculties of our nature, the essential characteristic of the human race" (Maimonides 1919: 14f.).

In his other major work, *Mishneh Torah,* he refers to the vocation of being holy like the Eternal One. Besides emphasizing the value and dignity of each individual, *imago Dei* also refers to the vocation of thinking and acting in accordance with him whose image the individual bears. However, the likeness between humankind and God consists more of an *analogia actionis* than of an *analogia entis* (cf. Kemp 2002: 185ff., 621). In the tradition so strongly influenced by Maimonides, there emerges a clear theological focus on the dual aspect of humankind: humans are inclined to both good and evil. But the interest is not first of all in the abstract origin of evil and of suffering, but more in ways to deal with the facts of life and the reality of suffering. By using suffering to achieve active moral renewal, the sufferer guards himself or herself against feelings of despair and impotence. This way of answering leads the person away from irrational forces that destroy life and focuses energy on using the freedom that remains the person's inherent possession. Kemp defines this classical Jewish position well: the human person cannot escape from the utter contingency and tragedies of human reality, but is challenged by the *imago Dei* that gives it its dignity not to just resign itself to fate, but to face and challenge it, and to thus change it to destiny (cf. 623).

An important twentieth-century Jewish voice was Martin Buber, who famously developed a highly personalistic "I-Thou" relationship as the focus of the truly lived life, and who also influenced Karl Barth significantly. Most important for my argument, though, are the ideas of the Jewish scholar Abraham Heschel. Heschel's theology was totally shaped by the fact that he escaped the horrors of the Holocaust while so many of his relatives and friends did not. In his famous speech "No Religion Is an Island," he stated: "I am a brand plucked from the fire [Zech. 3:2; Amos 4:11] in which my people was burned to death. I am a brand plucked from the fire of an altar of Satan on which millions of human lives were exterminated to evil's greater glory, and on which so much else was consumed: the divine image of so many human beings . . ." (Heschel 1991: 3).

This vivid and powerful image not only typifies Heschel's highly contextual and embodied theology, but it also strikingly supports my earlier and postfoundationalist warning against the danger of generic overabstraction in dealing with human uniqueness in theology: a theology not embedded in the experience of embodied faith runs the risk of distorting the reality of those experiences and even losing them in the process of translation from situation to conceptualization. For Heschel it was inconceivable that we would formulate and debate theological and philosophical issues while oblivious to, and alienated from, the experiences or insights that account for our raising those issues in the first place (cf. Heschel 1965: 2).

The idea that humans are created in the image of God was central to Heschel's thought, and he considered human dignity ultimately defined only by the fact that we humans are created in the image of God. For Heschel this led directly to one important question: How should a human being, created in the image of God, think, feel, and act? This was not however the problem of how to be good; it was the crucial question of how to be *holy* (cf. Heschel 1985: xxxi). Holiness was a crucial and central concept in Heschel's thought. It not only pointed to the absolute uniqueness of each and every human being as image of God, but also led to a dimension deeper than the dichotomy of good and evil: the biblical answer to evil is not the good but the holy, which raises us to a higher level of existence, where we are ultimately not alone when confronted with evil (cf. Kemp 2002: 243).

As created in the image of God, we humans are relational beings, and we are therefore needed, precious, and irreplaceable. The fact that Heschel referred so directly to the divine image of so many human beings who were destroyed in the Holocaust clearly shows how central the notion of the *imago Dei* was in his thought. Importantly for Heschel, therefore, in the biblical creation story, unlike in the Gilgamesh epic, the central question is not how the human being can escape death and become immortal, but rather how life can be made holy. Image and likeness do not lead to immortality, but to holiness (cf. Kemp 2002: 244). This notion of holiness is crucial for Heschel's understanding of human uniqueness: human beings are the only entities in nature with which sanctity in this specific sense is associated. All other sacred objects in space are made holy by humans. Human life is the only type of being that we consider intrinsically sacred, the only type of being we regard as supremely valuable (cf. Heschel 1965: 33).

For Heschel the image of God is not found in some Promethean "spark of the divine fire," or in some eternal spirit or soul, but in the whole human being, body and soul, the embodied human being. In fact, the image of God is not found *in* humans, but the image *is* the human. This also explains why for Heschel the *imago Dei* and the *imitatio Dei* are so directly related: to be created in God's image means that we can also act like God, and so attain holiness. In the end our human deeds can be sources for holiness. From this it should also be clear why Heschel would strongly contrast the biblical notion of God with the notion of God in classical theism, which for him implied going back to an idea of God as first cause, an a-pathetic and unmoved mover. For Heschel God has pathos, a pathos we are called to imitate (cf. Heschel 1962: 88f.).

It is clear that Heschel's ideas are infused with the classical rabbinical view that each human life is unique, irreplaceable, and above all holy. This human holiness is not just one of our human characteristics, but defines our capacity for *imitatio Dei* and for acting like God. Heschel regards our relational deeds, directed at other people, as sources of holiness: since our deeds are directed at others, and since we are the bearers of God's image, these deeds are considered to be directed at God as the Eternal One. Heschel thus regards God's compassion with humankind, as described by the prophets, as an inexhaustible source of respect, surprise, and awareness of the vocation of acting like him. God searches for us even before we are aware of this ourselves. This makes a human being who is restlessly searching for meaning by definition a bearer of meaning in fulfilling the human destiny to be in God's image.

With regard to his views on good and evil, the focus on the deed as the human contribution toward redemption of creation is crucial for Heschel. Implied here is a process of character education that holds that crisis is always an opportunity. Experiencing loss, illness, and suffering entails a challenge to transcend individual situations determined by fate, by now acting like God, that is, by the holiness of the deed. This also implies that suffering demands not primarily an *explanation* but an *answer* (cf. Kemp 2002: 626). I would phrase this important insight as follows: leading the life of the *imago Dei* implies living in the context of giving and endorsing meaning. This is why Heschel's reaction to the horrors of the Holocaust and his people burning to death on Satan's altar is so profoundly stirring: not only were the lives of millions of people destroyed on this altar, but also the divine image of as many human beings. This is also why Heschel could famously state: "A person is not just a specimen of the species called *Homo sapiens*. He is all of humanity in one. . . . The human is a disclosure of the divine. . . . To meet a human being is an opportunity to sense the image of God, the presence of God" (cf. Heschel 1991: 7f.).

Heschel clearly believed that to ask about human uniqueness is to seek to identify what is unique about the humanity of ourselves, and this is a task that goes beyond the scope of the sciences. In this sense human uniqueness is not just about human nature, but about what we as humans do with our nature (cf. Heschel 1965: 9). To ask about human uniqueness is to ask about which modes of being characterize the uniqueness of being human, what constitutes human existence, and what situations and sensibilities necessarily belong to being human (cf. 11). Heschel's embodied and highly contextual approach to anthropological issues clearly shines through when he argues that to talk about human nature or human uniqueness means to talk about myself as well as other selves. In other words, the subject I ask about is exceedingly close to me: I not only perceive it, but I am it (cf. 18). Against this background Heschel was not so puzzled by our closeness to animals, or by our animality. In asking the question about human nature, our problem is not the undeniable fact of its animality but rather the enigma of what human beings do, because of and in spite of, and apart from, their animality. The human being is a peculiar be-ing trying to understand its own uniqueness. And what Heschel thought we should be trying to understand was not first of all our animality, but our hu-manity (cf. 21). In this sense one could argue that the search for human origins is incomplete without the quest for human destiny. For Heschel, then, our question should never just be "what is the unique nature of the human spe-cies," but rather "what is the situation of the human individual." What is hu-man about a human being (cf. 28f.)? The exclamation of the psalmist, "I am fearfully and wonderfully made" (Ps. 139:14), expresses the sense of wonder we should feel at the mystery of our own existence. There is a depth of personal existence that cannot be fully illumined, that eludes our generalizations (cf. 31).

Heschel's understanding of the human condition and of relationality clearly challenges all baroque abstractions of human nature that are discon-nected from our physical bodies. It is futile and impossible to ponder human beings in general, since my understanding of, and my relation to, my own be-ing always intrudes into any reflection about *Homo sapiens*. Furthermore, in meeting another person I come upon familiarity: there are agreement of be-ing, a concurring of existence, a self beholding a self. I see what I am.

Looking at myself from the perspective of society or thinking compara-tively, I am an average person. Facing myself intimately, immediately, I re-gard myself as unique, as exceedingly precious, not to be exchanged for anything else. I would not like my existence to be a total waste, an utter ab-surdity. No one will live my life for me, no one will think my thoughts for me or dream my dreams. My own being, placed as it is in the midst of many beings, is not simply being here too, being around, being part of the environment. It is at the very center of my consciousness that I am distinct. (34f.)

With these words Heschel expressed what he saw as the most important ingredient of self-reflection: the preciousness of one's own existence. To my own heart my existence is unique, unprecedented, priceless, exceedingly pre-cious, and I resist the thought of gambling away its meaning. My existence as an event is an original, not a copy. No two human beings are alike. This kind of uniqueness goes hand in hand with the capacity to create novel events and meaning (cf. 35ff.). At exactly this point we find a remarkable transversal link to arguments made in my fourth and fifth lectures. If being human implies the unique ability to create symbolic meaning, and if our Paleolithic ancestors were indeed fully human, then we can also assume the following about these ancestors: the dimension of meaning is irrevocably indigenous to being hu-man. Our Cro-Magnon ancestors could not have been fully human without having the symbolic capacity to exist in a dimension of meaning. From within his historical context Heschel articulated it as follows, and in his own striking way: "The secret of being human is care for meaning. Man is not his own meaning, and if the essence of being human is concern for transcendent being, then man's secret lies in openness to transcendence, and openness to transcen-dence is a constitutive element of being human" (cf. 66).

As I will argue later, Heschel's ideas stunningly resonate with those of Emmanuel Levinas: for Heschel a human being, unique in this embodied sense, does not only have a body, it also has an embodied face. A face cannot be grafted and interchanged. A face is a message — it speaks — and as such is a living mixture of mystery and meaning. This most-exposed part of the body, the best known, is also the least describable, a synonym for an incarnation of uniqueness. This dramatically illustrates that the human face for Heschel first of all represents our total and complete embodiment as a unique physical event, and only then acquires a deeper metaphorical meaning for human relationality (cf. 38f.).

In a passionate plea for an embodied, concrete vision of human uniqueness, Heschel has argued that the human condition is vulnerable,[5] and is disclosed only in the thick of living, and in this very real sense the human deed is the distillation of the human self (cf. 94). We thus find our true human nature not in abstract self-consciousness, but in the reality of human living. Being human therefore is an act, not a thing, and its chief characteristic is not being, but what is done responsibly with being. By whatever we do, by every act we carry out, we either advance or obstruct the drama of redemption, and either reduce or enhance the power of evil (cf. 119). Against this background it is eminently clear what Heschel meant when he argued that humankind can no longer return to pure animality, and has long ago become a species sui generis, although biologically speaking we honor the deep ties to our animal past. Heschel's conclusion here is as profound as it is shocking: in *Homo sapiens* the opposite of humanness is not animality, but the demonic (cf. 101).

Heschel's important body of work illustrates the wealth of the Jewish tradition as far as the nature of the human person and the reality of good, evil, and suffering are concerned. In this case a theological anthropology was presented not as a set of abstract, philosophically tinted explanations, but as individual answers given for radically historical, contextual situations, displaying a surprisingly realistic view of the fundamental dual structure of human existence (cf. Kemp 2002: 628). *Methodologically,* I believe Heschel presents us with a highly postfoundationalist move over against many of the exotically baroque Christian abstractions that I dealt with in chapter 3. *Theologically,* Heschel's embodied view of the *imago Dei* strengthens those voices in contemporary Christian theology that are arguing against ephemeral abstract notions of what it means to be human. And in both these senses, I believe, the often neglected Jewish tradition can again become a powerful resource for Christian theological anthropology.

Human Uniqueness and the Limits of Interdisciplinarity

Edward Farley sets out to give a broad and comprehensive account of the biological or embodied dimension of the human condition, and his views on our embodied existence seem to converge quite specifically with those of Gordon Kaufman, Abraham Heschel, and Alasdair MacIntyre. Farley develops the

5. "Outwardly Homo sapiens may pretend to be satisfied and strong; inwardly he is poor, needy, vulnerable, always on the verge of misery, prone to suffer mentally and physically. Scratch his skin and you come upon bereavement, affliction, uncertainty, fear, and pain" (Heschel 1965: 51).

complexity of human distinctiveness by carefully defining the fact of being human as a multidimensional existence in three facets, namely, human individuality, relationality,[6] and the social. "Human reality" is the comprehensive term for the human form of life in which the three spheres of agency, relation, and the social converge. "Human condition" is the term for the same thing when approached from the perspective of its tragic situation and its encroachment by evil and redemption (cf. Farley 1990: xv).

By itself the human (biological) condition is neither good nor evil, but rather a set of capacities and tendencies that are the basis of, and are incorporated into, the distinctive experiencing life of human beings, that is, into language, embodiment, and ways of being spatial, social, and temporal. It is also the heritage of human phylogeny that makes possible everything from language to personhood, but carries with it also vulnerability and the possibility of extreme suffering. At the level of the biological we can speak of the vulnerability of the individual or species in a limiting or dangerous environment. As we shall see, Farley wants to go further and focus on the defining tragic nature of all human existence. To call the human condition "tragic" requires the personal dimension of full humanness, in other words, transcendence, but it still is never disconnected from the perils and vulnerabilities of the organic life we are embodied in (cf. 96).

It is precisely our embodied, biologically shaped individual existence that also facilitates the specificity of personal identity[7] and of transcendence. Farley's definition of human transcendence comes very close to my minimal definition of human uniqueness: we have the unique ability to understand features about ourselves; we can reflect on our desires, failures, and accomplishments, and weigh the outcomes of our actions. Human transcendence is this capacity to exist self-consciously in the face of discerned possibilities and to respond to situations in the light of what is discerned. Transcendence, then, defines the heart and the very possibility of being human and is what makes us moral, cognitive, and aesthetic agents (cf. 69). This ties in closely with the fact that, as human beings, our lived, temporal spaces have a very definite center, namely, our embodied selves. As personal agents we neither are bodies nor do we possess bodies. Whatever we say about our transcendence or consciousness, it is an embodied transcendence or consciousness that exists in the world in bodily relations and activities. And Farley's rather striking words here are reminiscent of the views of the evolutionary epistemologists we discussed in

6. Which Farley calls the *interhuman* (cf. 1990: xv).
7. Farley calls this specificity of personal existence *determinacy;* cf. 1990: 68.

my second chapter: our embodied selves are fields of initiating activities whose operations are our way of experiencing and relating to the world (cf. 71).

Most important theologically, however, is that dimension of humanness that Farley calls *the vulnerability of the personal being.* Here Farley's views converge strongly with those of Heschel and MacIntyre: vulnerability is the aspect of a living being that makes it able to be harmed and able to experience that harm in some form of suffering (cf. 72f.). Our vulnerability as human beings is complex precisely because we are multidimensional beings. As organic beings we are vulnerable to physical injury, disease, pain, and death. As social beings we are vulnerable to social incompatibility, social suffering, and oppressive social systems. We are vulnerable to the experience of suffering in very distinctive ways because we are personal, self-aware beings (cf. 72ff.).

The central vision of Farley's work aims at understanding how human evil and good arise in relation to these tragically structured spheres, with the reality of evil always meaning human evil.[8] Farley does not want to approach this issue as a systematic theologian, but in a truly pluralist, interdisciplinary way he sees his project on the human condition as crossing the borders that demarcate the theological disciplines. In this sense it has as much to do with ethics and moral theology as with systematic and philosophical theology, pastoral theology and psychology (cf. xvii). In a move that directly affects the interdisciplinary nature of his project, he first affirms the strong Jewish heritage of the Christian faith, but then also believes that the Christian movement neither reversed nor significantly altered the vision of evil and redemption of the Hebrew texts. Ultimately he wants to move beyond the specificity of a Christian interpretation and argues that the paradigm he is presenting will be more generally available and accessible than it would be if approached exclusively from a Christian position (cf. xviii).

In his attempt to focus on human distinctiveness, Farley highlights those enduring features that make up the human condition in everyday lived experience. To do this he has to move beyond those theologies that proceed so totally inside the circle of a privileged discourse, logic, or community that they are released from all broader, interdisciplinary criteria. In fact, to say that human evil and redemption can be understood without any use of philosophy, biology, sociology, linguistics, or psychology is tantamount to saying that human beings need no bodies, selves, societies, or discourse for understanding evil

8. Also see Farley 1990: xvi n. 4, where Farley explains his views regarding theological anthropology, and how his concept is related to the way Charles Hodge, Reinhold Niebuhr, and Wolfhart Pannenberg have broadened the notion of theological anthropology.

and redemptive change (cf. xxi). In this postfoundationalist move Farley is clearly consistent with his earlier focus on the embodied human being. The question is whether the options for the theologian here are really limited to either isolated, particularist theologies or post-Christian, secular theology. As I argued in my first chapter, a truly postfoundationalist theology offers a third option, that of retaining the specificity of contextual, theological integrity while at the same time reaching out in interdisciplinary discourse. The question that now emerges for Farley's proposal is whether his vision for human distinctiveness as an embodied human condition is helped or hindered by his move to a more generic, abstract, post-Christian theology.

I believe that in focusing on the enduring features of human reality, i.e., on the relational, the social, and the personal, Farley presents us with a powerful view of human uniqueness. He also successfully argues why these features are not abstract, unhistorical, or a-contextual universals, but are paradigmatic of the human condition that describes and illumines what is actually happening in the everyday worlds of human beings (cf. 2). It is in this sense, for Farley, that the primary symbol systems of the world faiths relate directly to recurring and typical features of our condition as it is tragically structured, and is finally open to redemptive change. The enduring features of human reality are therefore not so much unhistorical essences as they are features of a life-form that has endured over a very long biohistorical period (cf. 4). For Farley precisely a theological analysis would reveal how these features are receptive to, and the bearers of, evil and redemption, and as such are theologically relevant. The three spheres of human reality are interconnected, and as such describe the human way of existing in the world, or what Farley has called the human form of life (cf. 8). These features of the human condition describe characteristic powers or capacities of the lived human life, including the capacity to undergo and perpetrate evil and good. On this point Farley also provides us with an intriguing transversal link to my question about what would enable us to plausibly speculate about, or relate to, our Cro-Magnon ancestors: although the enduring features of human reality can never be seen as unhistorical essences, the features of human nature are so generically human that they would apply equally to archaic and postarchaic human beings (cf. 9). I think Farley is correct in arguing that we can assume that these distinctive human features were part of the makeup of our earliest *Homo sapiens* ancestors.

This is why it is important to understand clearly what Farley means by "the human condition." The term does not so much describe a collection of the features of human nature, as it describes how we humans respond and react to situations and contexts that evoke typical human reactions (cf. 27). Farley is correct in seeing this as requiring a distinctly interdisciplinary move: the problem of the human condition is intrinsically broader than the problems of specific sciences and specific disciplines. In fact, human condition is a category of experience and has to do with things we are perennially aware of, things that evoke our ongoing responses and deep postures, like suffering, relations with others, uncertainty about our futures, and death (cf. 27). In describing the features of human reality Farley argues that, aside from the dimensions of good and evil, the tragic is the most general and unifying feature of our human condition. The term "tragic" here refers to the vulnerability revealed in the typical human situation in which the conditions of well-being are interdependent with situations of limitation, frustration, challenge, and suffering. In this sense the human condition is not tragic simply because suffering is an aspect of it; it's tragic because sufferings of various sorts are necessary conditions of creativity, affection, and the experience of beauty (cf. 29). In this sense the human condition is ultimately defined by human transcendence, which is fundamentally shaped by the realities of tragedy, beauty, and creativity.

In unpacking the three spheres of human reality, the relational, the social, and individual agency, Farley develops strikingly similar notions to those of Heschel. This shines through in Farley's idea that the individual human agent has several dimensions of existence; while each of the three spheres of the human condition is interrelated and a necessary precondition for the other two, the relational or interhuman is primary to the other two spheres, in that it engenders the criterion for them. Borrowing from Levinas, and with shades of Heschel, Farley calls this criterion *the face* (cf. 190f., 280ff.). The idea that the deeply embodied, interhuman dimension of relationality is of primary importance for understanding human consciousness was an important theme in the work of Jean-Paul Sartre. Sartre argued that it is exactly through embodied self-consciousness that the human self looks for recognition as a self from other selves. Resonating closely with Heschel's and Levinas's notion of the "face," Sartre introduced the central concept of the "look" or "gaze": it is the look of another self-conscious being that makes me conscious of my own self, and at the same time conscious of the self who is not me (cf. Sartre 1956: 346f.). In being looked at by another, or gazed at, my self-consciousness is stirred acutely, but in such a way that I simultaneously realize the self-consciousness of the one who is looking at me. And in being seen by the other, I am jolted into a sharper level of self-consciousness than before (cf. O'Hear 2002: 118ff.). However, as Levinas has argued, for Sartre the encounter with the face of the other threatens my freedom, because it means that my freedom is now under the gaze of another freedom (Levinas 1969: 303).

For Levinas, however, to approach the face of the other is to put into question precisely my own freedom, and in that sense there is an essential normativity, or ethical exigency, in the face of the other, and it is the vulnerable face of the other that summons us to compassionate obligation (cf. 187ff., 207). Our "face" is therefore that depth of us that is exposed in the interpersonal sphere. It is our call to the other, our own vulnerable beauty. On Farley's interpretation it is also in the "communities of the face" that we work to overcome evil in each of the human spheres of existence (Farley 1990: 280f.; cf. also Tilley 1992: 2). Farley thus provides us with a nuanced and provocative account of human life as embodied and passionate, enhanced by virtues proper to each sphere and fractured by vices infecting all of them. Moreover, in each sphere of vulnerable human life Farley distinguishes the tragic from the evil. The tragic is a necessary human condition, but human evil is the sin-laden intensification of the tragic, rooted in idolatry (cf. Tilley 1992: 2). But Farley stops short of taking this powerful concept of embodied human uniqueness back into the contours of a specific contextual and particularist Christian theology.

For Farley it is in all the dimensions or spheres of human existence that we experience a gap between our strivings for fulfillment and our delimiting realizations. Thus the tragic dimension of human existence is not a product of sin, but a necessary and natural consequence of human existence. *Sin* occurs when we refuse to accept our finitude, and instead of living in reference to the ultimate horizon that alone can give meaning to our lives, we absolutize penultimate referents and allow evil to take over our lives. When this happens, we practice idolatry in the individual agential sphere, alienation in the relational sphere, and subjugation in the social sphere (cf. Tripole 2001: 569).

Toward the end of this book the newly redeemed "community of the face," like the *ecclesia* of the Christian faith, becomes the distinctive social and historical mediator for the whole redemptive process. In this way "communities of the face" effect redemption for all of human reality (cf. Taylor 1992: 576). Through the power of the face the redeeming presence of the divine, which in some sense must be personal, is sensed and experienced most of all in the relational, interhuman sphere. Redemption in the full sense tends, however, to be more an eschatological hope than an actual reality, and serves to bring the three different spheres of human reality together because of the humanizing element it brings to all three (cf. Carpenter 1992: 2).

In concluding this section, it is appropriate to ask what we have learned from Heschel and Farley about human uniqueness, and how well they grade out on interdisciplinarity in their respective theologies. We'll take Heschel first. On the first issue, a theological perspective of human uniqueness, it quickly became clear that Heschel's highly contextual and embodied approach to human uniqueness strikingly intersects with my own postfoundationalist caution against generic overabstraction in theology: a theology that does not find itself embedded in the experience of embodied faith runs the risk of distorting the reality of those experiences and even losing them in the process of translation from situation to conceptualization. For Heschel it was inconceivable that we would formulate and debate a theological and philosophical issue like human nature while oblivious to, and alienated from, the experiences or the insights that account for our raising those issues in the first place (cf. Heschel 1965: 2).

On the second question, how these scholars' approaches measure up against the challenge of my notion of interdisciplinarity, it is quickly and strikingly apparent how successful this methodology is. Heschel, of course, does not use contemporary philosophical categories for interdisciplinary dialogue, but his work on embodied human existence exhibits a total openness to scientific perspectives on human nature. More important is his implicit respect for the limitations of disciplinary boundaries. Heschel was deeply convinced that for a philosopher and theologian to ask about our humanity is to go beyond the scope of the sciences. His work is totally open to appropriate scientific perspectives on our embodied existence, while also demonstrating effectively the limitations of interdisciplinarity by drawing a clear line between science and theology on this very specific issue of the image of God.

By respecting the boundaries of the scientific approach, Heschel offers a comprehensive theological proposal about ultimate meaning in life, a proposal that by definition could not have come from any of the sciences. His work thus becomes a striking example of how asymmetrical reasoning strategies like theology and the sciences can intersect transversally on a carefully identified issue like human embodiment. Beyond this transversal moment, however, theology also offers a more comprehensive, complementary perspective on the deeper philosophical/theological meaning of what it means to be human. For such a concrete proposal from theology, there is no blueprint for how science should or could respond. On a postfoundationalist view, whether the theological perspective will be accepted as meaningful and enriching, or as irrelevant and speculative, will in the end depend on the specific scientist and his or her worldview.

Heschel's work illustrates the wealth of the Jewish tradition as far as the nature of the human person and the reality of good, evil, and suffering are concerned. His anthropology is not presented as philosophically tinted explanations but as an individual, personal answer given for radically historical, contextual situations, displaying a surprisingly realistic view of the fundamental dual structure of embodied human existence (cf. Kemp 2002: 628). At the same time, his philosophical and theological struggle with the reality of the *imago Dei* exemplifies nuanced interdisciplinarity, and qualifies as a highly postfoundationalist move over against the theoretical vagueness of many flamboyant Christian abstractions.

Farley's position on human uniqueness and on interdisciplinarity is more ambiguous. On the issues of human embodiment and human distinctiveness, his approach is quintessentially interdisciplinary. His thesis is that the condition of human persons, whatever else it is, is first of all the condition of living animals (cf. Farley 1990: 79). This clearly implies that our human specificity is the specificity of a species, and that our evolutionarily developed bodies are the bearers of human uniqueness. But when he develops a theology that would reach beyond isolated, particularist theologies, he ironically fails to meet the standards of a postfoundationalist, interdisciplinary approach. What Farley has gained by so specifically arguing for human embodiment and the concrete characteristics of the human condition now seems lost to a nonparticularist, abstract "metaphysics of the face." He has a highly contextual and concrete view of human nature, but the generic post-Christian theology that emerges does not even attempt to embed this embodied human and the human condition into the concrete particularity of a specific religion or lived religious faith.

The contrast to Heschel here is quite significant, and we find ourselves with an abstract, generic theology floating free from precisely the stark human realities of vulnerability, tragedy, and evil that his theology wants to address. In my first lecture I argued for a postfoundationalist theology that very consciously retains its embeddedness in disciplinary identity, even as it reaches out to other domains of discourse in interdisciplinary reflection. From a specifically Christian point of view, Farley could be criticized for, on the one hand, positioning himself within the Hebrew-Christian paradigm, while on the other hand discarding all critical elements from the Christian tradition, including the metaphors of sin and salvation. This leaves no room for the crucial contextuality and particularity of incarnation, crucifixion, and resurrection. In spite of a rich embodied anthropology, what is denied is a Christian view of the *imago Dei* and of redemption, and the result is a theology so generic and abstract that there is no Christ, no sin, no salvation, and no eschatology. In fact, the Christian viewpoint emerges as utterly undistinctive (cf. Tripole 2001: 569), and the heart of a Christian interpretation of the *imago Dei* is lost in translation.

Ironically, Farley's purpose was to show how the Hebrew-Christian paradigm of good and evil, or sin and redemption, illumines the human condition in its experiences of the tragic, of evil, and of liberation. In this radically interdisciplinary work, Farley did ingeniously explore the inner workings of human beings, using a creative, transversal blending of categories borrowed from psychology, sociobiology, linguistics, and philosophy. He is, however, less successful in maintaining the contextual integrity of the Christian paradigm (cf. 569), and from a postfoundationalist point of view this directly affects the credibility of his interdisciplinary approach. What was brilliantly gained in terms of human embodiment and concreteness was eventually lost with an abstract theology that floats above this concrete embodiment, and above the distinctive context of his own discipline.

Conclusion

In these lectures I have argued that Lord Gifford's charge of "promoting, advancing, teaching and diffusing the study of Natural Theology in the widest sense of the term"[9] can be deconstructed to reveal two important themes that reach out to us transversally across time. The first is a philosophical challenge to engage in what we would call a form of multidisciplinary thinking that may actually lead to quite specific interdisciplinary insights; and the second is a clear and unambiguous theological statement on the uniqueness of our human species, which can be optimally understood only in terms of our broader relationship to the universe and to God. What I have set out to do in these lectures is to see if there is a way that the heart of the Christian tradition of the *imago Dei* can be recovered and revisioned through an interdisciplinary dialogue with current scientific (specifically paleoanthropological) views on human uniqueness. For the Christian theologian, as became clear in chapter 3, this at the same time is the question of how to conceive of the power of canonical texts to author human identity effectively and creatively, and for the contemporary theologian to define human uniqueness imaginatively but responsibly. This clearly raised the question of the negotiability of the canonical boundaries of a crucially important doctrine like the *imago Dei*. It also, as became clear in our discussion of the work of Abraham Heschel and Edward Farley, raises the important question as to the possibilities, but also specific limitations, of a very concrete interdisciplinary dialogue between theology and the sciences.

9. Cf. *Lord Gifford's Will*, in Jaki 1986: 72, 74.

What we have certainly learned from this interdisciplinary research project is that we should not underestimate the transversal capacity of a tradition to absorb novelty and author new forms of understanding in cross-disciplinary conversation. We have also learned from the transversal nature of postfoundationalist reasoning that it is no longer possible to see theological reflection as an activity in which we can still follow universal rules for understanding. Not only is there no way of returning to modernity's notion of universal rationality, as we saw in chapter 1, but for an interdisciplinary theology there is no return possible to a premodern notion of tradition as a repository of privileged data and specially protected, exclusive criteria. My argument for interdisciplinarity has been precisely about the fact that Christian theology, as quintessentially public theology, should be answerable to canons of inquiry defensible within, and across, the various domains of our common discourse. And in this open, interdisciplinary dialogue we have learned that criteria for human uniqueness, whether in theology or the sciences, can never be the sole possession of one discipline, or be exclusively shaped by one disciplinary perspective only. Because of the transversal rationality of interdisciplinary discourse, not only shared interests and common concerns but also criteria from other reasoning strategies can be appropriated, precisely to enrich and enhance our understanding of that which has been identified as an interdisciplinary problem. As for the interdisciplinary problem of human uniqueness, this has certainly proved to be one way in which a multidisciplinary approach can lead to interdisciplinary results when we discover that criteria not only overlap, but can ultimately be shared in reasoning strategies as diverse as theology and science. Clearly, if no criteria are acceptable beyond the boundaries of a discipline, then the giving of reasons for arguments beyond the boundaries of that discipline would become impossible. If, however, there are interdisciplinary criteria, even if just limited to that brief but shared transversal overlap between disciplines, then a carefully demarcated interdisciplinary dialogue becomes possible. And in this interdisciplinary dialogue, our accountability for the giving of reasons, the providing of warrants for our views, becomes a cross-disciplinary obligation.

In chapter 1 I argued that:

1. A multidimensional or interdisciplinary understanding of rationality should enable us to move away from abstract, overgeneralized models or blueprints for doing interdisciplinary work, and specifically for engaging in the dialogue between Christian theology and the sciences. This should enable us to focus on developing, first contextually, then transversally,

the merits of each concrete interdisciplinary problem in terms of the very specific science or theology involved. In exactly this sense I have argued that an awareness of the radical social and historical contextuality of our rational reflection should always imply that the rather vague terms "theology and science" should be replaced by a focus on specific theologians who are trying to develop very specific kinds of theologies, and who are attempting to enter into disciplinary dialogue with very specific scientists working within the disciplinary context of specified sciences on clearly defined, shared problems or even research trajectories.

2. A postfoundationalist approach to interdisciplinary problems helps us to understand that we are rational agents situated in the rich, narrative texture of our social practices and traditions, and that our self-awareness and self-conceptions are indispensable starting points for interdisciplinary dialogue. Precisely because we are so embedded in the narrative structure of our social practices and traditions, the overall patterns of our experience reach back transversally in time to experiential patterns, contexts, and traditions of the past. It is against this background that I have argued for the epistemic importance of thinking of social context in terms of the very diverse research traditions in theology and the sciences. What this means in real-life interdisciplinary conversations is that our embeddedness in cultural and other traditions in a sense is unavoidable. A specific research tradition, however, is unavoidable only as a starting point, and never as a final destination. On this view a postfoundationalist approach helps to realize that we are not intellectual prisoners of our contexts or traditions, but are epistemically empowered to cross contextual, cultural, and disciplinary boundaries to explore critically the theories, meanings, and beliefs that we and others construct of our worlds.

3. As members of specific epistemic communities who would like to plausibly claim some form of expertise in our various fields of inquiry, we hope to discover in disciplines other than our own, clues, challenges, criteria, or other forms of persuasive evidence that will help us push the limits of our own disciplines. This forms the challenge at the heart of all interdisciplinary reflection: standing within specific research traditions, we may realize that a particular tradition may generate questions *that cannot be resolved by its own resources alone.* It is exactly this kind of interdisciplinary awareness, also and especially for the problem of human uniqueness, that should lead theologians to reach out for rational support to other disciplines. This is the reason why I have argued that, in theology at least, the "twilight zone of abstraction" is avoided only when

we realize that a crucially important notion like human uniqueness can no longer be discussed within the generalized terminology of a disciplinary metanarrative that ignores the sociohistorical context of the scientist(s) or theologian(s) who should be invited into this interdisciplinary space.

4. In this interdisciplinary case study on human uniqueness, I have argued for a revisioning of theology's public voice, and for the clearing of an interdisciplinary space where not only the diverse and pluralist forms of theological reflection but also important voices from the sciences might explore possible overlapping epistemological patterns as well as shared problems in ongoing interdisciplinary conversation. A postfoundationalist notion of rationality enables us to communicate across disciplinary boundaries, to move transversally from disciplinary context to disciplinary context, from one discipline to another. The tentative and shared mutual understanding we achieve through this I have named, following others, a wide reflective equilibrium. It is in this fragile, communal understanding that we may discover the strengths and limitations of interdisciplinary dialogue.

*   *   *

In chapter 2 I raised the troublesome question: How should theology respond to the way the sciences are challenging, and even deconstructing, notions of human uniqueness? Would any Christian theology that ventures forth bravely into interdisciplinary dialogue still in the end be able to maintain, for instance, that there is some deeper, divine purpose to being human, and by implication, also to human evolution? My answer to these and related questions has unfolded against the background of the theory of traditions developed briefly in the first chapter. As a starting point for my conversation with the sciences on human uniqueness, I focused on Charles Darwin and his profound influence on the notion of human nature in science. In my second chapter I argued that his understanding of human identity still functions as the canonical core of the ongoing discourse on human evolution, and that the powerful galaxy of meaning of these Darwinian views is also shaping our views of the evolution of human cognition. Darwin saw imagination as one of the "highest prerogatives of man," closely connected to our religious sensibilities, which he also thought were universal in all humans. But of all the faculties of the human mind, he saw reason and linguistic abilities at the summit, closely connected with our moral sense, which perhaps should be seen as the "highest distinction between man and the lower animals" (Darwin 1981: 106). The epistemic implications of these views on reason, imagination, consciousness, language ability, and moral awareness are, I believe, most clearly represented today in contemporary evolutionary epistemology. Arguments from evolutionary epistemology demonstrated the plausibility and importance of distinctions between biological and cultural evolution for the problem of human uniqueness, and how this issue is directly related to the problem of human origins. Furthermore, evolutionary epistemology clearly showed that the human propensity for metaphysical and religious beliefs should be seen as the result of specific interactions between early humans and their lifeworlds. In addition, it became very clear that the fact that theology has traditionally virtually ignored the question of the evolution of human cognition has not only added to the widespread estrangement between evolutionary views and many forms of Christian theology, but also reinforced esoteric, disembodied, and overly abstract notions of human uniqueness in much of contemporary theology.

Against this background I argued in chapter 2 that:

1. The primary hominid adaptation, in the sense of a true evolutionary innovation that established the uniqueness of our species, was bipedalism. Closely connected to this evolutionary fact are the increase in brain size, the development of technologies, and the eventual evolution of language. We humans are indeed "unique," as even Darwin would phrase it, as a result of our "superior" intellectual abilities and social habits. Even for Darwin, however, our "wonderful advancement" was ultimately dependent on the unique evolution of language. I have argued that Darwin's conception of the evolution of human cognition and language, of our powers of observation, memory, curiosity, imagination, reason, and moral sense, still functions as the canonical core of the ongoing discourse on human evolution. Moreover, Darwin's views on the evolution of human distinctiveness are still powerfully shaping current views on the evolution of human cognition, and the epistemic implications of these latter views are powerfully represented in some contemporary forms of evolutionary epistemology.

2. The focus of evolutionary epistemologists on the evolution of human cognition reveals cognition as the mediator between biology and culture, and in so doing sets the stage, as it were, for the all-important role of paleoanthropology in the wider debate about human origins.

3. Some evolutionary epistemologists have importantly argued that the study of human evolution can therefore clarify the preconditions of cul-

tural evolution, but that it cannot explain the particular paths a culture (or cultures) will take. In addition, one of the most crucial claims of evolutionary epistemology is that, not only has evolution produced cognitive phenomena, but evolution itself can be described as a cognition process, or more precisely a cognition-gaining process. This obviously implies that knowledge, and the ability for knowledge, is an information-processing procedure that would increase an organism's fitness.

4. It would be hard to imagine Darwin not agreeing with the idea that without cognition there would be no survival. For this reason the focus of evolutionary epistemologists on the fact that our interpreted experiences and expectations play a central role in the process of the evolution of knowledge is of extraordinary interdisciplinary significance and also all-important for my own postfoundationalist approach. I have argued that our expectations are always based on interpreted experiences, and that these experiences lead to new expectations. Evolutionary epistemology helps us to understand this epistemic connection as the result of long-term evolutionary processes.

5. Evolutionary epistemology thus reveals evolution as a holistic, belief-gaining process. On this view it becomes clear that all our beliefs, also our religious beliefs, have distant evolutionary origins and were established by mechanisms working reliably in the world(s) of our ancestors, even if on a broader cultural level our beliefs and convictions are not always explained by biological factors. This approach is validated by an important distinction between two levels of evolutionary epistemology: that of a natural history or biology of knowledge, and that of evolutionary epistemology as a metatheory for explaining the development of ideas, scientific theories, and religious views. On this evolutionary epistemological view we humans are, first of all, embodied beings, and as such what we do, think, and feel is conditioned by the materiality of our embodiment.

6. Evolutionary epistemology also explains why there is a "naturalness" to religious imagination and the human quest for meaning. Religious awareness, with its intimations of human limitations and our very human disposition to try to overcome these limitations, mirrors rather precisely our nature as reflective thinkers. In fact, when considering the crucial nonadaptive, cultural aspects of human cognition, we can argue that defining human characteristics like human knowledge, moral awareness, aesthetic appreciation, religious awareness, etc., in a sense transcend our biological origins. In this sense evolutionary epistemology helps us to understand that the study of human evolution clarifies the biological

preconditions of cultural evolution, but it cannot explain the particular paths that human culture will take through rational knowledge, moral awareness, aesthetic appreciation, and our religious disposition.

7. Even when some evolutionary epistemologists ultimately reject the value, significance, or realist claims of religion and religious belief, evolutionary epistemology still helps us understand that precisely because every human society has possessed religion of some sort, complete with origin myths that claim to explain the relationships of humans to the world around them, religious belief cannot be discounted from any discussion of those early human behaviors that we today regard as unique. This claim has turned out to be of crucial importance for this study of human uniqueness: if human cognition is the important link between biology and culture, and if only through paleoanthropology we can come to a fuller understanding of the cognitive capacities of our earliest human ancestors, then in the Upper Paleolithic some of our earliest ancestors met a challenge and confronted it through the formation of myth and ritual, and the spectacular material legacy of prehistoric cave paintings in southwestern France and the Basque Country in northern Spain.

8. If the origin of the human mind is closely tied to the kind of cognitive fluidity that includes symbolic and mythical dimensions, then the origins of our cognitive behavior are not fully understood unless we also take seriously the origins of religious behavior. On this view the prehistory of the human mind points to the naturalness of religions, and supports the broader argument for the rationality and plausibility of religious belief. For the theologian engaged in interdisciplinary dialogue, this will not provide any argument for the existence of God, but the naturalness of religious belief might give more credibility to the way theologians express themselves in more contextual ways when presupposing the reality of God within the disciplinary boundaries of theology itself.

*   *   *

In chapter 3 I turned to the notion of human uniqueness in theology and argued, first of all, that the history of ideas of Christian theological reflection clearly shows that theological traditions have always been extremely sensitive to the culture(s) in which they are embedded. I also argued that the rich history of notions of human uniqueness in theology suggests that the best way to get at this problem is by looking at how theological traditions, specifically the doctrine of the *imago Dei,* have evolved and responded to cultural pressure.

Since the sciences influence our cultural views of human origins and human nature so much today, this specific case study on human uniqueness developed by exploring the possibilities of transversal intersections between theology and paleoanthropology. Now we have to ask what kind of dialogue resulted, and what kinds of challenges were revealed as we uncovered shared concerns and overlapping interests between these very diverse reasoning strategies. We already know that the important notion of the *imago Dei* represents something at the very heart of the Christian tradition, but we also know that as a complex set of theological minitheories the *imago Dei* tradition never had an unchanging identity. However, I do believe that much of the distinctiveness of this canon, as embedded in the rich and shifting galaxy of meaning of this historical doctrine, ultimately is protected by its own gravitational pull, i.e., by the historical core of its original textual and theological identity. But we also know now that the core of the notion of human uniqueness in theology can turn out to be fluid and changing, so what would be the limits and boundaries that this galaxy of meaning would allow? Finally, and maybe most importantly, in our pursuit of the intelligibility and integrity of the doctrine of the *imago Dei,* is theology helped, or hindered, by ever increasing interdisciplinary voices from the sciences?

To arrive at some plausible answers to these questions, it will be helpful to briefly look back on the complex mosaic of meanings that has emerged from theology, and from the sciences, in the many attempts to define what is meant by human uniqueness. In my third chapter, interesting and very specific patterns were revealed in the evolving history of ideas of the notion of human uniqueness in Christian theology.

1. A careful analysis of Genesis 1:26-28 revealed that these verses recognize the primal human symbolically as the first human and as the significant forerunner of humanity, but more importantly as the link that defines the relationship between God and humanity. Against this background every human is created in the image of God, and these ancient texts are clear expressions of the uniqueness of human beings as walking representations of God on earth. In this ancient creation story we humans are seen as the culminating achievement of God: alone of all creatures, we are said to be made in God's image and invited into a personal relationship with God. In this very theological sense, then, we are indeed "alone in the world." In chapter 4 this biblical perspective would contrast strikingly with paleoanthropological views on human uniqueness where the idea of being alone in the world unambiguously points to the fact that we humans are the last of the hominids on this planet.

2. When considered within the rich context of other Genesis texts (3:22; 9:1-7) and Psalm 8, the notion of the human as the *imago Dei* emerges with a deeper and more sinister second meaning: humans are revealed as not only "crowned in glory," but as also deeply distorted, affected by hostility, affliction, arrogance, ruthlessness, and cunning, and inescapably caught between good and evil. In the Old Testament texts the first humans emerge as real-life, embodied persons of flesh and blood, and within the holism of Hebrew anthropology the notion of the *imago Dei* finally and strikingly functions as a hologram where the original image is visible from certain perspectives, but from others the reality of sin and evil is revealed and the tragic dimensions of human existence dominate. This is also the reason why I argued that the "image of God" texts are not only powerfully interactive with one another, but have to be linked directly to Genesis 3:22. There the image of God, theologically at least, achieves an enigmatic and ambiguous new level of meaning, when in addition to the original created likeness, "knowing good and evil," a "falling upwards" into moral awareness (cf. Peterson 2003: 179), emerges as a new and profound way of imaging God.

3. In the New Testament the image of God is tied directly to Jesus Christ. Moreover, Jesus so absolutely preempts the role of the image of God that the vocation and destiny of human beings can be realized only through a redemptive transformation of their spirit. In the long history of theological thought, the notion of the *imago Dei* has had a mosaic, checkered history. Sometimes it expressed important dimensions of the original ancient texts, and sometimes it soared free from the deepest intentions of these texts as it progressively evolved from substantive interpretations that highlighted reason, intellect, and rationality; functionalist interpretations that expressed our tasks as humans to be God's stewards on earth; androcentric interpretations that ignored the role and place of women; existentialist or relational interpretations that focused on our relationship with God and with one another; trinitarian notions that claimed to ground this relationality; and eschatological notions that focused on our openness to others and on the proleptic destiny of our finally becoming the image of God in the arrival of God's future.

4. In my critique of these many interpretations of the *imago Dei* in the history of Christianity, I tried to highlight the continuity of the core ideas of this central Christian doctrine and how they functioned as the gravitational pull of this powerful tradition. At the same time, I tried to show how we were lured into the "twilight zone of abstraction" where unem-

bodied theological notions of human uniqueness floated above body and nature in exotically baroque, overly abstract, metaphysical speculations. I also argued, however, that exciting recent developments in theological anthropology point to a retrieval of the earthy, embodied dimensions of humanness that we encountered in the ancient texts. In a striking image Robert Jenson sees *Homo sapiens* as the praying animal, and Adam and Eve as the first hominid group that, in whatever form of religion or language, by ritual action were embodied before God. On this view Christian theology is liberated from the obligation to stipulate morphological characteristics that would absolutely distinguish prehumans from humans in the process of evolutionary succession (cf. Jenson 1999: 59). In Philip Hefner's work the human being, as a product of biocultural evolution, emerges within natural evolutionary processes as a symbiosis of genes and culture, as a fully embodied being, as God's created cocreator (cf. Hefner 1993: 277). In Phyllis Bird's and Michael Welker's writings there is a very conscious move away from theological abstraction toward seeing the *imago Dei* in a highly contextualized, embodied sense that respects the sexual differentiation between men and women, even as they exercise responsible care and multiply and spread over the earth (cf. Welker 1999: 68).

5. It also became clear how easy it would be to criticize the notion of the *imago Dei* for missing the powerful thrust it should have had toward justice, human rights, and especially issues of sexism and heterosexism. In my brief historical overview of the history of the idea of the image of God, we saw that already in Calvin's work there was a strong suggestion that the image of God has important ethical implications, directly requiring human justice and mercy. For a number of theologians our "human uniqueness" is powerfully exemplified by the fact that we image God concretely in our love for others, and for the world for which we are responsible. This crucial idea was developed further in the work of Richard Middleton where, instead of the traditional picture of the *imago Dei* as a mirror reflecting God, this canonical notion emerges as a prism refracting God's presence through a multitude of sociocultural responsibilities and activities. For Middleton the *imago Dei* correctly implies an ethic of interhuman relationships and ecological practice, an idea powerfully resonating with George Newlands's argument for the radical ethical dimension of all interdisciplinary work in theology and science. Newlands ultimately roots ethics in the liberating character of the *imago Dei*, and rightly claims that an ethics of care implies care for, and solidarity

with, the marginalized at a fundamental, interdisciplinary level. Thus conceived, the *imago Dei* points to reconciliation, justice, and liberation; the issue of human rights is strikingly revealed to be at the very heart of any discussion of the *imago Dei*.

*   *   *

The most important aspect of my interdisciplinary conversation with the sciences on human uniqueness was my attempt to establish transversal links with those sciences that deal directly with human origins, i.e., paleoanthropology and archeology. In chapters 4 and 5 we saw that those characteristics that make us really human, i.e., language, self-awareness, moral awareness, consciousness, symbolic propensities, ritual and mythology, are precisely the characteristics that are the least visible in the prehistoric record. What is available to us for interpretation, however, is some of the most spectacular and earliest material evidence of symbolic behavior in humans, the Paleolithic cave paintings from France and the Basque Country in northern Spain, all painted toward the end of the last Ice Age. Various scholars have argued that the explicitly symbolic behavior of our Cro-Magnon ancestors should be seen as the hallmark of the behavioral transition from the Middle to the Upper Paleolithic in western Europe. This spectacular cave art, along with portable art, personal ornamentation, and the design and form of advanced stone tools, reflects the newly arrived human symbolic component that in time would define what it means to be human. To these highly embodied traits of human distinctiveness can be added a small number of other unique characteristics; *Homo sapiens* is the only surviving member of the family Hominidae, and in terms of this species specificity we certainly are "alone in the world." As such we are committed to bipedalism and have relatively large brains with the most complex neocortex of all primates. We are also identified by the unique presence of a spoken language; the remarkable cognitive fluidity to think, reason, plan, and generate mental symbols, especially as expressed in art and religion; and the bizarre inability to sustain prolonged bouts of boredom.

In chapters 4 and 5 I argued that:

1. There are remarkable methodological links between a postfoundationalist approach in theology and some of the most important methodological voices in contemporary paleoanthropology. This is one of the most important reasons why paleoanthropology, by focusing on human origins and modern human behavior, can intersect transversally with argu-

ments in theology and create a space for enhancing significantly theological notions of human uniqueness. Especially important in the current discussion are arguments for more local and contextual approaches to the interpretation of Paleolithic imagery. The archeological record reveals the past as a complex mosaic rather than just a linear trajectory, and in such a more holistic approach scientists take location and context absolutely seriously. It is also precisely these more contextual approaches that resonate with my postfoundationalist approach to interdisciplinary discourse.

2. Exactly this kind of holistic approach has shown that, before the remarkable transition of the Upper Paleolithic in western Europe, modern human behavior was appearing piecemeal in Africa as a stepwise progression and gradual assembling of the modern human adaptation. But the Upper Paleolithic evidence in southwestern Europe is still distinguished by a remarkable efflorescence of modern, symbolic, and aesthetic behavior, and in this sense we are still warranted to talk about a "creative explosion" of prehistoric imagery as exemplified by the famous cave paintings that I discussed in chapters 4 and 5. And scientists are right: it took the world a long time to acknowledge cave paintings and prehistoric imagery as a true cultural and aesthetic achievement. Thanks to this spectacular imagery, however, we are invited to "sail upstream" toward our remote origins as a species, and try to understand what it means that *Homo sapiens* have always lived in a dimension of meaning. Although we will never know, and should be careful not to project our own ideas onto these ethereal images, I have argued that there are good reasons for thinking that these paintings, drawings, and etchings could have functioned as links between what our Cro-Magnon ancestors saw as the "natural" and "supernatural" worlds. And this has opened up the possibility of shamanistic interpretations for at least some of the Paleolithic "art."

3. Moreover, if there are plausible arguments for the symbolic or even just tentative religious meaning of some of these paintings, then this symbolic heritage of our distant ancestors may reveal something about the emergence of the earliest forms of religion, and thus support the argument for the naturalness of religious faith. Therefore, even if we are not certain what exactly the spectacular cave paintings meant to the people who made them, it is clear that this prehistoric "art" reflected a view of their place in the world and a body of mythology, now all but vanished, that explained that place in the world. Clearly, in Upper Paleolithic "art" we are dealing with something that sets us apart from

all other animals, and even from our closest human ancestors. For some scientists, notably David Lewis-Williams and Jean Clottes, recent neuropsychological research on altered states of consciousness provides the principal access that we have to the mental and religious life of the people who lived in western Europe during the Upper Paleolithic. On this view some of the Upper Paleolithic imagery, similar to the later rock art of the south African San, demonstrates clearly how the universal aspects of shamanism are expressed quite contextually within specific local, cultural communities.

4. The fact that human uniqueness emerges in paleoanthropology as a highly contextualized and embodied notion, where the symbolizing minds of our distant ancestors are stunningly and physically revealed in prehistoric cave "art," also explains why paleoanthropologists, like evolutionary epistemologists, have linked the emergence of consciousness and of symbolic behavior directly to the emergence of religious awareness. These convergent arguments are strengthened by recent contextualized arguments for linking shamanistic explanations to the possible meaning and religious dimensions of prehistoric imagery. In chapter 5 I develop some of these central ideas on human uniqueness further, and I discuss the fact that precisely the imagination, productivity, and creativity that we associate with humans are very much a product of language. The majority view in the sciences today is that language, universal among humans, is the most evident of all uniquely human abilities. Language both permits and requires the ability to produce symbols in the cognitively fluid human mind, which can then be reshuffled and organized by the generative capacity that seems to be truly unique to our species. This also enables that most telling quality of our human consciousness and self-awareness — *inner experience,* the filter through which we view and interpret the world around us. On this view we can conclude that this capacity for self-awareness and consciousness, inextricably linked to our linguistic capacities, is our most conspicuously human characteristic.

5. In fact, some paleoanthropologists have argued that symbolic behavior should be seen as part and parcel of turning communication into language. Even more importantly, though, only a creature that already possessed a fully developed language could have used symbols separate from language, as in the famous imagery from the Upper Paleolithic. This idea was developed further by Terrence Deacon in his argument that we are the only species to have evolved the ability to communicate symbolically. Having symbolic minds, therefore, includes biologically unprecedented

ways of experiencing and understanding the world, from aesthetic experience to spiritual contemplation. Precisely the symbolic nature of *Homo sapiens* reveals language as our most distinctive human adaptation, and of crucial importance for the origins of moral and spiritual capacities. This is also the reason why mystical or religious inclinations can be regarded as an essentially universal attribute of human culture. In fact, for Deacon it is precisely this symbolic capacity that distinguishes humans from other species, and in this sense one could then say that the capacity for embodied spiritual experience can be understood as an emergent consequence of the symbolic transfiguration of cognition and emotions. In an important sense, therefore, the quest for meaning in prehistory is not only about the remote past, but it directly concerns our images of ourselves and what we today see as our distinctive humanness.

*   *   *

In chapter 6 I argued that in the work of Gordon Kaufman, Christian Smith, Abraham Heschel, Edward Farley, and Alasdair MacIntyre the theme of human embodiment has been even more powerfully developed in ways that enhance and complement what was earlier argued by theologians Jenson, Hefner, Bird, and Welker (chap. 3), as well as arguments for embodied human uniqueness by a significant group of contemporary paleoanthropologists, archeologists, and neuroscientists (chaps. 4 and 5). In this final chapter it becomes crystal clear that in Farley's interdisciplinary argument human uniqueness can never be defined as an abstract, intellectual, or spiritual capacity, because our embodied existence directly implies that our human specificity is the specificity of a species. And, for both Farley and MacIntyre, whatever our degree of difference from other animals may be, it is *our evolutionarily developed bodies* that are the bearers of human uniqueness, and it is this embodied existence that confronts us with the realities of vulnerability and affliction. For Heschel, exactly this vulnerability is deeply embedded in our bodily existence. For this reason the image of God is not found in some intellectual or spiritual capacity, but in the whole embodied human being, "body and soul." In fact, the image of God is not found *in* humans, but *is* the human, and for this reason *imago Dei* can be read only as *imitatio Dei:* to be created in God's image means we should act like God, and so attain holiness by caring for others and for the world.

What we find in the work of these scholars is a rediscovery of the meaning of embodiment for theological anthropology, and the beginnings of a revisioning of notions of human uniqueness and the *imago Dei* that resonate powerfully not only with the embodied, flesh-and-blood primal humans we encounter in the Genesis texts, but also with the embodied symbolic minds of our prehistoric ancestors, who in a burst of creativity and imagination left for us a spectacular material heritage in the cave paintings of the Upper Paleolithic. What can Christian theology now learn from these interdisciplinary insights gained from the sciences on the evolution of human uniqueness, and what happens if we connect transversally these conclusions about theological notions of human uniqueness with some of the results gleaned from the sciences on human uniqueness?

1. At the very least a serious interdisciplinary conversation with the sciences should inspire the theologian to revisit the way our construction of notions of the *imago Dei* is always deeply embedded in culture. This is why, in my third chapter, I analyzed and evaluated historical and contemporary interpretations of human uniqueness in theology. I argued there that the question of human identity or uniqueness in the biblical texts is ineluctably tied to the complex history of the notion of the *imago Dei*. But theologians are now also challenged to move beyond the disciplinary domain of theological reflection, and challenged, as we connect transversally with the science of paleoanthropology, to rethink what human uniqueness might mean for the human person, a being that has emerged biologically as a center of embodied self-awareness, consciousness, personal identity, and moral responsibility. Personhood, when richly reconceived in terms of imagination, symbolic propensities, and cognitive fluidity, may enable theology also to revision its notion of the *imago Dei* as a concept that acknowledges our close ties to our sister species in the animal world while at the same time challenging us to rethink our own species specificity, and in that sense our difference from other species, and what our symbolic and cognitively fluid minds might tell us about the emergence of the typically human propensity for religious awareness and experience. The emergence of this kind of mental complexity resonates with, and deeply enriches, theology's deepest convictions about human uniqueness and opens up arguments for the plausibility of a theological redescription of a phenomenon like the emergence of the human mind. After all, our ability to respond religiously to ultimate questions in worship and prayer is deeply embedded in our species' symbolic, imaginative nature.

2. This brings me to what I see as probably the most important interdisci-

plinary result of the multidisciplinary conversation between theology and paleoanthropology: if scientific contributions to understanding the issue of human uniqueness are taken seriously, the theological notion of the *imago Dei* is powerfully revisioned *as emerging from nature itself.* For the theologian this interdisciplinary move implies that God used natural history for religion and for religious belief to emerge as a natural phenomenon. Moreover, this move is validated by the significant discovery that the focus by some contemporary theologians on the radical embodied nature of our human condition stunningly intersects with transversally converging arguments about embodied human uniqueness from evolutionary epistemology, from paleoanthropology, and from the neurosciences. In all these very diverse disciplines, embodied human existence has emerged as crucial for defining human uniqueness in the sciences, as well as for the *imago Dei* in theology. To think of the "image of God" as having emerged from nature by natural evolutionary processes emphasizes our vital connection with nature precisely by focusing on our species specificity. In addition, this transversal, interpretative move also honors the intention of the classical biblical texts and does not necessarily imply that nature as a whole should now be seen as "created in the image of God,"[10] but, for theological reasons that are fair and compassionate, limits the notion of the *imago Dei* to *Homo sapiens.*

3. Therefore, I would conclude that interdisciplinary reasoning has here negotiated a shared, transversal space where theologians and scientists can explore a wide reflective equilibrium of agreement on what embodied existence means, and why it may have different but equally important consequences for different disciplines. In sharing this transversal moment, the theologian may be immeasurably enriched by taking on board the scientific implications of human embodiment for imagination, for creativity, and for our propensities for symbolic awareness and religious fulfillment. The scientist may be enriched by learning how these powerful symbolic and religious propensities cannot be discussed generically for all religions, but come alive only in the living faith of specific religious systems where they are augmented in ways that scientific methodology cannot anticipate. On this view the nuanced, sympathetic scientist would want to acknowledge that there is more to embodied human uniqueness than paleoanthropology or neuroscience could explain. The theologian should have learned, however, that overly abstract, disembod-

10. Contra Michollet 2000: 88f.

ied notions of human uniqueness not only betray the heart of his or her canonical, textual traditions, but also dangerously isolate theological discourse by destroying the possibility of interdisciplinary dialogue.

4. A revisioned interpretation of Lord Gifford's original charge not only revealed human uniqueness as a research topic for interdisciplinary dialogue, it also revealed much about the nature of interdisciplinarity itself. We have learned that the dialogue between the partners in two such asymmetrical discourses has strengths and weaknesses, possibilities and limitations. I have argued in these lectures that a multidisciplinary conversation can actually lead to true interdisciplinary results if the guidelines for a postfoundationalist approach are honored. We have also seen that the interdisciplinary dialogue between theology and science can break down if a certain point of no return is reached. When science claims a reductionist, scientistic worldview as the only valid view, as in Pascal Boyer's "explaining" of religion, theology as a research strategy is by definition explained away and all possibility of further interdisciplinary communication ceases. But with theology it is even more complex: interdisciplinary dialogue ceases to exist when overparticularist theologies retreat quite consciously from interdisciplinary dialogue, but also when theology leaves behind the particularity of its tradition(s) in favor of an abstract, generic religious metaphysics.

5. In addition to the possibilities and dangers of interdisciplinary conversation, there are also natural limitations to this kind of dialogue between disciplines. After sharing the rich resources of the transversal moment, interdisciplinarity points us back again to the broader boundaries of our own disciplines. A postfoundationalist approach thus opens up space for interdisciplinary dialogue, but it also reveals the limitations of the transversal moment, after which disciplinary lines of argument necessarily diverge again and move back to *intra*disciplinary contexts, carrying with them the rich interdisciplinary results of the multidisciplinary conversation. It is within the particularity of these specific contexts that theologians will bring back interdisciplinary results to impact a reimaging of human uniqueness within specific theological traditions. In the interdisciplinary conversation between theology and the sciences, as has become clear, the boundaries between our disciplines and reasoning strategies are porous, but that does not mean that deep theological convictions can be easily or uncritically transferred to philosophy, or to science, to function there as "data" in foreign systems. In the same manner, transversal reasoning does not mean that scientific data, paradigms, or

worldviews can be uncritically transported across disciplinary boundaries into theology, to there set the agenda, as it were, for theological reasoning. Transversal reasoning means that we also have to be alert to degrees of transversality, and that different theological approaches could have different degrees of success in interdisciplinary dialogue. Most importantly, though, theology and the sciences can share concerns, can indeed converge in their methodological approaches on specifically identified problems like the problem of human uniqueness. But precisely by also recognizing the limitations of interdisciplinarity, we can honor the disciplinary integrity of theology, and of the sciences.

6. In this specific case study on human uniqueness, this mutual, critical task always presupposed the richness of the interdisciplinary moment in which theology and paleoanthropology can find intriguing and mutually enriching, transversal connections on human uniqueness. In my third chapter I argued that the most responsible Christian theological way to look at human uniqueness is, first of all, to move away from esoteric and baroquely abstract notions of human uniqueness, and second, to return to embodied notions of humanness where our sexuality and moral awareness are tied directly to our embodied self-transcendence as believers who are in a relationship with God. In the fourth chapter I argued that, from a paleoanthropological point of view, human uniqueness emerged as a highly contextualized and embodied notion and is directly tied to the embodied, symbolizing minds of our distant prehistoric ancestors, as materially embodied in the spectacular cave paintings of the Upper Paleolithic. This opened up the possibility not only for converging arguments from both evolutionary epistemology and paleoanthropology for the presence of religious awareness in our earliest Cro-Magnon ancestors, but also for the plausibility of the larger argument: since the very beginning of the emergence of *Homo sapiens* those characteristics that made humans uniquely different from even their closest sister species — like consciousness, imagination, language, symbolic minds, and symbolic behavior — have always included religious awareness and religious behavior. Rethinking theologically the *imago Dei* as emerging from nature opens up theology to the interdisciplinary impact of the fact that the potential arose in the embodied human mind to undertake science and technology, to create art, and to discover the need and ability for religious belief. It is in this sense that we cannot understand early human behavior, and human nature itself, if we do not take this fundamental religious dimension into account.

7. The most challenging aspect of an interdisciplinary dialogue between theology and paleoanthropology may be for theology to lift up the specific limitations of this conversation. This implies a quite specific appeal from theology to the sciences, an appeal for a sensitivity to that which is particular to the broader, nonempirical or philosophical dimensions of theological discourse. This kind of disciplinary integrity means that Christian theology has an obligation to explore other issues that are crucial for understanding human uniqueness, issues that may not be empirically accessible. In this kind of interdisciplinary conversation theology can actually help to significantly broaden the scope of what is meant by "human uniqueness." The distinguishing characteristic of *Homo sapiens* is not solely a remarkable embodied brain, a stunning mental cognitive fluidity expressed in imagination, creativity, linguistic abilities, and symbolic propensities. But even more, as real-life, embodied persons of flesh and blood, *Homo sapiens* — we humans — are also affected by hostility, arrogance, vulnerability and dependence, ruthlessness and cunning, and therefore are inescapably caught between what we have come to call "good and evil." This experience of good and evil, and theological distinctions between evil, moral failure, sin, tragedy, and redemption, lies beyond the empirical scope of the fossil record, and therefore beyond the scope of science. But it is science that helps us better understand our evolutionarily developed bodies that are the bearers of human uniqueness, and it is precisely this embodied existence that confronts us with the realities of vulnerability, tragedy, and affliction. For the scientist drawn to the more comprehensive, complementary picture of the dimension of meaning in which *Homo sapiens* has existed since its very beginning, theology offers a promising key to understanding these profoundly tragic dimensions of human existence, but also to understanding why religious belief has provided our distant ancestors, and us, with dimensions of hope, redemption, and grace.

Bibliography

Augustine. 1968. *The Trinity.* Boston: Saint Paul Editions.

Bahn, Paul G. 1998. *Prehistoric Art.* New York: Cambridge University Press.

Bahn, Paul G., and Jean Vertut. 1997. *Journey through the Ice Age.* Berkeley and Los Angeles: University of California Press.

Bakhtin, Mikhail. 1981. *The Dialogic Imagination: Four Essays.* Austin: University of Texas Press.

Barbour, Ian. 2002. *Nature, Human Nature, and God.* Minneapolis: Fortress.

Barr, James. 1993. *Biblical Faith and Natural Theology: The Gifford Lectures for 1991, Delivered in the University of Edinburgh.* Oxford: Clarendon.

Barth, Karl. 1958. *The Doctrine of Creation.* Edinburgh: T. & T. Clark.

————. 1960. *Church Dogmatics.* III/2. Edinburgh: T. & T. Clark.

Berkouwer, Gerrit C. 1962. *Man: The Image of God.* Grand Rapids: Eerdmans.

Bevir, Mark. 2004. "Governance and Interpretation: What Are the Implications of Postfoundationalism?" *Public Administration* 82, no. 3.

Bird, Phyllis. 1981. "'Male and Female He Created Them': Gen 1:27b in the Context of the Priestly Account of Creation." *Harvard Theological Review* 74, no. 1.

Bonner, John T., and Robert M. May. 1981. Introduction to *The Descent of Man, and Selection in Relation to Sex,* by Charles Darwin. Princeton: Princeton University Press.

Boyer, Pascal. 2001. *Religion Explained: The Evolutionary Origins of Religious Thought.* New York: Basic Books.

Bratt, Jessica. 2005. "Wolfhart Pannenberg: Imago Dei as Gift and Destiny." Unpublished paper, Princeton Theological Seminary.

Brown, Delwin. 1994. *Boundaries of Our Habitations: Tradition and Theological Construction.* Albany: State University of New York Press.

Buber, Martin. 1958. *I and Thou.* New York: Scribner.

Callender, Dexter E. 2000. *Adam in Myth and History: Ancient Israelite Perspectives on the Primal Human.* Winona Lake, Ind.: Eisenbrauns.

Calvin, John. 1970. *Institutes of the Christian Religion.* Vol. 1. Grand Rapids: Eerdmans.

Campbell, Donald T. 1974. "Evolutionary Epistemology." In *Evolutionary Epistemology, Rationality, and the Sociology of Knowledge,* edited by Gerard Radnitzky and W. W. Bartley. La Salle, Ill.: Open Court.

Capps, Donald. 1999. "The Lesson of Art Theory for Pastoral Theology." *Pastoral Psychology* 47.

Carpenter, James A. 1992. Review of *Good and Evil: Interpreting a Human Condition,* by Edward Farley. *Anglican Theological Review* 74, no. 3.

Case-Winters, Anna. n.d. *The Promise of Process-Panentheism.* Burlington, Vt.: Ashgate. Forthcoming.

Changeux, Jean-Pierre, and Paul Ricoeur. 2000. *What Makes Us Think? A Neuroscientist and a Philosopher Argue about Ethics, Human Nature, and the Brain.* Princeton: Princeton University Press.

Clottes, Jean, and Jean Courtin. 1996. *The Cave beneath the Sea: Paleolithic Images at Cosquer.* New York: Harry N. Abrams.

Clottes, Jean, and David Lewis-Williams. 1998. *The Shamans of Prehistory: Trance and Magic in the Painted Caves.* New York: Harry N. Abrams.

Conard, Nicholas. 2003. "Paleolithic Ivory Sculptures from Southwest Germany and the Origins of Figurative Art." *Nature* 426.

Conkey, Margaret W. 1987. "New Approaches in the Search for Meaning? A Review of Research in 'Paleolithic Art.'" *Journal of Field Archeology* 14, no. 4.

———. 1997. "Beyond Art and between the Caves: Thinking about Context in the Interpretive Process." In *Beyond Art: Pleistocene Image and Symbol,* edited by Margaret Conkey, Olga Soffer, Deborah Stratmann, and Nina G. Jablonski. San Francisco: Allen Press.

Conway Morris, Simon. 1998. *The Crucible of Creation: The Burgess Shale and the Rise of Animals.* New York: Oxford University Press.

———. 2003a. *Life's Solution: Inevitable Humans in a Lonely Universe.* New York: Cambridge University Press.

———. 2003b. "The Paradoxes of Evolution: Inevitable Humans in a Lonely Universe." *Borderlands,* issue 2.

Corbey, Raymond, and Wil Roebroeks. 1997. Review of *Human Evolution, Language, and Mind: A Psychological and Archeological Inquiry,* by William Noble and Iain Davidson. *Current Anthropology* 38, no. 5.

Damasio, Antonio. 1999. *The Feeling of What Happens: Body and Emotion in the Making of Consciousness.* New York: Harcourt Brace.

d'Aquili, Eugene, and Andrew Newberg. 1999. *The Mystical Mind: Probing the Biology of Religious Experience.* Minneapolis: Fortress.

———. 2000. "Wired for Ultimate Reality: The Neuropsychology of Religious Experience." *Science and Spirit* 11, no. 2.

d'Aquili, Eugene, Andrew Newberg, and Vince Rause. 2001. *Why God Won't Go Away: Brain Science and the Biology of Belief.* New York: Ballantine Books.

Darwin, Charles. 1981. *The Descent of Man, and Selection in Relation to Sex.* Princeton: Princeton University Press.

————. 1985. *The Origin of Species.* New York: Penguin Books.

Davenport, Demorest, and Michael A. Jochim. 1988. "The Scene in the Shaft at Lascaux." *Antiquity* 62.

Davidson, Iain. 1997. "The Power of Pictures." In *Beyond Art: Pleistocene Image and Symbol,* edited by Margaret W. Conkey et al. San Francisco: Allen Press.

Deacon, Terrence. 1997. *The Symbolic Species: The Co-evolution of Language and the Brain.* New York: Norton.

————. 2003. "Language." In *Encyclopedia of Science and Religion,* vol. 2, edited by J. Wentzel Vrede van Huyssteen. New York: Macmillan Reference USA.

d'Errico, Francesco, and April Nowell. 2000. "A New Look at the Berekhat Ram Figurine: Implications for the Origins of Symbolism." *Cambridge Archeological Journal* 10, no. 1.

de Waal, Frans. 2003. "Response to Robert Proctor's 'Three Roots of Human Recency: Molecular Anthropology, the Refigured Acheulean, and the UNESCO Response to Auschwitz.'" *Current Anthropology* 44, no. 2.

Dickinson, Emily. 1960. "The Brain — Is Wider than the Sky." Poem 632, ca. 1862. In *The Complete Poems of Emily Dickinson,* edited by Thomas H. Johnson. Boston: Little, Brown.

Donald, Merlin. 1991. *Origins of the Modern Mind: Three Stages in the Evolution of Culture and Cognition.* Cambridge: Harvard University Press.

————. 1993. "Precis of *Origins of the Modern Mind: Three Stages in the Evolution of Culture and Cognition.*" *Behavioral and Brain Sciences* 16, no. 4.

————. 2001. *A Mind So Rare: The Evolution of Human Consciousness.* New York: Norton.

Douglass, E. Jane Dempsey. 1995. "The Image of God in Women as Seen by Luther and Calvin." In *The Image of God: Gender Models in Judaeo-Christian Tradition,* edited by Kari Elisabeth Borresen. Minneapolis: Fortress.

Edelman, Gerald. 1992. *Bright Air, Brilliant Fire: On the Matter of the Mind.* New York: Basic Books.

Fanlac, Pierre, ed. 1994. *The Font-De-Gaume Cave: Cave Painting, Protection, Conservation, Interventions.* Périgueux: Imprimerie Reymondie.

Farley, Edward. 1990. *Good and Evil: Interpreting a Human Condition.* Minneapolis: Fortress.

García-Rivera, Alejandro. 2003. *A Wounded Innocence: Sketches for a Theology of Art.* Collegeville, Minn.: Liturgical Press.

Gardner, Howard. 1983. *Frames of Mind: The Theory of Multiple Intelligences.* New York: Basic Books.

Gideon, Bethany. 2005. "Christianity in American Political Discourse: A Post-foundationalist Perspective." Senior thesis, Princeton Theological Seminary.

Gill, Jerry H. 1981. *On Knowing God.* Philadelphia: Westminster.

Gregersen, Niels. 1994. "Theology in a Neo-Darwinian World." *Studia Theologica: Scandinavian Journal of Theology* 48, no. 2.

———. 2003. "The Naturalness of Religious Imagination and the Idea of Revelation." *Ars Disputandi: The Online Journal for Philosophy of Religion* 3. www.arsdisputandi.org/. Accessed February 10, 2004.

Gregersen, Niels, and Ulf Görman, eds. 2002. *Design and Disorder: Perspectives from Science and Theology.* Edinburgh: T. & T. Clark.

Griffiths, Paul J. 2002. "Faith Seeking Explanation." Review of *Religion Explained: The Evolutionary Origins of Religious Thought,* by Pascal Boyer. *First Things,* no. 119.

Haack, Susan. 1995. *Evidence and Inquiry: Towards Reconstruction in Epistemology.* Oxford: Blackwell.

Hall, Douglas John. 1986. *Imaging God: Dominion as Stewardship.* Grand Rapids: Eerdmans.

Hančil, Tomáš. 1999. "Evolution, Culture and Theology: A Critical Evaluation of the Applicability of Evolutionary Epistemology for Theological Reasoning." Diss., Princeton Theological Seminary.

Hančil, Tomáš, and Margarete Ziemer. 2000. "Evolutionary Epistemology as a New Challenge in the Dialogue between Theology and Science." *CTNS Bulletin* 20, no. 3.

Haught, John F. 2002a. "The Darwinian Universe: Isn't There Room for God?" *Commonweal* 129, no. 2.

———. 2002b. *In Search of a God for Evolution: Paul Tillich and Pierre Teilhard de Chardin.* Lewisburg, Pa.: American Teilhard Association.

Hauser, M. D., Noam Chomsky, and T. W. Fitch. 2002. "The Faculty of Language: What Is It, Who Has It, and How Did It Evolve?" *Science* 298.

Hefner, Philip. 1993. *The Human Factor: Evolution, Culture, and Religion.* Minneapolis: Fortress.

———. 1998. "Biocultural Evolution and the Created Co-Creator." In *Science and Theology: The New Consonance,* edited by Ted Peters. Boulder, Colo.: Westview Press.

———. 2000. "Imago Dei: The Possibility and Necessity of the Human Person." In *The Human Person in Science and Theology,* edited by Niels Henrik Gregersen, Willem B. Drees, and Elf Gorman. Edinburgh: T. & T. Clark.

Heidegger, Martin. 1995. *The Fundamental Concepts of Metaphysics: World, Finitude, Solitude.* Bloomington: Indiana University Press.

Henshilwood, Chris, F. d'Errico, M. Vanhaeren, K. van Niekerk, and Z. Jacobs. 2004. "Middle Stone Age Shell Beads from South Africa." *Science* 304.

Herrmann, Eberhard. 1998. "Rationality, Warrant and Reflective Equilibrium." In

Reflective Equilibrium: Essays in Honor of Robert Heeger, edited by W. van der Burg and T. van Willigenburg. Dordrecht: Kluwer.

Herzfeld, Noreen. 2002. *In Our Image: Artificial Intelligence and the Human Spirit.* Minneapolis: Fortress.

Heschel, Abraham Joshua. 1962. *The Prophets II.* New York: Harper Torchbooks.

———. 1965. *Who Is Man?* Stanford: Stanford University Press.

———. 1985. *The Circle of the Baal Shem Tov: Studies in Hasidim.* Chicago: University of Chicago Press.

———. 1991. *No Religion Is an Island: Abraham Joshua Heschel and Interreligious Dialogue.* Edited by H. Kasimow and B. Sherwin. New York: Orbis.

Hilkert, Mary Catherine. 1995. "Cry Beloved Image: Rethinking the Image of God." In *In the Embrace of God: Feminist Approaches to Theological Anthropology,* edited by Ann O'Hara Graff. New York: Orbis.

Hochadel, Oliver. 2003. Response to "Three Roots of Human Recency: Molecular Anthropology, the Refigured Acheulean, and the UNESCO Response to Auschwitz," by Robert Proctor. *Current Anthropology* 44, no. 2.

Huxley, Thomas Henry. 1863. *Evidence as to Man's Place in Nature.* London: Williams and Norgate.

Jaki, Stanley L. 1986. *Lord Gifford and His Lectures: A Centenary Retrospect.* Edinburgh: Scottish Academic Press.

Jenson, Robert. 1983. "The Praying Animal." *Zygon: Journal of Science and Religion* 18, no. 3.

———. 1999. *Systematic Theology.* Vol. 2. New York: Oxford University Press.

Kagan, Jerome. 1998. *Three Seductive Ideas.* Cambridge: Harvard University Press.

Kaufman, Gordon D. 2004. *In the Beginning . . . Creativity.* Minneapolis: Fortress.

Keating, James. 2002. Review of *The Shaping of Rationality: Toward Interdisciplinarity in Theology and Science,* by Wentzel van Huyssteen. *The Thomist,* April 2002.

Kemp, Marcel. 2002. *Het Verscheurde Beeld.* Zoetermeer: Uitgeverij Boekencentrum.

Klein, Richard. 1999. *Human Career: Human Biological and Cultural Origins.* Chicago: University of Chicago Press.

Krüger, J. S. 1995. *Along Edges: Religion in South Africa; Bushman, Christian, Buddhist.* Pretoria: University of South Africa.

Lakatos, Imre. 1970. *Criticism and the Growth of Knowledge.* Cambridge: Cambridge University Press.

Lake, Mark. 1992. "Evolving Thought." *Cambridge Archeological Journal* 2, no. 2.

Laudan, Larry. 1977. *Progress and Its Problems: Toward a Theory of Scientific Growth.* Berkeley: University of California Press.

Levinas, Emmanuel. 1969. *Totality and Infinity: An Essay on Exteriority.* Pittsburgh: Duquesne University Press.

Lewin, Roger. 1993. *The Origin of Modern Humans.* New York: Scientific American Library.

Lewis-Williams, David. 2002. *The Mind in the Cave: Consciousness and the Origins of Art.* New York: Thames and Hudson.

Lewontin, Richard. 1974. *The Genetic Basis of Evolutionary Change.* New York: Columbia University Press.

Lieberman, Philip. 1999. Review of *Human Evolution, Language, and Mind: A Psychological and Archeological Inquiry,* by William Noble and Iain Davidson. *Anthropological Linguistics* 41, no. 4.

Lossky, Vladimir. 1974. *In the Image and Likeness of God.* Crestwood, N.Y.: St. Vladimir's Seminary Press.

Luther, Martin. 1958. *Commentary on Genesis.* Grand Rapids: Zondervan.

McBrearty, Sally, and Alison Brooks. 2000. "The Revolution That Wasn't: A New Interpretation of the Origin of Modern Human Behavior." *Journal of Human Evolution* 39, no. 5.

McClenon, James. 1997. "Shamanic Healing, Human Evolution, and the Origin of Religion." *Journal for the Scientific Study of Religion* 36, no. 3.

————. 2002. *Wondrous Healing: Shamanism, Human Evolution, and the Origin of Religion.* De Kalb: Northern Illinois University Press.

MacIntyre, Alasdair C. 1990. *Three Rival Versions of Moral Enquiry: Encyclopedia, Genealogy, and Tradition; Gifford Lectures Delivered in the University of Edinburgh in 1988.* Notre Dame: University of Notre Dame Press.

————. 1999. *Dependent Rational Animals: Why Human Beings Need the Virtues.* Chicago: Open Court.

McLeod, Frederick G., S.J. 1999. *The Image of God in the Antiochene Tradition.* Washington, D.C.: Catholic University of America Press.

Maimonides, Moses. 1919. *The Guide for the Perplexed.* London: George Routledge.

————. 1949. *The Mishneh Torah.* New York: Bloch Publishing.

Martindale, Colin. 1981. *Cognition and Consciousness.* Homewood, Ill.: Dorsey Press.

Mays, James Luther. 2005. "The Self in the Psalms and the Image of God." In *God and Human Destiny,* edited by R. Kendall Soulen and Linda Woodhead. New York: T. & T. Clark.

Meeks, Wayne A., gen. ed. 1989. *The HarperCollins Study Bible: New Revised Standard Version.* New York: HarperCollins.

Mellars, Paul. 1989. "Major Issues in the Emergence of Modern Humans." *Current Anthropology* 30, no. 3.

————. 1991. "Cognitive Changes and the Emergence of Modern Humans in Europe." *Cambridge Archeological Journal* 1, no. 1.

Merleau-Ponty, Maurice. 1962. *Phenomenology of Perception.* London: Routledge and K. Paul.

Michollet, Bernard. 2000. "Evolution and Anthropology: Human Beings as the 'Image of God.'" In *Evolution and Faith,* edited by B. van Iersel, C. Theobald, and H. Häring. London: SCM Press.

Middleton, J. Richard. 2005. *The Liberating Image: The Imago Dei in Genesis 1.* Grand Rapids: Brazos Press.

Miller, Patrick. 1978. "Genesis 1–11: Studies in Structure and Theme." *Journal for the Study of the Old Testament, Supplement Series* 8.

Mithen, Steven. 1996. *The Prehistory of the Mind: A Search for the Origins of Art, Religion, and Science.* London: Thames and Hudson.

———. 1997. "Pulling the Mind Apart." *Cambridge Archeological Journal* 7, no. 2.

———. 2000. Response to "A New Look at the Berekhat Ram Figurine: Implications for the Origins of Symbolism," by Francesco d'Errico and April Nowell. *Cambridge Archeological Journal* 10, no. 1.

Moltmann, Jürgen. 1981. *The Trinity and the Kingdom: The Doctrine of God.* San Francisco: Harper and Row.

———. 1985. *God in Creation: A New Theology of Creation and the Spirit of God.* San Francisco: Harper and Row.

———. 1992. *History and the Triune God: Contributions to Trinitarian Theology.* New York: Crossroad.

Munz, Peter. 1985. *Our Knowledge of the Growth of Knowledge: Popper or Wittgenstein?* London: Routledge and Kegan Paul.

———. 1993. *Philosophical Darwinism: On the Origin of Knowledge by Means of Natural Selection.* London: Routledge.

Newlands, George. 2005. "Science, Theology and Human Rights." Paper read at the Annual Meeting of the Highlands Institute for American Religious and Philosophical Thought, Highlands, N.C.

———. n.d. *Christ and Human Rights.* Ashgate. Forthcoming.

Niebuhr, Reinhold. 1942. *Nature and Destiny of Man: A Christian Interpretation.* Vol. 1. New York: Scribner.

Nielsen, Kai. 1987. "Searching for an Emancipatory Perspective: Wide Reflective Equilibrium and the Hermeneutical Circle." In *Anti-Foundationalism and Practical Reasoning,* edited by Evan Simpson. Edmonton: Academic Press.

Noble, William, and Iain Davidson. 1996. *Human Evolution, Language, and Mind: A Psychological and Archeological Inquiry.* Cambridge: Cambridge University Press.

Novakovic, Ivica. 2004. "Theology: Speculative or Combinatorial?" Ph.D. diss., Princeton Theological Seminary.

O'Hear, Anthony. 2002. *Beyond Evolution: Human Nature and the Limits of Evolutionary Explanation.* Oxford: Clarendon.

Oomen, Palmyre. 2003. "Neurotheology." In *Encyclopedia of Science and Religion,* vol. 2, edited by J. Wentzel Vrede van Huyssteen. New York: Macmillan Reference USA.

Osmer, Richard. 2000. "A New Clue for Religious Education in a New Millennium? Cross-Disciplinary Thinking and the Quest for Integrity and Intelligibility." In

Forging a Better Religious Education in the Third Millennium, edited by James
Michael Lee. Birmingham, Ala.: Religious Education Press.

Pannenberg, Wolfhart. 1970. *What Is Man? Contemporary Anthropology in Theological Perspective.* Philadelphia: Fortress.

―――. 1985. *Anthropology in Theological Perspective.* Philadelphia. Westminster.

―――. 1991. *Systematic Theology.* Grand Rapids: Eerdmans.

Parker, Sue T. 1997. Review of *Human Evolution, Language, and Mind: A Psychological and Archeological Inquiry,* by William Noble and Iain Davidson. *American Antiquity* 62, no. 3.

Peacocke, A. R. 1993. *Theology for a Scientific Age: Being and Becoming — Natural, Divine, and Human.* Minneapolis: Fortress.

Peterson, Gregory R. 1999. "The Evolution of Consciousness and the Theology of Nature." *Zygon* 34, no. 2.

―――. 2003. *Minding God: Theology and the Cognitive Sciences.* Minneapolis: Fortress.

Philo of Alexandria. 2001. *On the Creation of the Cosmos according to Moses.* Leiden and Boston: Brill.

Plassard, Jean, and Marie-Odile. 1995. *Visiting Rouffignac Cave.* Paris: Editions Sud Quest.

Plotkin, Henry C. 1993. *Darwin Machines and the Nature of Knowledge.* Cambridge: Harvard University Press.

Popper, Karl R. 1998. *Conjectures and Refutations: The Growth of Scientific Knowledge.* London: Routledge.

Potts, Richard. 1996. *Humanity's Descent.* New York: Morrow.

―――. 2004. "Sociality and the Concept of Culture in Human Origins." In *The Origins and Nature of Sociality,* edited by Robert W. Sussman and Audrey R. Chapman. New York: Walter de Gruyter.

Proctor, Robert. 2003. "Three Roots of Human Recency: Molecular Anthropology, the Refigured Acheulean, and the UNESCO Response to Auschwitz." *Current Anthropology* 44, no. 2.

Proudfoot, Wayne. 2000. Review of *The Mystical Mind: Probing the Biology of Religious Experience,* by E. d'Aquili and A. Newberg. *Christian Century,* November 8, 2000.

Rad, Gerhard von. 2001. *Old Testament Theology.* Louisville: Westminster John Knox.

Rescher, Nicholas. 1988. *Rationality: A Philosophical Inquiry into the Nature and the Rationale of Reason.* New York: Oxford University Press.

―――. 1990. *Evolution, Cognition, and Realism: Studies in Evolutionary Epistemology.* Lanham, Md.: University Press of America.

―――. 1992. *A System of Pragmatic Idealism.* Vol. 1, *Human Knowledge in Idealistic Perspective.* Princeton: Princeton University Press.

―――. 1993. *A System of Pragmatic Idealism.* Vol. 2, *The Validity of Values.* Princeton: Princeton University Press.

Rolston, Holmes. 1987. *Science and Religion: A Critical Survey.* New York: Random House.

————. 1996. "Science, Religion, and the Future." In *Religion and Science: History, Method, and Dialogue,* edited by W. Mark Richardson and J. Wildman. New York: Routledge.

————. 1999. *Genes, Genesis, and God: Values and Their Origins in Natural and Human History; The Gifford Lectures, University of Edinburgh, 1997-1998.* Cambridge: Cambridge University Press.

Rouse, Joseph. 1987. *Knowledge and Power: Toward a Political Philosophy of Science.* Ithaca, N.Y.: Cornell University Press.

————. 1996. *Engaging Science: How to Understand Its Practices Philosophically.* Ithaca, N.Y.: Cornell University Press.

Runehov, Anne. 2004. "Sacred or Neural? Neuroscientific Explanations of Religious Experience: A Philosophical Evaluation." Ph.D. diss., University of Uppsala.

Sartre, Jean-Paul. 1956. *Being and Nothingness; An Essay on Phenomenological Ontology.* New York: Philosophical Library.

————. 1960. *The Transcendence of the Ego: An Existentialist Theory of Consciousness.* New York: Hill and Wang.

Schneider, Robert. 2001. "Can We Talk? Theology and Science in Interdisciplinary Conversation." *The Cresset,* Easter 2001.

Schrag, Calvin. 1989. "Rationality between Modernity and Postmodernity." In *Lifeworld and Politics: Between Modernity and Postmodernity; Essays in Honor of Fred R. Dallmayr,* edited by Stephen K. White. Notre Dame, Ind.: University of Notre Dame Press.

————. 1992. *The Resources of Rationality: A Response to the Postmodern Challenge.* Bloomington: Indiana University Press.

————. 1994. "Transversal Rationality." In *The Question of Hermeneutics: Essays in Honor of Joseph J. Kockelmans,* edited by T. J. Stapleton. Dordrecht: Kluwer.

Schüssler Fiorenza, Francis. 1984. *Foundational Theology: Jesus and the Church.* New York: Crossroad.

Shirin, Andrey V. 2005. "Postfoundationalist *Zhivoznaniye:* Splitting the Difference between American Pragmatism and the Russian Tradition of All-Unity." Diss., Princeton Theological Seminary.

Shults, F. LeRon. 1999. *The Postfoundationalist Task of Theology: Wolfhart Pannenberg and the New Theological Rationality.* Grand Rapids: Eerdmans.

————. 2003. *Reforming Theological Anthropology: After the Philosophical Turn to Relationality.* Grand Rapids: Eerdmans.

Simek, Jan F. 1998. Review of *Human Evolution, Language and Mind: A Psychological and Archeological Inquiry,* by William Noble and Iain Davidson. *Antiquity* 72, no. 276.

Sinclair, Anthony. 2003. "Art of the Ancients." *Nature* 426.

Smith, Christian. 2003. *Moral, Believing Animals: Human Personhood and Culture.* New York: Oxford University Press.

Smith, David L. 2002. "Religion Explained: A Review of Pascal Boyer." *Metapsychology Online Book Reviews,* December 19, 2002.

Soffer, Olga, and Margaret Conkey. 1997. "Studying Ancient Visual Cultures." In *Beyond Art: Pleistocene Image and Symbol,* edited by Margaret W. Conkey, Olga Soffer, Deborah Stratmann, and Nina G. Jablonski. San Francisco: Allen Press.

Solberg, Mary M. 1997. *Compelling Knowledge: A Feminist Proposal for an Epistemology of the Cross.* Albany, N.Y.: SUNY Press.

Stanesby, Derek. 1988. *Science, Reason, and Religion.* London and New York: Routledge.

Stenmark, Mikael. 1995. *Rationality in Science, Religion, and Everyday Life: A Critical Evaluation of Four Models of Rationality.* Notre Dame, Ind.: University of Notre Dame Press.

Stewart, Ian. 1998. *Life's Other Secret: The New Mathematics of the Living World.* New York: Wiley.

Stoeger, William R. 1988. *Physics, Philosophy, and Theology: Common Quest for Understanding.* Vatican City: Vatican Observatory.

Sullivan, Christopher. 2002. "French Underground: Painted Caves of Perigord a Subterranean World Revealing Art in Its Very Infancy." *Newark Sunday Star-Ledger,* September 15, 2002.

Tattersall, Ian. 1998. *Becoming Human: Evolution and Human Uniqueness.* New York: Harcourt Brace.

———. 2002. *The Monkey in the Mirror: Essays on the Science of What Makes Us Human.* New York: Harcourt.

———. 2003. "Response to Robert Proctor's 'Three Roots of Human Recency: Molecular Anthropology, the Refigured Acheulean, and the UNESCO Response to Auschwitz.'" *Current Anthropology* 44, no. 2.

Tattersall, Ian, and Kenneth Mowbray. 2003. "Human Evolution." In *Encyclopedia of Science and Religion,* vol. 1, edited by J. Wentzel Vrede van Huyssteen. New York: Macmillan Reference USA.

Taylor, Mark Kline. 1992. Review of *Good and Evil: Interpreting a Human Condition,* by Edward Farley. *Journal of Religion* 72.

Thomas Aquinas. 1911. *Summa Theologica (The Summa Theologica of St. Thomas Aquinas).* London: Thomas Baker.

Tilley, Terrence. 1992. Review of *Good and Evil: Interpreting a Human Condition,* by Edward Farley. *Theology Today* 48, no. 4.

Towner, W. Sibley. 2001. *Genesis.* Louisville: Westminster John Knox.

Tracy, David, and Frank Reynolds, eds. 1992. *Discourse and Practice.* Albany: State University of New York Press.

Tripole, Martin R. 2001. Review of *Good and Evil: Interpreting a Human Condition,* by Edward Farley. *Theological Studies* 52, no. 3.

van Huyssteen, Wentzel J. 1989. *Theology and the Justification of Faith: Constructing Theories in Systematic Theology.* Grand Rapids: Eerdmans.

———. 1997. *Essays in Postfoundationalist Theology.* Grand Rapids: Eerdmans.

———. 1998. *Duet or Duel? Theology and Science in a Postmodern World.* Harrisburg, Pa.: Trinity.

———. 1999. *The Shaping of Rationality: Toward Interdisciplinarity in Theology and Science.* Grand Rapids: Eerdmans.

Welker, Michael. 1999. *Creation and Reality.* Minneapolis: Fortress.

Welsch, Wolfgang. 1996. *Vernunft: Die Zeitgenössische Vernunftkritik und das Konzept der transversalen Vernunft.* Frankfurt am Main: Suhrkamp Taschenbuch.

———. n.d. *Reason and Transition: On the Concept of Transversal Reason.* http://www2.uni-jena.de/welsch/start.html. Accessed October 13, 2005.

Wills, Christopher. 1998. *Children of Prometheus: The Accelerating Pace of Human Evolution.* Reading, Mass.: Perseus Books.

Wright, Robert. 2000. *Nonzero: The Logical of Human Destiny.* New York: Pantheon Books.

Wuketits, Franz M. 1990. *Evolutionary Epistemology and Its Implications for Humankind.* Albany, N.Y.: SUNY Press.

Index

58-64, 70, 77, 88, 95-97, 112, 122, 147, 166, 191-215, 221, 226, 233, 240-70, 274-76, 280, 290-91, 298-303, 311, 319, 321, 324; altered states of, 206-8, 220, 240-60, 268, 319; embodied, 49, 276; fragmented, 243; human transcendent, 20, 291; intensified trajectory of, 244; levels of, 42; ordinary, 244; panhuman, 205; religious, 218; shifting, 244-50; spectrum of states of, 243; subjective, 166

Conscious self-awareness, 15, 48

Contextuality, 4-44, 113-14, 159-60, 241, 247, 306, 309; disciplinary, 113, 159-60; radical, 2

Convergence, xvi, 43, 57-59, 113, 167, 230-37, 267

Conway Morris, Simon, 39, 55-59

Copernican revolution, 85, 166

Corbey, Raymond, 232

Cougnac, cave of, xii, 183-85, 211, 251, 254-55

Creation, 42, 71-75, 116-30, 135, 141-57, 167, 181, 194-95, 212-14, 240, 276, 280, 293-96, 314; biblical account of, 150, 295; Priestly account of, 117-23, 135, 151-57

Creative Explosion, 64, 66, 177-79, 188, 318

Creativity, 28, 66, 190, 196-97, 229-31, 280, 290, 303, 319, 321, 325; serendipitous, 280-82. *See also* Kaufman, Gordon

Cro-Magnon, 63-64, 148, 170-71, 181, 186-92, 204-13, 218-20, 234, 238, 247, 267, 275, 285, 289, 298, 302, 317-18, 324

Crucifixion, 306

Culture: emergence of, 86, 99-100; Hominid, 222, 226; human, 18, 70, 86, 91, 97, 100, 148-50, 196, 202, 222-23, 239, 261, 267, 275, 279, 288-89, 313, 320; intellectual, 33, 39; material, 225, 268, 287; postmodern, 10; primate, 222; scientific, 18; transmissible, 38, 48, 99-100; Upper Paleolithic, 181, 202

Cyril of Alexandria, 128

Damasio, Antonio, 42, 243, 248

D'Aquili, Eugene, 256-60

Darwin, Charles, xv, 38, 49, 67-109, 164-66, 187, 191, 204, 236, 237, 284, 310-12; on human cognition, 67-75, 112; on human

uniqueness, 67-75, 79-81; on morality/conscience, 73; on rationality, 79; on religion, 72

Darwinian canon, 164

Darwinian revolution, 166

Darwinism, 38, 55, 77-82, 98-99

Darwinists, "hard" or "ultra," 57, 59, 99

Davenport, Demorest, 253-54

Davidson, Iain, 52, 200-202, 228-33, 238-39, 247, 265, 275

Dawkins, Richard, 57, 147

Deacon, Terence, 103, 234-40, 261-65, 267, 275, 319-20

Deafferentation, 257

Dehumanization, 156

Deleuze, B. Gilles, 21

Demut, 119-20, 293. *See also* Likeness

D'Errico, Francesco, xi, 199

Developmental plasticity, 81

De Waal, Frans, 67

Diagnostic trait, 237

Differentiation: geographic, 222-23; racial, 51; sexual, 150-54, 274, 316

DNA (deoxyribonucleic acid), 55-59, 66, 169

Dolphins, 285-87

Domains, cognitive, 4, 12, 42, 194-96, 214, 265

Dominion, 117, 120-22, 128-35, 141, 150-56, 293

Donald, Merlin, 103

Dordogne region caves, 170, 182-85

"Dotted Horses" in Pech-Merle, 183, 251-52

Douglass, Jane Dempsey, 129-31

Dreams/dreaming, 71, 207, 243-50, 298

Ecology, 135, 150, 158, 221-23, 235, 279-81, 316; adaptation because of, 224, 237; crisis of, 150; imperialism of, 150; responsibility for, 158, 161

Eden, 119-22

Eikōn. See Image

Eland, 172, 207, 244

Eldredge, Niles, 62, 188

Electron spin, 64

Embeddedness, 18, 24-26, 46, 75, 83, 103, 113-19, 127, 131, 160, 242, 280, 306, 309

Glossolalia, 255
God. *See* Image of God
Gorillas, 223
Gould, Stephen Jay, 57-66, 188
Grammar, 36, 235
Great apes, 36, 47, 52, 166, 188, 221, 223
Greek philosophy, 125-26, 130
Gregersen, Niels, 144, 261-68
Griffiths, Paul, 264
Guattari, Felix, 21

Haack, Susan, 13
Haeckel, Ernst, 70-71
Hallucinations, 205-10, 243-50, 254-56;
  pricking sensations, 255; somatic, 255-56
Hančil, Tomáš, 102-9, 218-19
Handprints, 173, 209, 230, 251-52
Haught, John F., 262
Hauser, M. D., 225
Hebrew Bible, 119-20, 124-25
Hebrew-Christian paradigm, 306-7
Hector, Kevin, 283
Hefner, Philip, 104, 147-48, 157, 215, 274-81, 316, 320
Heidegger, Martin, 133, 286
Henshilwood, Chris, xi, 178-79
Herder, J. G., 140
Heritage, cultural, 39, 239
Hermeneutics, 15, 22-23, 26, 34, 41, 114, 141-42, 157
Herrmann, Eberhard, xi, 28-31
Herzfeld, Noreen, 126, 132-38
Heschel, Abraham, 271, 276, 294-307, 320
Heterosexism, 132, 316
Heuristic structures, 16; culture as third-level, 84; instinct as primary, 83; intelligence as secondary, 83; potential of, 242; transversality as device of, xv, 112
Hildegard from Bingen, 244
Hilkert, Mary Catherine, 129, 132
Historicity, 280-83
History: embodied, 105, 219, 271; evolutionary, 54-58, 70, 88, 92, 99, 166, 187, 190-94, 261, 281-82, 290; Hominid, 53-54; human, 170-74, 280-84; of ideas, 126, 158, 281-82, 292, 321; intellectual, 2, 117, 126; natural, 73, 91, 97-98, 196-98, 221, 279-84, 312, 322;

primeval, 119; of theology, 117-18, 132, 150, 161, 164
Hochadel, Oliver, 50
Hohle Fels, 170, 211
Holistic operator, 258
Holocene period, 177
Holy/holiness, 129, 131, 143-45, 274, 294-96, 320
Hominidae, 203, 317
Hominids: brain of, 235-36; culture of, 222, 226; dehumanizing of early, 50-51; early, 50-54, 187, 224; early diversity of, 51-52; fossil diversity of, 51-54. *See also* Evolution: Hominid
Homo creatus, 127
Homo erectus, 54, 61-66, 187
Homo ergaster, 187
Homo habilis, 52, 54, 61-64, 187, 223
Homo neanderthalensis. See Neanderthal
Homo peccator, 127
Homo sapiens, xiv-xvii, 36-37, 42, 47-67, 76, 84, 103, 113, 116, 140, 148, 162, 165, 169, 176-96, 220-39, 249, 268, 274-75, 297-302, 316-25; anatomically modern, 50-51; behaviorally modern *(Homo sapiens sapiens),* 50-51, 176-77, 196, 206
Homo symbolicus, 237
Human condition, xv, 36, 136, 154, 192, 218, 265, 277-92, 297-307, 322
Human identity, xv, 49, 67-75, 106, 145, 156, 164, 284, 307, 310, 321
Human rights, 132, 158, 161, 274, 316-17
Humans: behavior of, as linguistic and essentially interactive, 231; capacity of, for self-awareness, xvii-xviii, 13-24, 37-48, 59, 88, 95, 147, 161, 191, 215, 274, 309, 319; cognitive evolution of, xvii, 38, 45-109, 200, 262; embodied uniqueness of, 43, 162, 215, 231, 304, 320-22; evolution of language of, 62-63, 74, 232-34, 239, 265, 287, 311; as fully human, 47-54, 106, 137, 141, 191, 244-46, 275, 298; as moral, believing animals, 288-91; primal, 118-24, 150, 160, 167, 314, 321; as rational animals, 37, 126, 283-85; as symbiosis of genes and culture, 148, 274, 316; relationship of, to God, 7-8, 39, 121, 124, 136-38, 147-57, 267-

Pluralism, 2-5, 12-41, 114-18, 160, 169-76, 264, 269, 310; authentic, 30; easy, 26, 30, 114

Polanyi, Michael, 5, 77

Popper, Karl R., 77-79, 91, 100

Postfoundationalism: approach of, to interdisciplinarity, 34, 41, 45, 69, 113-16, 139, 159, 174-76, 270, 282, 309, 318; approach of, to theology, 29, 115, 144-45, 164, 317; epistemology of, 4, 40, 92, 164; and fallibilism and provisionalism, 180; rationality of, xiv, 10-41, 159, 310. *See also* Foundationalism; Nonfoundationalism

Postmodernity, 2, 12, 23, 39

Potts, Richard, 221-26, 233, 239, 261, 265-68, 287-88

Prayer, xviii, 22, 43, 122, 146-47, 158, 218, 267, 321

Prehistoric art. *See* Art

Pricking sensations, 255

Primatology, 221-23

Problem-oriented thought, 243

Proctor, Robert, 47, 50-54, 65-66

Protestant Scholastics, 127

Protolanguage, 42, 200-201, 232

Proudfoot, Wayne, 260

Psychology, cognitive, 68, 108, 220, 261, 270

Psychotropic substances, 244, 255

Punctuated equilibrium, 57-66, 188, 227

Quantitative operator, 258

Rationality: biological origins of, 13, 49, 60, 89, 105, 191, 219-20, 271; embodied, 21-22, 69, 87; human, xv, 3-24, 34, 40-46, 60, 69-94, 105, 133, 159, 214, 261, 265; interdisciplinary understanding of, 3, 5, 13, 34, 308, 322; multidimensional understanding of, 13, 21, 41, 308; postfoundationalist notion of, xiv, 10-41, 159, 310; scientific, 10, 95; substantive, 3; theological, 17, 104, 219, 324; transversal, 12-23, 41, 69, 219, 308, 323-24; tribal, 26, 114; universal, 3-12, 69, 308. *See also* Interdisciplinarity; Tranversality

Rational knowledge, 39, 48, 88, 92-97, 313

Rational progress, 3

Rational selection, 38, 48

Realistic fantasy, 243

Reason. *See* Rationality

Recency, 48-51, 66

Reconciliation, 158, 161, 317

Recursion, 225

Reductionism, 17, 55-57, 84, 89, 92, 94, 102-5, 112, 159, 218-19, 258-70, 277, 323; genetic, 55, 84; scientistic, 105, 112, 219, 259, 270, 323; view of, of religion, 94, 263

Reformation, 126, 129

Relationality, 8, 137-43, 151-58, 214, 276-78, 297-303, 315; I-Thou, 152-53, 294; trinitarian, 137-43

Relativism, 3, 10, 14, 24-30, 114, 241

Religion: Abrahamic, 167; awareness of, xviii, 18, 433, 96-97, 105-6, 147, 203-12, 217-20, 267-68, 312, 319; Darwin's conception of, 72; experience of, xvi-xvii, 16-17, 189, 206, 215, 220, 247, 255-69; first religions, 107, 218, 252; meaning of, 161, 189, 318; naturalness of belief in, 18, 94-105, 112, 205, 218, 256-68, 313, 318; propensity for belief in, xvi-xviii, 18, 39, 43, 48-49, 59, 94-97, 215, 218, 258, 265, 289, 311, 321

Rescher, Nicholas, 12, 33, 37-39, 48-49, 59, 76, 80, 191

Resurrection, 124, 161, 306

Revelation, 1, 6, 53, 206, 247, 277

Reverie, 243

Reynolds, Frank, 9

Ricoeur, Paul, 8-9

Righteousness, 116, 127, 129, 131, 136, 142

Ritual, 42, 52, 67, 146-48, 161, 171, 182-89, 204-13, 246, 252, 257, 274, 285, 313

Ritual action, 146, 274, 316

Roebroecks, Wil, 232

Rolston, Holmes, III, 15, 38, 48, 99-100, 265-66

Rouffignac, cave of, 184-86, 210

Rouse, Joseph, 5, 16

Runehov, Anne, 260

Sacrifice, 116, 290

Salon Noir sanctuary, 184, 251

Sapiens. See Homo sapiens